where to weekend around

WASHINGTON, D.C.

Fodor's

Fodor's Travel Publications   New York   Toronto   London   Sydney   Auckland

Fodor's Where to Weekend Around Washington, D.C.

Editor: John D. Rambow

Editorial Production: Tom Holton

Editorial Contributors: Laura Knowles Callanan, Kristi Delovitch, Kevin Myatt, Pete Nelson, Karyn-Siobhan Robinson, Sarah Sper, CiCi Williamson

Maps: David Lindroth, *cartographer;* Bob Blake and Rebecca Baer, *map editors*

Cover Art: Jessie Hartland

Book Design: Fabrizio La Rocca, *creative director;* Guido Caroti, *art director;* Sophie Ye Chin, *designer*

Production/Manufacturing: Robert B. Shields

Copyright

First Edition

ISBN 1–4000–1302–X

ISSN 1547–6774

Special Sales

Fodor's Travel Publications are available at special discounts for bulk purchases for sales promotions or premiums. Special editions, including personalized covers, excerpts of existing guides, and corporate imprints, can be created in large quantities for special needs. For more information, contact your local bookseller or write to Special Markets, Fodor's Travel Publications, 1745 Broadway, New York, New York 10019. Inquiries from Canada should be directed to your local Canadian bookseller or sent to Random House of Canada, Ltd., Marketing Department, 2775 Matheson Boulevard East, Mississauga, Ontario L4W 4P7. Inquiries from the United Kingdom should be sent to Fodor's Travel Publications, 20 Vauxhall Bridge Road, London SW1V 2SA, England.

PRINTED IN THE UNITED STATES OF AMERICA

10 9 8 7 6 5 4 3 2 1

Where to Weekend Around Washington, D.C.

What are you doing this weekend? Just the word *weekend* implies such promise—a break from the workaday rhythm, a bit of downtime, a chance to see friends and family, a good time to be had by all. Two things are certain: there aren't enough weekends, and they're always too short. You can make them feel longer, however, by going away, seeing someplace different, and really leaving the concerns of home life behind. And, surprise, planning a weekend getaway doesn't have to be stressful, regardless of whether you're deciding where to go next month or next weekend. That's where this book comes in.

Where to Weekend Around Washington, D.C. helps you plan trips to 24 destinations within 250 mi of the city. In the dozens of towns and parks we describe, you'll find hundreds of places to explore. Some may be places you know; others may be new to you. This book makes sure you know your options so that you don't miss something that's right around the next bend—even practically in your backyard—just because you didn't know it was there. Maybe you usually spend your summers in Rehoboth. Why not consider St. Mary's City for a change, or go in May or October instead? Perhaps your favorite inn is booked solid and you can't wait to get away, or you're tired of eating at the same three restaurants in Bucks County. With the practical information in this book, you can easily call to confirm the details that matter and study up on what you'll want to see and do and where you'll want to eat and sleep. Then toss *Where to Weekend Around Washington, D.C.* in your bag for the journey.

Although there's no substitute for travel advice from a good friend who knows your style and taste, our contributors are the next best thing—the kind of people you would poll for weekend ideas if you knew them.

Laura Knowles Callanan has lived in South Central Pennsylvania for nearly 25 years. She especially enjoys writing about travel, food, the arts, and entertainment for area newspapers and other publications. Her favorite local places include Landis Valley Museum and Central Market in Lancaster, the elegant Hotel Hershey and Spa, and the antiques shops of New Hope.

Kristi Delovitch lives in Capitol Hill. She began her writing career as a news reporter and in recent years has written travel programs for PBS as well as sections of *Fodor's Washington, D.C.* and *Fodor's Virginia and Maryland.* Her favorite escape is Ocean City, where she consumes massive quantities of Thrasher's french fries and steamed blue crabs each summer.

Kevin Myatt lives in Roanoke. As the hiking and weather columnist for www.roanoke.com, it probably comes as no surprise that his favorite weekend getaways involve seeing remote mountaintops and snowflakes—such as greeting the first snow of the winter every year at Mountain Lake, west of town. A newspaper writer and editor for 14 years, Kevin also works as a copy editor at *The Roanoke Times.*

Pete Nelson, a resident of the northern Chesapeake Bay area since the early 1980s, covered Maryland's and Virginia's Eastern Shore for this edition. After a career of more than 20 years in hospitality marketing, he now writes regularly for local and regional lifestyle magazines. He has twice updated regions for *Fodor's Virginia and Maryland.*

Karyn-Siobhan Robinson is a native of central Virginia and has lived in Dupont Circle since 1991. She loves driving to Richmond on Route 301 and exploring the restaurants, antiques stores, and other shops that line the highway. It's a favorite trip in the fall when the leaves change. Charlottesville's wineries are always a welcome get-away, and she couldn't live without frequent summertime trips to Southern Maryland for the produce.

The author of six books, **CiCi Williamson** has been a food and travel writer and syndicated newspaper columnist for more than two decades. A resident of McLean, Virginia, and the daughter of a U.S. Naval officer, her inherited wanderlust has enticed her to visit every U.S. state and more than 80 countries on six continents.

Contents

How to Use This Book

Our goal is to cover the best sights, activities, lodgings, and restaurants in their category within each weekend-getaway destination. Alphabetical organization makes it easy to navigate through these pages. Still, we've made certain decisions and used certain terms that you need to know about. For starters you can go on the assumption that everything you read about in this book is recommended by our writers and editors. It goes without saying that no property mentioned in the book has paid to be included.

ORGANIZATION

Bullets on the map, which follows this section, correspond to the chapter numbers. Each chapter focuses on one getaway destination; the directional line at the start of each chapter tells you how far it is from the city. The information in each chapter's What to See & Do section is arranged in alphabetical order, broken up by town in many cases. Parks and forests are sometimes listed under the main access point. Where to Stay and Where to Eat follow, with suggestions for places for all budgets, also arranged alphabetically and usually by town as well. The Essentials section provides information about how to get there and other logistical details.

For ideas about the best places for shopping, sightseeing with kids, and visiting Civil War sites, flip to the Fodor's Choice listings, which follow the map. Pit Stops are places to pull off the highway, stretch your legs, and grab a snack.

WHAT TO SEE & DO

This book is loaded with sights and activities for all seasons, budgets, lifestyles, and interests, which means that whether you want to go sailing or visit a pre-colonial mansion, you'll find plenty of places to explore. Admission prices given apply to adults; substantially reduced fees are almost always available for children, students, and senior citizens.

Where they're available, sightseeing tours are listed in their own section. Sports are limited to area highlights. Biking is an option most everywhere, so we give details only when facilities are extensive or otherwise notable. The same can be said of shopping, but we tell you about shopping standouts such as Lambertville's antiques stores and the outlet malls near Williamsburg. Use Save the Date as a timing tool, for events you wish to attend (and perhaps crowds you'd prefer to avoid).

WHERE TO STAY

The places we list—including homey B&Bs, mom-and-pop motels, grand inns, chain hotels, and luxury retreats—are the cream of the crop in each price and lodging category.

Baths: You'll find private bathrooms unless noted otherwise.

Credit cards: AE, D, DC, MC, and V following lodging listings indicate whether American Express, Discover, Diners Club, MasterCard, or Visa are accepted.

Facilities: We list what's available but we don't specify what costs extra. When pricing accommodations, always ask what's included. The term *hot tub* denotes hot tubs, whirlpools, and Jacuzzis. Assume that lodgings have phones, TVs, and air-conditioning and that they permit smoking, unless we note otherwise.

Closings: Assume that hostelries are open all year unless otherwise noted.

Meal plans: Hostelries operate on the European Plan (EP, with no meals) unless we specify that they use the Continental Plan (CP, with a Continental breakfast), Breakfast Plan (BP, with a full breakfast), or Modified American Plan (MAP, with breakfast and dinner).

Prices: Price categories are based on the price range for a standard double room during high season, excluding service charges and tax. Price categories for all-suites properties are based on prices for standard suites.

WHAT IT COSTS

$$$$	over $250
$$$	$200–$250
$$	$150–$200
$	$90–$150
¢	under $90

WHERE TO EAT

We make a point of including local food-lovers' hot spots as well as neighborhood options, with options for all budgets.

Credit cards: AE, D, DC, MC, and V following restaurant listings indicate whether American Express, Discover, Diners Club, MasterCard, or Visa are accepted.

Dress: Assume that no jackets or ties are required for men unless otherwise noted.

Meals and hours: Assume that restaurants are open for lunch and dinner unless otherwise noted. We always specify days closed and meals not available. When traveling in the off season, be sure to call ahead.

Reservations: They're always a good idea, but we don't mention them unless they're essential or are not accepted.

Prices: The price categories listed are based on the cost per person for a main course at dinner or, when dinner isn't available, the next most expensive meal.

WHAT IT COSTS

$$$$	over $25
$$$	$18–$25
$$	$13–$18
$	$7–$13
¢	under $7

ESSENTIALS

Details about transportation and other logistical information end each chapter. Be sure to check Web sites or call for particulars.

AN IMPORTANT TIP

Although all prices, opening times, and other details in this book are based on information supplied to us at press time, changes occur all the time in the travel world, especially in seasonal destinations, and Fodor's cannot accept responsibility for facts that become outdated or for inadvertent errors or omissions. So always confirm information when it matters, especially if you're making a detour to visit a specific place.

Let Us Hear from You

Keeping a travel guide fresh and up-to-date is a big job, and we welcome any and all comments. We'd love to have your thoughts on places we've listed, and we're interested in hearing about your own special finds. Our guides are thoroughly updated for each new edition, and we're always adding new information, so your feedback is vital. Contact us via e-mail in care of editors@fodors.com (specifying *Where to Weekend Around Washington, D.C.* on the subject line) or via snail mail in care of *Where to Weekend Around Washington, D.C.* at Fodor's, 1745 Broadway, New York, NY 10019. We look forward to hearing from you. And in the meantime, have a great weekend.

—*The Editors*

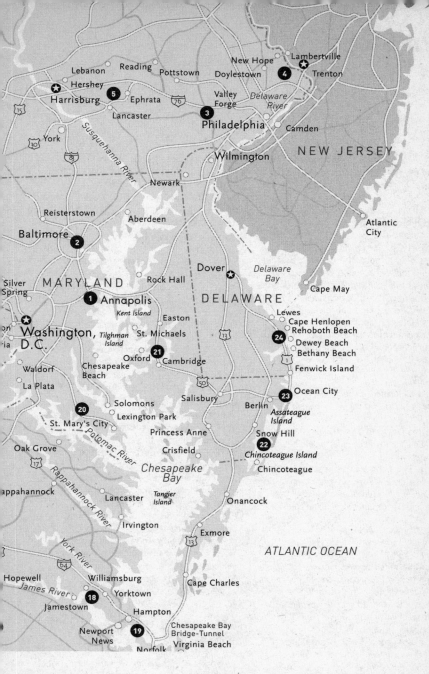

Pit Stops

Off the major thoroughfares outside the city and beyond the highway rest stops, these places offer a quick bite (and a rest room).

I-81

Wright's Dairy Rite
Exit 222 to U.S. 250 North; left onto U.S. 11
This old hangout of the Statler Brothers still offers curbside service; orders are brought to your car. Try the homemade onion rings, the hot dogs, and one of the nine different kinds of thick milk shakes, available in nine different flavors. You can even order that 1950s staple, a malted. > 346 Greenville Ave., Staunton, tel. 540/886-0435. AE, D, MC, V.

I-83

Kitchen Kettle Village
Rte. 30 East and then 6½ mi east on Rte. 340
At this group of 32 shops and restaurants you can sample jams and relishes, eat some funnel cake, listen to a little street jazz. The Kling House Restaurant here serves classic American fare with a Pennsylvania Dutch influence. > Rte. 340, 10 mi east of Lancaster, Intercourse, tel. 717/768-8261, www.kitchenkettle.com. D, MC, V. Closed Sun.

I-95

Aunt Sarah's Pancake House
Exit 104 on Rte. 207, Carmel Church exit
Pancakes rule at this homey pancake house. Be sure to try the boysenberry syrup. If you're not in the mood for pancakes, the honey-dipped fried chicken—served with more honey on the side for dipping—is delicious. > 23496 Welcome Way Dr., Carmel Church, tel. 804/448-3660. MC, V.

RTE. 50/301 NORTH

Angler's Restaurant and Marina
½ mi from Exit 42
On the mainland side of Kent Narrows, in the shadow of the Kent Narrows drawbridge, sits Angler's, one of the oldest eateries in the region. Join linemen and watermen, interstate travelers, and transplanted residents for a crabmeat omelet (available until 3) or dinner entrées such as Angler's Famous Lump Crab Cakes, from 5 on. > South Side of Kent Narrows Bridge, Grasonville, tel. 410/827-6716, www.anglersrestaurant.com. AE, D, MC, V.

Cantler's Riverside Inn
Off Rte. 179
You wind through a maze of neighborhoods on the outskirts of downtown Annapolis before coming to this creek-side crab shack. In addition to the steamed crabs, clams, and traditional Maryland fish dishes served here, you can also always expect rowdy crowds. For a true Eastern Shore experience chow down at one of the waterside deck's long communal tables. > 458 Forest Beach Rd., Annapolis, tel. 410/757-1311. AE, D, MC, V.

Gourmet Carry-Out
Rte. 8 South exit, after crossing the Chesapeake Bay Bridge
Beyond the first traffic light and just past the Bay Bridge Airport, look for the Gourmet Carry-Out on the right, next to the Citgo. At this incongruous location, part of the Kent Island Depot convenience store, is some of the best food in the area. The international take-out specialties include fajitas, paella, curried chicken, beef burgundy, and stir-fries. There's also broad selection of beverages available, include beer and wine. > 320 Romancoke Rd., Stevensville, tel. 410/604-3000, www.kidepot.com. AE, D, MC, V.

RTE. 301 SOUTH

Twin Kiss
6 mi south of Waldorf
When it's hot, the lines here get long, but don't let them keep you away. Stop the car, because Twin Kiss is worth the wait. The Twin Kiss is a twist of chocolate and vanilla soft ice cream. Milk shakes here are thick and made from scratch, as is the root beer. You can get hot dogs, hamburgers, and other diner fare, too. > 7415 Crain Highway, La Plata, tel. 301/934-4025. No credit cards.

Fodor's Choice

The towns, sights, places, and other travel experiences listed on this page are Fodor's editors' and writers' top picks for each category.

CIVIL WAR SITES
Antietam Battlefield > chapter 7
Appomattox Court House, Lynchburg > chapter 14
Dr. Samuel A. Mudd House, Waldorf > chapter 20
Gettysburg > chapter 6
Richmond > chapter 17

FALL COLORS
Bucks County > chapter 4
Charlottesville > chapter 15
Fredericksburg > chapter 16
Shenandoah Valley > chapters 11 and 14

SHOPPING
Annapolis outlets > chapter 1
King of Prussia Mall > chapter 3
Lahaska > chapter 4
Lightfoot > chapter 18
Rehoboth Outlets > chapter 24
Rockvale Square Outlets, Lancaster > chapter 5

STATE AND NATIONAL PARKS
Assateague Island National Seashore > chapter 22
Gettysburg National Military Park > chapter 6
Potomac Highlands > chapter 10
Shenandoah Valley > chapters 11 and 14

WINERIES
Central Virginia Vineyards > chapter 12
Mount Hope Estate and Winery, Lancaster > chapter 5
Nissley Winery, Lancaster > chapter 5
Shenandoah Valley > chapters 11 and 14

WITH KIDS
Baltimore > chapter 2
Historic Triangle > chapter 18
Ocean City > chapter 23
Pennsylvania Dutch Country > chapter 5

HISTORIC HOUSES
Fonthill, Doylestown > chapter 4
Fredericksburg > chapter 16
Hampton Roads > chapter 19
Monticello > chapter 15
Richmond > chapter 17

Annapolis

40 mi east of Washington, D.C.

1

Revised by CiCi Williamson

SAILS AND SAILORS are the main attraction in "Crabtown." However, even before the tony yacht clubs and the United States Naval Academy were built, Annapolis assured its spot in early-American history by serving as the nation's first peacetime capital (1783–84). The city's considerable colonial and early republican heritage is largely intact and, because it's all within walking distance, highly accessible. Annapolis has one of the highest concentrations of 18th-century buildings in the nation, including more than 50 that predate the Revolutionary War. Maryland is the only state in which the homes of all its signers of the Declaration of Independence still exist—they're all in Annapolis. You can tour three of the four—the homes of Charles Carroll, Samuel Chase, and William Paca.

On a peninsula bounded by the Severn and South rivers and the western shore of the Chesapeake Bay, Annapolis is the mid-Atlantic's sailing capital and also the gateway to southern Maryland and the Atlantic Ocean beaches. Since their founding in the mid-1600s, the counties of Anne Arundel, Calvert, Charles, and St. Mary's have all been supported through tobacco fields and fishing fleets.

In 1649 a group of Puritan settlers moved from Virginia to a spot at the mouth of the Severn River, where they established a community called Providence. Lord Baltimore—who held the royal charter to settle Maryland—named the area around this town Anne Arundel County, after his wife; in 1684 Anne Arundel Town was established across from Providence on the Severn's south side. Ten years later, Anne Arundel Town became the capital of Maryland and was renamed Annapolis—for Princess Anne, who later became queen. It received its city charter in 1708 and became a major port, particularly for the export of tobacco. In 1774 patriots here emulated their Boston counterparts (who had thrown their famous tea party the previous year) by burning the *Peggy Stewart*, a ship loaded with taxed tea.

Although it has long since been overtaken by Baltimore as the major Maryland port, Annapolis is still a popular pleasure-boating destination. On warm sunny days, the waters off City Dock become center stage for an amateur show of powerboaters maneuvering through the heavy traffic. Annapolis's enduring nautical reputation derives largely from the presence of the United States Naval Academy, whose strikingly uniformed midshipmen—destined to become Naval and Marine Corps officers—throng the city streets in crisp white uniforms in summer and navy blue in winter.

As you travel through town, keep an eye out for two beautiful houses designed by William Buckland, colonial America's foremost architect. To find out more about the city's heritage, visit the Banneer-Douglass Museum as well as the plaque at the spot Kunta Kinte—immortalized in Alex Haley's *Roots*—arrived at the city dock.

During the 20th century, the Annapolis area emerged as a prime residential community for the Annapolis–Baltimore–Washington, D.C., metro triangle, but despite the subdivisions and shopping centers, the city retains the allure of stunning water vistas, scenic roads, historic sites, and many unique hotels and restaurants. A word of advice: bring dependable walking shoes for the cobblestones and brick sidewalks of the historic district.

WHAT TO SEE & DO

Banneker-Douglass Museum What was once a church is now a museum with changing exhibits, lectures, films, and literature about the African-American experience in Maryland. It's named for Frederick Douglass, the 19th-century abolitionist, and Benjamin Banneker, a Maryland astronomer, surveyor, and mathematician who helped Pierre-Charles L'Enfant survey what would become D.C. > 84 Franklin St., tel. 410/216–6180, www.marylandhistoricaltrust.net. Free. Tues.–Fri. 10–3, Sat. noon–4.

Charles Carroll House This birthplace and city home of the only Catholic to sign the Declaration of Independence has 18th-century terraced gardens that overlook Spa Creek. One of the wealthiest men in colonial America, Carroll was educated abroad, studying law in France and England. He served in the Maryland legislature and later became one of the state's first two U.S. senators. After leaving public office, he became a businessman and entrepreneur. The restored 1720 house's wine cellar was added in the 19th century. > 107 Duke of Gloucester St., tel. 410/269–1737 or 888/269–1737, www.annapolis.org. $4. Fri. and Sun. noon–4, Sat. 10–2; other times by appointment.

Chase-Lloyd House The prominent colonial architect William Buckland built the Chase-Lloyd House. In 1774 the tobacco planter and revolutionary Edward Lloyd IV completed work begun five years earlier by Samuel Chase, a signer of the Declaration of Independence and future Supreme Court justice. The first floor is open to the public and contains more of Buckland's handiwork, including a parlor mantelpiece with tobacco leaves carved into the marble. (Buckland was famous for his interior woodwork; you can see more of it in the Hammond-Harwood House across the street, and in George Mason's Gunston Hall in Mason Neck, Virginia.) The house, furnished in a mixture of 18th-, 19th-, and 20th-century pieces, has a staircase that parts dramatically around an arched triple window. For more than 100 years the house has served as a home for elderly women, who live upstairs. > 22 Maryland Ave., tel. 410/263–2723. $2. Mar.–Dec., Mon.–Sat. 2–4.

Hammond-Harwood House Ninety percent of this 1774 home is original. One of the States' finest examples of colonial five-part Georgian architecture (a single block with two connecting rooms and wings on each side), the Hammond-Harwood House is the only verifiable full-scale example of William Buckland's work. It was also his final project, as he died the year the house was completed. Exquisite moldings, cornices, and other carvings appear throughout (note especially the garlands of roses above the front doorway). The house was meant to be a manorial wedding present from Matthias Hammond, a planter and revolutionary, to his fiancée, but she jilted him before the house was finished. Hammond died a bachelor in 1784. The Harwoods took over the house toward the turn of the 19th century. Today it's furnished with 18th- and early-19th-century furniture and paintings, including portraits by Charles Willson Peale. The garden is tended with regard to period authenticity. > 19 Maryland Ave., tel. 410/263–4683, www.hammondharwoodhouse.org. $6, $10 combination ticket with William Paca House. Apr. 15–Oct., daily noon–5; Jan. and Feb., weekends noon–4; Nov., Dec., and Mar.–Apr. 14, Mon.–Sat. 10–4, Sun. noon–4.

Annapolis's Midshipmen

THE U.S. NAVAL ACADEMY (USNA) in Annapolis is on the section of the Severn River that flows into the great Chesapeake Bay. Its "Yard," the 338-acre campus of the academy, is open to local joggers, bikers, dog-walkers, and those just walking through.

All students—who must receive their appointment by a member of Congress—attend free of charge and receive their uniforms as well as a monthly stipend for incidental expenses. Upon graduation, the new officers are required to serve a minimum of five years in the Armed Forces. The great majority make the Navy a career.

The USNA began quite modestly as the Naval School in 1845 on 10 acres of old Fort Severn. In 1850, a new curriculum was created that required midshipmen—"amidship" sailors already aboard U.S. naval vessels who were selected for their officer potential—to study four years and train aboard ship each summer. The origi-nal student body of 60 has grown to a brigade of some 4,000 men and women. There were 7 faculty members when the school began; today there is a group of 580, drawn from the ranks of the civilian as well as the military.

Women were first accepted in 1976 after Congress authorized admission of women to all service academies. Now more than 200 young women enter with each plebe (first-year) class, and share the title of midshipmen with their male classmates. You may view a replica midshipman's room of Bancroft Hall (the world's largest dormitory) at the USNA Armel-Leftwich Visitor Center.

Historic Annapolis Foundation Museum Store The Historic Annapolis Foundation operates its museum store in a warehouse that held supplies for the Continental Army during the Revolutionary War. Here you can shop, check out a diorama of the city's 18th-century waterfront, and rent taped narrations for the 90-minute walking tours. > 77 Main St., tel. 410/268–5576, www.hafmuseumstore.com. Free. Sun.–Thurs. 10–6, Fri. and Sat. 10–9. Variable extended hrs in summer.

King of France Tavern Adjacent to the Treaty of Paris Restaurant in the Maryland Inn is this mid-18th-century tavern. In addition to live jazz on Friday and Saturday and blues on Sunday, local artists sponsored by radio station WRNR (for "Rock 'N' Roll") perform on Monday. General George Washington is said to have lost a horse in a poker game held here. > 16 Church Circle, tel. 410/263–2641, www.annapolisinns.com.

Kunta Kinte Plaque and Alex Haley Memorial The three-sided obelisk and plaque beyond Market Square at the head of City Dock commemorates the 1767 arrival of the African slave immortalized in Alex Haley's *Roots*. The memorial to Alex Haley includes bronze sculptures portraying Haley reading to three children of different ethnic backgrounds. > www.kintehaley.org.

London Town House and Gardens Maryland's largest archaeological site, this National Historic Landmark is on the South River, 8 mi from Annapolis. The three-story waterfront brick house, built by William Brown in 1760, has 8 acres of woodland gardens. The 17th-century tobacco port of London, made up of 40 dwellings, shops, and taverns, disappeared in the 18th century, when its buildings were abandoned and left to decay. The excavation of the town is still going on. From April to September, you can join the dig one Saturday each month (call for schedule). Docents conduct 30- to 45-minute house tours; allow more time to wander the grounds. From March 15 to December, house tours leave on the hour (the last is at 3). > 839 Londontown Rd., Edgewater, tel. 410/222–1919, www.historiclondontown.com. $6. Grounds Mar. 15–Dec., Mon.–Sat. 10–4, Sun. noon–4; Jan.–Mar. 14, Tues.–Sat. 10–3.

Maryland State Archives Genealogists use the public search room for family history and historical research. Collections include original land, court, government, business, and church records; newspapers; photographs; and maps. In the lobby are changing exhibits and a gift shop. > 350 Rowe Blvd., tel. 410/260–6400 or 800/235–4045, www.mdarchives.state.md.us. Free. Wed.–Fri. 8–4:30, Sat. 8:30–noon and 1–4:30 (closed 1st Sat. of each month).

Maryland State House Completed in 1780, the State House is the oldest state capitol in continuous legislative use; it's also the only one in which the U.S. Congress has sat (1783–84). It was here that General George Washington resigned as commander in chief of the Continental Army and the Treaty of Paris was ratified, ending the Revolutionary War. Both events took place in the Old Senate Chamber, which is filled with intricate woodwork (featuring the ubiquitous tobacco motif) attributed to colonial architect William Buckland. Also decorating this room is the painting *Washington at the Battle of Yorktown,* a masterpiece by the Revolutionary War period's finest portrait artist, Charles Willson Peale. The Maryland Senate and House now hold their sessions in two other chambers in the building. Also on the grounds is the oldest public building in Maryland, the tiny redbrick **Treasury**, built in 1735. > State Circle, tel. 410/974–3400. Free. Weekdays 8:30–5; weekends 10–4; ½-hr tour daily at 11 and 3.

Middleton Tavern On weekends this historic restaurant presents local and regional acoustic musicians in the Corner Bar lounge. The Oyster Shooter—raw oysters served in a shot glass with vodka and cocktail sauce and washed down with beer—supposedly originated here. The upstairs piano bar is open on Friday and Saturday nights. > City Dock, tel. 410/263–3323, www.middletontavern.com.

St. Anne's Church St. Anne's Episcopal parish was founded in 1692; King William III donated the Communion silver. The first St. Anne's Church, built in 1704, was torn down in 1775. The second, built in 1792, burned down in 1858. Parts of the walls survived and were incorporated into the present structure, built the next year. The churchyard contains the grave of the last colonial governor, Sir Robert Eden. > Church Circle, tel. 410/267–9333. Free. Daily 8–5:30.

St. John's College Here is the alma mater of Francis Scott Key, lyricist of "The Star-Spangled Banner." However, since 1937, the college has been best known as the birthplace of the Great Books curriculum, which includes reading the works of great authors from Homer to Faulkner and beyond. All students at the college follow the same curriculum for four years, and classes are conducted as discussions rather than lectures. Climb the gradual slope of the long, brick-paved path to the impressive golden cupola of McDowell Hall, the third-oldest academic building in the country. Founded as King William's School in 1696, St. John's was chartered under its current name in 1784. St. John's grounds once held the last living Liberty Tree (the trees under which the Sons of Liberty convened to hear patriot-orators plan the Revolution against England). Wounded in a 1999 hurricane, the 400-year-old tulip poplar was removed; its progeny stands to the left of McDowell Hall. The **Elizabeth Myers**

Mitchell Art Gallery (tel. 410/626–2556), on the east side of Mellon Hall, presents exhibits and special programs that relate to the fine arts. > 60 College Ave., at St. John's St., tel. 410/263–2371, www.sjca.edu.

Thurgood Marshall Memorial Born in Baltimore, Maryland, Thurgood Marshall (1908–93) was the first African-American Supreme Court Justice and was one of the 20th century's foremost leaders in the struggle for equal rights under the law. Marshall won the decision in *Brown v. Board of Education,* in which the Supreme Court in 1954 overturned the doctrine of "separate but equal." Marshall was appointed as United States solicitor general in 1965 and to the Supreme Court in 1967 by President Lyndon B. Johnson. The 8-foot statue depicts Marshall as a young lawyer. > State House Sq., bordered by Bladen St., School St., and College Ave.

United States Naval Academy Probably the most interesting and important site in Annapolis, the Naval Academy runs along the Severn River and abuts downtown Annapolis. Midshipmen (the term used for women as well as men) enter from every part of the United States and many foreign countries to undergo rigorous study. The academy, established in 1845 on the site of a U.S. Army fort, occupies 329 waterfront acres. The centerpiece of the campus is the bright copper-clad dome of the interdenominational **U.S. Naval Academy Chapel.** Beneath it lies the crypt of the Revolutionary War naval officer John Paul Jones, who, in a historic naval battle with a British ship, uttered the inspirational words, "I have not yet begun to fight!"

Near the chapel in Preble Hall is the **U.S. Naval Academy Museum & Gallery of Ships** (118 Maryland Ave., tel. 410/293–2108), which tells the story of the U.S. Navy through displays of model ships and memorabilia from naval heroes and fighting vessels. The U.S. Naval Institute and Bookstore is also in this building. Admission for the museum, institute, and bookstore is free; hours are Monday through Saturday from 9 to 5 and Sunday from 11 to 5.

On the grounds, midshipmen go to classes, conduct military drills, and practice for or compete in intercollegiate and intramural sports. **Bancroft Hall,** closed to the public, is one of the largest dormitories in the world (it houses the entire 4,000-member Brigade of Midshipmen). The **Statue of Tecumseh,** in front of Bancroft Hall, is a bronze replica of the USS *Delaware*'s wooden figurehead, "Tamanend." It's decorated by midshipmen for athletics events, and for good luck during exams, students pitch pennies into his quiver of arrows. If you're there at noon in fair weather you can see midshipmen form up outside Bancroft Hall and parade to lunch to the beat of the Drum and Bugle Corps.

Adjoining Halsey Field House is the **USNA Armel-Leftwich Visitor Center** (52 King George St., tel. 410/263–6933), which has exhibits of midshipmen life—including a mock-up of a midshipman's room—and the *Freedom 7* space capsule flown by astronaut Alan Shepard, who was a graduate of USNA. Walking tours of the Naval Academy led by licensed guides leave from here. Note that you must have a photo ID to be admitted through the Academy's gates, and only cars used for official Department of Defense business may enter the grounds. > www.navyonline.com. Grounds tour $6.50. USNA Armel-Leftwich Visitor Center: Mar.–Dec., daily 9–5; Jan. and Feb., daily 9–4. Guided walking tours generally leave Mon.–Sat. 10–3 and Sun. 12:30–2:30; call ahead to confirm.

William Paca House and Garden Paca (pronounced "PAY-cuh") was a signer of the Declaration of Independence and a Maryland governor from 1782 to 1785. His house was built in 1765, and its original garden was finished in 1772. Inside, the main floor (furnished with 18th-century antiques) retains its original Prussian-blue and soft-gray color scheme. The second floor contains a mixture of 18th- and 19th-century pieces. The adjacent 2-acre gentlemen's pleasure garden provides a longer perspective on the back of the house, plus worthwhile sights of its own: parterres (upper terraces), a Chinese Chippendale bridge, a pond, a wilderness area, and formal arrangements. An inn, Carvel Hall, once stood on the gardens. After the inn was demolished in 1965, it took eight years to rebuild the gardens, which are planted in 18th-century perennials. > 186 Prince George St., tel. 410/263–5553, www.annapolis.org. House and garden $8, combination ticket with Hammond-Harwood House $10. House and garden mid-Mar.–Dec., Mon.–Sat. 10–5, Sun. noon–5; Jan.–mid-Mar., Fri. and Sat. 10–4, Sun. noon–4.

Tours

Annapolis Walkabout Experts on historic buildings take you around the Historic District and the United States Naval Academy ($8). Several tours leave from the visitor center at 26 West Street. > 223 S. Cherry Grove Ave., tel. 410/263–8253. Apr.–Oct., weekends 11:30.

Discover Annapolis Tours Matthew Grubbs provides hour-long narrated history and architecture tours of Annapolis in a mini-bus. Tours cover local history, the Severn River, and the United States Naval Academy, and can be tailored to include African-American history. The bus tour leaves from the visitor center daily April through November and on most weekends December through March and costs about $12. > 31 Decatur Ave., tel. 410/626–6000, www.discover-annapolis.com.

Legacy Promotions Janice Hayes-Williams, an Annapolis native, offers guided walking tours of colonial Annapolis streets not often visited by most tourists. Tours focus on historic African-American sites and include the homes of several signers of the Declaration of Independence. > 835 Spa Rd., tel. 410/280–9745.

LIBERTÉ, The Schooner In addition to private charters, the 74-foot, three-masted ship offers Sunday-brunch sails in May and June. Captain Chris lives on the schooner. > Chart House Restaurant dock, tel. 410/263–8234, www.theliberte.com.

Schooner Woodwind and the Schooner Woodwind II Between April and October, these twin 74-foot boats sail two to four times a day (except Monday) and also make some overnight trips. > Annapolis Marriott Hotel dock, 80 Compromise St., tel. 410/263–7837, www.schooner-woodwind.com.

Self-guided Walking Tours The Historic Annapolis Foundation Museum Store rents audiotapes for two self-guided walking tours: "Historic Annapolis Walk with Walter Cronkite" and "Historic Annapolis African-American Heritage Audio Walking Tour." The cost for each is $5. > 77 Main St., tel. 410/268–5576, www.hafmuseumstore.com.

Three Centuries Tours Guides wear colonial-style dress and take you to the state house, St. John's College, and the Naval Academy. Tours ($9) depart daily April through October at 10:30 from the visitor center and at 1:30 from the City Dock information booth. > 48 Maryland Ave., tel. 410/263–5401, www.annapolis-tours.com.

Watermark Cruises When the weather's good, this company runs boat tours that last from 40 minutes to 7½ hours and go as far as St. Michaels on the Eastern Shore ($6–$35). > City Dock, tel. 410/268–7600 or 410/268–7601, www.watermarkcruises.com.

Sports

SAILING

Annapolis Sailing School Billed as America's oldest and largest sailing school, the school offers two-hour basic lessons for the inexperienced. In addition, live-aboard,

cruising, and advanced-sailing programs are available, as are boat rentals. > 601 6th St., Annapolis, tel. 410/267–7205 or 800/638–9192, www.annapolissailing.com.
Annapolis Yacht Club The club sponsors sailboat races at 6 PM each Wednesday from mid-May through early September in Annapolis Harbor. > Eastport bridge, Annapolis, tel. 410/263–9279, www.annapolisyc.com.
Womanship Run by women and primarily for women who want to go on multiday sails, Womanship also has programs for girls (ages 12–17), for mother/daughter partners, for couples, and for family groups, and can custom-design classes for special needs or desires. Men are welcome to take classes as half of a couple or as part of a group. > 137 Conduit St., Annapolis, tel. 410/267–6661 or 800/342–9295, www.womanship.com.

Shopping

Stores along Maryland Avenue as well as on Main Street in downtown Annapolis sell antiques and fine art, fashions, arts and crafts, home furnishings, and gifts and souvenirs, as well as nautical clothing and other necessities for seasoned salts and would-be sailors alike. Dealers in fine antiques also abound along Maryland Avenue. Other shops are in nearby West Annapolis.

ANTIQUES
Annapolis Antique Gallery A consortium of 35–40 dealers sells Victorian and art deco pieces. > 2009 West St., tel. 410/266–0635.
Ron Snyder Antiques Next door to the Annapolis Antique Gallery, these seven tastefully decorated rooms display 18th- and 19th-century American furniture. > 2011 West St., tel. 410/266–5452.

Save the Date

MAY
Maryland Maritime Heritage Festival The proud seafaring heritage of Maryland is celebrated in a weekend of exhibits, traditional Chesapeake Bay watercraft, antique and classic boats, maritime art exhibits, and artists, musicians, singers, and storytellers. > City Dock Annapolis, tel. 410/263–9446, www.mdmaritimefestival.com.

AUGUST
Kunta Kinte Heritage Festival Families are at the heart of this celebration of the heritage, culture, history, music, and cuisine of Africans, African-Americans, and African-Caribbeans. > St. John's College, tel. 410/349–0338, www.kuntakinte.org.

SEPTEMBER
Maryland Seafood Festival Live music is in the air at this event, where you can taste seafood and other regional favorites. Activities include the Maryland Crab Soup Cook-off, beach bingo, face painting, beach golf, treasure hunts, a petting zoo, rock wall climbing, and beach volleyball. Many unique local arts and crafts are also on display. > Sandy Point State Park, tel. 410/268–7682, www.mdseafoodfestival.com.

OCTOBER
Boat Shows The nation's two oldest and largest in-water boat shows are held on back-to-back weeks: United States Sailboat Show and United States Power Boat Show. All the new racing and cruising sailboats from U.S. and foreign builders make up the first show. The next covers motorboats, including trawlers and luxurious yachts. > Annapolis City Dock, tel. 410/268–8828, www.usboat.com.

WHERE TO STAY

Annapolis Inn An extraordinarily elegant B&B, this circa-1770 house has an intimate and richly colored dining room and parlors, decorated in a style in keeping with the era of the original home. The master suite has a formal sitting room and two fire-places. All suites have a king-size bed with imported luxury linens, and bathrooms include two whirlpool baths. The third-floor suite's sundeck offers a view of the Naval Academy Chapel, the state capitol, and a glimpse of the harbor. There's generally a two-night minimum on weekends. > 144 Prince George St., 21401, tel. 410/295–5200, fax 410/295–5201, www.annapolisinn.com. 3 suites. Dining room, in-room data ports, some in-room hot tubs, free parking; no kids, no smoking. AE, MC, V. BP. **$$$$**

Annapolis Marriott Waterfront You can practically fish from your room at the city's only waterfront hotel. Rooms, done in a modern style with mauve quilted bed-spreads, have either balconies over the water or large windows with views of the harbor or the historic district. The outdoor bar by the harbor's edge is popular in nice weather. > 80 Compromise St., 21401, tel. 410/268–7555 or 800/336–0072, fax 410/269–5864, www.annapolismarriott.com. 150 rooms. Restaurant, in-room data ports, cable TV, gym, boating, 2 bars, laundry service, concierge, business services, meeting rooms, parking (fee), no-smoking rooms. AE, D, DC, MC, V. **$$$$**

Best Western Annapolis This well-maintained two-story motel is a good value. Although it's set away from traffic intersections, it's just 3 mi from the United States Naval Academy. Guest rooms, entered from the parking lot, are decorated in forest green with quilted floral bedspreads. There's an outdoor covered deck for enjoying breakfast or your own picnic. From U.S. 50, take Exit 22 and follow the signs to Riva Road North. The motel is in a business park on your left. > 2520 Riva Rd., 21401, tel. 410/224–2800 or 800/638–5179, fax 410/266–5539, www.bestwestern.com. 142 rooms. In-room data ports, pool, gym, laundry service, meeting rooms, free parking. AE, D, DC, MC, V. CP. **¢–$**

Gibson's Lodgings Three detached houses from three decades—1780, 1890, and 1980—are operated together as a single inn. One of the house's hallways is strikingly lined with mirrors. Guest rooms are furnished with pre-1900 antiques. One first-floor room, which has a private bath and porch, is designed for disabled access. Free parking in the courtyards is a big advantage in the heart of this small colonial-era city (the houses are opposite the United States Naval Academy). Continental breakfast is served in the formal dining room of the 18th-century Patterson House. > 110–114 Prince George St., 21401, tel. 410/268–5555 or 877/330–0057, fax 410/268–2775, www.avmcyber.com/gibson. 21 rooms, 17 with bath. Dining room, some in-room data ports, cable TV in some rooms, meeting rooms, free parking; no TV in some rooms, no kids under 5, no smoking. AE, MC, V. CP. **$–$$**

Historic Inns of Annapolis A stay in one of these 18th-century inns will add still more historic charm to your Annapolis visit. Registration for all three is at the 51-room **Governor Calvert House**, built in 1727 for the Maryland chief executive, who was also cousin to the fifth Lord Baltimore. At 23 State Circle, the 25-room **Robert Johnson House** was built for the Annapolis barber in 1772 by his grandson. The **Maryland Inn**, with 34 guest rooms and 10 suites, has some rooms that date back to the Revolutionary era. It's at 16 Church Circle (the entrance is on Main Street). The Treaty of Paris Restaurant, the King of France Tavern, and the Drummer's Lot Pub serve all three inns. Guest rooms are individually decorated with antiques and reproductions; all have coffeemakers and hair dryers, and some have kitchenettes, sitting suites, or whirlpools. > 58 State Circle, 21401, tel. 410/263–2641 or 800/847–8882, fax 410/268–3613, www.annapolisinns.com. 110 rooms, 10 suites. Restaurant, in-room data ports, some in-room hot tubs, some kitchenettes, health club, bar, pub, laundry service, concierge, business services, meeting rooms, parking (fee), no-smoking rooms. AE, D, DC, MC, V. **$$**

Loews Annapolis Hotel Although its redbrick exterior blends with the city's 18th-century architecture, the interior is airy, spacious, and modern. The lobby is done in light green and brown; the parquet floor has a herringbone pattern. Guest rooms come with coffeemakers and terry robes. A free hotel shuttle bus takes you anywhere you want to go in Annapolis. > 126 West St., 21401, tel. 410/263–7777 or 800/235–6397, fax 410/263–0084, www.loewsannapolis.com. 210 rooms, 7 suites. 2 restaurants, room service, in-room data ports, minibars, gym, hair salon, bar, dry cleaning, laundry service, concierge, concierge floor, business services, meeting rooms, airport shuttle, parking (fee), no-smoking floors. AE, D, DC, MC, V. **$$**

O'Callaghan Hotel When this Irish-owned and -operated hotel opened in 2002 in a former Holiday Inn, it was the city's first new downtown hotel in more than two decades. The lush carpets, in deep blues, golds, and other colors, and floor-length drapes were custom-made in Ireland (most of the attentive staff is from the Emerald Isle as well). Meeting rooms are named after counties in Ireland, and maps and pictures of the Old Country adorn the elegant guest rooms. The first-floor restaurant and bar overlooks West Street and carries a limited but fine selection of entrées. > 174 West St., 21401, tel. 410/263–7700, fax 410/990–1400, www.ocallaghanhotels.com. 120 rooms, 2 suites. Restaurant, cable TV with movies and video games, health club, bar, concierge, laundry services, business services, meeting rooms, parking (fee). AE, MC, V. **$$$$**

Scotlaur Inn This family-owned bed-and-breakfast takes up the two floors above Chick and Ruth's Delly. Rooms are papered in pastel colonial prints, and hobnail bedspreads cover the beds. All rooms have private baths, irons, ironing boards, and hair dryers. Breakfast is downstairs. > 165 Main St., 21401, tel. 410/268–5665, fax 410/269–6738, www.scotlaurinn.com. 10 rooms. Restaurant; no smoking. MC, V. CP. **¢–$**

William Page Inn Built in 1908, this dark-brown, cedar-shingle, wood-frame structure was the local Democratic party clubhouse for 50 years. Today its wraparound porch is furnished with Adirondack chairs. The slope-ceiling third-floor suite with dormer windows includes an Italian-marble bathroom with whirlpool. Breakfast is served in the common room. There's a two-night minimum for weekend stays. > 8 Martin St., 21401, tel. 410/626–1506 or 800/364–4160, www.williampageinn.com. 4 rooms, 2 with bath; 1 suite. Some in-room hot tubs, free parking, no-smoking rooms; no kids under 12. MC, V. BP. **$–$$$**

WHERE TO EAT

Aqua Terra This funky restaurant gives history-minded Annapolis an alternative to the colonial-style establishments that predominate in downtown. Inside are bare floors, blond-wood furniture, an open kitchen, and a handsome granite counter under a row of blue teardrop-shape lamps. The menu changes with each season, but always employs seafood, beef, and pasta as regular features. A summer menu included Cajun New York strip: a handsome cut of beef topped with pink curls of shrimp, butter, and chopped garlic. The summer's linguine is tossed with lumps of crab, fresh tomatoes, and shallots. > 164 Main St., tel. 410/263–1985. AE, MC, V. **$–$$$**

Breeze The blues, sand tones, teak, and beach glass all intimate a contemporary flair at this relaxed restaurant. Chef Shane Henderson taps into the rich bounty of the Chesapeake region—from both water and land. His menu includes rockfish with fried green tomatoes and a leek and lobster salad. A favorite is Crab 3 Ways: crab cake, crab dip, and crabmeat in a champagne-butter sauce. > Loews Annapolis Hotel, 126 West St., tel. 410/295–3232. AE, D, DC, MC, V. $$$–$$$$

Café Normandie Ladder-back chairs, wooden beams, skylights, and a four-sided fireplace make this French restaurant homey. Out of the open kitchen—with its blue-and-white ceramic tiles—comes an astonishingly good French onion soup, made daily from scratch. Puffy omelets, crepes, and seafood dishes are other specialties. The restaurant's brunch (Friday through Sunday) offers American and French dishes, including poached eggs in ratatouille, eggs Benedict, seafood omelets, pancakes, waffles, and croissants and muffins made from scratch. > 185 Main St., tel. 410/263–3382. AE, D, DC, MC, V. $$–$$$$

Cantler's Riverside Inn Opened in 1974, this local institution was founded by Bay waterman Jimmy Cantler. The no-nonsense interior has wooden blinds and floors, nautical items laminated beneath tabletops, and metal chairs. Food is served with disposable dinnerware; if you order steamed crabs, your "tablecloth" will be brown paper. Outdoor dining is available seasonally. Boat owners can tie up at the dock; drivers must fight for parking during the busy summer season. Specialties are steamed mussels, clams, and shrimp as well as Maryland vegetable crab soup, seafood sandwiches, oysters, crab cakes, and numerous finfish. To get here from U.S. 50, take Exit 29A onto Busch's Frontage Road. At the flashing light, turn right onto St. Margaret's Road and follow for 2.3 mi. Turn left onto Brown's Woods Road; then take the first right onto Forest Beach Road and follow it to the end. > 458 Forest Beach Rd., St. Margaret's, tel. 410/757–1311, www.cantlers.com. AE, D, DC, MC, V. $–$$$

Carrol's Creek You can walk, catch a water taxi from City Dock, or drive over the Spa Creek drawbridge to this local favorite in Eastport. Whether you dine indoors or out, the view of Annapolis and its harbor is spectacular. The all-you-can-eat Sunday brunch is of special note, as are the seafood specialties. A menu standout is macadamia-encrusted mahimahi, which is served over sweet mashed potatoes with a mango compote. > 410 Severn Ave., Eastport, tel. 410/263–8102, www.carrolscreek.com. AE, D, DC, MC, V. $$–$$$$

Chick and Ruth's Delly Deli sandwiches (named for local politicos), burgers, subs, milk shakes, and other ice cream concoctions are the bill of fare at this counter-and-table institution, which has been here since 1965. > 165 Main St., tel. 410/269–6737, www.chickandruths.com. No credit cards. ¢–$$

El Toro Bravo A local favorite, this inexpensive, authentic Mexican restaurant is family-owned. The wooden colonial exterior conceals colorful, south-of-the-border scenes hand-painted on the interior walls, hanging plants, and padded aqua booths. There's usually a line but takeout is available. Lunch and dinner specials include enchiladas, fish tacos, grilled shrimp, and steak. The guacamole is made on the premises. > 50 West St. (1 block from visitor center), tel. 410/267–5949. AE, D, DC, MC, V. ¢–$

Harry Browne's Sitting unobtrusively across from the imposing State House, this understated establishment is a popular place to entertain special friends and visitors. A deserved reputation for quality Continental cuisine and attentive service assures bustle here year-round, and during the busy days of the legislative session (early January into early April) and special weekend events at the Naval Academy, advance reservations are a must. The menu clearly reflects the city's maritime culture, but also has other seasonal specialties, such as rack of lamb and wild mushroom ravioli. Live Irish music is performed in the lounge every Monday night. The sidewalk café is open, when the weather allows, April through October. > 66 State Circle, tel. 410/263–4332. AE, D, DC, MC, V. $$$–$$$$

McGarvey's Saloon and Oyster Bar An Annapolis institution open since 1975, this dockside eatery and watering hole is full of good cheer, great drink, and grand food. A heritage of seasonal shell- and finfish dishes, the finest burgers and steaks, as well as unstinting appetizers, make the McGarvey's menu one of the most popular in the area. The full menu is available daily until 11 PM. > 8 Market Space, tel. 410/263–5700. AE, DC, MC, V. ¢–$$$

Middleton Tavern Oyster Bar and Restaurant Horatio Middleton began operating this "inn for seafaring men" in 1750; Washington, Jefferson, and Franklin were among its patrons. Today, two fireplaces, wood floors, paneled walls, and a nautical theme give it a cozy charm. Seafood tops the menu; the Maryland crab soup and broiled Chesapeake Bay rockfish are standouts. Try the tavern's own Middleton Pale Ale, perhaps during a weekend blues session in the upstairs piano bar. Brunch is served on weekends, and you can dine outdoors in good weather. > 2 Market Space, City Dock at Randall St., tel. 410/263–3323. AE, D, MC, V. ¢–$$$$

Phillips Annapolis Harbor With a panoramic view of the harbor, this city-dock eatery belongs to a group of popular local restaurants whose forte is Maryland-style seafood. The bar and lounge is on the ground floor; the dining room, on the second floor. The restaurant's skylights and glassed-in all-season room keep things sunny. Specialties include buckets of mussels, clams on the half shell, lump crab cocktail, crab-stuffed flounder, seafood platters, and a clambake for two. > 87 Prince George St. (12 Dock St.), tel. 410/990–9888. AE, D, DC, MC, V. $$–$$$$

Rams Head Tavern A traditional English-style pub also houses the Fordham Brewing Company, which you can tour. The Rams Head serves better-than-usual tavern fare, including spicy shrimp salad, crab cakes, and beer-battered shrimp, as well as more than 170 beers—26 on tap—from around the world. Brunch is served on Sunday. The nightclub-like Rams Head Tavern On Stage brings in nationally known folk, rock, jazz, country, and bluegrass artists. Dinner-show combo specials are offered; the menu has light fare. > 33 West St., tel. 410/268–4545, www.ramsheadtavern.com. AE, D, MC, V. $–$$$$

Treaty of Paris Restaurant Period reproduction furniture and fabrics decorate this handsome, 18th-century dining room. For dinner, you may want to try such Continental dishes as beef Wellington or seafood choices such as crab imperial, twin lobster tails, and crab cakes. Colonial Tea Time is Wednesday from 3 to 4. > Maryland Inn, 16 Church Circle, tel. 410/263–2641. AE, D, MC, V. $$$–$$$$

ESSENTIALS

Getting Here

Although you can get to Annapolis on a bus, it's far easier to see all the city's many sites via car. If you confined yourself to the Historic District, you could see everything on foot—but even that confined area would require a great deal of walking.

BY BUS

Bus service between Washington, D.C., and Annapolis is geared toward commuters rather than vacationers. Weekday mornings and afternoons, buses arrive at and depart from the Navy–Marine Corps Stadium parking lot, from College Avenue by the state buildings, and also from St. John's

College. On weekends Greyhound makes one trip daily, arriving at and departing from the stadium.

LINES **Academy Bus Lines** > Tel. 800/992–0451, www.academybus.com.**Dillons Bus Service** > Tel. 410/647–2321 or 800/827–3490, www.dillonbus.com. **Greyhound Lines** > Tel. 609/345–6617 or 800/231–2222, www.greyhound.com. **Mass Transit Administration** (MTA) > Tel. 410/539–5000, www.mtamaryland.com.

BY CAR

Annapolis is normally 35–45 minutes by car from Washington, D.C., on U.S. 50 (Rowe Blvd. exit). During rush hour (weekdays 3:30–6:30 PM), however, it takes about twice as long.

Parking spots on Annapolis's historic downtown streets are scarce, but there are some parking meters for 50¢ an hour (maximum two hours). You can park on residential streets free where allowable; the maximum parking time is to hours. You can pay $4 ($8 for recreational vehicles) to park at the Navy–Marine Corps Stadium (to the right of Rowe Blvd. as you enter town from U.S. 50), and ride a shuttle bus downtown for 75¢. Parking is also available at garages on Main Street and Gott's Court (adjacent to the visitor center); on weekdays parking is free for the first hour and $1 an hour thereafter; on weekends it costs $4 a day.

PARKING

Visitor Information

From April to October the information booth on City Dock, adjacent to the harbormaster's office, is open and stocked with maps and brochures.

CONTACTS **Annapolis & Anne Arundel County Conference & Visitors Bureau** > 26 West St., tel. 410/280–0445, www.visit-annapolis.org. Daily 9–5. **City Dock Information Booth** > Dock St. parking lot, tel. 410/280–0445.

Baltimore

40 mi north of Washington, D.C.

2

Revised by Kristi Delovitch

THIS UNDERRATED PORT CITY is often overshadowed by the political dramas of the capital city to the south. But Baltimore has a unique identity, one that the film director and Baltimore native John Waters characterized as "gloriously decrepit [and] inexplicably charming." Quirky and down-to-earth, Baltimore is an easily accessible reprieve from Washington's frantic pace and high-voltage decision making. What most people who come to town remember are the laid-back waterfront restaurants, the long-standing ethnic neighborhoods, the offbeat museums, and unmistakable icons like the harbor and the Baltimore Orioles.

After Ellis Island, Baltimore was the second-largest port of entry for U.S. immigrants, and that past lives on in its many distinct neighborhoods. The Inner Harbor is the heart of the city: the Maryland Science Center and the National Aquarium, both in this area, remain Baltimore's two most popular attractions. Massive renovations of the downtown and Inner Harbor, begun in the 1980s, have also brought Port Discovery, Baltimore's children's museum; the conversion of the city's old power plant into a sports and entertainment complex; an expanded convention center; and a new stadium for the Ravens, the city's football team.

Federal Hill, which overlooks the Inner Harbor, is one of the oldest neighborhoods in Baltimore. Fort McHenry, whose still-waving flag inspired Francis Scott Key to write "The Star-Spangled Banner," is here. Federal Hill Park, named when Maryland ratified the Constitution, has what may be the best view in town.

Before the Inner Harbor took away its title, Fells Point was the city's main port. Settled in 1730 by Quaker shipbuilder William Fell, the area is best known today for its boisterous weekends, when swarms of partyers fill the cobblestone streets and move from one casual bar to the next. In spite of the exuberant nightlife, Fells Point's narrow lanes and redbrick buildings retain their charm. Head to the Fells Point Maritime Museum to find out more about the neighborhood's seafaring past; you might also want to check out the many shops specializing in antique accessories and knick-knacks: these are concentrated on Eastern, Fleet, and Aliceanna streets.

Little Italy, which covers 12 blocks just east of the Inner Harbor, has been Italian since the mid-1800s, when workers arrived here for the promise of railroad jobs. By 1900, every home in the neighborhood was Italian. A century later, this residential area still holds numerous trattorias and bakeries.

Once a run-down collection of industrial buildings and working-class houses, Canton is now a community of restaurants, former canneries and factories converted into condos and shops, and row houses restored to their 19th-century appearance. O'Donnell Square, flanked by a stone church and an old fire station, holds many good eateries and bars. You can reach Canton via water taxi from Fells Point or the Inner Harbor.

Mount Vernon, with its collection of white marble steps, 19th-century row houses, and tree-shaded streets, is one of the nation's most beautiful neighborhoods. Once the home of the city's elite, Mount Vernon is now known for museums, churches, and cultural institutions that include the Peabody Conservatory of Music. The 500–1000 blocks of North Charles form a restaurant row. Popular ethnic restaurants like Helmand, the city's first Afghan restaurant, line the main drag. Most of Baltimore's antiques shops can be found along the 700 and 800 blocks of North Howard Street, which form the western border of Mount Vernon. The 40 shops here represent more than 70 dealers. Some of the shops are cluttered with kitsch; others hold elegant furniture and fine art.

Wherever you decide to sightsee, keep in mind that there's one view that can't be seen from any neighborhood in the city—that's the one from the harbor itself. Whether you see it on a harbor cruise, paddleboat, or a water taxi, the city's evolving skyline is well worth the trip.

WHAT TO SEE & DO

American Dime Museum It's no surprise that Baltimore, a town with a sense of humor about itself and others, embraces this tribute. "Dime Museums," traveling collections of man-made and natural curiosities popular in the 1800s, were called that after the typical cost of admission. Baltimore's most eccentric museum is dedicated to these carnival sideshows, displaying a collection of colorful artifacts: sideshow banners, props, and believe-it-or-not displays that include a "Feegee mermaid" and a "genuine" unicorn. > 1808 Maryland Ave., Midtown, tel. 410/230–0263, www.dimemuseum.com. $5. Wed.–Fri. noon–3, weekends noon–5.

American Visionary Art Museum The nation's museum and education center for self-taught or "outsider" art has won great acclaim by both museum experts and those who don't usually consider themselves art aficionados. Seven galleries exhibit the unusual creations—paintings, sculptures, relief works, and pieces that defy easy classification—of untrained "visionary" artists working outside art's mainstream. There are only a few permanent pieces in the museum; exhibitions turn over every nine months. Past exhibitions have included art about angels and art by female victims of domestic violence. The museum's restaurant, the Joy America Cafe, has a view of the Baltimore Harbor and an exuberant menu to match its playful name. > 800 Key Hwy., Federal Hill, tel. 410/244–1900, www.avam.org. $8. Tues.–Sun. 10–6.

Atomic Books The store's motto, "literary finds for mutated minds," gives some idea of the small-press publications, comics, 'zines, and videos sold here. The formidable selection of pop-culture toys includes lunch boxes, cookie jars, and stickers. Those who like Atomic Books really, really like it. > 1100 W. 36th St., Hampden, tel. 410/662–4444, www.atomicbooks.com.

Babe Ruth Birthplace and Museum This modest brick row house, just three blocks from Oriole Park at Camden Yards, was the birthplace of "the Bambino." Although Ruth was born here in 1895, his family never actually lived here; they lived in a nearby apartment, above a tavern run by Ruth's father. The row house and the adjoining buildings make up a museum devoted to Ruth's life and to the Orioles. Film clips, rare photos of Ruth, a score book from Ruth's first professional game, and many other artifacts can be found here, along with Orioles memorabilia that includes bats and other items associated with Cal Ripken Jr. The museum often stays open until 7 PM when the Orioles are playing a night game at home. > 216 Emory St., Downtown,

Where Locals Dine

HEAD FOR THE MARKETS *if you want to eat with the people that live here. Baltimore has seven indoor food markets, all of them at least 100 years old. Inside are Chesapeake Bay seafood, imported cheeses, fresh flowers, other produce, and meats. The most famous, Lexington Market, is also America's oldest municipal market. Of the 140 merchants in Lexington Market (Lexington St., between Paca and Eutaw Sts., West Baltimore, 410/685–6169), a few stand out as famous Baltimore brands. Faidley's Seafood is the most famous place in Baltimore for crab cakes. Though Faidley's also has cheaper alternatives, which use claw meat and back fin, indulge in the $12.95 Jumbo Lump Cake. You can eat it standing at the no-frills counter. Other local favorites include Pollock Johnny's sausages, and Bergers Bakery, famous for the indulgent chocolate top cookie, which is crowned by a huge glob of icing. Because the market is in a high-crime area, limit your visit to daylight hours.*

Federal Hill's Cross Street Market (410/276–9498), on the corner of Light Street, is a popular alternative to Lexington. The market slopes downward, and at the bottom is Tony's Sushi, known for its sushi happy hour and a popular oyster raw bar. Also inside is the Cross Street Cheese Company, which carries a wide selection of domestic and imported cheeses.

At the top of Fells Point, Broadway Market (Broadway and Fleet) is a great option for a quick bite after walking the neighborhood's cobblestones. A large building in the middle of Thames Street, Broadway holds the famous Fells Point Chicken as well as Broadway Seafood, which serves very fresh shucked oysters.

tel. 410/727–1539, www.baberuthmuseum.com. $6. Apr.–Oct., daily 10–5; Nov.–Mar., daily 10–4.

Baltimore Maritime Museum The three docked vessels and the restored lighthouse that make up this museum give a good sense of Baltimore's and the nation's maritime heritage and power. The submarine USS *Torsk*, painted like a giant shark, was nicknamed the "Galloping Ghost of the Japanese Coast." It sunk the last two Japanese warships in World War II. The lightship *Chesapeake*, built as a floating lighthouse in 1930 and now out of commission, remains fully operational. The *Taney* is a Coast Guard cutter that saw action at Pearl Harbor. Built in 1856, the Seven Foot Knoll Lighthouse marked the entrance to the Baltimore Harbor from the Chesapeake Bay for 133 years before its move to the museum. > Pier 3, Inner Harbor, tel. 410/396–3453, www.baltomaritimemuseum.org. $6. Mar.–Dec., Sun.–Thurs. 10–5:30, Fri. and Sat. 10–6:30; Jan. and Feb., Fri.–Sun. 10:30–5.

Baltimore Museum of Art Roughly 100,000 paintings, sculptures, and decorative arts are on exhibit at this impressive museum, where the holdings include works by Matisse, Picasso, Cézanne, Gauguin, van Gogh, and Monet. The museum also owns the world's second-largest collection of Andy Warhol works, and many pieces of 18th- and 19th-century American painting and decorative arts. The neoclassical main building was designed by John Russell Pope, the architect of Washington's National Gallery. > 10 Art Museum Dr., Charles Village, tel. 410/396–7100, www.artbma.org. $7, free 1st Thurs. of month. Wed.–Fri. 11–5, weekends 11–6, 1st Thurs. of month 11–8.

Baltimore Museum of Industry Inside an 1865 oyster cannery, this tribute to the city's industrial and labor history is worth the ½-mi walk south of the Inner Harbor along Key Highway. Here, you can watch and help operate the functional re-creations of a machine shop, a print shop, a cannery, and a garment workroom. When enough children are in the museum, an interactive kids cannery is organized: work like this was often carried out by children in the early 1900s. Docked outside is a restored steam-driven tugboat that covered the waterfront in the first half of the 20th century. > 1415 Key Hwy., Federal Hill, tel. 410/727–4808, www.thebmi.org. $6. Mon.–Sat. 10–5, Sun. noon–5.

Dr. Samuel D. Harris National Museum of Dentistry Appropriately, this unusual museum is on the Baltimore campus of the University of Maryland, the world's first dental school. Housed in a Roman Renaissance revival–style building, the museum has exhibits on the anatomy and physiology of human and animal teeth and the history of dentistry; you can also play a tune on the "Tooth Jukebox." One popular exhibit displays the dental instruments used in treating Queen Victoria in the mid-19th century, and the museum also has a set of George Washington's dentures. Quirky finds in the gift shop include denture boxer shorts and chairs shaped like giant molars. > 31 S. Greene St., Downtown, tel. 410/706–0600. $4.50. Wed.–Sat. 10–4, Sun. 1–4.

Fells Point Maritime Museum Opened in 2003, this former trolley-car barn is now a museum that focuses on the port's golden age, from the mid-1700s to the 1830s, when Fells Point's ship industry was very important. Among the many seafaring exhibits are 23 models of Baltimore clipper ships. The Maryland Historical Society's collection of artifacts are also on display. > 1724 Thames St., Fells Point, tel. 410/732–0278 or 410/685–3750, www.mdhs.org. $4. Thurs.–Mon. 10–5.

Fort McHenry Francis Scott Key wrote the words for "The Star-Spangled Banner" as he watched the redcoats bombard Fort McHenry during the War of 1812. A visit to the fort includes a 16-minute history film, guided tour, and frequent living-history displays (including battle reenactments) on weekends. To see how the formidable fortifications might have appeared to the British, catch a water taxi from the Inner Harbor to the fort instead of driving. > E. Fort Ave., Locust Point, from Light St., take Key Hwy. for 1½ mi and follow signs, tel. 410/962–4290, www.nps.gov/fomc. $5. Memorial Day–Labor Day, daily 8–8; Labor Day–Memorial Day, daily 8–5.

Harborplace and The Gallery Part of Baltimore's move toward urban renewal, this development was built in 1980. The two airy, glass-enclosed structures each have a different function: the Light Street Pavilion has two stories of food courts and restaurants and the Pratt Street Pavilion is dedicated mainly to retail stores. Jugglers, bands, and other street performers entertain the crowd at an outdoor amphitheater between the two pavilions, and paddleboats can be rented south of the Pratt Street building. A skywalk from the Pratt Street Pavilion leads to the **Gallery,** a four-story shopping mall with 70 more shops, including J. Crew, Coach, and Godiva Chocolatiers. Harborplace and the Gallery have extended summer hours; some restaurants open earlier for breakfast, and most close very late. > 100 Pratt St., Inner Harbor, tel. 410/332–4191, www.harborplace.com. Mon.–Sat. 10–9, Sun. 10–6.

Maryland Historical Society More than 200,000 objects, including period furnishings, textiles, costumes, and toys, serve to celebrate Maryland's history and heritage. The Radcliffe Maritime Collection tells the history of the Chesapeake Bay and the Port of Baltimore. Two major attractions are the original manuscript of "The Star-Spangled Banner" and the world's largest collection of 19th-century American silver. The exhibit Looking for Liberty in Maryland focuses on individuals who made large contributions to the state, including Francis Scott Key, Barbara Fritchie, and the signers of the Declaration of Independence. > 201 W. Monument St., Midtown, tel. 410/685–3750, www.mdhs.org. $8. Wed.–Sun. 10–5.

Maryland Science Center This science center, known as the Maryland Academy of Sciences when it began in 1797, is one of the oldest scientific institutions in the United States. The three floors of interactive exhibits cover the Chesapeake Bay, applied science, natural history, and outer space and serve as an invitation to engage, experiment, and explore. There's a planetarium, a simulated archaeological dinosaur dig, and an IMAX movie theater with a screen five stories high. > 601 Light St., Inner Harbor, tel. 410/685–5225, www.mdsci.org. Museum $12, IMAX tickets $7.50, combination $15.50. Sept.–June, weekdays 10–5, Sat. 10–6, Sun. noon–5; July and Aug., weekdays 10–5, weekends 10–6.

Mount Vernon Square One of the most beautifully designed public spaces in the world, Mount Vernon Square acquired its ground and name when John Eager Howard donated the highest point in Baltimore as a site for a memorial to George Washington. With the monument as its center, the square is composed of four parks, each a block in length, that are arranged around Mount Vernon Place (which runs east–west) and Washington Place (north–south). The sculptures in the parks deserve a close look; of special note is a bronze lion by Barye in the middle of West Mount Vernon Place. Northeast of the monument is Mount Vernon Methodist Church, built in the mid-1850s on the site of Francis Scott Key's home and place of death. Take a moment to admire the brownstones along the north side of East Mount Vernon Place. They're excellent examples of the luxurious mansions built by 19th-century residents of Baltimore's most prestigious address.

National Aquarium in Baltimore The most-visited attraction in Maryland has more than 10,000 fish, sharks, dolphins, and amphibians dwelling in 2 million gallons of water. They're joined by the reptiles, birds, plants, and mammals inside the center's rain-forest environment, a glass pyramid 64 feet high. In the Marine Mammal Pavilion, seven Atlantic bottlenose dolphins give several entertaining shows a day that highlight their agility and intelligence. The aquarium's famed shark tank and Atlantic coral reef exhibits are spectacular; you can wind through an enormous glass enclosure on a spiral ramp while hammerheads glide by. Timed tickets may be required on weekends and holidays; purchase these early in the day. > Pier 3, Inner Harbor, tel. 410/576–3800, www.aqua.org. $17.50. Mar.–June, Sept., and Oct., Sat.–Thurs. 9–5, Fri. 9–8; July and Aug., Mon.–Thurs. 9–6, Fri.–Sun. 9–8; Nov.–Feb., Sat.–Thurs. 10–5, Fri. 10–8; visitors may tour for up to 2 hrs after closing.

Oriole Park at Camden Yards Since its opening in 1992, this baseball stadium has inspired other cities to emulate its nostalgic design and state-of-the-art amenities. Home of the Baltimore Orioles, Camden Yards bustles on game days but is accessible in the off-season as well. The Eutaw Street promenade, between the warehouse and the field, is open daily and has a view of the stadium; look for the brass baseballs embedded in the sidewalk that mark where home runs have cleared the fence, or visit the Orioles Hall of Fame display and the monuments to retired Orioles. (The glove on the Babe Ruth statue was placed on the wrong hand, making for a citywide debate.) Daily tours take fans to many of the ballpark's nooks and crannies, from the immense JumboTron scoreboard to the dugout to the technologically advanced beer delivery system. > 333 W. Camden St., Downtown, tel. 410/685–9800 general information, 410/547–6234 tour times, 410/481–7328 tickets to Orioles home games, www.theorioles.com. Eutaw St. promenade free, tour $5. Eutaw St. promenade daily 10–3, otherwise during games and tours.

Port Discovery—The Baltimore Children's Museum Designed to offer a different experience for every visitor, this interactive museum is like no other—adults are encouraged to play every bit as much as the children. On the three-story KidWorks, a sort of futuristic jungle gym, children can climb, crawl, slide, and swing their way through stairs, slides, ropes, zip-lines, and tunnels, and even traverse a narrow foot-bridge three stories up; there is a smaller version of KidWorks for toddlers. > 35 Market Pl., Inner Harbor, tel. 410/727–8120, www.portdiscovery.com. $11. Memorial Day–Labor Day, daily 10–6; Labor Day–Memorial Day, Tues.–Sat. 10–5, Sun. noon–5.

The Power Plant What once really was the city's power plant is now a bustling day-and nighttime retail and dining complex that includes a Hard Rock Cafe, a Barnes & Noble, and an ESPN Zone: its 35,000 square feet are devoted to sports, entertainment, and dining. Designed by Disney and ESPN, the two-level facility is supposed to feel like a stadium. Diners can participate in virtual-reality sports activities or watch their favorite teams on TV. ESPN occasionally broadcasts live from the Zone, especially during and after Baltimore Orioles baseball games or other local sporting events. > Pier 5, 601 E. Pratt St., Inner Harbor, No phone.

Senator Theatre Built around 1939, this 900-seat movie house in northern Baltimore is on the National Register of Historic Places. With art-deco style, velvet curtains, and a retro lobby, it's a great place to view the new and classic films screened here (the owner is a huge George Lucas fan)—nearly every movie made in Maryland premieres here. The theater also hosts film festivals (hosts include Baltimore personalities like Barry Levinson) and musical performances. No children under five are admitted. > 5904 York Rd., North Baltimore, tel. 410/435–8338, www.senator.com. No credit cards. $8. Daily.

Star-Spangled Banner House Built in 1793, this federal-style home was where Mary Pickersgill sewed the 15-star, 15-stripe flag that flew above Fort McHenry in 1814 and that inspired Francis Scott Key to write "The Star-Spangled Banner." The house contains federal furniture and American art of the period, including pieces from the Pickersgill family. Outdoors, a map of the United States has been made of stones from corresponding states. A museum connected to the house tells the history of the War of 1812. > 844 E. Pratt St., Inner Harbor East, tel. 410/837–1793, www.flaghouse.org. $5. Tues.–Sat. 10–4.

USS Constellation Launched in 1854, the USS *Constellation* was the last—and largest—all-sail ship built by the U.S. Navy. Before the Civil War, as part of the African Squadron, she saw service on antislavery patrol; during the war, she protected Union-sympathizing U.S. merchant ships from Confederate raiders. You can tour the *Constellation* for a glimpse of life as a 19th-century navy sailor, and children can muster to become Civil War–era "powder monkeys." Recruits receive "basic training," try on replica period uniforms, participate in a gun drill, and learn a sea chantey or two before being discharged and paid off in Civil War money at the end of their tour of duty. > Pratt and Light Sts., Inner Harbor. tel. 410/539–6238, www.constellation.org. $6.50. May–mid-Oct., daily 10–6; mid-Oct.–Apr., daily 10–4.

Vaccaro's With the strong smell of Italian coffee, glass cases of homemade desserts, and a rainbow of gelato, Vaccaro's is the unrivaled king of desserts in Little Italy. Heavy crowds pack into the two-story building after dinner for a coffee, cordial, or one of the store's famous cannoli (thousands are shipped nationally each year). Monday night is all you can eat and drink for $11 (this price excludes alcohol). Although there are locations around the city, the original Little Italy location is unique, with the most character. > 222 Albemarle, Little Italy, tel. 410/685–4905, www.vaccarospastry.com.

Walters Art Museum The 30,000 works of art at the Walters provide an organized overview of human history from the 3rd millennium BC to the early 20th century. The original museum (1904) houses Renaissance and baroque paintings as well as a sculpture court. Two other buildings hold Egyptian, Greco-Roman, Byzantine, and Ethiopian

art collections, among the best in the nation, along with many 19th-century paintings.
> 600 N. Charles St., Mount Vernon, tel. 410/547–9000, www.thewalters.org. $8, free
Sat. 11–1. Tues.–Sun. 10–5.

Washington Monument Erected in 1829, the marble Doric column is arguably the
oldest formal monument to the nation's first president. The 178-foot monument was
designed by Robert Mills, who also designed the more famous Washington Monument in the nation's capital. If you're lucky enough to catch the monument when it's
open, you may climb the 228 steps to its top for a bird's-eye view of the city. Otherwise, walk around the gardens surrounding the monument and enjoy the neighborhood from this beautiful prospect. > N. Charles St., Mount Vernon, tel.
410/396–0929, www.wam.umd.edu/~jlehnert/welcome.html. $1.

Westminster Cemetery and Catacombs The city's oldest cemetery is the final resting place of Edgar Allan Poe and other famous Marylanders, including 15 generals
from the American Revolution and the War of 1812. In the early 1850s a city ordinance
demanded that burial grounds be part of a church, so a building was constructed
above part of the cemetery, creating the catacombs beneath. In the 1930s the school-
children of Baltimore collected pennies to raise the necessary funds for Poe's monument and those who visit continue the tradition by leaving a few pennies on his
grave. In one of Baltimore's quirkier traditions, each year on Poe's birthday, January
19, the "Poe Toaster," a mysterious, cloaked stranger, leaves one red rose and a bottle
of cognac on the writer's grave. > W. Fayette and Greene Sts., Downtown, tel.
410/706–2072. Daily 8–dusk.

Tours

Clipper City Tall Ship Cruises The *Clipper City*, a replica of a 19th-century schooner,
hosts two-hour cruises of the Inner Harbor that include Fort McHenry. The main deck
has a custom canopy in case of poor weather conditions. The ship sets sail Monday
through Saturday at noon and 3 and Sundays at 3 and 6. The cost is $12 per person.
Evening and Sunday-brunch cruises are also available. Some summer weekend
cruises include live reggae bands ($20 a person). > Light St., next to Maryland Sci-
ence Center, Inner Harbor, tel. 410/539–6277, www.sailingship.com.

Discovery Channel Ducks These old World War II vessels give the only tour in town
that crosses both land and water. The 80-minute amphibious bus tour takes you
through Mount Vernon, Fells Point, Little Italy, and the Inner Harbor. Tickets are
$21.95 for adults. The ticket kiosk is between the visitor center and the Maryland Sci-
ence Center in the Inner Harbor. Tours are available April to November from 10 to 5.
> 25 Light St., Suite 300, Inner Harbor, tel. 410/727–3825,
www.discoverychannelducks.com.

Harbor Cruises' *Lady Baltimore* and *Bay Lady* The narrated tours aboard these
two ships cover Fells Point, Fort McHenry, and the Patapsco River. Lunch and dinner
cruises are on fully enclosed decks; the top deck is open air. The daily cruises range in
price from $12.50 to $54 per person. > 301 Light St., Inner Harbor, tel. 410/727–3113
or 800/695–2628, www.harborcruises.com.

***Minnie V* Cruises** aboard this skipjack, a Chesapeake sailing craft for dredging oys-
ters, cover topics that include harbor landmarks, the history of the U.S. Naval Academy, and the Great Baltimore Fire. At the peak of Baltimore's oyster industry (in the
late 19th century), more than 1,000 of these vessels were on the bay. Tours are available March–November on Tuesday and Thursday evenings; reservations are essential. > Pier 1, Fells Point, tel. 410/685–0295.

Sports

BASEBALL

Baltimore Orioles The American League's Orioles play at Oriole Park at Camden Yards, a beautiful baseball-only stadium from 1992 that harks back to the very first ballparks. The stadium is open for tours daily. > Camden Yards, 333 W. Camden St., tel. 410/685–9800 tickets, 410/547–6234 tour info, www.theorioles.com. Games $9–$35. Apr.–Oct.

FOOTBALL

Baltimore Ravens The Ravens—named after Poe's famous work—play out their National Football League season at PSINet Stadium at Camden Yards. The team's marching band is the same one that played during the days of the Baltimore Colts. Even after the Colts left Baltimore and the city was teamless, the band continued to practice in anticipation of a new team. > Camden Yards, 1101 Russell St., 21230, tel. 410/230–8010, www.baltimoreravens.com. Games $20–$200. Games Sept.–Jan.; tours daily 10–2.

HORSE RACING

Pimlico Race Course This 140-acre, 95,000-capacity venue is probably best known as the home of the Preakness, the second jewel of horse racing's Triple Crown. The rest of the spring and early summer, the track hosts daily thoroughbred and simulcast racing. > 5201 Park Heights Ave., tel. 410/542–9400, www.pimlico.com. $3 stands, $5 box, except during Preakness. Mar.–June, Wed.–Fri. 2:05 post time, weekends 1:05.

Save the Date

MAY

Preakness Celebration Hot-air-balloon launches, parades, concerts, and other events are all held throughout the city during the week leading up to the running of the Preakness Stakes in mid-May. The grand finale is the race itself, held at the Pimlico Race Course. > Tel. 410/837–3030 festivities, 410/542–9400 race tickets, www.preaknesscelebration.org and www.pimlico.com.

JULY

Artscape Visual, literary, and performing arts are celebrated in the Mount Royal neighborhood. A wine tasting, children's activities, street theater, and concerts are all part of the weeklong celebration. > Tel. 410/837–4686, www.artscape.org.

SEPTEMBER

Baltimore Book Festival This late-September celebration of literature brings with it author signings, storytelling sessions, children's activities, and walking tours. > Mt. Vernon Pl. off Charles St., tel. 410/752–8632, www.bop.org/calendar/events/book_index.html.

NOVEMBER

Thanksgiving Parade Santa Claus receives his official holiday welcome as floats and bands fill the streets along the Inner Harbor. The parade starts off at Eutaw and Pratt streets, travels along Pratt Street, and disbands at Market Place. > Tel. 410/837–4636, www.bop.org.

DECEMBER

New Year's Eve Extravaganza This nonalcoholic celebration includes fireworks, parades, music, and themed parties for all ages. > Inner Harbor, tel. 410/837–4636 or 800/282–6632, www.bop.org/calendar/events/newyears.html.

Night of 100 Elvises Elvis may be gone, but he's still the King. This annual event at Lithuanian Hall, just west of downtown, pays him homage with live bands, dancing, and a dozen or so "tribute artists." There's even a life-size Elvis ice sculpture. You can show up in a tux or a rhinestone jumpsuit—it's all allowed in the name of a good time. Drinks and food are available, and the proceeds benefit local charities. > 851 Hollins St., tel. 410/494–9558 or 888/494–9558, www.nightof100elvises.com.

WHERE TO STAY

Abacrombie This five-story gray-stone row house is from 1890. The guest rooms are basic compared to the more royal furnishings in the sitting parlor, which has high ceilings and original planked wood floors. A large stuffed badger named Abacrombie vigilantly overlooks the breakfast tables from the mantel. The rooms all are done in Victorian style, though each room is distinctive. Some have four-poster beds and many, especially those on top floors, have striking city views. > 58 W. Biddle St., 21201 Bolton Hill, tel. 410/244–7227, fax 410/244–8415, www.badger-inn.com. 12 rooms. Restaurant, bar, cable TV, business services. AE, D, DC, MC, V. CP. **$–$$**

Admiral Fell Inn This elegant inn is at the center of action in funky Fells Point, and no other evokes Baltimore's past so well. By joining together buildings constructed between the late 1770s and the 1920s, the owners created a structure that resembles one small hotel. The rooms, which vary in shape, all have four-poster canopy beds. Three suites and eight rooms have whirlpool baths. Some hallways have a few stairs, and some rooms face a quiet, interior courtyard: if steps or street noise are a hindrance to your comfort, let the reservation agent know. > 888 S. Broadway, Fells Point 21231, tel. 410/522–7377, 800/292–4667 outside MD, fax 410/522–0707, www.admiralfell.com. 77 rooms, 3 suites. 3 restaurants, in-room data ports, some in-room hot tubs, cable TV, 3 bars, business services, free parking, some pets allowed. AE, DC, MC, V. CP. **$–$$$**

Baltimore Marriott-Waterfront The city's tallest hotel and the only one directly on the Inner Harbor itself, this upscale 32-story Marriott has an elegant, neoclassical interior that uses multihued marbles, rich jewel-tone walls, and striking photographs of Baltimore architectural landmarks. Although it is at the eastern end of the Inner Harbor, all downtown attractions are within walking distance; there is also a water taxi stop right by the front door. Most rooms have unobstructed views of the city and harbor; ask for one that faces west toward downtown for a splendid panorama of the waterfront and skyscrapers. > 700 Aliceanna St., Inner Harbor East, 21202, tel. 410/385–3000, fax 410/385–0330, www.marriott.com. 729 rooms, 22 suites. Restaurant, coffee shop, indoor pool, health club, lounge, business services, parking (fee). AE, D, DC, MC, V. **$$$–$$$$**

Harbor Court Hotel The entrance to Baltimore's most prestigious hotel is set back from the street by a brick courtyard that provides an immediate sense of tranquility. A grand spiral staircase dominates the lobby, which is decorated in an English country style. Guest rooms include such deluxe touches as twice-daily maid service, plush bathrobes, and televisions in the bathrooms; amenities in the suites include 6-foot marble tubs with separate shower, canopied four-poster beds, and CD players. Waterside rooms have a good view of the harbor, but courtyard rooms are quieter. > 550 Light St., Inner Harbor 21202, tel. 410/234–0550 or 800/824–0076, fax 410/659–5925, www.harborcourt.com. 202 rooms, 25 suites. Restaurant, bar, in-room data ports, refrigerators, room service, cable TV, tennis court, pool, gym, hot tub, massage, racquetball, business services, airport shuttle, parking. AE, D, DC, MC, V. **$$$$**

Inn at 2920 An upscale row house that was once a brothel and tavern is now an engaging hotel option. A smooth marriage of old and new charms, the 1880 brick building has exposed brick walls, copper ceilings, and stark, modern furnishings. The Bordello Room has a king-size canopy bed with rich, red linens and a two-person whirlpool bath lined with limestone tile. The breakfast changes daily, depending on what is found at the local farmers' market, but interesting offerings like white sweet-potato home fries and sage sausage are often on the menu. The inn is a quick walk from O'Donnell Square, where there are many bar and restaurant options. > 2920 Elliott St., Canton, 21224, tel. 410/342–4450, fax 410/342–6436, www.theinnat2920.com. 4 rooms. Dining room, fans, in-room hot tubs, cable TV, in-room VCRs, hot tub, Internet; no kids under 12, no smoking. AE, MD, V. BP. $$

Mr. Mole Bed & Breakfast Dating back to the 1860s, this elegant redbrick building in a neighborhood just west of Mount Vernon was owned by a series of merchants. The five guest rooms are whimsically decorated and come with fresh flowers and a direct-dial phone with voice mail. The Dutch-style breakfast typically consists of fresh fruits, Amish cheeses and meats, homemade breads, and coffee cake. Mr. Mole Bed & Breakfast, which gets its name from a character in the children's book *The Wind in the Willows*, is within walking distance of many attractions, including Howard Street's Antiques Row. > 1601 Bolton St., Bolton Hill, 21217, tel. 410/728–1179, fax 410/728–3379, www.mrmolebb.com. 3 rooms, 2 suites. In-room data ports, business services; no kids under 10, no smoking. AE, D, DC, MC, V. CP. $–$$

Scarborough Fair Two blocks from the Inner Harbor, this Georgian brick house from 1801 is one of the oldest in the areas. On the exterior are gabled roofs and Flemish-bonded brickwork, a traditional style characteristic of the neighborhood. Rooms are done with a blend of contemporary and colonial-era furnishings. The second-floor Round Hill room includes Victorian-era reproductions as well as a gas fireplace and double Jacuzzi. Refreshments are served in the afternoon. > 1 E. Montgomery St., Federal Hill, 21202, tel. 410/837–0010, fax 410/783–4635, www.scarborough-fair.com. 6 rooms. Dining room, some in-room hot tubs, cable TV, free parking; no room phones, no kids. AE, D, MC, V. BP. $$

Tremont Plaza Hotel Built in the 1960s as an apartment house, the 13-story Tremont is now an all-suites hotel that's elegant but still comfortable. The lobby and hotel restaurant, 8 East, are intimate and private—qualities attracting some guests who might be easily recognized. The suites come in two sizes: both have a toaster oven and a coffeemaker (complete with freshly ground beans). The Tremont is near Mount Vernon's cultural attractions and restaurants, and the concierge will also help you arrange local transportation, which in most cases is free of charge. > 222 St. Paul Pl., 21202, tel. 410/727–2222 or 800/873–6668, fax 410/244–1154, www.tremontsuitehotels.com. 60 suites. Restaurant, kitchenettes, cable TV, bar, concierge, business services, parking (fee), some pets allowed. AE, D, DC, MC, V. CP. $–$$

WHERE TO EAT

Babalu Grill It's one of the most entertaining restaurants in town. From the prominent portrait of Desi Arnaz to the conga drum bar stools to the live salsa music on weekends, this place is all about fun. The house cocktail, the *mojito*, is a Cuban drink of rum, sugarcane, and mint that will help you catch the Babalu spirit. Many of the classic Cuban dishes on the menu come from owner Steve DeCastro's family recipes, including the savory *ropa vieja* (a stew of shredded beef) and seafood paella, brimming with shrimp, shellfish, and chorizo. The bar serves an impressive selection of obscure rums and tequilas, and the wine list focuses on South American and Spanish vintages. > 32 Market Pl., Inner Harbor, tel. 410/234–9898. AE, D, DC, MC, V. Closed Mon. No lunch Sat.–Wed. **$$–$$$$**

Blue Agave Restaurante y Tequileria To create his authentic regional Mexican and American Southwestern dishes, chef and owner Michael Marx flies in chilies from New Mexico and spices and chocolate from Oaxaca. Every sauce and salsa is made daily to create pure, concentrated flavors—the traditional mole sauces in which the restaurant specializes are delicious. Dishes such as grilled quail served with both green and spicy yellow moles, or the more familiar chicken enchiladas with mole poblano, demonstrate the kitchen's mastery. They stock more than 80 different kinds of tequila, and you won't find a finer margarita anywhere; try the deep purple version made from prickly-pear juice. The tequila flight serves as a good introduction to the different varieties of this liquor. > 1032 Light St., Federal Hill, tel. 410/576–3938. AE, D, MC, V. Closed Tues. and Wed. No lunch. **$–$$**

Brewer's Art The two elegant dining rooms here are inside a tastefully redone mansion—and the copper-tank brew house is in back. The restaurant tries to be young and urbane, with an ambitious menu, a well-chosen wine list, and the Belgian-style beers it brews: try the potent Resurrection ale. The dishes employ high-quality, locally available ingredients to create country fare that is both hearty and sophisticated. The classic steak frites are a best bet, as are the fresh homemade ravioli, made with seasonal ingredients such as pumpkin in fall and tomatoes and artichokes in summer. > 1106 N. Charles St., Mount Vernon, tel. 410/547–6925. AE, D, DC, MC, V. Closed Mon. **$$–$$$**

Charleston The kitchen here may have a South Carolina low-country accent, but it's also fluent in the fundamentals of French cooking. Inside the glowingly lighted dining room, such classics as she-crab soup, crisp cornmeal-crusted oysters, and spoon bread mesh beautifully with more elegant fare, such as squab roasted with apples. Best bets are Southern-inspired dishes such as shrimp sautéed with andouille and Cajun ham served over creamy grits. The wine list has more than 250 vintages, and the superb waitstaff is attentive but unobtrusive. > 1000 Lancaster St., Fells Point, tel. 410/332–7373. Reservations essential. AE, D, MC, V. Closed Sun. No lunch. **$$$$**

Corks This restaurant excels at pairing its New American cuisine with domestic wines from its list of over 300 vintages. For every entrée, the menu includes a suggested wine that's available by the glass. For example, the braised pork shank might be paired with a Central Coast syrah. Themed wine dinners (such as an East Coast vs. West Coast competition of dishes and wines) are planned for the third Thursday of each month. > 1026 S. Charles St., Federal Hill, tel. 410/752–3810. Reservations essential. AE, D, DC, MC, V. No lunch. **$$$**

Helen's Garden You must walk through a narrow, brick-lined tunnel to get to this eclectic bistro. The earth-tone palate and the worn wooden floor of the interior give it a casual elegance. Dishes include pecan-crusted brook trout with horseradish potatoes and shrimp sautéed with peanuts, basil, lime, and garlic. You can either sit in one of the three dining rooms or the backyard patio, and if you taste a wine you like, you may be able to buy a bottle to go—many are available for purchase. > 2908 O'-Donnell St., Canton, tel. 410/276–2233. Reservations essential. D, MC, V. Closed Mon. **$$–$$$$**

Helmand Baltimore's first Afghan restaurant is a great option for vegetarians. Lively crowds pack into the small, no-frills space. Interesting items such as panfried baby pumpkin and leek-filled ravioli share the menu with the very tasty kebobs. Instead of ordering one entrée, consider getting three or four appetizers, which allows you to get more exposed to the eclectic choices. The owner, a local celebrity, is a brother of the temporary ruler of postwar Afghanistan. > 806 N. Charles St., Mount Vernon, tel. 410/752–0311. Reservations essential. AE, DC, MC, V. $–$$

Joy America Cafe Part of the American Visionary Art Museum, Baltimore's most creative kitchen overlooks the harbor, and the appropriately unconventional menu does the museum justice. The food is inspired by New World cuisines: the American Southwest, Latin America, and the Caribbean. The chili-spiced shrimp ceviche with lime and coconut milk as well as the guacamole, prepared table-side, are full of exuberant flavor. Sunday brunch fare includes interesting twists such as crab omelets and *huevos rancheros* (Mexican-style eggs) with sweet potatoes. > American Visionary Art Museum, 800 Key Hwy., Federal Hill, tel. 410/244–6500. AE, DC, MC, V. Closed Mon. $$–$$$$

La Scala Mahogany chairs, multicolor tablecloths, and tile floors make this low-key, family-owned restaurant look upscale. Dishes include standard regional Italian fare like eggplant Parmesan and veal chops. Specialties include grilled Caesar salad, shrimp Luana, and weekly fish specials. Many of the most popular items, including the gnocchi, are made in-house. The cannoli is only available half the year, when the chef's mother visits from Italy and employs her secret recipe. > 1012 Eastern Ave., Little Italy, tel. 410/783–9209. AE, D, DC, MC, V. No lunch. $$–$$$

Louisiana Fells Point's most elegant dining room resembles a spacious, opulent parlor. The menu mixes Creole and classic French with a touch of New American; the wine list is expansive but thoughtful. The lobster bisque, with a dollop of aged sherry added at the table by one of the impeccable waiters, is sublime, and the crawfish étouffée is a worthy follow-up. > 1708 Aliceanna St., Fells Point, tel. 410/327–2610. AE, DC, MC, V. No lunch. $$$–$$$$

Nacho Mama's A wooden statue of Elvis marks the entrance to this extremely popular bar and restaurant. Inside, a funky mixture of sports and Elvis memorabilia hangs from the ceiling and walls. Try a National Bohemian ("Natty Bo" to regulars) as you wait for a table. In addition to the south-of-the-border fare, burgers and salads are also served. The spinach salad with feta, roasted red peppers, and avocado dressing is especially good. During the annual Night of 100 Elvises, the regulars have to make room for many impersonators, who convene here to admire the scenery. > 2907 O'Donnell St., Canton, tel. 410/675–0898. AE, MC, V. ¢–$$

Obrycki's Crab House It's Baltimore's crab house of choice—and tasting the steamed crabs yourself will help you understand why. Beyond that, the seafood menu is standard and the food just fair. Talk-show host Oprah Winfrey, once a Baltimore television personality, still has Obrycki's crab cakes mailed to her. > 1727 E. Pratt St., Fells Point, tel. 410/732–6399. AE, D, DC, MC, V. Closed mid-Dec.–early Mar. $$–$$$$

Papermoon Diner Inside an unassuming little house is this restaurant, where the furniture is mismatched and high ceilings are crisscrossed with vibrantly painted pipes and ducts. Lava lights bubble, and mannequins, in various stages of undress, are posed. Old-fashioned comfort foods like meat loaf with mashed potatoes and gravy and mac and cheese are on the menu along with dishes like angel-hair pasta with garlic and basil. The Papermoon is open 24 hours. > 227 W. 29th St., Charles Village, tel. 410/889–4444. MC, V. ¢–$

Red Maple There's no sign outside this theatrical and stylish joint: the picture of a small red maple tree on the front door is the only way to know you're in the right place. The striking, minimalist space is warmed by a fireplace, candles, and sumptuous suede banquettes. The food is equally arresting: it's Asian-inspired appetizers, artfully conceived and beautifully presented. Consider the tiny whole ginger-garlic baby vegetables, spilling from a faux "grocery sack" fashioned from a crisp wonton wrapper. The 16 different small plates are fairly cheap, but it's easy to run up your tab when they're each so compelling. > 930 N. Charles St., Mount Vernon, tel. 410/547–0149. AE, DC, MC, V. No lunch. **$**

Rusty Scupper When viewed from this tourist favorite, sunsets are magical: you can see the sun sink slowly into the harbor as lights twinkle on in the city's skyscrapers. The interior is decorated with light wood and windows from floor to ceiling; the house specialty is seafood, particularly the jumbo lump crab cake, but there are also beef, chicken, and pasta dishes. Reservations are essential on Friday and Saturday. > 402 Key Hwy., Inner Harbor, tel. 410/727–3678. AE, D, DC, MC, V. **$$$–$$$$**

Soigné Polished but relaxed, a bit of New York's SoHo in South Baltimore, Soigné presents an Asian- and French-influenced fusion menu amid attractively spare, comfortable surroundings. The creative menu succeeds beautifully with such ambitious dishes as seared foie gras with scallops: the combined richness of these two components is leavened with caramelized mango in a sake-spiked sauce. The lemongrass sorbet, with pineapple-mint salsa and rose peppercorns, is one of the most fascinating (and delicious) desserts in town. > 554 E. Fort Ave., Locust Point, tel. 410/659–9898. Reservations essential. AE, D, MC, V. Closed Sun. No lunch. **$$–$$$**

ESSENTIALS

Getting Here

A 45-minute drive by car is the easiest way to get to Baltimore. On weekdays, avoid leaving in the early morning or early evening to miss both city's rush hours. It's relatively easy to navigate Baltimore by car; clear signs mark most attractions.

Greyhound Bus Lines and Amtrak both have daily service to Baltimore. The Maryland Area Rail Commuter (MARC) rail line, however, only runs on weekdays. Most trains depart and arrive Baltimore at Penn Station.

Most attractions are either a reasonable walk or a short cab ride from the Inner Harbor. Though Baltimore does have a light-rail and metro system, they are somewhat limited, and using the Downtown Area Shuttle bus (DASH) can involve a number of transfers. The water taxi is a reasonably priced, interesting way to see the city.

BY BUS

Baltimore's shuttle bus, DASH, stops at many downtown locations every 5 minutes on weekdays and every 20 minutes on weekends. Rides, which cost 50¢ individually, are included as part of the MTA's $3 all-day transportation pass. DASH stops are convenient to Mount Vernon, the Inner Harbor, and Camden Yards.

DEPOTS **Downtown Area Shuttle (DASH)** > Tel. 800/231–2722, www.godowntownbaltimore.com. **Trailways-Greyhound Bus Terminal** > 210 W. Fayette St., tel. 800/231–2722, www.greyhound.com.

LINE **Downtown Area Shuttle bus (DASH),** > Tel. 800/231–2722, www.godowntownbaltimore.com.

BY CAR

From Washington, D.C., take the Beltway, I–95 (I–495), to I–95 North toward Baltimore/College Park. Merge onto I–395 North via Exit 53 and head toward downtown Baltimore. The route is well marked.

Most downtown streets are one-way. Streets are identified as east or west based on their orientation to Charles Street, or as north or south based on their orientation to Baltimore Street. Because the city's traffic lights are often not properly synchronized, you're often left waiting at long red lights. Be patient. The speed limit in most parts of the city is 25 mph.

Parking can be difficult to find downtown. Meters cost $1 per hour, and fines run $20 or more for expired meters. Parking garages are a good alternative; they're easy to find along Pratt Street between Camden Yard and the Inner Harbor. Daily prices average $15. Many downtown attractions are within easy walking distance of the garages, and many of those that are not can be reached via water taxi.

BY TRAIN

MARC weekday commuter trains run to and from Washington's Union Station to either Camden Station, convenient for baseball games, or Penn Station, best for everything else. The trains run approximately every 30 minutes in the morning and every hour from the afternoon to the evening. The cost is $5.75 one-way and $10.25 for a round-trip.

Amtrak also operates regularly scheduled passenger trains from Washington to Baltimore. An expensive but easy way to travel, it's also the only option when MARC trains are not running.

Baltimore's Mass Transit Administration (MTA) runs the city's light-rail, subway, bus service, and commuter trains. The MTA's one-day pass ($3) allows unlimited use of the light-rail, the metro, and the bus system. Individual rides on the light-rail and the metro cost $1.35.

LINES **Amtrak** > Tel. 800/872–7245, www.amtrak.com. **Mass Transit Administration** > 6 St. Paul St., tel. 410/539–5000.
STATION **Penn Station** > 1500 N. Charles St., tel. 410/291–4165, www.mtamaryland.com.

BY WATER TAXI

A water taxi is an inexpensive, easy, and safe way to see the city. Two companies run daily water taxi service: Ed Kane's Water Taxis are blue and white, and Seaport Taxis are cream and green. Taxis make regularly spaced stops at 16 sights, including the Inner Harbor, Little Italy, the Aquarium, Harborplace, and the Science Center. A map, available from the visitor center, shows the stops, which are all clearly marked by waterfront signs.

Water taxis operate year-round, but stops are much more frequent May through September, averaging one every 15–18 minutes at most stops. The cost for a day pass is $6 for adults. When you exit the taxi make sure to get your hand stamped: this allows you continuous rides all day. (A day pass is not transferable between the two taxi companies.)

LINES **Ed Kane's Water Taxis** > 1732 Thames St., tel. 410/563–3901 or 800/658–8947, www.thewatertaxi.com. **Seaport Taxi** > Tel. 410/675–2900.

Visitor Information

Baltimore's official visitor center is on the Inner Harbor, near the Maryland Science Center. In addition to carrying brochures, the center also runs a booking service for restaurants, hotels, and attractions.

CONTACT **Baltimore Area Convention and Visitors Association** > Between Light Street Pavilion and Maryland Science Center, Inner Harbor, 21202, tel. 877/225–8466, www.baltimore.org.

Valley Forge

140 mi northeast of Washington, D.C.

3

Updated by Laura Knowles Callanan

JUST A HALF HOUR OUTSIDE OF PHILADELPHIA lies what was once the headquarters of the Revolutionary Army. No battles were ever fought at Valley Forge, but the soldiers nevertheless faced abundant troubles as they waited to take part in the conflict.

The lush Valley Forge National Historical Park, made up of 3,600 acres of open fields, flowering trees, hillsides, and woodlands, is quiet today—but this is a far cry from its condition when General George Washington was here. In 1777 the army had just lost the nearby battles of Brandywine, White Horse, and Germantown. While the British occupied Philadelphia, Washington's soldiers were forced to endure blizzards, inadequate food and clothing, damp quarters, and disease. Many men deserted, and 2,000 soldiers died due to the conditions—more than were killed at Brandywine and Germantown combined.

The men, from various parts of the country, set up camp quickly. The construction of shelters ranged from adequate to downright poor. Because troops were clothed and equipped by the states from which they came, some were better prepared for the harsh winter than others. In the month of February alone, the army dwindled to 6,000 men. Spring proved to be the only relief.

The troops did win one victory that winter—a war of will. The forces slowly regained strength and confidence under the leadership of Prussian drillmaster Friedrich von Steuben. In June 1778 Washington led his troops away from Valley Forge in search of the British. Fortified, the Continental Army was able to carry on the fight for five years more.

Relics of the encampment still lie throughout the park. Washington's original stone headquarters have been restored and furnished, and the grounds are scattered with 50 reconstructed log huts. Reminders of the park's role in the Revolutionary War include statues and monuments that pay tribute to General "Mad Anthony" Wayne, Baron Friedrich von Steuben, and "Patriots of African Descent."

Begin at the visitor center, where you can pick up a map. While there, be sure to take some time to view the actual weapons and tools used by Washington's troops (some quite rare), and watch an 18-minute video on what life was like that winter.

A trip around the park can be done in one of four ways—car, bus, walking, or bicycling. The 10-mi car tour takes visitors to the huts, Washington's headquarters, the Arch memorial, and various encampments and artillery fields. On hot and humid days, the automobile and bus tours are most popular. On the bus tour, you can disembark to take photographs or have a picnic and then catch the next bus that comes along. Buses run every 30 minutes. Only one stop, George Washington's cathedral, offers food and beverages so those planning to make a day out of the visit may want to pack a picnic lunch and enjoy one of the many picnic areas. For those looking for a workout or a more leisurely tour of the area, a paved bike and walking path is the answer.

Valley Forge is the main draw to the region, but other popular stops include Mill Grove, the home of naturalist John James Audubon; the studio and residence of craftsman Wharton Esherick; and the vast King of Prussia Plaza & Court shopping complex.

In contrast to Valley Forge's fields, King of Prussia is part of bustling suburbia, with residential areas, stylish accommodations and restaurants, and upscale shopping. Originally called Reeseville after the family that was the major landholder in the area, King of Prussia was renamed in the 1850s after an inn that was once the focal point of the community. Among the attractions here are the 1704 Harriton House, restored to its early-18th-century grandeur, and Swiss Pines, which has Japanese-style gardens.

WHAT TO SEE & DO

Fort Washington State Park Washington and his men camped in the area until moving on to Valley Forge. This 493-acre park has 3½ mi of hiking trails, an observation deck for bird-watching, a creek in which you can fish, picnic facilities, a 400-foot slope for sledding, and a 1.7-mi loop for cross-country skiing. Pets are allowed in the park, but dogs must be on a leash. > 500 Bethlehem Pike, Fort Washington, tel. 215/591–5250 or 888/727–2757, www.dcnr.state.pa.us. Free. Daily 8 AM–dusk.

Harriton House Once the home of Charles Thomson, Secretary of the Continental Congresses, this estate has been restored to its 18th-century appearance with period furnishings. Back in Thomson's time, the estate was formed from a land grant of 700 acres. The 16½ acres that remain now include a nature park with walking paths. > 500 Harriton Rd., Bryn Mawr, tel. 610/525–0201, www.harritonhouse.org. $2. Wed.–Sat. 10–4.

The Highlands Built by Anthony Morris, Speaker of the Pennsylvania Senate from 1793 to 1794, this late-Georgian–style mansion is on 44 acres of land. Madison, Monroe, and Jefferson were all guests (in fact, Madison may have met his future wife, Dolley, here). The estate has a 2-acre formal garden and nine outbuildings, including a barn and a springhouse from 1799. > 7001 Sheaff La., Fort Washington, tel. 215/641–2687. $4. House tours weekdays 1:30 and 3; gardens daily dawn–dusk.

Hope Lodge An 18th-century mansion that was occupied until the 1950s and never modernized, the lodge has its original colonial shape and is mainly furnished with items correct to the area. A perfect example of Georgian architecture, the home was built between 1743 and 1748 by Samuel Morris, a Quaker businessman. Revolutionary troops camped on the estate in 1777 on their way to Valley Forge. > 553 Bethlehem Pike, tel. 215/646–1595, www.ushistory.org/hope. $4. Wed.–Sat. 9–5, Sun. noon–5.

Mennonite Heritage Center This center serves as an introduction to the Mennonites, members of a group of strict religious sects that include the Amish. Those in nearby Pennsylvania Dutch Country emigrated from Germany in the early 1700s to pursue William Penn's promise of religious freedom. Designed to look like an early Mennonite meetinghouse, the center has rotating and permanent exhibits that illustrate Mennonite life in the 20th century. > 565 Yoder Rd., Harleysville 19438, tel. 215/256–3020, www.mhep.org. Free. Tues.–Fri. 10–5, Sat. 10–2, Sun. 2–5.

Mill Grove The first American home of Haitian-born artist and naturalist John James Audubon (1785–1851) is now a museum displaying his major works, including original prints, his paintings of birds and wildlife, and a "double-elephant" folio of his *Birds of America*. Built in 1762, the house has an attic restored to a studio and taxidermy room. The surrounding Audubon Wildlife Sanctuary is 175 acres, with 5 mi of hiking trails. > Audubon and Pawlings Rds., Audubon, tel. 610/666–5593. Free. Museum Tues.–Sat. 10–4, Sun. 1–4; grounds Tues.–Sun. dawn–dusk.

The Plaza and The Court at King of Prussia These two joined-together upscale malls contain more than 35 restaurants, 350 shops and boutiques, and nine major department stores, including Bloomingdale's, Nordstrom, Neiman Marcus, Lord & Taylor, Williams-Sonoma, J. Crew, Banana Republic, and Pottery Barn. > Rte. 202 at the Schuylkill Expressway, 160 N. Gulph Rd., tel. 610/265–5727 for the Plaza, 610/337–1210 for the Court, www.kingofprussiamall.com. Mon.–Sat. 10–9:30, Sun. 11–6.

Swiss Pines The soothing beauty of the elegant Japanese gardens arises from the vast collection of azaleas, rhododendron, fishponds, waterfalls, and a pathway that winds through herb and ground-cover gardens. Children under 12 are not allowed. > Charlestown Rd., Malvern, tel. 610/933–6916. Free. Wed.–Fri. 10:30–3:30, Sat. 9–1.

Valley Forge National Historical Park Stop first at the National Park Service's visitor center to see the 18-minute orientation film (shown every 30 minutes), view exhibits, and pick up a map for a 10-mi self-guided car tour of the attractions in the 3,600-acre park. At Muhlenberg Brigade, the reconstructed huts show what life was like for soldiers during their 6-month winter encampment. There's also a demonstration here of how muskets were loaded and fired.

Another stop, the National Memorial Arch, pays tribute to the soldiers who suffered through the brutal winter. Other sites include the bronze equestrian statue of General Anthony Wayne, in the area where his Pennsylvania troops were encamped; Artillery Park, where the soldiers stored their cannons; and the Isaac Potts House, which served as Washington's headquarters.

The park, run by the National Park Service, provides a quiet escape from the busy world, and is especially beautiful in spring, when trees are in bloom, and in fall, when the wooded areas are ablaze with color. The park contains 6 mi of jogging and bicycling paths and hiking trails, and you can picnic at any of three designated areas. A leisurely visit to the park takes no more than half a day. > Rtes. 23 and 363, tel. 610/783–1077, www.nps.gov/vafo. Washington's headquarters $2, park free. Visitor center and Washington's headquarters daily 9–5; park grounds daily 6 AM–10 PM.

Wharton Esherick Museum Esherick (1887–1970), the "Dean of American Craftsmen," was best known for his sculptural furniture. The museum houses 200 examples of his work—paintings, woodcuts, furniture, and wood sculptures. The studio, in which everything from the light switches to the spiral staircase is hand-carved, is one of his monumental achievements. The museum is 2 mi west of Valley Forge National Historical Park. > 1520 Horseshoe Trail, tel. 610/644–5822, www.levins.com/esherick.html. $9. Mar.–Dec., Sat. 10–5, Sun. 1–5 for hourly guided tours (reservations required). Group tours (at least 5 people) weekdays.

Tours

Valley Forge National Historical Park Bus Tour During this narrated minibus tour, you can get off to visit sites and then reboard. Tours run from mid-May through September; times vary. The cost is $6. > Visitor Center, Rte. 23 and N. Gulph Rd., tel. 610/783–1077.

Save the Date

JANUARY

Greater Philadelphia Sport, Travel, and Outdoor Show Held at the Fort Washington Expo Center, this four-day show highlights the latest boats, fishing gear, and hunting equipment. There are also cooking exhibits and booths with information on area resorts and travel destinations. > Tel. 215/641–4500. $9.

JUNE

March out of Valley Forge Six months after the commemoration of Washington's entry into Valley Forge comes this celebration of the troops' departure. The festivities, which include the firing of muskets, last longer than the march itself. > Tel. 610/783–1077, www.nps.gov/vafo.

DECEMBER

March into Valley Forge Each year on December 19, Pennsylvanians and others reenact the 1777 march of George Washington and his 12,000 troops into Valley Forge. You can experience the glowing campfires, an encampment, living history-demonstrations, and tours of the park. > Tel. 610/783–1077, www.nps.gov/vafo.

WHERE TO STAY

Great Valley House of Valley Forge This 300-year-old stone farmhouse still has its original fireplaces, random-width wood floors, iron door hinges, and a pre-1700 stone sink. The Peaches and Cream room is furnished with a Victorian queen canopy bed and an antique footed bathtub, the Rose and Grey room with a canopied queen bed and a sink made from an antique Singer sewing machine, and the Cranberry room with an antique brass double bed and a sitting area with a queen sofa bed. Breakfast is served in the pre–Revolutionary War kitchen in front of a 12-foot-wide fireplace. > 1475 Swedesford Rd., Malvern 19355, tel. 610/644–6759, www.greatvalleyhouse.com. 3 rooms. In-room data ports, cable TV, pool, Internet. AE, D, DC, MC, V. BP. $–$$

Historic General Warren Inne Built in 1745, this inn was once a carriage stop. It was later owned by a grandson of William Penn. The suites' furnishings take their cue from the inn's earliest history, with quilts on the bed and much wooden colonial-style furniture. Nearly all suites have a fireplace, and one has a Jacuzzi. > Old Lancaster Hwy., Malvern 19355, tel. 610/296–3637, fax 610/296–8084, www.generalwarren.com. 8 suites. Restaurant, in-room data ports, cable TV, in-room VCRs; no kids under 12. AE, DC, MC, V. CP. $–$$

Radisson Valley Forge Hotel/Scanticon Hotel These two hotels share a 15-story building that overlooks Valley Forge National Historical Park. Some of the suites are furnished with over-the-top themes that include "Caesar's Palace" and the *Titanic*. Guest rooms are standard, with large desks. > 1160 1st Ave., King of Prussia 19406, tel. 610/337–2000 or 800/267–1500, fax 610/337–2564, www.radissonvalleyforge.com. 328 rooms; Radisson 39 suites, Scanticon 160 suites. 3 restaurants, room service, in-room data ports, some in-room hot tubs, cable TV with video games, pool, gym, health club, hot tub, sauna, spa, steam room, laundry service, business services; no pets. AE, D, DC, MC, V. $$–$$$$

Wayne Hotel This Tudor-style building was built in 1906 in what's now a genteel suburb of Philadelphia. It was a nursing home, church, and synagogue before becoming a hotel again in 1985. The Wayne has an impressive wraparound porch and a lobby filled with palms, and its guest rooms are individually furnished with reproductions of Victorian furniture. > 139 E. Lancaster Ave., Wayne 19087, tel. 610/687–5000 or

800/962–5850, fax 610/687–8387, www.waynehotel.com. 40 rooms. Restaurant, in-room data ports, cable TV, pool, bar, business services, airport shuttle, free parking, no-smoking rooms. AE, D, DC, MC, V. BP. ¢–$$

Wyndham Valley Forge In the Chesterbrook Corporate Center, the rooms at this all-suites hotel include a spacious living room and separate bedroom, and a worktable with an Aeron chair. > 888 Chesterbrook Blvd., Wayne 19087, tel. 610/647–6700, fax 610/889–9420, www.wyndham.com. 229 suites. Restaurant, in-room data ports, minibars, refrigerators, cable TV, indoor pool, exercise equipment, hot tub, sauna, bar, business services, airport shuttle. AE, D, DC, MC, V. $$

WHERE TO EAT

Bertolini's Authentic Trattoria The sauces and pasta here keep people coming back to this chain restaurant. Characteristic dishes are the *fazzoletto con funghi* ("handker-chiefs" of pasta topped with a mushroom sauce) and the *tagliolini al frutti di mare* (thin noodles with seafood). Also on the menu are minestrone, classic pizzas, and tiramisu. > 160 N. Gulph Rd., King of Prussia, tel. 610/265–2965. AE, DC, MC, V. $–$$$

Blue Grotto Restaurant Soft lighting and candlelit tables make this hotel restaurant, known for its seafood, a good place for romance. There's a kids' menu and a Sunday brunch. > Radisson Valley Forge Hotel, 1160 1st Ave., King of Prussia, tel. 610/337–2825. AE, D, DC, MC, V. No dinner Sun. No lunch. $$–$$$

Chumley's Steakhouse With its soft light, the lounge is an intimate place to talk or listen to live music on Friday or Saturday. The restaurant in this 18th-century brick building has dark wooden tables and chairs and the windows are draped with cur-tains. You can choose from Angus beef and lobster tail stuffed with crabmeat. > Radisson Valley Forge Hotel, 1160 1st Ave., King of Prussia, tel. 610/337–2000. AE, DC, MC, V. No lunch weekends. $$$

Historic General Warren Inne The General Warren, inside a stone building from the 1700s, is known for its restaurant as well as its lodgings. Salads as well as some of the more dramatic entrées are prepared table-side. You can dine by candlelight in-doors, or outdoors overlooking the vegetable garden. The restaurant is known for its turtle soup, beef and chicken dishes, and beef Wellington salad. Lunchtime brings a more casual and much less expensive roster of dishes. > Old Lancaster Hwy., Malvern, tel. 610/296–3637, www.generalwarren.com. AE, DC, MC, V. Closed Sun. No lunch Sat. $$$–$$$$

Jefferson House Bouillabaisse, baked jumbo lump crab, Black Angus filet mignon, and a seasonal game plate of boar and venison are the specialties at this stately Georgian mansion on 11 acres of lush grounds. After dinner, you can stroll around the duck pond and Italian gazebos. > 2519 DeKalb Pike, Norristown, 4 mi northeast of King of Prussia, tel. 610/275–3407. AE, DC, MC, V. No lunch Sat. $$–$$$$

Kennedy Supplee Restaurant French cuisine with an accent on regional specialties is served in this 1852 Italianate mansion, overlooking the park. Nine elegant rooms be-decked with chandeliers and marble floors are a fitting backdrop for entrées such as sautéed quail with juniper berries and wine sauce and seared buffalo tenderloin with morels. The lunch menu leans more to Italian classics such as veal piccante and pasta puttanesca. > 1100 W. Valley Forge Rd., tel. 610/337–3777, www.kennedysupplee.com. Jacket required. AE, MC, V. No lunch weekends. $$$–$$$$

Kimberton Inn You can take a stroll through the 4½ acres of gardens on the grounds of this 1796 tavern, known for its fresh seafood, steaks, rack of lamb, and crab cakes.

There's live music Friday and Saturday, and there's a three-course, prix-fixe Sunday brunch ($22). > Kimberton and Hares Hill Rd., Kimberton, tel. 610/933–8148, www.kimbertoninn.com. AE, D, DC, MC, V. No lunch. $$$–$$$$

Lily Langtry's Dinner Theater In this lavishly appointed restaurant-cabaret, the menu is American and Continental, but the campy Las Vegas–style entertainment—corny comedians, showgirls, and some singers and dancers—is the real draw. There are matinee lunch and evening dinner shows. > Radisson Valley Forge Hotel, 1160 1st Ave., King of Prussia, tel. 610/337–5459, www.lilylangtrys.com. Reservations essential. AE, D, DC, MC, V. Closed Mon. $$$$

Palace of Asia Traditional Indian music and artwork decorate the interior. There's a full bar and the menu has chicken tandoori, chicken tikka masala, lamb, and vegetarian dishes such as cooked okra. There's a brunch on weekends. > Best Western Fort Washington Inn, 285 Commerce Dr., Fort Washington, tel. 215/646–2133. Reservations essential. AE, D, DC, MC, V. $–$$$

ESSENTIALS

Getting Here

BY CAR
A car is a must when traveling around the Valley Forge and King of Prussia area. To get here, take I–95 toward Baltimore. Outside of Wilmington, take Route 202 to King of Prussia. Take Route 363 to North Gulph Road and follow signs to Valley Forge National Park.

Visitor Information

CONTACTS **King of Prussia Chamber of Commerce** > 1150 1st Ave., 19406, tel. 610/265–1776. **Valley Forge Convention and Visitors Bureau** > 600 W. Germantown Pike, Suite 130, Plymouth Meeting 19462, tel. 610/834–1550 or 800/441–3549, www.valleyforge.org. **Valley Forge Country Funline** > Tel. 610/834–8844.

Bucks County

New Hope is 175 mi north of Washington, D.C.

4

Revised by Laura Knowles Callanan

A CLASSIC AMERICAN GETAWAY, Bucks County is 625 square miles of covered bridges, stone barns, hills, and waterways. It's an area that manages to pair relaxing countryside with cosmopolitan innovation.

The area's roots run deep. The very founder of Pennsylvania, William Penn, made his home here. His house, a brick Georgian-style mansion on the banks of the Delaware, was built in the 1600s (it has since been faithfully reconstructed). And that famous painting of George Washington and his troops crossing the Delaware? The actual event happened a few miles down the road from the county's largest town, New Hope.

Until the 20th century, Bucks County remained rural, its land given over to woods, mills, and farms. In the late 1800s, an art colony took root, and in 1930s New York luminaries, including writer Dorothy Parker and lyricist Oscar Hammerstein II, began to make the area their home. Pearl S. Buck wrote that she chose to live here because it was "where the landscapes were varied, where farm and industry lived side by side, where the sea was near at hand, mountains not far away, and city and countryside were not enemies."

In intervening years Bucks County has become known for its art galleries and antiques, for summer theater and bed-and-breakfasts. Many people are drawn by the natural beauty—artists seeking to capture the outdoors are a common sight. The wooded countryside is appealing in spring and summer, but nothing compares to the vivid golds, oranges, and yellows that fall brings.

Take your time and stay awhile, so you can discover the delights of one of the inns here. Many of the area's hotels and restaurants are inside former houses, barns, and mills that were built up to a half century before the Revolution. Few joys compare to savoring a hearty meal, turning in for a blissful night's sleep, and then spending a day driving leisurely along the Delaware on the tree-shaded River Road (Route 32).

As you travel, you might be lucky enough to come upon one of the area's 12 remaining covered bridges (there were originally 36). Romantics may call them "kissing bridges" or "wishing bridges," but the roofs were built to protect the supporting beams from the ravages of the weather. The visitors guide published by the Bucks County Conference and Visitors Bureau includes a map showing the bridges' locations.

Bucks County's towns are clustered along the Delaware River and are generally close to Route 202, which runs west from New Hope, one of the county's most popular destinations. Settled in the early 1700s as the industrial village of Coryell's Ferry, New Hope was once the state's terminal for stagecoaches and for ferry traffic along the Delaware. It's now better known as a tourist, rather than a transportation, hub. Its narrow streets and alleys are lined with historic buildings, antiques shops, galleries, and some very tantalizing ice cream parlors.

You'd do well to explore the town on foot: many of the most interesting sights and shops are clustered along four blocks of Main Street and on the cross streets of Mechanic Street, Ferry Street, and Bridge Street. They all lead to the Delaware River, not far from where George Washington made his historic crossing. Many inns and restaurants lay claim to having hosted Washington, and when you see the proverbial plaque stating that GEORGE WASHINGTON SLEPT HERE, it's probably true.

Summer weekends in New Hope can be frantic, with traffic jammed along Main Street and parking very difficult to find. Midweek and off-season visits allow for a slower-paced exploration. To escape the crowds, you might want to take a ride on a mule-pulled barge that glides along the Delaware Canal, or venture across the Delaware River bridge to the small town of Lambertville, New Jersey—a calmer adjunct to Bucks County.

Along Lambertville's tree-lined streets are Federal row houses, imposing Victorians, and an abundance of art galleries, antiques shops, restaurants, and B&Bs. In the self-described "Antiques Capital of New Jersey," you can find collectibles from the 1950s as well as furniture and decorative pieces from the 1700s. But one of Lambertville's chief pleasures doesn't involve commerce at all: the towpath along the Delaware Canal is a bucolic retreat for running, biking, or just a stroll.

West of New Hope, on Route 202, is the town of Lahaska, the region's center for shopping. Its Peddler's Village, a group of 75 stores, can be a rewarding place to search for antiques and fine reproduction furniture, handcrafted chandeliers, hand-woven wicker, and homespun fabrics. The nearby village of Buckingham, which dates to the colonial era, remains primarily rural, with many large produce and dairy farms.

Farther to the west is the county seat of Doylestown, an important coach stop during the 18th century. The town was the home of the multifaceted and eccentric Henry Chapman Mercer, who managed to be a master potter and a self-taught architect as well as the curator of American and Prehistoric Archaeology at the University of Pennsylvania. When Mercer died in 1930, he left a legacy of artistic creativity, along with a bizarre concrete castle, a museum displaying 50,000 implements and tools, and a pottery and tile factory that still makes Mercer tiles. A few miles north of Doylestown, near Dublin, is the home of Pearl S. Buck (1892–1973).

Point Pleasant, to the north of New Hope, is reminiscent of England's Cotswolds, with roads that resemble corkscrews, bridge-keeper lodges, and gorgeous vistas. Two covered bridges are a few miles northwest of town. In tiny Lumberville, a bit to the south, you can picnic along the Delaware Canal or on Bull's Island, accessible by the footbridge across the Delaware River. The Lumberville Store, open since 1770, is the focus of village life—it's the place to mail letters, buy groceries and picnic supplies, and rent a bicycle.

Pennsbury Manor, near Morrisville on the Delaware River, is a reconstruction of the Georgian-style mansion and plantation that William Penn built as his country estate. Formal gardens, orchards, an icehouse, a smokehouse, a bake-and-brew house, and collections of tools attest to the self-sufficient nature of Penn's early community, and the living-history demonstrations provide a glimpse into daily life in 17th-century America.

WHAT TO SEE & DO

DOYLESTOWN

Fonthill Henry Chapman Mercer's unique house, designed in 1910, was modeled after a 13th-century Rhenish castle—and made entirely out of reinforced concrete. Outside, the mansion bristles with turrets and balconies. Inside, the multilevel structure is mazelike: Mercer built his castle from the inside out, without blueprints. The Gothic doorways, abruptly appearing stairways, dead ends, and nooks follow closely on each other. Fonthill's prints and engravings are enhanced by the house itself: the ceilings and walls are embedded with tiles from Mercer's own kilns and with ancient tiles from around the world. As a final touch, every room has a different shape. > E. Court St. and Swamp Rd. (Rte. 313), tel. 215/348–9461, www.fonthillmuseum.org. $7. Mon.–Sat. 10–5, Sun. noon–5. Hr-long guided tours, last tour at 4.

James A. Michener Art Museum A native of Doylestown, the best-selling novelist endowed this museum, which emphasizes regional and national art of the 19th and 20th centuries. The Pennsylvania impressionists, who worked in the area in the early 1900s, are represented by such artists as Edward Redfield and Daniel Garber. Because the buildings and grounds were once the Bucks County Jail (1884), a 23-foot-high fieldstone wall surrounds the outdoor sculpture garden, Gothic-style warden's house, and seven exhibition galleries. There is also a re-creation of Michener's Doylestown study. The Michener Wing has a library, archives, and a room with 12 interactive exhibits honoring prominent Bucks County arts figures that include Pearl S. Buck and Oscar Hammerstein II. > 138 S. Pine St., tel. 215/340–9800, www.michenermuseum.org. $6. Tues., Thurs., Fri. 10–4:30, Wed. 10–9, weekends 10–5.

Mercer Museum On display in this museum is Henry Chapman Mercer's collection of tools, which includes more than 50,000 objects and seeks to represent every craft. As an archaeologist, Mercer worried that the rapid advance of progress would wipe out evidence of American productivity in the days before the industrial age. From 1895 to 1915 he scoured the back roads of eastern Pennsylvania, buying up folk art, tools, and everyday objects. This must be one of the most incredible attics in the world: the four-story central court is crammed with log sleds, cheese presses, fire engines, boats, and bean hullers, most of them suspended by wires from the walls and ceiling. The Spruance Library, on the third floor, holds 20,000 books on Bucks County history. > 84 S. Pine St., tel. 215/345–0210, www.mercermuseum.org. $6. Mon. and Wed.–Sat. 10–5, Tues. 10–9, Sun. noon–5.

Moravian Pottery and Tile Works This factory, on the grounds of the Fonthill estate, still produces the arts-and-crafts-style picture tiles that have adorned Graumann's Chinese Theater in Hollywood, among other buildings. As author and Bucks County resident James Michener described them, the tiles are done "in powerful earth colors that glow with intensity and unforgettable imagery." Reproductions of Mercer's tiles can be purchased in the Tile Works Shop. The factory, built in 1912, resembles a Spanish mission. > 130 Swamp Rd. (Rte. 313), tel. 215/345–6722. $3. Daily 10–4:45; 45-min self-guided tours every ½ hr; last tour at 4.

National Shrine of Our Lady of Czestochowa Since its opening in 1966, this shrine has drawn millions of pilgrims, including Pope John Paul II, many U.S. presidents, and Lech Walesa. The complex includes a modern church with huge panels of stained glass that portray the history of Christianity in Poland and the United States (the area has a large population of Polish Americans). The gift shop and bookstore sell religious gifts, many imported from Poland, and the cafeteria serves hot Polish and American

food on Sunday. > Ferry Rd. off Rte. 313, tel. 215/345–0600, www.polishshrine.com. Free. Daily 9–4:30; church opens daily at 7:15 AM for 7:30 and 8 Mass.
Pearl S. Buck House Green Hills Farm, Buck's country home (built in 1835), is where she wrote nearly 100 novels (including *The Good Earth*), children's books, and works of nonfiction. Filled with the writer's collection of Asian and American antiques and personal belongings, the house bears the imprint of the girl who grew up in China and became the first American woman to win both the Nobel and Pulitzer prizes. Pearl S. Buck International, which supports displaced children in Asia, has offices on the 60-acre property. Buck herself raised seven adopted children and cared for many others. > 520 Dublin Rd., off Rte. 313, Perkasie, tel. 215/249–0100 or 800/220–2825, www.pearl-s-buck.org. $6. Mar.–Dec., farmhouse tours Tues.–Sat. at 11, 1, and 2, Sun. at 1 and 2.

LAMBERTVILLE, NJ

Holcombe-Jimison Farmstead Museum On display here are farming equipment, a country kitchen, a rural post office, a combination doctor and dentist office, a blacksmith shop, a print shop, and a carpentry shop. From spring through fall, the herb garden showcases old-fashioned varieties. The museum is just north of Lambertville on Route 29 at the last exit of the Route 202 toll bridge. > Route 29, tel. 609/397–2752 or 908/782–6653. Donations accepted. May–Oct., Sun. 1–4, Wed. 9–noon.
Marshall House This house, run by the Lambertville Historical Society, is a look at Lambertville in the middle of the 19th century. Inside are furnishings from 1843, quilts, and a display devoted to shad fishing. Group tours can be arranged by appointment year-round. > 62 Bridge St., tel. 609/397–1898. Donations accepted. Early Apr.–Oct., weekends 1–4; guided walking tours on 1st Sun. at 2.

LANGHORNE

Sesame Place The good times roll, crawl, climb, and jump at this theme park, where there are 15 water rides and more than 50 play activities for children ages 2 to 13. One highlight is Sesame Neighborhood, a replica of the beloved street from the popular PBS program. Kids can spend time with their favorite Sesame Street characters on Cookie Mountain, Ernie's Bed Bounce, and the Vapor Trail roller coaster (Super Grover is the mascot). There's also an interactive stage show, Elmo's World Live, and a large water park. > 100 Sesame Rd., off Oxford Valley Rd. near junction of U.S. 1 and I-95, tel. 215/752–7070, www.sesameplace.com. $37, parking $8. Mid-May–mid-Sept., daily 10–8; early May and mid-Sept.–mid-Oct., weekends; call for spring and fall hrs.

MORRISVILLE

Historic Fallsington The pre-Revolutionary village of Fallsington is where William Penn attended Quaker meetings. Exhibits at the village amount to a three-century survey of American architecture, from a simple 17th-century log cabin to the Victorian excesses of the late 1800s. The restored buildings have been restored and are open for guided tours. > 4 Yardley Ave., off Tyburn Rd. W (off U.S. 13), Fallsington, tel. 215/295–6567, www.bucksnet.com/hisfalls. $4. Mid-May–Oct., Mon.–Sat. 10:30–3:30, Sun. 12:30–3:30.
Pennsbury Manor Reconstructed in 1938–39, the Georgian-style mansion and plantation duplicates the original, built by William Penn in the 1680s as his country es-

tate. On a gently sloping hillside overlooking the Delaware River, the original 8,400 acres are used for living-history demonstrations of what life was like in 17th-century America. The property includes formal gardens, orchards, an icehouse, a smoke-house, and a combination bakery-brewery. Penn's estate reveals that as governor of the colony he enjoyed the good life of a country gentleman, with the finest provisions and a multitude of servants. > 400 Pennsbury Memorial Rd., Tyburn Rd. E off U.S. 13, between Morrisville and Bristol, tel. 215/946–0400. $5. Tues.–Sat. 9–5, Sun. noon–5. Tours Mar.–Nov., weekdays at 10, 11:30, 1:30, 3:30, Sat. at 11, 12:30, 2, 3:30, Sun. at 12:30, 1:30, 2:30, 3:30; Dec.–Feb., weekdays at 11 and 2, weekends at 2.

NEW HOPE

Bucks County Playhouse Housed inside one of New Hope's original gristmills, New Hope's theatrical company stages revivals of Broadway musicals, including *On the Town, Titanic,* and *The Scarlet Pimpernel.* The season runs from April through December. > 70 S. Main St., tel. 215/862–2041, www.buckscountyplayhouse.com.

New Hope Canal Boat Company Beginning in 1832, coal barges went along the Delaware Canal. Now the canal is a state park, and you can ride one of the boat company's mule-pulled barges. The one-hour narrated tour travels past Revolutionary-era cottages, gardens, and artists' workshops. A barge historian and folk singer entertains aboard the 60-passenger boat. > New and S. Main Sts., tel. 215/862–0758, www.canalboats.com. $8. Apr., Fri.–Sun. 12:30, 3; May–Oct., daily noon, 1:30, 3, 4:30.

Parry Mansion The eight rooms of this stone house, built in 1784, are filled with furnishings that date from 1775 to 1900, representing over a century of changing tastes in wall decoration, upholstery, and accessories. Built by the lumber-mill owner Benjamin Parry, the house was occupied by five generations of his family. > S. Main and Ferry Sts., tel. 215/862–5652, www.parrymansion.org. $5. May–Dec., Fri.–Sun. 1–5.

Washington Crossing Historic Park It was on the frigid Christmas night of 1776 that George Washington and his 2,400 soldiers set out crossing the icy Delaware, taking the Hessian solders by surprise, and capturing Trenton. A 1917 granite statue of Washington marks their point of departure that snowy night. Memorials and attractions are divided between the Lower and the Upper Park, which are about 5 mi apart.

In the Lower Park, the fieldstone Memorial Building and visitor center, on Route 32, 7 mi south of New Hope, displays a reproduction of Emanuel Leutze's famous painting of the crossing (The original hangs in New York's Metropolitan Museum of Art.) The McConkey Ferry Inn, near the Memorial Building, is where Washington and his staff had Christmas dinner while waiting to cross the river.

In the Upper Park, about 5 mi north of the Memorial Building on Route 32, stop at Bowman's Hill Tower, named after a surgeon who sailed with Captain Kidd. Washington used the hill as a lookout point. You can get a much better view of the countryside than he did by riding the elevator up the 110-foot-tall memorial tower. It's open April through November, Tuesday through Sunday 10–4:30. Also in the Upper Park is the Taylor Mansion, a completely restored house from the 1800s.

A half mile north of Bowman's Hill Tower, the 100-acre **Wildflower Preserve** (tel. 215/862–2924) showcases hundreds of species of wildflowers, trees, shrubs, and ferns native to Pennsylvania. Take the guided tour (offered April through October for $3 per person or $5 per family) or follow the short trails, which will bring you back to your starting point. At the same location, the Platt Bird Collection displays more than

100 stuffed birds and 600 eggs. The Thompson-Neely House, an 18th-century farmhouse, is furnished just as it was when the colonial leaders sat in the kitchen and planned the attack on Trenton. > Rtes. 532 and 32, tel. 215/493–4076, www.phmc.state.pa.us. Parking in picnic areas $1 per car; 45-min walking tour $4. Park Tues.–Sat. 9–5, Sun. noon–5. Tours Tues.–Sat. at 9, 10, 11, 1, 2, 3; Sun. at noon, 1, 2, 3; Apr.–Oct., additional tour at 4.

Tours

Bucks County Carriages The horses that pull the carriages for these 20-minute tours are "parked" at the Logan Inn in New Hope, near the bakery in Peddler's Village, and at the Lambertville Station. There are daytime and evening rides depending on the season and departure location. A ride to a catered picnic and customized tours are available by reservation. > Tel. 215/862–3582.

Coryell's Ferry Ride and Historic Narrative This half-hour sightseeing ride on the Delaware runs from mid-April through October. It's run in a pontoon boat that seats 27. > Tel. 215/862–2050.

Executive Events Inc. This company's tours are conducted in 28-passenger mini-vans. Some trip themes include covered bridges, historic mansions, arts, wineries, antiques, and shopping. > Tel. 215/766–2211.

Sports

TUBING

Bucks County River Country Canoe and Tube Each year more than 100,000 people—from toddlers to grandparents—negotiate the Delaware on this company's inner tubes. From April through October, a bus transports people upriver to begin three- or four-hour tube or raft rides down to the base. No food, cans, or bottles are permitted on the tube rides. Wear lots of sunscreen and sneakers you don't mind getting wet; life jackets are available at no charge. Reservations are required for the trips, which cost around $18 per person for an inner tube and $22 for a raft on weekends. River Country also rents rafts and kayaks. > Byron Rd. at River Rd., tel. 215/297–5000, www.rivercountry.net.

Shopping

Bucks County has long been known for antiques shops full of everything from fine examples of early-American craftsmanship to fun kitsch. There are formal and country furnishings as well as American, European, and Asian antiques. Many shops are along a 4-mi stretch of U.S. 202 between Lahaska and New Hope and on intersecting country roads. Stores are generally open on weekends, with weekday hours by appointment only; it's best to call first.

New Hope's streets are lined with shops selling crafts and handmade accessories, art, antiques, vintage items, and contemporary wares. Union Street heading north from Bridge (as well as its cross streets) is lined with antiques shops, furniture stores, and art galleries. This is where the serious antiques collectors shop. Walk across the bridge from New Hope to Lambertville, New Jersey, for dozens more shops.

Many artists live in Bucks County, and numerous galleries showcase their paintings, prints, and sculpture. The New Hope Information Center can tell you about area galleries.

In Lahaska, throngs of shoppers head to the boutiques at Peddler's Village. There are also many outlet stores, and antiques shops abound on U.S. 202 between New Hope and Lahaska.

LAHASKA

Peddler's Village In the early 1960s, Earl Jamison bought a 6-acre chicken farm, moved local 18th-century houses to the site, and opened a collection of specialty shops and restaurants. Today the 75 shops in the 42-acre village peddle books, cookware, toys, leather goods, clothes, jewelry, contemporary crafts, art prints, candles, and other decorative items. The Grand Carousel, a restored 1922 Philadelphia Toboggan Company creation, still operates. Children love the Giggleberry Fair, with kid-pleasing games and rides. Seasonal events include the Strawberry Festival in May, the Teddy Bear's Picnic in July, and the Scarecrow Festival in September. > U.S. 202 and Rte. 263, tel. 215/794–4000, www.peddlersvillage.com.

Penn's Purchase Factory Outlet Stores The 40 stores here sell merchandise at 20%–60% off regular retail prices. The brands represented include Adidas, Coach, Easy Spirit, Geoffrey Beene, Izod, Nine West, Orvis, and Nautica. All 15 buildings in this complex have been designed in an early-American style that blends in with Peddler's Village, right across the road. > 5881 York Rd., at U.S. 202, tel. 215/794–0300, www.pennspurchase.com.

LAMBERTVILLE, NJ

A Mano Gallery Have a look at A Mano for wood and iron furniture as well as jewelry, clay, glass, and wearable art. > 36 N. Union St., tel. 609/397–0063.

America Antiques & Designs This store carries decorative arts, eclectic 19th- and 20th-century artifacts, and furniture. > 5 S. Main St., tel. 609/397–6966.

Broadmoor Antiques The 10 galleries at this location are packed with decorative and antique items. > 6 N. Union St., tel. 609/397–8802.

Coryell Street Antiques Proprietor Charles A. Buttaci has an ever-changing selection of fine art, period antiques, paintings, grandfather clocks, and Kentucky rifles displayed inside a Victorian house. > 51 Coryell St., tel. 609/397–5700. Closed Mon.–Wed.

David Rago Auctions Art, textiles, and household furnishings are brought to David Rago's auction block year-round. > 333 N. Main St., tel. 609/397–9374, www.ragoarts.com.

Golden Nugget Antique Flea Market Dozens of vendors set up their wares at this flea market. > 1850 River Rd., tel. 609/397–0811. Closed Mon.–Tues. and Thurs.–Fri.

Orchard Hill Collection This store carries a fine collection of Dutch-colonial antiques and handcrafted furniture. > 22 N. Union St., tel. 609/397–1188.

The Urban Archaeologist Italian and Greek objects for the house and garden are what the Urban Archaeologist does best. > 63 Bridge St., tel. 609/397–9588.

NEW HOPE

Farley's Bookshop This store's crowded shelves hold plenty of choices, including a good selection of books about the area. > 44 S. Main St., tel. 215/862–2452, www.farleysbookshop.com.

Golden Door Gallery Specializing in works by Bucks County painters, sculptors, and printmakers, the Golden Door also displays work by artists from other parts of the country. > 52 S. Main St., tel. 215/862–5529. Closed Mon.

Hobensack & Keller This store sells antique and reproduction garden ornaments, cast-iron furniture, fencing, and Oriental rugs. > Bridge St., tel. 215/862–2406.

Katy Kane Head here for antique, vintage, and designer clothing; accessories; and fine linens. The shop is open by appointment only. > 34 W. Ferry St., tel. 215/862–5873.

Olde Hope Antiques Hooked rugs, Pennsylvania German textiles, hand-painted furniture, and folk art are on offer at this appointment-only store. > Creamery Rd., tel. 215/297–0200.

Pink House Magnificent European 18th- and 19th-century furnishings and textiles are on offer at this antiques store. > W. Bridge St., tel. 215/862–5947.

Save the Date

APRIL

Annual Shad Festival On the last weekend of the month of April, Lambertville celebrates its favorite fish, marking the warm weather of spring. The Shad Festival is organized by the Lambertville Area Chamber of Commerce and includes works by the local artists, craftspeople, and musical performances. At Lewis Fishery, New Jersey's only commercial fishery, you can watch shad being hauled in. The Riverside Shad Dinner, held on Sunday, serves grilled shad, chowder, and other fish-based dishes. > www.lambertville.org.

DECEMBER

Washington's Crossing Reenactment Past and present seem to merge, almost magically, during the annual Christmas Day reenactment of George Washington crossing the Delaware. Locals don colonial uniforms and brave the elements in small boats. At nearby restaurants later in the day, you may discover troops, still in uniform, enjoying their holiday fare. > Rte. 32, Washington Crossing Historic Park, tel. 215/493–4076.

WHERE TO STAY

Bucks County has relatively limited lodging options for families; larger inns, hotels, and motels are the best bets. There are numerous choices for couples: accommodations ranging from modest to elegant can be found in historic inns, small hotels, and B&Bs. Most hostelries include breakfast in their room rates. Plan and reserve early— as much as three months ahead for summer and fall weekends. You should also ask about minimum stays; many accommodations require a two-night minimum stay on weekends and a three-night minimum on holiday weekends. Many inns prohibit or restrict smoking. Since some inns are historic homes furnished with fine antiques, the owners may discourage bringing children or may have age restrictions.

DOYLESTOWN

Doylestown Inn In the middle of town at the crossroads of Route 611 and U.S. 202, this Victorian hotel dates to 1902. It has been completely refurbished, with guest rooms on the third floor. Dark woods and traditional furniture set the tone in the guest rooms, some of which have whirlpool tubs and fireplaces. Mercer tiles are in the lobby. > 18 W. State St. 18901, tel. 215/345–6610, fax 215/345–4017, www.doylestowninn.com. 11 rooms. Restaurant, in-room data ports, minibars, free parking. AE, D, DC, MC, V. CP. $–$$

Pine Tree Farm This colonial farmhouse from 1730 has light and airy guest rooms that have been decorated with cheerful country antiques. The largest and most popular room has a white twig bed and a dressing table in the bathroom. The glass-enclosed garden room in the rear of the house overlooks 16 acres of pine trees. Breakfast, served poolside in summer, may include Grand Marnier French toast and fresh-baked muffins; lighter fare is also available. There's a two-night minimum stay.

> 2155 Lower State Rd., 18901, tel. 215/348–0632. 3 rooms. Pool, pond; no smoking. AE, MC, V. BP. **$$**

LAHASKA

Ash Mill Farm This country B&B is a handsome 18th-century fieldstone manor house set on 10 acres. High ceilings, ornate moldings, and deep-sill windows add character to the parlor; rooms have family antiques, reproductions, and thoughtful extras such as hair dryers and down comforters on canopy or four-poster beds. After-noon refreshments are available. The porch has a view of resident sheep. This B&B is just south of Lahaska. > 5358 York Rd. (Rte. 202), Holicong 18928, tel. 215/794–5373, www.ashmillfarm.com. 3 rooms, 2 suites. MC, V. BP. **$**

Barley Sheaf Farm Once the home of George S. Kaufman, who cowrote such classic plays as *The Man Who Came to Dinner* and *You Can't Take It with You*, these 30 acres includes a 1740 fieldstone house, a duck pond, a pool, and a meadow full of sheep. A hearty breakfast is served on the sunporch. Barley Sheaf Farm is a mile west of La-haska. > 5281 York Rd. (U.S. 202), Holicong 18928, tel. 215/794–5104, fax 215/794–5332, www.barleysheaf.com. 15 rooms. Pool, badminton, croquet, meeting room. AE, MC, V. BP. **$–$$**

Golden Plough Inn The main building of this inn has 22 spacious guest rooms, many of which come with four-poster beds, rich fabrics, and cozy window seats—along with modern conveniences. Some rooms have a fireplace or whirlpool bath. Other guest rooms are scattered about the village in an 18th-century farmhouse, a historic carriage house, and in Merchant's Row. There is a complimentary Continen-tal breakfast or a credit toward breakfast on the à la carte menu at the Spotted Hog. > Peddler's Village, Rte. 202 and Street Rd., 18931, tel. 215/794–4004, fax 215/794–4000, www.goldenploughinn.com. 42 rooms, 24 suites. Restaurant, refriger-ators, cable TV. AE, D, DC, MC, V. CP. **$–$$**

LAMBERTVILLE, NJ

Historic Lambertville House Rooms in this former stagecoach stop, built in 1823, are furnished with a mix of antiques and period pieces. Most have whirlpool tubs, and some have fireplaces. The handsome stone building overlooks Lambertville's small downtown; it's also steps away from North Union Street's antiques shops and the bridge to New Hope. On the first floor is Left Bank Libations, a cozy bar with an inviting outdoor porch open in season. > 32 Bridge St., 18938, tel. 609/397–0200 or 888/867–8859, fax 609/397–0511, www.lambertvillehouse.com. 20 rooms, 6 suites. Bar. AE, MC, V. BP. **$$**

Inn at Lambertville Station Guest rooms at this small hotel overlook the Delaware River and are decorated with antiques and reproduction furnishings. Suites have sit-ting areas and gas fireplaces. > Bridge St. and the Delaware, 08530, tel. 609/397–8300 or 800/524–1091, fax 215/862–0277, www.lambertvillestation.com. 37 rooms, 8 suites. Restaurant, bar. AE, MC, V. BP. **$–$$**

Martin Coryell House Bed & Breakfast This elegant inn is classically decorated with a chinoiserie mural, a hand-painted dining room ceiling inspired by a New Orleans ballroom, and Bradbury & Bradbury wallpapers. The six rooms and suites are filled with romantic touches, such as whirlpool tubs for two, claw-foot tubs, fireplaces, and plush feather beds. > 111 N. Union St., 08530, tel. 609/397–8981, fax 609/397–0755, www.martincoryellhouse.com. 3 rooms, 3 suites. Internet, free parking; no kids under 12. AE, MC, V. CP. **$$–$$$$**

Woolverton Inn Surrounding this stone manor on the Delaware are more than 300 acres of farm- and woodland: it's a secluded hideaway. The plush rooms, decorated with antiques, are done in soothing color schemes. Rooms include fluffy feather beds and some have whirlpool baths and fireplaces. > 6 Woolverton Rd., Stockton 08559, tel. 609/397–0802, fax 609/397–0987, www.woolvertoninn.com. 3 rooms, 5 suites, 5 cottages. Meeting rooms. AE, MC, V. BP. **$–$$$**

NEW HOPE

Best Western New Hope Inn Just a few minutes from New Hope and 30 minutes from Sesame Place, this Best Western is the place to consider when the B&Bs are booked or you want to stay only one night. Nicely outfitted, the hotel's amenities also make it a good fit for families with children. > 6426 Lower York Rd. (Rte. 202), 18938, tel. 215/862–5221 or 800/467–3202, fax 215/862–5847, www.bwnewhope.com. 152 rooms. Restaurant, in-room data ports, cable TV with video games, tennis court, pool, gym, bar, playground, dry cleaning, laundry facilities, business services, some pets allowed (fee), no-smoking rooms. AE, D, DC, MC, V. **¢–$**

Hotel du Village The large old stone boarding school has been transformed into an inn surrounded by flowers, creating the feel of an English manor house. The guest rooms have country furniture and elegant artwork. > 2535 N. River Rd. (Rte. 32), 18938, tel. 215/862–9911, fax 215/862–9788, www.hotelduvillage.com. 19 rooms. Dining room, 2 tennis courts, pool, bar; no room phones, no smoking. AE, DC. CP. **$**

Logan Inn George Washington is said to have stayed at least five times at this 1727 inn. Rooms have original and reproduction colonial and Victorian furnishings and canopy beds; some also have river views. The Continental breakfast of muffins, fruit, cereals, and juices is served on the tented patio. > 10 W. Ferry St., 18938, tel. 215/862–2300, www.loganinn.com. 16 rooms. Restaurant, in-room data ports, cable TV. AE, D, DC, MC, V. CP. **$–$$**

Mansion Inn This elegant Victorian inn was built in 1865. Even the English gardens feel pleasantly private. Inside, Depression glass, local art, antiques, and comfortable furniture fill the high-ceilinged yellow and beige sitting rooms. Guest rooms have antique pieces, plush linens, and modern baths; some have fireplaces and whirlpool tubs. Breakfast may include fresh muffins, an egg dish, or French toast. There's a two-night minimum on weekends and 3 nights on holidays. > 9 S. Main St., 18938, tel. 215/862–1231, fax 215/862–0277, www.themansioninn.com. 7 rooms, 5 suites. Cable TV, pool; no smoking. AE, MC, V. BP. **$$–$$$$**

Wedgwood Inn The Wedgwood Inn B&B includes an 1870 Victorian done in shades of blue, with a porch and gabled roof, as well as a federal-style 1840 stone manor house and the 1870 Aaron Burr House. Outside are lush gardens; the interiors are furnished with Wedgwood pottery and fireplaces. Five rooms have two-person whirlpool tubs. Breakfast is served on the sunporch, gazebo, or in your room. Tennis and pool privileges are available. > 111 W. Bridge St., 18938, tel. 215/862–2570, www.new-hope-inn.com/wedgwood. 15 rooms, 4 suites. Some cable TV, concierge, some pets allowed; no TV in some rooms, no smoking. AE, MC, V. CP. **¢–$$**

WHERE TO EAT

DOYLESTOWN

Black Walnut Cafe Inside an 1846 town house, this restaurant, with original plank hardwood floors and white tablecloths, looks traditional. However, the American cooking includes innovative global touches, such as Brazilian lobster tails with shiitake mushroom dumplings. > 80 W. State St., tel. 215/348–0708. AE, D, DC, MC, V. Closed Mon. and Tues. No lunch. $$–$$$$

Cafe Arielle This French bistro serves delicious grilled seafood dishes, including tuna steaks, as well as prime meats. The interior is furnished in a country-French style, with striking artwork. > Doylestown Agricultural Works, 100 S. Main St., tel. 215/345–5930. AE, DC, MC, V. Closed Mon. and Tues. No lunch weekends. $$$–$$$$

LAHASKA

Carversville Inn An out-of-the-way location has made this circa-1813 inn one of the area's best-kept secrets. The regional Southern food served here includes such flavorful dishes as Gulf shrimp étouffée or roast tenderloin of pork in a sauce of rosemary and garlic. > Carversville and Aquetong Rds., Carversville, tel. 215/297–0900. AE, MC, V. Closed Mon. $$$

Jenny's Bistro American regional cuisine is served in a Victorian or a country-French room. Balsamic-glazed ahi tuna and filet mignon with cheddar cheese, bacon, and horseradish sauce are favorites. You can hear piano music Friday and Saturday nights. > Peddler's Village, Rte. 202 and Street Rd. AE, D, DC, MC, V. No dinner Mon., except in Dec. $$$–$$$$

Spotted Hog This casual country bistro serves American cuisine such as New York strip steak, grilled chicken with melted Monterey Jack cheese in an oyster-sherry sauce, Philly cheesesteaks, barbecued ribs, pizza, and pasta. The bar stocks 35 American microbrewery beers. The Spotted Hog is the only restaurant in Peddler's Village to serve breakfast. > Golden Plough Inn, Peddler's Village, Rte. 202 and Street Rd., tel. 215/794–4000. AE, D, DC, MC, V. $–$$$

LAMBERTVILLE, NJ

DeAnna's Known for its homemade ravioli and pasta dishes (Gorgonzola cream sauce is a specialty), DeAnna's is cozy and bohemian. Banquettes in the main dining room have colorful overstuffed cushions. There's another, more formal, dining room, as well as a lovely outdoor, covered patio that's perfect for alfresco dining in the warm-weather months. > 18 S. Main St., at Lilly St., tel. 609/397–8957. No credit cards. Closed Mon. No lunch. BYOB. $–$$

Full Moon This funky, casual eatery has an eclectic menu that includes Asian, Cajun, and Mediterranean dishes. Specialties for breakfast include omelets and egg dishes, and for lunch there's hearty meat loaf, along with vegetarian offerings such as Portobello mushrooms topped with cheese and sautéed with onions and peppers in pesto olive oil. Dinner, served on Friday and Saturday only, might include seafood bisque, baked artichoke, or grilled pork chops seasoned with Cajun spices. > 23 Bridge St., tel. 609/397–1096. No credit cards. Closed Tues. No dinner Sun.–Thurs. $–$$$

Hamilton's Grill Room Casually elegant, the Grill Room has earned a fine reputation for its changing menu of simply prepared Mediterranean-inspired meat and fish dishes. The open grill, the centerpiece of the main dining room, figures heavily in the kitchen's preparations. Starters might include shad roe with capers, butter, and lemon, or chilled asparagus and calamari escabèche; entrées might include grilled breast and leg of duck with dates and almonds or grilled tuna with avocado chutney. > 8½ Coryell St., tel. 609/397–4343. Reservations essential. AE, MC, V. No lunch. BYOB. **$$$**

Inn at Lambertville Station This inn's restaurant and bar are housed in an 1867 stone building designed by Thomas Ustick Walter, architect of the U.S. Capitol's dome. The American dishes include such classics as pork loin, roast duck, and roasted Atlantic salmon with a sauce of lemon, dill, and garlic. There's also a casual pub that serves sandwiches and snacks. > Bridge St. and the Delaware, 08530, tel. 609/397–8300 or 800/524–1091, fax 215/862–0277, www.lambertvillestation.com. AE, MC, V. **$$–$$$**

NEW HOPE

Havana Bar and Restaurant Grilled specialties are what stand out amid the American and contemporary fare here. Options include sesame onion rings, a grilled eggplant and Brie sandwich, and a newfangled hamburger with Gorgonzola cheese and spiced walnuts. The bar is enlivened by jazz, blues, and dance bands from Thursday through Sunday nights and by karaoke on Monday. The view of Main Street you get here, especially from the patio, makes Havana ideal for people-watching. > 105 S. Main St., tel. 215/862–9897. AE, D, DC, MC, V. **$–$$$**

Hotel du Village Inside a former school, this restaurant serves country-French fare. The dining room is Tudor style, but you might prefer the sunporch. Dishes include tournedos Henri IV, a beef fillet with béarnaise sauce; sweetbreads with mushrooms in Madeira sauce; and fillet of sole in curried butter. Try one of the extravagant desserts. > 2535 N. River Rd. (Rte. 32), 18938, tel. 215/862–9911, fax 215/862–9788, www.hotelduvillage.com. AE, DC. Closed Mon. and Tues. No lunch. **$$$**

La Bonne Auberge Inside a pre-Revolutionary farmhouse, La Bonne Auberge serves classic French cuisine. Some specialties include rack of lamb and poached Dover sole with a champagne and lobster sauce. The four-course prix-fixe menu ($50; available Wednesday and Thursday) is a good deal. The restaurant is within a development called Village 2; travel directions are provided when you call for a reservation. > Village 2 off Mechanic St., tel. 215/862–2462, www.bonneauberge.com. Reservations essential. Jacket required. AE, MC, V. Closed Mon. and Tues. No lunch. **$$$$**

Logan Inn Inside this restored inn from 1727 are elegant colonial dining rooms as well as the Garden Room, decorated with stained glass. When the weather cooperates, patio dining is popular. In addition to lunch and dinner, the Logan's friendly restaurant also serves a popular bar menu throughout the day. It includes such favorites as nachos, buffalo wings, and salads. > 10 W. Ferry St., 18938, tel. 215/862–2300, www.loganinn.com. AE, D, DC, MC, V. **$–$$$**

Martine's The beam ceiling, plaster-over-stone walls, and fireplace make Martine's look like an English pub. The eclectic menu includes filet mignon au poivre, pasta, duckling, and a steamed seafood mélange. Try the French onion soup. Outdoor dining is on a small patio. > 7 E. Ferry St., tel. 215/862–2966. AE, MC, V. **$$–$$$**

Mother's At one of New Hope's most popular dining spots, it's the desserts, including chocolate mousse pie and apple walnut cake, that really stand out. Homemade soups, pastas, and unusual pizzas are also on the extensive menu, but your best bet for good food is to visit for breakfast. In summer meals are also served in the garden. Expect to wait; it's often crowded here. > 34 N. Main St., tel. 215/862–9354. AE, D, MC, V. **$$–$$$**

Odette's In 1961 Parisian actress Odette Myrtil Logan converted this former canal lock house into a restaurant that resembles a French country bistro. The Continental menu, which changes seasonally, includes such choices as pine nut–crusted swordfish and roasted rack of veal. The Sunday brunch is buffet style. You may want to request a dining room that has a river view. Entertainment consists of a nightly session around the piano bar, legendary among local show-tune buffs, plus regular appearances by nationally known cabaret performers. > S. River Rd., ½ mi south of Bridge St., tel. 215/862–2432, www.odettes.com. AE, DC, MC, V. Reservations essential. $$–$$$$

ESSENTIALS

Getting Here

Bucks County is a large area—40 mi long and up to 20 mi wide—and is almost impossible to tour without a car. Main roads include River Road (Route 32), U.S. 202, and Rte. 611. One great pleasure of a visit here can be exploring country back roads.

BY CAR

A car is a must when traveling the roads of Bucks County. In small, popular towns like New Hope, however, parking can be a challenge. Park where you are staying or hope for some luck in finding public parking spaces.

Visitor Information

CONTACTS **Bucks County Conference and Visitors Bureau,** > 3207 Street Rd., Bensalem 19020, tel. 800/836–2825, www.bccvb.org. **Central Bucks Chamber of Commerce,** > First Union Bank Bldg., 115 W. Court St., Doylestown 18901, tel. 215/348–3913, www.centralbuckschamber.org. **Lambertville Area Chamber of Commerce,** > 239 N. Union St., Lambertville, NJ 08530, tel. 609/397–9066, www.lambertville.org. **New Hope Information Center,** > 1 W. Mechanic St., at Main St., New Hope 18938, tel. 215/862–5880 for automated menu, 215/862–5030 for a travel counselor, www.newhopepa.com.

Pennsylvania Dutch Country

Lancaster is 125 mi north of Washington, D.C.

5

Revised by Laura Knowles Callanan

BLENDING THE OLD WITH THE NEW, Lancaster County is a place with rolling fields of corn and wheat, green pastures full of horses and Holstein cattle, and horse-drawn buggies being driven down back roads. Despite the county's growth, there are still areas where time seems to have stood still. The scenery can take your breath away here. Later on, you can savor hearty Pennsylvania Dutch cooking and go shopping for fresh produce, baked goods, antiques, and quilts.

Today the county's main roads are lined with souvenir shops and sometimes crowded with cars and buses of tourists. Land is valuable here, and many farmers have sold their property. But despite the commercialism and development, you can still find general stores, one-room schoolhouses, country lanes, and tidy farms that exist as they have for decades and even centuries.

Lancaster, in the center of the county, makes a good base for exploring the surrounding countryside and has plenty to see in its own right. Dating back to 1710, it was the largest inland city in the colonies. For one day, September 27, 1777, Lancaster became the national capital, as Congress fled the British entering Philadelphia. Today, Lancaster's rich heritage is captured in many historic districts and in the Central Market at Penn Square. Other nearby sights include Wheatland, the home of U.S. president James Buchanan, and the Landis Valley Museum, devoted to rural life before 1900.

Lancaster County holds the country's largest and oldest settlement of Pennsylvania Dutch, or Plain People, a name they use to differentiate themselves from the "fancy" folk of the modern world. The roughly 85,000 Plain People that live here belong to about 41 different sects, including Amish, Mennonites, and Brethren. The members vary in how strictly they live, with some traveling by horse and buggy and others driving black cars with bumpers painted black, so that they won't be too showy. Still others live quite like most other Americans. (The Pennsylvania Dutch, by the way, are not Dutch at all—it's a corruption of *Deutsch*, meaning German. Most Plain People descend from German and Swiss immigrants who immigrated here to escape religious persecution.)

Roughly a quarter of the Plain people are Old Order Amish, one of the more conservative sects. Men begin to grow a beard (with no mustache) upon marriage, and they wear several different styles of hats to distinguish their age, status, and religious district. Amish women wear black full-length dresses, capes, and aprons. Those who have been baptized wear white organdy caps and don't cut their hair.

The Amish way of life has changed very little since their ancestors settled here in the early 1700s. Because of their religious beliefs, most shun telephones, electricity, and other trappings of modern civilization. They continue to use kerosene or gas lamps, horse-drawn buggies instead of cars, and wear conservative clothing that pins instead of buttons. (A few Amish do use telephones and even the Internet to promote their quilt and furniture businesses.) Of course, in turning their backs on the modern world, the Amish and other Plain People have attracted its attention.

When you are visiting among the Amish, remember to respect their values. Many believe that photographs and videos with recognizable reproductions of themselves violate the commandment against making graven images. Respect their beliefs, and don't videotape or take photos.

Most Amish families farm, using teams of mules to plow, plant, and harvest their crops, which include tobacco. When the tobacco leaves mature in September, whole families take to the fields to cut stalks, after which they hang them in rows from floor to ceiling in sheds.

Most of the area's Amish community is east of Lancaster, between Routes 340 and 23, in towns with names such as Blue Ball, Paradise, and Bird-in-Hand. Strasburg, to the southeast, has sights for train buffs. No more than 12 mi north of Lancaster, Lititz is a lovely town, as are Marietta and Manheim. Ephrata is one of the few places where you can see the rich traditions of the Amish mesh with modern. Its residents stage full-scale musicals in summer: the works are about Ephrata itself. Intercourse, another center of Amish life, was named for its location at the intersection, or intercourse, of two roads (today's Routes 340 and 772).

A visit to Hershey, the chocolate company town 30 mi northwest of Lancaster, can be easily combined with a trip to Pennsylvania Dutch Country. Founded in 1903 by confectioner Milton S. Hershey, a descendant of Mennonites, Hershey has continued to branch out from the same center business that began here a century ago. Today, Hershey is home to a huge amusement park, a sports arena, a theater and concert halls used by acclaimed performers, and even a spa that employs chocolate-based treatments.

WHAT TO SEE & DO

EPHRATA

Ephrata Cloister The three restored buildings here are part of what remains of a religious communal society founded in 1728 by German immigrant Conrad Beissel. The monastic society of brothers and sisters lived a life of work, study, and prayer. They ate one meal a day of grains, fruits, and vegetables and encouraged celibacy. The society was best known for its a cappella singing and its Fraktur (calligraphic documents with folk art decorations), as well as for its publishing center and the medieval German style of its buildings. The last member died in 1813. Guides lead 45-minute tours of three restored buildings, after which you can browse through the stable, print shop, and craft shop. There is also on-site archaeological research. > Rtes. 272 and 322, Ephrata, tel. 717/733–6600, www.cob-net.org/cloister.htm. $6. Mon.–Sat. 9–5, Sun. noon–5.

Green Dragon Farmers Market and Auction Fridays bustle at this 30-acre farmer's market, one of the state's largest. In the morning livestock and agricultural commodities are auctioned (small animals are auctioned in the evening). Throughout the day, local Amish and Mennonite farmers tend many of the 400 indoor and outdoor stalls that sell meats, fruits, vegetables, fresh-baked pies, and dry goods. There's also a flea market. > 955 N. State St., off Rte. 272, Ephrata, tel. 717/738–1117, www.greendragonmarket.com. Fri. 9–9.

HERSHEY

Hershey Gardens What was once a single 3½-acre plot of 7,000 rosebushes has grown to include 10 theme gardens on 23 landscaped acres, along with 1,200 varieties of roses and 22,000 tulips. The gardens come to life in spring as thousands of bulbs burst into bloom. Flowering displays last until fall, when late roses open. Kid-oriented areas include a butterfly house and a children's garden. > Hotel Rd. near Hotel Hershey, tel. 717/534–3492, www.hersheygardens.org. $7. Apr.–Sept., daily 9–6; Oct., daily 9–5.

Hershey Museum Milton S. Hershey, who founded the town and just about everything in it, is the subject of this museum. The main exhibition, *Built on Chocolate*, including chocolate-bar wrappers and cocoa tins from different eras, and black-and-white photos of the town from the '30s, '40s, and '50s juxtaposed with color photos of the same sites today. There are also exhibits that document the daily lives of the Pennsylvania Dutch, a display of Native American art, and artifacts from Hershey's personal collection. There's also a hands-on children's area. > 170 W. Hersheypark Dr., tel. 717/534–3439, www.hersheypa.com. $6. Daily 10–5.

Hersheypark At this 100-acre park you can enjoy over 60 thrilling and nostalgic rides. Begun in 1907, Hersheypark is one of the country's most attractive theme parks. Standout rides include the Comet, a wooden roller coaster from 1946, and a carousel built in 1919 with 66 hand-carved wooden horses. Newer rides include the Lightning Racer double-track wood racing coaster, the Great Bear steel inverted roller coaster, and the Roller Soaker—half roller coaster, half water ride. Costumed Hershey's Bars and Reese's Peanut Butter Cups characters roam the park, which also has five theaters for musicals and other performances. > Hersheypark Dr., Rte. 743 and U.S. 422, tel. 717/534–3090, www.hersheypa.com. $35.95, includes ZooAmerica. Memorial Day–Labor Day, daily 10–10 (some earlier closings); May and Sept., weekends only, call for hrs.

Hershey's Chocolate World At the town's official visitor center, this 10-minute automated ride takes you through the steps of producing chocolate, from picking the cocoa beans to making candy bars in Hershey's candy kitchens. There is also a 3-D show with entertainment by chocolate product characters. You can also taste-test Hershey confections, and buy gifts in a spacious conservatory filled with tropical plants. > Park Blvd., tel. 717/534–4900, www.hersheypa.com. Free. Daily 9–5; extended hrs in summer.

ZooAmerica This 11-acre wildlife park holds more than 200 animals of 75 North American species, including roadrunners, bison, and prairie dogs. The settings are designed to duplicate the animals' natural habitats. > Hersheypark, Rte. 743 and U.S. 422, tel. 717/534–3860. $7 (or included in Hersheypark admission price). Mid-June–Aug., daily 10–8; Sept.–mid-June, daily 10–5.

INTERCOURSE

Amish Country Homestead On the guided tour of the nine furnished rooms in this re-creation of an Old Order Amish house, you can learn about the culture and clothing of the Amish and how they live without electricity and other modern conveniences. > Plain & Fancy Farm, Rte. 340 between Bird-in-Hand and Intercourse, tel. 717/768–3600. $6.95. July–Oct., Mon.–Sat. 9:45–6:45; Apr.–June and Nov., Mon.–Sat. 9:45–4:15; Dec.–Mar., weekends 9:45–4:15.

Amish Farm and House The 40-minute tours through this 10-room, circa-1805 house cover its Old Order Amish style and furnishing. A map guides you to the animals, waterwheel, lime kiln, and barns on the 25-acre farmstead. > 2395 Lincoln Hwy.

E (U.S. 30), Smoketown, tel. 717/394–6185, www.amishfarmandhouse.com. $6.95. Apr., May, Sept., and Oct., daily 8:30–5; June–Aug., daily 8:30–6; Nov.–Mar., daily 8:30–4.

People's Place What's billed as a "people-to-people interpretation center" is an excellent introduction to the Amish, Mennonite, and Hutterite communities. A 30-minute multiscreen slide show titled *Who Are the Amish?* includes perceptive narration and close-ups of Amish life. 20Q (short for 20 Questions), an interactive family museum, highlights the differences between Amish and Mennonite societies. Children can try on bonnets and play in the "feeling box." Don't miss the collection of wood carvings by Aaron Zook. There's a bookstore, too. > 3513 Old Philadelphia Pike (Rte. 340), Intercourse, tel. 717/768–7171 or 800/390–8436, www.thepeoplesplace.com. $8. Memorial Day–Labor Day, Mon.–Sat. 9:30–8; Labor Day–Memorial Day, Mon.–Sat. 9:30–5.

LANCASTER

Central Market A must-see stop, the oldest continuously operating farmer's market in the United States began as open-air stalls in 1742; the Romanesque building is from 1889. Here local people shop for fresh fruit and vegetables, meats (try the Lebanon bologna), ethnic foods, fresh flowers, and such baked goods as sticky buns and shoofly pie. > Penn Sq., tel. 717/291–4723. Tues. and Fri. 6–4, Sat. 6–2.

Demuth Foundation Charles Demuth (1883–1935), one of America's first modernist artists, found inspiration for his watercolors in the geometric shapes of machines and modern technology, as well as flowers in his mother's garden. At his restored 18th-century home, studio, and garden, a few of his works are usually on display. The complex includes a museum shop and the oldest operating tobacco shop in the country (1770). > 120 E. King St., tel. 717/299–9940, www.demuth.org. Donations accepted. Feb.–Dec., Tues.–Sat. 10–4, Sun. 1–4.

Dutch Wonderland The 44 acres of games and rides at this amusement park are suited for families with younger children. The roller coaster, merry-go-round, and giant slide are all quite tame. Diving shows and concerts are also staged here. > 2249 U.S. 30, east of Lancaster, tel. 717/291–1888, www.dutchwonderland.com. $25.95 for unlimited rides. Memorial Day–Labor Day, daily 10–6 or later; Labor Day–Oct. and Easter–Memorial Day, weekends 10–6.

Hans Herr House The oldest house in Lancaster County is also one of the best examples of medieval-style German architecture in North America. The subject of several paintings by Andrew Wyeth, the house was the colonial home of his ancestors, the Herr family. Today the house is owned by the Lancaster Mennonite Historical Society, which educates the public about the Mennonite religion through exhibits in its visitor center. The 45-minute tours cover the grounds and the 1719 sandstone house, a former Mennonite meeting place. > 1849 Hans Herr Dr., 5 mi south of Lancaster off U.S. 222, tel. 717/464–4438, www.hansherr.org. $4. Apr.–Nov., Mon.–Sat. 9–4.

Heritage Center Museum The Old City Hall is now a museum documenting colonial history and the culture of the Pennsylvania Dutch settlers. The museum showcases works Lancaster County artisans and craftspeople have made—clocks, furniture, homemade toys, Fraktur, and Pennsylvania long rifles. > King and Queen Sts. on Penn Sq., tel. 717/299–6440, www.lancasterheritage.com. Donations accepted. May–Dec., Tues.–Sat. 10–5.

Historic Rock Ford Plantation This 1794 Georgian-style mansion was owned by General Edward Hand, Revolutionary War commander, George Washington's adjutant, and member of the Continental Congress. Eighteenth-century antiques and folk art are inside, and the Kauffman Barn contains changing exhibits. > Lancaster County Park, 881

Rock Ford Rd., tel. 717/392–7223, www.rockfordplantation.org. $5. Apr.–Oct., Tues.–Fri. 10–4, Sun. noon–4. Yuletide tours Thanksgiving–Christmas, weekends only.

Landis Valley Museum This outdoor living-history museum is devoted to the Pennsylvania German rural life and folk culture before 1900. Started by brothers Henry and George Landis, the farm and village are now operated by the Pennsylvania Historical and Museum Commission. You can visit more than 15 historical buildings, from a farmstead to a country store. There are demonstrations of skills such as spinning and weaving, pottery making, and tinsmithing. Many of the crafts made are for sale in the Weathervane Shop. > 2451 Kissel Hill Rd., off Oregon Pike (Rte. 272), tel. 717/569–0401, www.landisvalleymuseum.org. $9. Mar.–Dec., Mon.–Sat. 9–5, Sun. noon–5.

Mount Hope Estate and Winery This elegant 19th-century mansion and its surrounding gardens have been placed on the National Register of Historic Places. Originally built in 1800 in the federal style, the house was give Victorian touches and enlarged in 1895 to its current 32 rooms. Turrets, hand-painted 18-foot ceilings, Egyptian marble fireplaces, gold-leaf wallpaper, and crystal gas chandeliers are just some of the decorative elements. The winery bottles about 30 different wines; complimentary tastings are held in the wine shop. > 5 mi north of Manheim on Rte. 72, ½ mi from Pennsylvania Tpke. Exit 20, tel. 717/665–7021 Ext. 125. Mon.–Sat. 10–5, Sun. 11–5; house tours by special arrangement.

Nissley Vineyards and Winery Estate You can see how grapes grow on a self-guided tour at this 52-acre winery, which also holds tastings and allows picnicking on its grounds. In summer there is a musical concert series with a cost for admission. > 140 Vintage Dr., northwest of Marietta near Bainbridge, 1½ mi off Rte. 441, tel. 717/426–3514, www.nissleywine.com. Free. Mon.–Sat. 10–5, Sun. 1–4.

Wheatland James Buchanan, the only Pennsylvanian president, served from 1857 to 1861. The 15th president's restored 1828 federal mansion and outbuildings display his furniture as it was during his lifetime. A one-hour tour includes a profile of the only bachelor to occupy the White House. Around Christmas there are candlelight tours with costumed guides. > 1120 Marietta Ave., Rte. 23, 1½ mi west of Lancaster, tel. 717/392–8721, www.wheatland.org. $5.50. Apr.–mid-Dec., daily 10–4.

Wright's Ferry Mansion In this 1738 stone lived the English Quaker Susanna Wright, a silkworm breeder whose family helped open colonial Pennsylvania west of the Susquehanna. Inside is period furniture in the Philadelphia William & Mary and Queen Anne styles and a great collection of English needlework, ceramics, and glass. > 38 S. 2nd St., Columbia, tel. 717/684–4325. $5. May–Oct., Tues., Wed., Fri., and Sat. 10–3.

STRASBURG

Amish Village After you take a guided tour through an authentically furnished Amish house, you can wander through the village itself, where there are a barn and house, a one-room schoolhouse, a blacksmith shop, a village store, and an operating smokehouse built by Amish craftsmen. > Rte. 896 between U.S. 30 and Rte. 741, Strasburg, tel. 717/687–8511. $6.50. Mar.–mid-May, Sept., and Oct., daily 9–5; mid-May–Aug., daily 9–6; Nov.–Feb., house tours weekends 10–4.

Choo-Choo Barn, Traintown, USA What started as a family hobby in 1945 with a single train chugging around the Groff family Christmas tree now has its own building. This 1,700-square-foot display of Lancaster County in miniature has 20 trains mainly in O-gauge, with 150 animated scenes, including an authentic Amish barn raising, a huge three-ring circus with animals and acrobats, and a blazing house fire, with fire engines rushing toward it. Periodically, the overhead lights dim for night, when street-lights and locomotive headlights glow in the darkness, and a nighttime baseball game gets underway. > Rte. 741 East, tel. 717/687–7911, www.choochoobarn.com. $5. Apr.–Dec., daily 10–5.

National Toy Train Museum At the showplace of the Train Collectors Association, you can see antique and 20th-century toy trains. The museum has five huge operating layouts, with toy trains from the 1800s to the present, plus hundreds of locomotives and cars in display cases. There are special hands-on layouts for kids every Friday from June through August. > Paradise La. just north of Rte. 741, tel. 717/687–8976, www.traincollectors.org. $3. May–Oct. and Christmas wk, daily 10–5; Apr. and Nov.–late Dec., weekends 10–5.

Railroad Museum of Pennsylvania and the Railway Education Center Across the road from the Strasburg Rail Road, this museum holds 75 pieces of train history, including 13 colossal engines built between 1888 and 1930; 12 railroad cars, among them a Pullman sleeper; sleighs; and railroad memorabilia that documents the history of Pennsylvania railroading. More than 50 of the pieces of equipment are kept indoors in the Rolling Stock Hall. > Rte. 741, Strasburg, tel. 717/687–8628, www.rrmuseumpa.org. $7. May–Oct., Mon.–Sat. 9–5, Sun. noon–5; Nov.–Apr., Tues.–Sat. 9–5, Sun. noon–5.

Strasburg Rail Road When this train began in 1832, it was built to carry milk, mail, and coal. Now you can take it on a 45-minute round-trip excursion through Amish farm country from Strasburg to Paradise. Called America's oldest short line, the Strasburg run has wooden coaches pulled by an iron steam locomotive. You can lunch in the dining car, or buy a box lunch at the station, and have a picnic at Groff's Grove along the line. Visit the Reading Car No. 10, a restored business car that carried the top brass of the Philadelphia and Reading Railroad back in the early 1900s. There are special train rides planned around Christmas and Halloween. > Rte. 741, tel. 717/687–7522, www.strasburgrailroad.com. $9.25. Mid-Feb.–mid-Apr. and Nov.–mid-Dec., weekends noon–2; mid-Apr.–Oct., weekdays 11–4, weekends 11–5 or later. Dinner train boards at 6:30. Trains depart every hr, depending on season; call for schedule.

Tours

Aaron & Jessica's Buggy Rides These four tours, each about 3½ mi, cover the countryside in an authentic Amish carriage. > Plain & Fancy Farm, Rte. 340 between Bird-in-Hand and Intercourse, tel. 717/768–8828, www.amishbuggyrides.com. $10. Mon.–Sat., 8 AM–dusk.

Abe's Buggy Rides During this 2-mi trip down country roads in an Amish carriage, Abe chats about the customs of the Pennsylvania Dutch. > 2596 Old Philadelphia Pike (Rte. 340), tel. 717/392–1794. $10. Mon.–Sat. 9 AM–dusk.

Historic Lancaster Walking Tour This 90-minute stroll through town is conducted by costumed guides, who cover about 50 points of architectural and historical interest. There are also themed tours and group tours. Tours of the six-square-block area depart from the visitor center downtown. > S. Queen and Vine Sts. near Penn Sq., Lancaster, tel. 717/392–1776. $7. Apr.–Oct., Mon., Wed., Thurs., and Sun. at 1, Tues., Fri., and Sat. at 10 and 1; Nov.–Mar., by reservation only.

Shopping

U.S. 30 is lined with outlets of varying quality; be sure to check the retail prices of whatever you want before you leave home. On Sunday fans of yesteryear frequent the huge antiques malls along Route 272 between Adamstown and Denver. As many as 5,000 dealers may turn up on Extravaganza Days, held in late spring, summer, and early fall.

ADAMSTOWN

Renninger's Antique and Collector's Market Thousands of collectors and dealers come to this huge market, open Sunday year-round from 7:30 to 5. Nearly 400 indoor stalls overflow with every conceivable type of antique; when the weather cooperates, the outdoor flea market adds to the selection, and there are food stands, too. > Rte. 272, ½ mi north of Pennsylvania Tpke. Exit 21, tel. 717/336–2177.

Shupp's Grove The oldest of the antiques markets in Adamstown is in a shady grove. Tables are piled with antiques, art, and collectibles. The market is open weekends from April through October, 7–5. > Off Rte. 897, south of Adamstown, tel. 717/484–4115, www.shuppsgrove.com.

Stoudt's Black Angus Antiques Mall More than 500 dealers display old books and prints, estate jewelry, linens, china and glassware, coins, and plenty of furniture, inside and out. There's also a restaurant. Stoudt's is open Sunday 7:30–5. > Rte. 272, Adamstown, tel. 717/484–4385.

Ten Thousand Villages Operated by the Mennonite Central Committee, Ten Thousand Villages is an alternative trading organization (ATO) designed to benefit artisans in low-income countries. The vast store stocks more than 3,000 items—jewelry, Indian brass, onyx, needlework, baskets, toys, handwoven rugs, and clothing—from more than 30 countries. The Oriental Rug Room has hand-knotted Persians, Bokharas, kilims, dhurries, and Afghani tribal rugs. Sales in January and July offer excellent bargains. You can sample a different country's cuisine each week in the Nav Jiwan Tea Room. > Rte. 272, north of Ephrata Cloister, tel. 717/721–8400, www.tenthousandvillages.com.

HERSHEY

Crossroads Antiques Mall About 90 dealers in antiques and collectibles are in this mall, which is shaped like a high dome. Crossroads is open Thursday to Monday, 10–5:30. > Intersection Rtes. 322 and 743, tel. 717/520–1600. Closed Tues. and Wed.

Ziegler's in the Country This 1850s homestead has several buildings from that era. The air-conditioned barn has space for 92 dealers and an herb and body-products shop (open weekends). > Rte. 743, tel. 717/533–1662, www.zieglersantiques.com. Closed Tues. and Wed.

LANCASTER

Kitchen Kettle Village A showcase of local crafts, the 32 shops here are devoted to decoy carving; furniture making; leather tooling; relish-, jam-, and jelly making; and tin punching. The Kling House serves homemade local recipes, and there are stands for ice cream, fudge, and funnel cake. The shops are closed Sunday. > Rte. 340, Intercourse, tel. 717/768–8261 or 800/732–3538.

Olde Mill House Shoppes One of Lancaster's oldest country stores, Olde Mill House stocks a fine choice of pottery, folk art, country and Shaker furniture, and custom handcrafted early-American reproduction interior and exterior lighting. > 105 Strasburg Pike, Lancaster, tel. 717/299–0678.

Rockvale Square Outlets With more than 120 stores, from Bass to Nike, this is the largest outlet center in the area. > U.S. 30 and Rte. 896, Lancaster, tel. 717/293–9595.

Tanger Outlet Center This collection of 65 outlets includes Banana Republic, Ralph Lauren, and Eddie Bauer. > 311 Outlet Dr., Rte. 30 E, Lancaster, tel. 717/392–7260, www.tangeroutlet.com.

Weathervane Shop Among the few places that carry fine local crafts is the Landis Valley Museum shop, which includes many items made on-site. You can get tin, pottery, leather, braided rugs, weaving, and cane chairs here. > 2451 Kissel Hill Rd., off Oregon Pike (Rte. 272) Lancaster, tel. 717/569–9312.

Save the Date

MAY

Wheels Wheels Wheels More than 200 antique cars and cycles line the streets of downtown Lancaster during this annual event, usually held the weekend after Mother's Day. You can taste food from city vendors and listen to live music. > Tel. 717/291–4758.

JUNE–SEPTEMBER

Music at Gretna Nationally known artists perform chamber music and jazz in two different locations, once a week from June through September. > Mount Gretna Playhouse, Mount Gretna; Leffler Performance Center, 1 Alpha Dr., Elizabethtown 17022, tel. 717/964–3836. $15–$20.

AUGUST–OCTOBER

Pennsylvania Renaissance Faire For several months, the grounds of the Mount Hope Estate and Winery are transformed into a 16th-century English village ruled by Queen Elizabeth I. There are human chess matches, jousting and fencing tournaments, knighthood ceremonies, street performances, craft demonstrations, jesters, medieval food, and Shakespearean plays performed on outdoor stages. > 5 mi north of Manheim on Rte. 72, ½ mi from Pennsylvania Tpke. Exit 20, tel. 717/665–7021, www.parenfaire.com. $21.95. Mid-Aug.–mid-Oct., weekends 10–6:30.

OCTOBER

Harvest Days Every Columbus Day weekend more than 80 crafts and harvest activities are demonstrated for this celebration of the fall harvest. > Landis Valley Museum, tel. 717/569–0401. $7.

DECEMBER

Victorian Christmas Tours Each year, between Christmas and New Year's, Wheatland is dressed in Victorian Christmas finery for the holiday season. Day and candlelight tours are available. > Wheatland, 1120 Marietta Ave., tel. 717/392–8721. $6.50.

WHERE TO STAY

ADAMSTOWN

Inns of Adamstown These two elegant Victorian inns are less than a half block from each other. Both the Adamstown and the Amethyst inns have spacious rooms with handmade quilts, fresh flowers, and lace curtains. A number of the rooms have whirlpools, fireplaces, and steam showers. Set high on a hill, the Amethyst is painted with deep eggplant, green, and five other colors. There's even an Old English sheepdog to greet you. The hearty Continental breakfast is served each morning in the Adamstown Inn's dining room. > 62 W. Main St., 17522, tel. 717/484–0800 or 800/594–4808, www.adamstown.com. 8 rooms. AE, MC, V. CP. ¢–$$

BIRD-IN-HAND

Bird-in-Hand Family Inn The rooms are simple, clean, and comfortable, and the staff is friendly at this family-run motel. > 2740 Old Philadelphia Pike (Rte. 340), 17505, tel. 717/768–8271 or 800/537–2535, fax 717/768–1768, www.bird-in-hand.com/familyinn.

125 rooms, 4 suites. Restaurant, refrigerators, miniature golf, tennis court, 3 pools (2 indoor), lake, gym, hot tub, bicycles, basketball, playground. AE, D, DC, MC, V. **$**

Village Inn of Bird-in-Hand The Victorian flavor of this three-story country-style inn, built in 1734 to serve travelers along the Old Philadelphia Pike, is tempered by the modern comforts of cable TV and whirlpools in some rooms. An evening snack and a two-hour tour of the area are included in rates, as are pool and tennis privileges at the nearby Bird-in-Hand Family Inn. > 2695 Old Philadelphia Pike (Rte. 340), 17505, tel. 717/293–8369 or 800/914–2473, www.bird-in-hand.com/villageinn. 5 rooms, 6 suites. No-smoking rooms. AE, D, MC, V. CP. **¢–$**

EPHRATA

Smithton Inn This B&B, a former stagecoach inn from 1763, has been lovingly and authentically restored. The hand-tooled furniture, woodwork, and architectural detail are true to the period. Some rooms have fireplaces and canopy beds; the third-floor suite has a skylight, cathedral ceiling, and Franklin stove fireplace. Nice touches abound: oversize pillows, nightshirts, and flowers. Feather beds are available upon request when you book a room. Outside are a lily pond, a fountain, English lawn furniture, and a huge dahlia garden. There's complimentary coffee and tea. > 900 W. Main St., at Academy Dr., 17522, tel. 717/733–6094 or 877/755–4590, www.historicsmithtoninn.com. 7 rooms, 1 suite. AE, MC, V. BP. **¢–$$**

HERSHEY

Hotel Hershey The grande dame of Hershey, this gracious Mediterranean villa–style hotel is a sophisticated resort with plenty of options for recreation, starting with the golf course that surrounds the hotel. Inspired by the fine European hotels Milton S. Hershey encountered in his travels, the hotel abounds in elegant touches, from the mosaic-tile lobby to rooms with maple armoires, paintings from local artists, and tile baths. Dining options include the Iberian Lounge, the Fountain Café, the casual Clubhouse Café, and the formal Circular Dining Room, which overlooks the gardens, fountains, and reflecting pools. The spa's treatments here include a chocolate bean polish, a cocoa butter scrub, a chocolate fondue wrap, and whipped cocoa bath. Carriage rides, a ropes course, and nature trails are all on the property. > Hotel Rd. 17033, tel. 717/533–2171 or 800/533–3131, www.hersheypa.com. 234 rooms, 20 suites. 3 restaurants, coffee shop, room service, 2 18-hole golf courses, 1 9-hole golf course, 3 tennis courts, 2 pools (1 indoor), gym, sauna, spa, bicycles, basketball, lounge, baby-sitting, laundry service, concierge, business services, meeting rooms. AE, D, DC, MC, V. **$$$$**

LANCASTER

King's Cottage An elegant 1913 Spanish Mission–revival mansion on the National Register of Historic Places is now a B&B. The blend of decorative and architectural elements encompasses Chippendale-style furniture in the dining room and an art deco fireplace and stained-glass windows. Several rooms have whirlpools and fireplaces, including the first-floor bedroom chamber. An outdoor goldfish pond and a patio with seating are pleasant in warmer weather. The price includes full breakfast and afternoon tea; a small kitchen is available for those staying here. > 1049 E. King St., 17602, tel. 717/397–1017 or 800/747–8717, fax 717/397–3447, www.kingscottagebb.com. 7 rooms, 1 cottage. Dining room, in-room data ports, library, free parking; no smoking. D, MC, V. BP. **$$–$$$$**

Willow Valley Family Resort and Conference Center Smorgasbord meals, large rooms, a duck pond, and indoor pools make this large, stylish resort a great family place. Rooms are spread out over three buildings; those in the Atrium Building surround a striking skylighted lobby. The extensive Sunday brunch in the Palm Court is a favored feast. Since the resort is owned by Mennonites, liquor isn't permitted on the premises. > 2416 Willow St. Pike, 17602, tel. 717/464–2711 or 800/444–1714, fax 717/464–4784, www.willowvalley.com. 342 rooms, 50 suites. 2 restaurants, 9-hole golf course, 2 tennis courts, 3 pools (2 indoor), hot tub, sauna, steam room, basketball, recreation room, playground, business services, meeting rooms. AE, D, DC, MC, V. $

LITITZ
Swiss Woods Innkeepers Werner and Debrah Mosimann designed this chalet while they were still living in Werner's native Switzerland. On the edge of the woods overlooking Speedwell Forge Lake, it's an airy building with light pine and contemporary country furnishings. Extensive flower gardens surround the house. Each room has its own patio or balcony, and goose-down comforters are on all the beds. > 500 Blantz Rd., Lititz 17543, tel. 717/627–3358 or 800/594–8018, fax 717/627–3483, www.swisswoods.com. 6 rooms, 1 suite. Boating, fishing, hiking. AE, D, MC, V. BP. $$–$$$

MOUNT JOY
Rocky Acre Farm The ideal family getaway, this 200-year-old stone farmhouse was once a stop on the Underground Railroad. At this dairy farm, children love the abundance of kittens, roosters, and sheep, as well as the fishing and boating in the creek. There are also free pony, barrel train, and tractor rides. > 1020 Pinkerton Rd., Mount Joy 17552, tel. 717/653–4449, www.rockyacre.com. 8 rooms, 2 efficiency units. Boating, fishing. No credit cards. BP. $

STRASBURG
Hershey Farm Restaurant and Motor Inn This motel just south of Bird-in-Hand overlooks flower and vegetable gardens, a picture-perfect pond, and a farm. Ask for one of the large rooms in the newer building. The handy restaurant serves a complimentary breakfast smorgasbord and reasonably priced buffet and à la carte meals that employ homegrown produce. Walking trails are throughout the grounds. > Rte. 896, Strasburg 17572, tel. 717/687–8635 or 800/827–8635, fax 717/687–8638, www.hersheyfarm.com. 57 rooms, 2 suites. Restaurant, pool, playground, no-smoking rooms. AE, D, MC, V. BP. $
Limestone Inn Bed and Breakfast Richard and Denise Waller are gracious hosts in this 1786 Georgian home, listed on the National Register of Historic Places. A formal living room, a library, and a sitting room with a fireplace serve as common areas; there's a small garden with a fishpond outside. The bedrooms have Amish quilts and four-poster beds, and some of the bathrooms have old-fashioned clawfoot soaking tubs. The hearty breakfast might include apple pancakes with apple-cider syrup or a strata (an egg and bread casserole) with country sausage. The B&B is in the center of the village, within walking distance of many Strasburg attractions. > 33 E. Main St., 17579, tel. 717/687–8392 or 800/278–8392, fax 717/687–8366, www.thelimestoneinn.com. 6 rooms. Dining room, library. AE, D, MC, V. BP. $–$$

WHERE TO EAT

Influenced by the hearty German cooking of their ancestors, Pennsylvania Dutch food uses ingredients from local farms. The plentiful and basic meals often include fried chicken, ham, roast beef, dried corn, buttered noodles, mashed potatoes, chowchow (pickled vegetables), bread, pepper cabbage, and more. Desserts include the famous shoofly pie, which is made with molasses and brown sugar; dried apple pie; and rich cream pies. Be sure to try a *fastnacht* (Pennsylvania Dutch for doughnut).

Some traditional meals are started with the seven sweets and sours, small helpings of pickled foods, vegetables, pies, cakes, and puddings.

ADAMSTOWN

Silk City Diner At this classic diner with chrome fixtures, checkerboard floors, and a jukebox of old-time hits, the big helpings and consistent quality keep the parking lot full. The large menu includes baked meat loaf, grilled chicken, country-fried steak, and club sandwiches. The many desserts are made on the premises and include chocolate chip cheesecake and éclairs. > 1640 North Reading Road(Rte. 272), Stevens, tel. 717/335–3833. AE, DC, MC, V. ¢–$$

Stoudt's Black Angus Prime rib cut from certified Angus beef is the specialty of this Victorian-style restaurant, adjacent to the Black Angus Antiques Mall. Also notable are its raw bar and German dishes such as Wiener schnitzel. Stoudt's beer, brewed next door, is on tap. On weekends from August through October, a Bavarian Beer Fest with German bands and a pig roast takes over Brewery Hall. There are brewery tours Saturday at 3 and Sunday at 1. > Rte. 272, tel. 717/484–4385. AE, DC, MC, V. No lunch Mon.–Thurs. $$–$$$$

BIRD-IN-HAND

Good 'N Plenty At Good 'N Plenty, you share a table with about a dozen other customers and are treated to huge servings of hearty regional fare, including traditional sweets and sours of pickled vegetables, pastries, and puddings. More than 650 can be served at this bustling family-style restaurant, set within a remodeled Amish farmhouse. > Rte. 896, ½ mi north of U.S. 30, tel. 717/394–7111. MC, V. Closed Sun. and Jan. $–$$

Miller's Smorgasbord The lavish spread here has a good selection of Pennsylvania Dutch foods. The breakfast buffet (served daily June through October and on weekends November through May) is sensational, with omelets, pancakes, and eggs cooked to order, fresh fruits, pastries, bacon, sausage, and potatoes. > 2811 Lincoln Hwy. E (U.S. 30), Ronks, tel. 717/687–6621. AE, D, MC, V. $

Plain & Fancy Farm Come to this family-style restaurant for heaping helpings of stick-to-your-ribs Pennsylvania Dutch food. Also on the grounds are specialty shops selling art, quilts, and baked goods, and other attractions including Aaron & Jessica's Buggy Rides, the Amish Experience theatrical presentation, and a tour group. > Rte. 340 between Bird-in-Hand and Intercourse, tel. 717/768–4400. AE, MC, V. $$

EPHRATA

Lily's on Main Chef and manager Steve Brown's food draws on regional American dishes for its inspiration. Favorite dishes include raspberry chicken with Brie and almonds, and horseradish-crusted Atlantic salmon. You can also dine on lighter fare, such as a panini sandwich or Lily's special salad with fresh greens and vegetables. The food is artistically presented on tables draped with crisp white linens and topped with a single lily. The gorgeous view overlooking town is another reason to dine here. > Brossman Business Complex, 124 E. Main St., Ephrata, tel. 717/738–2711. AE, D, DC, MC, V. $$–$$$

Nav Jiwan Tea Room This soothing café is often adventurous. Each week brings cuisine from a different country, such as India, Mexico, Laos, Haiti, Ethiopia, Nepal, Philippines, Tanzania, and Thailand. The lunch entrées are prepared in an authentic style and served by volunteers. A bountiful Friday-evening buffet is a sampling of foods from the featured country. > Ten Thousand Villages, 240 N. Reading Rd., Ephrata, tel. 717/721–8400. D, MC, V. Closed Sun. No dinner Mon.–Thurs. or Sat. ¢–$

Restaurant at Doneckers The Inns at Doneckers is made up of three properties from the 1770s to the 1920s that have been tastefully furnished with French country antiques and decorated with hand stenciling. Classic and country French cuisine is served amid colonial antiques downstairs, and in country-garden surroundings upstairs. Dishes include rainbow trout *en croute* and roast duckling with sweet potato dumplings. The service is attentive and the wine cellar extensive. > The Inns at Doneckers, 318–333 N. State St., Ephrata 17522, tel. 717/738–9502 or 800/377–2206, www.doneckers.com. 35 rooms, 10 suites, 2 lofts. Restaurant, shops. AE, D, DC, MC, V. Closed Wed. and Sun.

LANCASTER

Gibraltor An unexpected addition to Lancaster County, Gibraltor's Mediterranean cuisine emphasizes fresh, beautifully prepared seafood. The enticing tapas include flash-fried calamari and steamed mussels. The menu changes every few weeks, but might include lobster risotto, seared Chilean sea bass, and grilled yellowfin tuna with basil pesto. The golden yellows used throughout the restaurant are complemented by striking blue goblets. The restaurant's Aqua Bar is a big hit with the Friday-evening crowd, which comes for cocktails and tapas. > 931 Harrisburg Pike at College Sq., across from Franklin & Marshall College, Lancaster, tel. 717/397–2790, fax 717/397–3622. AE, MC, V. Closed Sun. ¢–$

Lancaster Dispensing Co. Fajitas, salads, sandwiches, and pizzas with pita crusts are served until midnight in this stylish, boisterous, Victorian pub. The imported beer selection is vast. There's live music on weekends. > 33–35 N. Market St., Lancaster, tel. 717/299–4602. AE, D, MC, V. $

Log Cabin Consistency is the appeal here: several generations have made this their special-occasion place for classic fare such as *filet au poivre* with brandy Dijon sauce. The steaks, as well as lamb chops and seafood, are prepared on a charcoal grill in this 1928 expanded log cabin on a wooded hillside. An impressive collection of 18th- and 19th-century American paintings help make the 10 candlelit dining rooms elegant. > 11 Lehoy Forest Dr., off Rte. 272, Leola, tel. 717/626–1181, www.logcabinrestaurant.com. AE, MC, V. No lunch. $$–$$$$

The Meritage Hidden away in a quiet corner of Lancaster, Meritage has a warm and intimate dining area with a stone-and-brick wall. In warm weather, the enclosed outdoor dining area is a delight. Selections include hazelnut sea scallops, Atlantic salmon with pearl pasta, and mesquite-marinated flank steak. The wine list is extensive. > 51 N. Market St., Lancaster, tel. 717/396–1189. AE, D, DC, MC, V. Closed Sun. and Mon. $$–$$$$

The Pressroom The menus look like newspapers, and headline banners hang over the bar in this casual bistro in an old warehouse. The open kitchen has an exposed baking hearth. Sandwiches, named after comics characters, include the Marmaduke tuna salad and the Blondie breaded flounder. There's also a decent selection of salads, pizza, and pasta dishes. In summer, the patio is a pleasant outdoor dining spot. > 26–28 W. King St., Lancaster, tel. 717/399–5400. AE, MC, V. ¢–$

LITITZ

Cat's Meow Owners David Matos and Michael Hewett welcome you to the roaring '20s at this speakeasy-like restaurant inside a restored 1869 railroad house hotel. Appetizers, sandwiches, and entrées include broiled crab-cake sandwich, seafood Gabrielle with shrimp, scallops and clams, and excellent tenderloin tips with mushrooms. > 215 S. Charlotte St., Manheim, tel. 717/664–3370. AE, D, MC, V. $–$$$
1764 Restaurant Built in 1764, the General Sutter is the oldest continuously run inn in Pennsylvania. Its 1764 Restaurant has a menu with some artistic flair: favorites include crab cakes, elk medallions, and Pennsylvania trout. There are also twilight menus and a Friday-night lobster feast. In warm weather, the brick patio is a favorite place to eat. > 14 E. Main St., corner of Rtes. 501 and 772, Lititz 17543, tel. 717/626–2115, fax 717/626–0992, www.generalsutterinn.com. AE, D, MC, V. $$–$$$$

MOUNT JOY

Bube's Brewery The only intact pre-Prohibition brewery in the country contains four unique restaurants. The Bottling Works, in what was the bottling plant, serves steaks, light dinners, salads, burgers, and subs at lunch and dinner. Alois's presents prix-fixe six-course international dinners (reservations required; closed Monday) in a Victorian hotel attached to the brewery. The dinner-only Catacombs serves traditional steak and seafood dishes in the brewery's aging cellars below street level. A feast master presides over a medieval-, pirate-, or Roman-theme dinner (reservations required) every Sunday night. Wine and ale flow, musicians entertain, and diners participate in the festivities. The shady outdoor Biergarten Restaurant is open in summer. > 102 N. Market St., Mount Joy, tel. 717/653–2056. AE, D, MC, V. $–$$$$
Groff's Farm Abe and Betty Groff's 1756 farmhouse restaurant is known for its hearty Mennonite fare. Candlelight, fresh flowers, and original Groff Farm country fabrics and wall coverings contribute to the homeyness. House specialties include chicken in a cream sauce, farm relishes, and cracker pudding. Dinner begins with seven sweets and sours. Lunch is à la carte, dinner either à la carte or family style, but served at your own table. Groff's Farm also has an 18-hole golf course, pro shop, and sports bar. Reservations are essential for dinner. > 650 Pinkerton Rd., Mount Joy, tel. 717/653–2048. AE, D, DC, MC, V. Closed Sun. and Mon. $$–$$$

ESSENTIALS

Getting Here

A car is the easiest way to explore the many sights in the area; it also lets you get off the main roads and into the countryside. Lancaster County's main arteries are U.S. 30 (also known as Lincoln Highway) and Route 340 (sometimes called the Old Philadelphia Pike). Some pleasant back roads can be found between Routes 23 and 340. Vintage Road is a country road running north over U.S. 30 and then along Route 772 west to Intercourse. You get a look at some of the farms in the area and also see Amish schoolhouses, stores, and the Amish themselves. Remember to slow down for horse-drawn buggies when you're driving on country roads.

BY CAR

From Washington, D.C., take Route 295 North to I–95 to Baltimore, then to I–695 North to I–83 to York, Pennsylvania, where you connect to Route 30 East to Lancaster. The trip takes about two hours and 15 minutes.

BY TRAIN

Amtrak has regular service from Philadelphia's 30th Street Station to the Lancaster Amtrak station. You can connect from Washington, D.C. The total trip takes about two hours.

INFORMATION **Amtrak** > 53 McGovern Ave., tel. 215/824–1600 or 800/872–7245, www.amtrak.com.

Visitor Information

The Pennsylvania Dutch Convention & Visitors Bureau screens the presentation "Lancaster County: People, Places & Passions," which serves as a good introduction to the area. The Mennonite Information Center, established to "interpret the faith and practice of the Mennonites and Amish to all who inquire," has information on local inns and Mennonite guest homes as well as a 20-minute video about the Amish and Mennonite people. The Center can also arrange to have local Mennonite guides accompany you in your car to country roads, produce stands, and Amish crafts shops as well as acquaint you with their religion.

CONTACTS **Mennonite Information Center** > 2209 Millstream Rd., Lancaster 17602-1494, tel. 717/299–0954 or 800/858–8320, www.mennoniteinfoctr.com. **Pennsylvania Dutch Convention & Visitors Bureau** > 501 Greenfield Rd., Lancaster 17601, tel. 717/299–8901, 800/723–8824, www.padutchcountry.com.

Gettysburg

83 mi north of Washington, D.C.

6

Updated by Laura Knowles Callanan

OVER THREE DAYS OF FIGHTING, 51,000 AMERICANS were killed, wounded, or counted as missing during Gettysburg, the bloodiest battle of the Civil War. This marked a turning point. Although the struggle raged on for almost two more years, the Confederate forces never recovered from their losses in this rural area, where cornfields turned into battlefields, and orchards became graveyards.

It wasn't until four months after the battle, in November 1863, that President Abraham Lincoln came to dedicate the Gettysburg National Cemetery, next to the battlefield. "The world will little note, nor long remember, what we say here, but it can never forget what they did here," he said in words that proved as enduring as the changes the battle wrought. At the 6,000-acre national military park as well as at 20 museums in Gettysburg itself, you can recapture some sense of those days.

Over a thousand monuments and markers are scattered throughout the park, easily navigated through 35 mi of road. Little Round Top, on the southern end of Cemetery Ridge, is a key area of the battlefield. Still piled high with the loose rocks and large boulders that made it a natural defensive position, the spot marks the end of the Union line. Devil's Den marks the Union position on July 2, 1863, the second day of battle, when Confederate troops pushed the Union forces from this area. That afternoon, George Rose's wheat field, also marked, was strewn with more than 4,000 dead and wounded.

Other important sites include Culp's Hill, an important anchor for the right flank of the Union line at Gettysburg, and Seminary Ridge, the main Confederate position west of Gettysburg for the last two days of the battle. The Angle marks the Union position on July 3, 1863, when soldiers stopped Confederate general George E. Pickett's charge. During this battle, troops destroyed the peach orchard owned by Joseph Sherfy during the battle, ransacking his house, tearing apart fences, burning his barn to the ground, and covering his fields with the dead.

On the park's outskirts, the new visitor center and museum that's being built will allow the park to better preserve and display its extensive collection of Civil War artifacts. Also underway is the long-term restoration of the battlefield to its 1863 condition.

When planning your visit, keep in mind that summer months and weekends can be quite crowded at this popular destination—every July, thousands of volunteers arrive to dress in period uniforms and reenact the three-day battle. Crowds begin thinning out after Labor Day, but weekends remain busy through November and again as spring begins.

WHAT TO SEE & DO

Cyclorama Center The Gettysburg Cyclorama is a 360-foot, circular oil painting of Pickett's Charge. One of the last surviving paintings of its kind, it's been on display since 1884. There is also a 20-minute film on the battle. > Taneytown Rd., adjacent to the visitor center, tel. 717/334–1124. $3. Showings daily every 30 mins, 9–4:30.

Eisenhower National Historic Site President and Mrs. Dwight D. Eisenhower bought this 230-acre complex of three farms in 1950, using it as a weekend retreat, sanctuary, and meeting place for world leaders. From 1961 until the 34th president's death in 1969, it was the Eisenhower's full-time residence. The brick-and-stone farmhouse is preserved in 1950s style, with a number of outbuildings. The farm adjoins the battlefield and is administered by the Park Service, which sells daily ticketed tours on a first-come, first-served basis at the Gettysburg National Military Park Visitor Center. Shuttle buses depart to the farm from there. > 250 Eisenhower Farm La., off Millerstown Rd., tel. 717/338–9114, www.nps.gov/eise. $7. Call ahead for shuttle bus departure times.

General Lee's Headquarters In this old stone house from the 1700s, General Robert E. Lee drew up plans for the Gettysburg battle. The house now holds a collection of Civil War artifacts and a museum store. > 401 Buford Ave., 8 blocks west of Lincoln Sq., tel. 717/334–3141, www.civilwarheadquarters.com. $3. Mar.–Nov., daily 9–5 (extended summer hrs).

Gettysburg National Military Park It was here that General Robert E. Lee and his Confederate troops encountered the Union forces of General George Meade. The 6,000 acres are adorned with markers and monuments honoring the battle's losses. More than 30 mi of marked roads lead through the park, highlighting key battle sites. If you're up for a hike, check out the many trails that wind through the battlefield. They include the High Water Mark Trail (1 mi; begins at the Cyclorama Center); the Big Round Top Loop Trail (1 mi); and paths winding through the enormous rocks, caves, and crevices that hid Confederate sharpshooters in Devil's Den. For a longer hike, ask about the 9-mi Billy Yank Trail or the 3½-mile Johnny Reb Trail. Lincoln's Gettysburg Address was delivered at **Gettysburg National Cemetery** (off Baltimore Pike, free, Daily dawn–dusk) during its dedication on November 19, 1863. More than 7,000 are interred here, including more than 3,500 from the Civil War. > 97 Taneytown Rd., tel. 717/334–1124, www.nps.gov/gett. Free. Park roads 6 AM–10 PM.

Gettysburg Railway You can take 90-minute and four-hour trips on a diesel train. The theme rides include Civil War raids, a ride with Lincoln, dinner trips, fall foliage, a Santa train, an Easter bunny train, and a Halloween ghost train. > 106 N. Washington St., tel. 717/334–6932 or 888/948–7246, fax 717/334–4746, www.gettysburgrail.com. $10. Thurs.–Sun., 10–3.

Jennie Wade House Jennie Wade was the only civilian casualty in the Battle of Gettysburg, and her home and its furnishings have been preserved. The story the museum tells amounts to a snapshot of life in the Civil War era. > 758 Baltimore St., tel. 717/334–4100. $5.95. Daily 9–6.

Land of Little Horses The largest herd of Falabella miniature horses lives at this amusement park. Daily events include pig races, carousel rides, saddle rides, train rides, and an arena show. There's also a museum and nature area with more than 100 animals. > 125 Glenwood Dr., tel. 717/334–7259, www.landoflittlehorses.com. $7. Memorial Day–late Aug., Mon.–Sat. 10–5, Sun. noon–5; Apr., May, Sept., and Oct., Sat. 10–5, Sun. noon–5.

Lincoln Train Museum The 12-minute ride here reenacts the sights and sounds of Lincoln's journey from Washington to Gettysburg in November 1863 to dedicate the

National Cemetery. Actors portray the reporters and officials on the train. You can also see the 1890 caboose, model train display, and military rail collection. > 425 Steinwehr Ave., Gettysburg, tel. 717/334–5678. $5.95. May and June, daily 9–7; June–Aug., daily 9–9; Sept.–late Nov., daily 9–5.

Schriver House George and Henrietta Schriver lived with their two children here during the war. After George joined the Union troops and his family fled to safety, the home was taken over by Confederate sharpshooters, two of whom were killed in its garret during the battle. The restored four-floor home received the Pennsylvania State Historic Preservation Award. > 309 Baltimore St., tel. 717/337–2800, www.schriverhouse.com. $6. Apr.–Nov., Mon.–Sat. 10–5, Sun. noon–5; Dec., Feb., and Mar., weekends noon–5.

Soldier's National Museum What was once the headquarters for Union general Oliver O. Howard during the Battle of Gettysburg became the Soldiers National Orphanage after the war. It now has 60 displays of more than 5,000 Civil War items. > 777 Baltimore St., Gettysburg, tel. 717/334–4890 or 717/334–6296. $5.95. June–Labor Day, daily 9–9; Mar., Apr., and mid-Oct.–Thanksgiving, daily 9–5; May and Sept.–mid-Oct., daily 9–7.

Shopping

Gettysburg has numerous shops with handmade crafts and furniture, antiques, gifts, Civil War memorabilia, and books. Tourist shops sell T-shirts, postcards, and other less expensive keepsakes; homemade quilts and furniture, handcrafted by the local Amish community, are south of town. Stop at one of the many roadside markets north of Gettysburg for fresh fruits and vegetables at bargain prices.

Downtown, along the streets radiating from Lincoln Square, are stores selling clothing, crafts, books, art, and hard-to-find items. In the tourist district, many shops along Steinwehr Avenue sell bullets and relics excavated from the battlefield. A few you might want to visit include Mel's Antiques and Collectibles (33 Foth Alley), Arrow Horse International Market and Antiques (51 Chambersburg St.), Codori's Gift Shop (2 York St.), Irish Brigade Gift Shop (504 Baltimore St.), and Farnsworth Military Impressions (401 Baltimore St.).

Gallon Historical Art This art gallery shows original paintings and prints of Gettysburg battle scenes by Dale Gallon, the town's artist-in-residence. > 9 Steinwehr Ave., tel. 717/334–8666, www.gallon.com.

Horse Soldier In this museum-like store of military antiques, you can see everything from bullets to discharge papers. As you might expect, Civil War items get the most attention. The store's Soldier Genealogical Research Service can help you find your ancestors' war records prior to 1910. > 777 Baltimore St., tel. 717/334–0347. Closed Wed.

Save the Date

MAY

Apple Blossom Festival During this three-day festival in early May you can take an orchard tour, eat apple foods, buy handmade crafts, and watch music and other kinds of performances. Arendtsville is 10 mi northwest of Gettysburg. > South Mountain Fairgrounds, Arendtsville, tel. 717/677–7444.

JUNE–JULY

Civil War Heritage Days The many events that take place during these two months—lectures, memorabilia collectors' shows, and fireworks, among others—are held to commemorate the anniversary of the battle of Gettysburg. The first week of

July brings reenactors, who dress in period uniforms and costumes to commemorate the three-day battle. > Tel. 717/334–6274.

OCTOBER

Apple Harvest Festival Apple cider, caramel apples, and apple butter all have pride of place at this festival, held the first two weekends in October. There are also free hayrides, scarecrow making, and crafts. > South Mountain Fairgrounds, Arendtsville, tel. 717/677–9413, www.appleharvest.com.

WHERE TO STAY

Baladerry Inn During the Battle of Gettysburg, this 1812 home, on 4 acres with a gazebo, served as a field hospital. You can stay in the original home or a newer addition. The rooms, given floral names like Primrose and Garden, are bright and airy; some have private patios and fireplaces. > 40 Hospital Rd., 17235, tel. 717/337–1342, fax 717/337–1342, www.baladerryinn.com. 8 rooms, 1 suite. Tennis court; no room TVs, no kids under 12. AE, D, DC, MC, V. BP. **$–$$**

Battlefield Bed & Breakfast Inn Here you can stay in an 1809 stone farmhouse on more than 30 acres. In keeping with a B&B that faces the South Cavalry Battlefield, rooms are named for generals or infantry divisions that fought here or fired upon the property. The beds are covered in handmade quilts, and Civil War regalia appears throughout the property. > 2264 Emmittsburg Rd., 17325, tel. 717/334–8804, fax 717/334–7330, www.gettysburgbattlefield.com. 6 rooms, 2 suites. Pond, children's programs (ages 5 and up), playground; no room TVs, no smoking. AE, D, MC, V. CP. **$–$$**

Best Western Gettysburg Hotel The hotel is a pre–Civil War structure in the heart of the downtown historic district; prominent guests have included Carl Sandburg, Henry Ford, and General Ulysses S. Grant. Rooms are furnished in traditional style, and suites have fireplaces and whirlpool baths. Ask about the cannonball from the battle that is still embedded in the brick wall across the street. > 1 Lincoln Sq., 17325, tel. 717/337–2000, fax 717/337–2075, www.gettysburg-hotel.com. 126 rooms. Restaurant, room service, in-room data ports, in-room hot tubs, microwaves, refrigerators, cable TV, pool, hot tub, bar, laundry service, business services, free parking, no-smoking rooms. AE, D, DC, MC, V. **$–$$$**

Brafferton The original stone town house, a half block from Lincoln Square, was built in 1786, the brick addition in 1815. The town house once served as a chapel. Some suites have their own entrance and exposed-brick walls. > 44 York St., 17325, tel. 717/337–3423, fax 717/334–8185, www.brafferton.com. 5 suites, 9 rooms. No room phones, no TV in some rooms, no smoking. AE, D, MC, V. BP. **$–$$**

Brickhouse Inn Bed and Breakfast The guest rooms, named for states that fought in Gettysburg, are furnished with antiques and reproductions and come with ceiling fans and pastel or off-white walls. The wood floors are all original. There are two formal parlors in the main 1898 brick Victorian house; two guest rooms are in a separate house next door. > 452 Baltimore St., 17325, tel. 717/338–9337 or 800/864–3464, fax 717/338–9265, www.brickhouseinn.com. 7 rooms. Free parking; no smoking. AE, D, MC, V. BP. **$**

Farnsworth House Inn This inn is an early-19th-century federal brick house that Confederate sharpshooters occupied during the Battle of Gettysburg. You can take a tour of the house and cellar, rumored to be haunted. Each Victorian guest room is lushly decorated with period sewing machines, Victrolas, and antique clothing; some have claw-foot bathtubs. An art gallery and bookstore are on the premises. > 401 Baltimore

St., 17325, tel. 717/334–8838, fax 717/334–5862, www.farnsworthhousedining.com. 11 rooms. Restaurant, shops, library, business services; no room phones. AE, D, MC, V. CP. $–$$

Gaslight Inn Many original details from this 1872 mansion are intact, including its Italianate front. Some rooms have fireplaces, some have double-wide Jacuzzis, and several of the showers are 5-foot stalls with steam spas. On the second floor there's a deck with views of the garden. > 33 E. Middle St., 17325, tel. 717/337–9100, fax 717/337–1100, www.thegaslightinn.com. 9 rooms. Dining room, cable TV, some in-room VCRs, some hot tubs, free parking, business services; no kids under 8. AE, D, MC, V. BP. $–$$

Gettystown Inn Across from the National Cemetery, this inn is on the grounds of the Dobbin House restaurant. The 1860s home has period furnishings, four-poster beds, and Civil War–era artifacts. > 89 Steinwehr Ave., 17325, tel. 717/334–2100, fax 717/334–6905, www.dobbinhouse.com. 4 rooms, 3 suites. Restaurant, some kitchenettes, refrigerators; no phones in some rooms, no TV in some rooms, no kids under 5, no smoking. AE, D, MC, V. CP. $

Herr Tavern and Publick House Antiques set the scene in this antebellum tavern and inn 1 mi from the town square. All rooms have fireplaces, and some have Jacuzzis. Sitting on the front porch, you can see a pond with a water garden. > 900 Chambersburg Rd., 17325, tel. 717/334–4332 or 800/362–9849, fax 717/334–3332, www.herrtavern.com. 18 rooms. Restaurant, some microwaves, some refrigerators, cable TV, some hot tubs; no kids under 12, no smoking. D, MC, V. CP. ¢–$$

James Gettys Hotel Just off the town square, this four-story all-suites hotel was established in 1804—the main staircase is original. The individually decorated rooms are decorated in a country style. When you've had enough sightseeing, you can relax with full English afternoon tea at the neighboring Thistlefields tearoom. > 27 Chambersburg St., 17325, tel. 717/337–1334, fax 717/334–2103, www.jamesgettyshotel.com. 11 suites. Restaurant, kitchenettes, microwaves, refrigerators, cable TV, laundry service, business services; no smoking. AE, D, MC, V. CP. $

Keystone Inn Bed and Breakfast Leaded glass windows, polished wood floors, and lots of lace and flowers are inside this three-story Victorian, built in 1913. The huge wraparound porch is outfitted with wicker furniture. The rooms, done in pastels and with lots of woodwork, include books and comfortable chairs for reading. > 231 Hanover St., 17325, tel. 717/337–3888. 4 rooms, 1 suite. Library. D, MC, V. BP. ¢–$

Lightner Farmhouse Bed and Breakfast Nineteen acres surround this 1862 farmhouse, which served as a hospital for Union troops during the battle of Gettysburg. The common room is filled with oak furniture, and the guest rooms' color schemes also take their cue from various kinds of wood, including maple and oak. > 2350 Baltimore Pike, 17325, tel. 717/337–9508, www.lightnerfarmhouse.com. 4 rooms, 2 suites. No smoking. D, MC, V. BP. $

CAMPING

Artillery Ridge Campground You can pitch a tent or park an RV a mile south of the Gettysburg National Military Park Visitor Center. Horse owners can even bring their horses on vacation with them. > 610 Taneytown Rd., 17325, tel. 717/334–1288, www.artilleryridge.com. 45 tent sites, 105 camper or RV sites. Flush toilets, dump station, drinking water, laundry facilities, showers, fire grates, picnic tables, public telephone, general store, swimming (pool), fishing, bicycles, horseback riding. D, MC. ¢

WHERE TO EAT

Dobbin House Listed on the National Register of Historic Places, this tavern and inn puts its waiters in period clothing. The building, the oldest in Gettysburg, was a stop on the Underground Railroad and a hospital during the Civil War. You can eat your meal while reclining under a bed canopy, part of the restaurant's seating area. The food, a nod to the colonial past, includes prime rib, roast duck over apples with a citrus-orange sauce, or a pork tenderloin with raspberry sauce. For dessert there's apple pie and pecan pie. > 89 Steinwehr Ave., tel. 717/334–2100, fax 717/334–6905. Reservations essential. AE, D, MC, V. No lunch. $$–$$$$

Dunlap's Restaurant and Bakery This casual family restaurant is owned by a couple who fell in love with the town and bought the restaurant after visiting their son at Gettysburg College. You can get burgers, sandwiches, salads, and American classics like chicken and dumplings. Be sure to save room for a piece of cake or pie. > 90 Buford Ave., tel. 717/334–4816, www.dunlapsrestaurant.com. D, MC, V. ¢–$

Farnsworth House Inn You can eat like a fortunate Civil War soldier here: wild game pie, peanut soup, pumpkin fritters, and spoon bread are all served in the antiques-filled dining room. The historic home, riddled by bullets during the war, has an attic full of war memorabilia that you can examine. > 401 Baltimore St., tel. 717/334–8838, www.farnsworthhousedining.com. Reservations essential. AE, D, MC, V. $–$$

Gettysbrew Restaurant and Brewery Inside a building used as a field hospital by the Confederates during the Civil War, Gettysbrew has a patio overlooking the surrounding farmland. Standouts include beer-cheese soup, sandwiches on focaccia bread, buffets with 10 cold salads and six hot entrées, and handcrafted root beer and sodas. > 248 Hunterstown Rd., tel. 717/337–1001. D, MC, V. No lunch weekdays. $–$$

Gingerbread Man Brass fixtures, exposed brick walls, and Civil War photographs and prints make up the interior of the Gingerbread Man. Chili, New York deli–style sandwiches, hearty salads, and other classics are the offerings here, where there's also an extensive kids' menu. > 217 Steinwehr Ave., tel. 717/334–1100, www.thegingerbreadman.net. AE, D, DC, MC, V. $–$$

Herr Tavern and Publick House Built in 1815, this tavern, the first Confederate hospital, survived a direct hit from artillery during the Battle of Gettysburg. You can eat in the dining room, with a view of the battlefield, or on the porch. Choose from cream of crab soup, prime rib, and chicken stuffed with crabmeat and Mornay sauce. Dessert offerings include cheesecake, pecan pie, or apple dumplings. > 900 Chambersburg Rd., tel. 717/334–4332. D, MC, V. No lunch Sun. $$–$$$$

Historic Cashtown Inn The menu at this historic inn is reminiscent of home-cooked food from the Civil War era, with choices such as steaks, seafood, pecan-crusted chicken, and crab cakes. The restaurant is in an old building with a walk-up porch, 8 mi west of downtown Gettysburg. > 1325 Old Rte. 30, Cashtown, tel. 717/334–9722 or 800/367–1797, www.cashtowninn.com. AE, D, MC, V. Closed Mon. No lunch Sun. $–$$

Lincoln Diner Locals flock to this 24-hour diner for its American classics as well as cakes, pies, and pastries. You can get breakfast at any time. > 32 Carlisle St., tel. 717/334–3900. No credit cards. ¢–$

The Pub and Restaurant Tex-Mex dishes, chicken marsala, broiled scallops, jambalaya, pitas, and burgers are all available at this casual, friendly restaurant downtown. There's also an impressive selection of beer. > 20–22 Lincoln Sq., tel. 717/334–7100, www.the-pub.com. AE, MC, V. $–$$$

ESSENTIALS

Getting Here

A car is the easiest way to explore the many sights in the area; it lets you get off the main roads and into the countryside.

BY CAR

To get to Gettysburg, take I–270 North to U.S. 15 North, near Frederick. You you are just outside of Gettysburg, take Route 134 (Taneytown Rd.) to the national park's visitor center.

Visitor Information

The Gettysburg National Military Park Visitor Center distributes a free map with an 18-mi driving tour through the battlefield, as well as an orientation program, Civil War exhibits, and current schedules of ranger-conducted programs and talks. The park service also provides free walking-tour maps. Private, licensed guides may also be hired at the center. To best understand the battle, begin by viewing the Electric Map ($3), which uses colored lights to illustrate deployments and clashes during the three-day battle.

CONTACTS **Gettysburg Convention and Visitors Bureau** > 89 Steinwehr Ave., tel. 717/334–2100, www.gettysburg.com. **Gettysburg National Military Park Visitor Center** > 97 Taneytown Rd., tel. 717/334–1124, www.nps.gov/gett.

Frederick

45 mi northwest of Washington, D.C.

7

Revised by Kristi Delovitch

THE MARYLAND MOUNTAINSIDE stretches from the rolling farmland of the Piedmont region to the remote mountaintops of Garrett County and the Appalachians. The region's largest city, Frederick, has one of the best-preserved historic districts in Maryland, perhaps second only to that of Annapolis. About the same size as Old Town Alexandria, the 50-block district is made up of tree-shaded streets lined with buildings from the 18th and 19th centuries, and brick walks that connect lovely courtyards. Eclectic shops, museums, antiques stores, and fine restaurants all help attract crowds of weekend visitors here, where a horse-drawn carriage is a popular way to tour the area.

Because of its proximity to Washington, Frederick became a staging area for many important events in American history. Ben Franklin helped plan aspects of the French and Indian War from Braddock Heights, a mountain on Frederick's western edge. Meriwether Lewis stopped by before meeting up with William Clark on their trek westward. During the Civil War, Confederate and Union troops often clashed on the streets of Frederick—including before the Battle of Antietam, fought in 1862 on the other side of the green mountains that border Frederick to the west. (Frederick was so close to the Union–Confederate line that the bloody battles of Antietam and Monocacy were often fought between neighbors.) When Antietam was over, Abraham Lincoln himself passed through town. In the present day, convenient rail transportation and greater number of businesses along the I–270 corridor have made Frederick a bedroom community for Washington. This has brought many upscale stores and restaurants to Main Street and throughout town. When planning your visit, keep in mind that that many restaurants and stores are closed on Sunday.

With rising home prices in the nation's capital, Frederick has increasingly become a bedroom community for Washington. More people who work in Washington are able to live in Frederick because of the convenient rail transportation and the expanding number of businesses on the 270 corridor. For Frederick this means more upscale restaurants and stores in the historic main street and an increase in amenities for the rest of the city. Remember when planning a weekend visit that many restaurants and stores remain closed on Sunday. Frederick is surrounded by pastures and countryside as well as a few small towns. New Market, the self-proclaimed antiques capital of Maryland, is just a few miles east of downtown Frederick. A general store and antiques shops line this 200-year-old town's Main Street. Nearby, in the even smaller burgs of Taneytown and Middleton, are luxurious inns with restaurants that draw the well heeled.

Outside of Frederick are rolling pastures, rugged mountains, and hardwood forests, where white-tail deer, wild turkey, and even black bear roam among stretches of oak, hickory, and maple. Today, campers, hikers, hunters, and those seeking an escape from Washington and the suburbs head to these hills. Agriculture is the leading industry in the county: many of the dairy products, meats, fruits, and vegetables used in

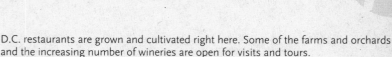

D.C. restaurants are grown and cultivated right here. Some of the farms and orchards and the increasing number of wineries are open for visits and tours.

WHAT TO SEE & DO

Barbara Fritchie House and Museum From this modest brick cottage, a reproduction of the original, it's easy to imagine Dame Fritchie sticking her white-capped head out of a second-floor window and waving a Union flag at Confederate troops. Poet John Greenleaf Whittier made her famous; his poem "Barbara Fritchie" appeared in the *Atlantic Monthly* a year after Confederate troops passed through Frederick. His stirring account of Fritchie defiantly waving the flag at the invading Confederates stirred patriotism and made the 95-year-old woman a heroine. Her unusual life, at least as told by Whittier, has fascinated history enthusiasts around the world. Even British prime minister Winston Churchill visited the house; on his way to Camp David with President Franklin Roosevelt, he stood outside and recited Whittier's poem: "Shoot if you must, this old gray head, but spare your country's flag. . . ." > 154 W. Patrick St., tel. 301/698–0630. $2. Apr.–Sept., Mon. and Thurs.–Sat. 10–4; Oct. and Nov., Sat. 10–4, Sun. 1–4.

Candy Kitchen This family-owned business has been hand dipping their chocolates since 1902. Favorites include seasonal fudges like key lime pie in summer and pumpkin pie in the fall but just about anything that gets packaged in the Kitchen's signature soft pink box is popular—and good. Lines circle the building for long-stem strawberries dipped in chocolate, sold for Mother's Day and Valentine's Day. > 52 N. Market St., tel. 301/698–0442 or 866/869–8898. Mon.–Sat. 10–6; Sun. 1–5.

Community Bridge Mural What was once made of unadorned concrete is now a work of art. After having close to 3,000 realistic-looking stones and other objects painted on it, this bridge in the center of historic Frederick is now covered with "ivy," and many beautiful designs. > S. Carroll St. on Carroll Creek, tel. 301/228–2888, bridge.skyline.net.

Everedy Square & Shab Row What was once a complex of buildings that manufactured kitchen utensils and wares is now downtown's center for retail shops, restaurants, and boutiques. People flock to the two large antique stores here, as well as Tauraso's, a festiva Italian restaurant. > Church St. and East St., tel. 301/662–4140.

Frederick Coffee Co. and Café This large coffee shop is in a renovated garage whose bays are now windows that overlook the Everedy Square complex. Among the many events here are Irish music on Tuesday, poetry on Wednesday, and folk and jazz on Saturday, Sunday, and Monday nights. The coffee beans are roasted in-house. > 100 East St., tel. 301/698–0039. Daily.

Mount Olivet Cemetery Some of Frederick's most famous sons and daughters, including Francis Scott Key and Barbara Fritchie, rest in this 1854 cemetery. Also here are the remains of more than 800 of the Confederate soldiers killed during the battles of Antietam and Monocacy. > 515 S. Market St., tel. 301/662–1164. Daily sunrise–sunset.

National Museum of Civil War Medicine With historic photographs, artifacts, and documents, the story of medicine, is told through the journey of Peleg Bradford, a young Union private from Maine. The Civil War, in which two-thirds of its 620,000 fatalities resulted from disease, led to advances in the transportation of the wounded, hospital care, surgery, and prostheses. The more than 3,000 medical artifacts on display in this museum include the only known surviving Civil War surgeon's tent and a horse-drawn Civil War ambulance. The building housing the museum was where the dead were embalmed after the Battle of Antietam; today, it's a popular stop for city

ghost tours. > 48 E. Patrick St., tel. 301/695–1864, www.civilwarmed.org. $6.50.
Mon.–Sat. 10–5, Sun. 11–5.

Rose Hill Manor Park/The Children's and Farm Museum Although this lovely
Georgian manor is intended as a place for elementary-school kids to study local
and regional history, it's more than just that. Maryland's first governor, Thomas
Johnson, lived here from 1798 to 1819, and guided tours of his gracious home
cover its owners and lifestyles. During the tour, children can card wool, weave on a
table loom, play with reproductions of old toys, and dress in period costumes. Also
open are several outbuildings, including a log cabin, icehouse, smokehouse, blacksmith shop, and large shed housing a carriage collection. You can also wander
through herb, vegetable, and rose gardens. > 1611 N. Market St., tel. 301/694–1648,
www.co.frederick.md.us/parks/rosehill.html. $4. Apr.–Oct., Mon.–Sat. 10–4, Sun.
1–4; Nov., Sat. 10–4, Sun. 1–4.

Schifferstadt Architectural Museum Believed to be the oldest house in Frederick,
this unusual stone structure was built in 1756 by German immigrants. Spared from
the wrecking ball by preservation-minded citizens, the house is considered one of the
finest examples of German architecture in America. Because the rooms are barren,
it's easy to observe structural details such as the sandstone walls, which are 2½ feet
thick. > 1110 Rosemont Ave., tel. 301/663–3885. $3. Apr.–mid-Dec., Tues.–Sat. 10–4,
Sun. 1–4.

Wonder Book & Video Away from downtown, this massive bookstore stocks
more than a million new and used books, videos, and CDs. There's also a second
location at 425 South Jefferson Street. > 1306 W. Patrick St., tel. 301/694–5955,
www.wonderbk.com. Daily 10–10.

NEARBY

Antietam Battlefield The fields that held the bloodiest single-day battle of the Civil
War is 25 mi from Frederick. Over 23,000 soldiers were killed, wounded, or missing. A
theater at the visitor center shows a 26-minute movie every half hour and a one-hour
documentary at noon every day. The 8½-mi self-guided driving tour of the battlefield
takes you through the three phases of the battle and ends at Antietam National
Cemetery, where 4,776 Union soldiers were laid to rest. > MD-65, Sharpsburg, tel.
301/432–5124, www.nps.gov/anti. 3-day pass: $3 a person, $5 a family. June–Aug.,
daily 8:30–6; Sept.–May, 8:30–5.

Berrywine Plantations and Linganore Winecellars Linganore Winery sits on the
230-acre Berrywine Plantation, 20 mi from Frederick. The family-owned vineyard is
Maryland's largest producer of wine. Though some of its 30 wines are made from
standard grape varieties, Berrywine is best known for its mead and its wines made
from raspberries and other fruits. In addition to tours and tastings, the winery holds
many musical events here, including the Swingin' Blues Wine Festival in May, June's
Classic Motown Wine Festival, and the Reggae Festival in July. > 13601 Glissans Mill
Rd., Mt. Airy, tel. 410/795–6432, www.linganore-wine.com. Free. Weekdays 10–5, Sat.
10–6, Sun. noon–6. Tours daily at noon, 2, and 4.

Monocacy National Battlefield This battlefield was the site of a little-known, highly
lopsided confrontation between 12,000–13,000 Confederates and 5,800 Union
troops. Many historians believe that this Union victory on July 9, 1864, thwarted a
Confederate invasion of Washington, D.C. Although the Union troops were outnum-
bered, they delayed the Rebels by burning a bridge along the Monocacy. This tactic,
along with some intensive fighting in the river, delayed the Confederates' approach to
Washington, and allowed the federal government time to bolster its forts. The farm-

land surrounding the battlefield remains largely unchanged. An electronic map in the visitor center explains the battle. Monocacy is 2 mi south of Frederick via MD-355. > 4801 Urbana Pike, Frederick, tel. 301/662–3515, www.nps.gov/mono. Free. Daily 8–4:30 (until 5:30 Memorial Day–Labor Day).

New Market General Store This general store from 1881 went on to become a post office, a butcher shop, and a candy store. Now it's a general store once again, selling quirky ointments, fudge, and Christmas ornaments (year-round). Quilts, preserves, and reproductions of Windsor chairs, all made locally, are also for sale. There's also a little café here serving breakfast all day as well as Maryland crab-cake sandwiches and other light fare, including over 25 varieties of wraps. > 26 W. Main St., New Market, tel. 301/865–6313, www.newmarketgeneralstore.com. Mon., Tues., Thurs., and Fri. 9–5; Sat. 9–6; Sun. 10–6.

Tours

Candlelight Ghost Tour of Frederick Most of this company's walking tours include stops at "haunted" locations such as the Civil War Medicine Museum, where dead soldiers were embalmed during the Civil War. Additional tours are available in October, in time for Halloween. > Frederick, tel. 301/845–7001 or 301/668–8922, www.frederickcarriage.com.

Carriage Tour of Historic Frederick A horse-drawn carriage tour is a good way to get a sense of Frederick's 18th- and 19th-century buildings. Half-hour ($50) and hour tours ($75) seat four people and are offered year-round; reservations are required. > 19 E. Church St., Frederick, tel. 301/845–7001, www.frederickcarriage.com.

Covered Bridge Tour A free brochure available at the visitor center maps out a self-guided driving tour that takes you to the three covered bridges in Frederick County. The drive winds through Maryland's scenic farmland up to the northern section of Frederick County near Catoctin State Park. The bridge at Loy Station is an ideal stopping point for a picnic lunch. The visitor center is open daily 9–5. > 19 E. Church St., Frederick, tel. 301/228–2888, www.visitfrederick.org.

Sports

GOLF

P.B. Dye Golf Club Consistently rated one of the most difficult courses in the area, this golf course (7,036/5,391; 72/73; 74.6/71.5) has Maryland's only G2 Bent Grass Greens, the same in Pinehurst's Number 2 course. A weekend round of golf is $89. > 9526 Dr. Perry Rd., Ijamsville, tel. 301/607–4653, www.pbdyegolf.com.

Whiskey Creek One of more than a dozen courses in Frederick County, the 18-hole Whiskey Creek (7001/5,296; 72/72; 74.5/70.5), designed by Erny Els and about 10 mi south of Frederick, is occasionally visited by avid golfers from presidential administrations. Perks at this course include the global positioning system in the golf carts, which shows the yardage to the next hole. The 18-hole course is $90 on the weekend. > 4804 Whiskey Court, Ijamsville, tel. 888/883–1174, www.whiskeycreekgolf.com.

HIKING

Appalachian Trail Crossing the spine of South Mountain just west of Frederick, the Appalachian Trail runs from the Potomac River to the Pennsylvania line in Frederick County. Several well-known viewing points can be found along Maryland's 40-mi stretch, including Annapolis Rocks and Weverton Cliffs. The best access points that have parking available are Gathland State Park, Washington Monument State Park, and Greenbrier State Park. The Appalachian Trail Conference has more information.

Catoctin Mountain National Park The park, made up of 5,000 acres of forested and mountainous terrain, holds 26 mi of hiking trails, thousands of white-tail deer, and Camp David, the official presidential retreat. You can pick up detailed trail maps at the visitor center. You can also get a topographic map and a compass for use on either a 1-mi or a 5-mi orienteering course. > 6602 Foxville Rd., Thurmont, tel. 301/663–9388 or 301/663–9330, www.nps.gov/cato.

Cunningham Falls State Park A gorgeous 78-foot waterfall is the main attraction at this park. All hiking trails lead to a platform for viewing the falls. The Lower Trail is an easy ½ mi from the swimming lake; the ¾-mi Cliff Trail goes through rougher terrain. The swimming lake has lifeguards, boat rentals, and a concession stand from Memorial Day to Labor Day. Picnic areas are at South Beach and North Beach. You can get a trail map from the entrance kiosk, where you pay admission. > 14039 Catoctin Hollow Rd., Thurmont, tel. 301/271–7574, www.dnr.state.md.us/publiclands/western/cunninghamfalls.html. $3.

CONTACT **Appalachian Trail Conference** > 799 Washington St., Harpers Ferry, WV 25425, tel. 304/535–6331, www.atconf.org.

EQUIPMENT **The Trail House** > 17 S. Market St., Frederick, tel. 301/694–8448, www.trailhouse.com.

Save the Date

MAY

Beyond the Garden Gates Garden Tour The annual weekend garden tour includes six private gardens and three public gardens. The self-guided tour is $12; tickets can be purchased at the visitor center. > 19 E. Church St., Frederick, tel. 301/694–2489 or 301/228–2888, www.cityoffrederick.com.

Swinging Blues Wine Festival at Linganore Wine Cellars A 15-minute drive on Route 75 through New Market brings you to this vineyard's festival. The live blues performances are supplemented with a wine tasting and a guided tour of the grounds and the wine-making machinery. You can bring your own beach chair and blanket. > 13601 Glissans Mill Rd., Mt. Airy, tel. 410/795–6432, www.linganore-wine.com.

JUNE

Frederick Festival of the Arts Live music and screenings of local and regional independent films take place along the canal, just off Frederick's main street. You can canoe or kayak in the canal, or just browse at the many stands filled with regional artworks. > Frederick, tel. 301/694–9632, www.frederickarts.org.

JULY

Reggae Wine Festival at Linganore Winery This mid-month festival brings to Linganore live blues performances each day as well as wine tastings and tours. > 13601 Glissans Mill Rd., Mt. Airy, tel. 410/795–6432, www.linganore-wine.com.

AUGUST

Wings Over Frederick Each year in mid-August the Frederick Municipal Airport hosts this popular air show. Attractions include vintage planes and live stunt planes shows. Every year World War II fighter planes reenact the bombing of Pearl Harbor. > Frederick, tel. 301/631–5357, www.wingsoffreedomairshow.org.

OCTOBER

Catoctin Colorfest Drawing over 70,000 attendees, Colorfest is the area's largest arts-and-crafts show. Vendors crowd the small town of Thurmont. Parking in the town is difficult, but free shuttle buses are there to take you to the festival. > Thurmont, www.colorfest.org.

Family Festival at the Farm This self-guided tour showcases the agriculture of Frederick County by visits to a dozen working farms. Exhibits include pumpkin patches, a dairy farm, and even a full-scale professional rodeo. Brochures mapping the free tour are available at the visitor center. > 19 E. Church St., Frederick, tel. 301/631–3037, www.cityoffrederick.com.

WHERE TO STAY

Linganore Hills Inn This restored all-brick Georgian federal was built in 1850 and overlooks the Monocacy River halfway between Frederick and New Market. It was once a mill and part of a dairy farm. The small rooms are furnished with reproductions of antiques. You can lounge on the spacious back porch or wander the inn's 5 acres, which still hold a springhouse. The old-fashioned country-style breakfast is served with French toast, pancakes, and fresh fruit. > 6229 Linganore Rd., 21701, tel. 301/668–1020, fax 301/668–1021, www.linganorehillsinn.com. 4 rooms. No TV in some rooms. No credit cards. BP. $

McCleery's Flat On antiques row, this French-style town house has an unbeatable location, just a short walk from restaurants and shops. The home, built in 1876, is furnished with many antiques. Many guest rooms, outfitted with antique furniture and brightly colored walls, also have balconies and working fireplaces. The Caroline McCleery suite includes an impressive king-size Victorian poster bed and a bathroom with a whirlpool tub, a separate shower, and even a chandelier. > 121 E. Patrick St., 21701, tel. 301/620–2433 or 800/774–7926, www.fwp.net/mccleerysflat. 3 rooms, 2 suites. No kids under 15, no smoking. AE, DC, MC, V. BP. $

NEARBY

Inn at Buckeystown This 1897 Victorian is in a town just outside of Frederick. Resembling a dollhouse, the inn is furnished with kitschy accents, lace linens, and furnishing that include sleigh beds. Dinner is available by reservation. Book well in advance for the murder-mystery dinners, held monthly. A formal tea is offered Wednesday, Fridays, and alternate Sundays for $18–$25. > 3521 Buckeystown Pike, Buckeystown 21717, tel. 301/874–5755 or 800/272–1190, www.innatbuckeystown.com. 3 suites, 7 rooms (2 with bath). Restaurant. AE, D, MC, V. BP. $–$$

Stone Manor Part of a 114-acre working farm, this inn is inside an 18th-century stone house, since expanded. The majestic Stone Manor, with 10 working fireplaces, has six suites individually decorated with floral-print armchairs and sofas, antique reproductions, and canopy or carved four-poster beds. Breakfast is served in one of the three lovely dining rooms or in the suites—but the five-course dinner ($69) is the main event. > 5820 Carroll Boyer Rd., Middletown 21769, tel. 301/473–5454, fax 301/371–5622, www.stonemanor.com. 6 suites. Restaurant, in-room VCRs, business services, meeting rooms; no room phones, no smoking. AE, D, DC, MC, V. BP. $$–$$$$

Strawberry Inn B& B This 1840 farmhouse is the oldest B&B in Frederick County. Rooms in the restored home are tastefully decorated with antiques. In summer, the back porch, covered with grapevines, is the setting for the old-fashioned breakfast. The comfortable sitting room has a working fireplace. > 17 W. Main, New Market 21774, tel. 301/865–3318. 3 rooms, 1 suite. No credit cards. BP. $

CAMPING

Catoctin Mountain Park–Owen's Creek Campground Six miles from the visitor center on the west side of the park, Owen's Creek has basic tent and RV sites. Each site includes a 9- by 12-foot tent pad, a picnic table, and a grill, but no water or electric hookups. There are two bathhouses, one with showers. Twenty cabins are available at Camp Misty Mount. > Foxville Rd., Thurmont 21788, tel. 301/663–9388, www.nps.gov/cato. 51 tent or RV sites. Flush toilets, showers. Reservations not accepted. No credit cards. Closed Nov.–mid-Apr. ¢

Ole Mink Farm Eighteen miles north of Frederick in the Catoctin Mountains, Ole Mink Farm sits on 34 wooded acres. Luxury cabins have fireplaces, fully equipped kitchens, and bathrooms with hot showers. The Hide and Seek cabin has a large stone fireplace and an old-fashioned claw-foot bath. If you prefer a bit more roughing it, camping cabins come with a propane stove top, a microwave, and a small refrigerator, but no bathroom. There's also a four-bedroom Coffee Hollow that can sleep two families. The farm has a native trout stream and a fishing pond stocked with blue gill, trout, bass, and catfish. > 12806 Mink Farm Rd., Thurmont 21788, tel. 301/271–7012 or 877/653–6465, fax 301/271–4856, www.oleminkfarm.com. 9 cabins, 6 with bath. Swimming (indoor pool). Reservations essential. AE, D, MC, V. ¢–$

William Hauck Campground Just ½ mi from Cunningham Falls itself, this campground is close to a swimming lake and hiking trails. Lifeguards, rental canoes, rowboats, paddleboats, and a food concession are available from Memorial Day to Labor Day. There are nine one-room cabins, each with electricity. If you want a bit more privacy, try the Manor Area campground near Catoctin Iron Furnace Trail. Reservations are highly recommended May through September. > 14039 Catoctin Hollow Rd., Thurmont 21788, tel. 301/271–7574, 888/432–2267 reservations, www.dnr.state.md.us/publiclands/western/cunninghamfalls.html. 150 tent or RV sites (30 with electric hookups), 9 cabins; Manor Area: 31 tent or RV sites (10 with electric hookups). Showers, swimming (lake). MC, V. Closed Nov.–Mar. ¢

WHERE TO EAT

Cafe Kyoko Above a downtown Frederick bakery, Cafe Kyoko overlooks busy Patrick Street. The sparsely decorated dining room is nevertheless inviting: there are wooden booths up front by the window, exposed rafters, and ceiling fans. Popular dishes on the menu, a mix of Japanese, Thai, and other Asian cuisines, are sushi and Thai curry dishes. The less adventuresome might prefer chicken teriyaki, steak, and seafood entrées. The wine and beer selection is limited. > 10 E. Patrick St., tel. 301/695–9656. AE, MC, V. No lunch Sun. $–$$$

Firestone's In a 1920s-era building whose earlier incarnations include a bank, a sporting goods store, and an Irish pub, Firestone's is a casual place for good American fare. At first glimpse, it seems more like a local pub, with a wooden bar dominating the main floor. Look more closely, and the white linens covering the tables become noticeable. Steak and seafood predominate the menu, which also offers a few surprises, including marinated and roasted Portobello mushrooms stacked with onions, peppers, eggplant, and zucchini. Desserts are made on the premises. > 105 N. Market St., tel. 301/663–0330. AE, D, MC, V. Closed Mon. $$–$$$$

Isabella's The opening of this Spanish eatery added some flair to downtown Frederick's predominantly American restaurant scene. Most people head here for the tapas, which include lamb, beef, chicken, and seafood served with spices, herbs, and some wonderful sauces. Try the littleneck clams steamed in beer, garlic, cilantro, pepper, and tomato; the grilled lamb chops, served with a black currant sauce; or the chili shrimp, sautéed in hot oil, garlic, peppers, and caramelized onions. Three or four tapas makes a meal. Most of the wines are South American. > 44 N. Market St., tel. 301/698–8922. AE, D, MC, V. Closed Mon. **$$–$$$$**

Red Horse A local institution and landmark—note the red horse on the roof—the Red Horse is primarily a steak house. The rustic dining room has a stone fireplace, exposed rafters, and a large wagon-wheel chandelier. The service is first-rate; you can watch your steak being grilled from behind a window. A cigar parlor on a lower level serves cognac, port, sherry, and bourbon. > 996–998 W. Patrick St., tel. 301/663–3030. AE, D, DC, MC, V. No lunch weekends. **$$–$$$$**

Tasting Room Huge glass windows showcase the modern interior of this restaurant that began as a wine bar. Of the roughly 150 wines available, 40 are offered by the glass ($5–$17). Dishes change each season; most are a fusion of American, Asian, and French cuisine. Asian chicken salad, coq au vin, and lobster whipped potatoes, made with fresh Maine lobster and chive butter, are popular items. Over 45 specialty martinis are available, including a fresh lime beer martini. > 101 N. Market St., tel. 240/379–7772. AE, DC, MC, V. Closed Sun. **$$–$$$$**

Tauraso's Restaurant In summer, this popular Italian restaurant draws a big crowd that overflows into the massive outdoor dining area. The standard Italian menu includes a different fish special each night. The brick-oven pizza is a local favorite, as is the pan-seared grouper. Other dishes include eggplant Parmesan and cioppino, a seafood stew. For a more casual meal, try the pub. Tauraso's is one of the few restaurants in the area that serves Sunday brunch. > 6 N. East St. Reservations essential. AE, D, DC, MC, V. **$–$$$**

NEARBY

Mealey's Once a store and hotel, Mealey's is now a busy restaurant decorated with antiques—appropriate, given its New Market location. A large stone fireplace dominates the spacious main dining room, which is often filled to capacity on weekend evenings and Sunday afternoons; smaller dining rooms offer more privacy. Beef and Chesapeake Bay seafood are the specialties. Desserts are worth saving room for—especially the bread pudding, served with a bourbon-vanilla sauce. > 8 Main St., New Market, tel. 301/865–5488. AE, D, DC, MC, V. Closed Mon. **$$–$$$$**

Village Tea Room An 1876 New Market home is now small tearoom serving salads, sandwiches, and fabulous homemade pies. The local favorite is the bumble berry pie, made of apples, rhubarb, blackberries, raspberries, and strawberries. Summer meals are served alfresco on the lawn. > 81 W. Main St., New Market, tel. 301/865–3450. AE, D, DC, MC, V. Closed Mon. No dinner Tues.–Thurs. and Sun. **¢–$**

Zest Light pours into this small restaurant and bounces off its caramel-color wood floors and brightly painted walls. The fairly innovative menu includes such dishes as a bison and gulf shrimp casserole. Trained in popular D.C. kitchens, the chef uses local greens, pork, beef, and lamb. Take a moment to examine the wine collection on display at the back of the space and the impressive collection of cookbooks next to the women's rest room. > 11791 Fingerboard Rd., Monrovia, tel. 301/865–0868. AE, D, MC, V. Closed Sun. and Mon. **$$–$$$**

ESSENTIALS

Getting Here

The fastest and easiest way to get to Frederick is by car. Driving also gives you a chance to explore the countryside surrounding Frederick.

BY BUS

Greyhound Lines provides daily transportation to Frederick from Washington, D.C. Frederick Transit provides bus service within Frederick and to outlying towns, including Thurmont, Emmitsburg, Jefferson, and Walkersville. Shuttle buses transport commuters to the Washington Metro at Shady Grove and Maryland's commuter train at Point of Rocks. The shuttle fare is $1.

DEPOT **Maryland Area Rail Commuter (MARC) Train Station** > 100 S. East St., Frederick 21701, tel. 301/663–3311.

BUS LINES **Frederick Transit** > Tel. 301/694–2065, www.co.frederick.md.us. **Greyhound Lines** > Tel. 800/231–2222, www.greyhound.com.

BY CAR

Frederick is 45 mi from Washington, and about an hour's drive. Take the Capital Beltway to I–270 North toward Rockville/Frederick. Travel about 30 mi and then merge onto MD-85 North (Buckeystown Pike) via Exit 31A, heading toward Market Street. Turn left onto MD-355 (Urbana Pike), which takes you into the downtown historic district.

Parking in the historic district is easy to find. Metered parking is plentiful on Market Street, and it's free after 5 PM. There are also two municipal garages in which it costs $1 to park.

BY TRAIN

The Maryland Area Rail Commuter line runs from Frederick southwest to Point of Rocks on the Potomac River and then onto Washington, D.C. Amtrak service is available from Washington, D.C., to Frederick.

LINES **Amtrak** > Tel. 800/872–7245, www.amtrak.com. **MARC** > Tel. 800/325–7245, www.mtamaryland.com.

STATION **Frederick Train Station** > 100 S. East St., Frederick, tel. 301/663–3311.

Visitor Information

At Frederick's visitor center you can pick up brochures of historic sites and maps for a self-guided tour. The center also organizes guided 90-minute walking tours with costumed guides. Tours begin at 1:30 PM and are available on holidays and weekends from April through December.

CONTACT **Frederick visitor center** > 19 E. Church St., Frederick, tel. 301/228–2888 or 800/999–3613, www.visitfrederick.org. Tour $5.50. Daily 9–5.

The C&O Canal

Harpers Ferry is 67 mi northwest of Washington, D.C.

8

By CiCi Williamson

WHEN THE C&O CANAL WAS BUILT in the 1860s, water routes were an essential method to get goods from point A to B. Nowadays, the canal and the towns along it are reminders of how much has changed, as well as great places from which to begin a weekend spent in communion with the outdoors.

Now dry in portions, the canal runs 185-mi west from Washington, D.C., stretching along the Potomac River past Harpers Ferry and Paw Paw in West Virginia. During a weekend, you can "take the waters" in a long-standing natural spa, walk or bike along the canal's towpath, and go for a hike in a nearby park. You can also take a ride in a canal boat, canoe or kayak, and even take a trip on a vintage train car pulled by a steam engine.

In the 18th and early 19th centuries, the Potomac River was the main transportation route between Cumberland, Maryland—one of the most important ports on the nation's frontier—and the seaports of the Chesapeake Bay. Tobacco, grain, whiskey, furs, iron ore, timber, and other commodities were sent down the Potomac to Georgetown and Alexandria, which served as major distribution points for both domestic and international markets.

Although it served as a vital link with the country's western territories, the Potomac had some drawbacks: rapids and waterfalls between Cumberland and Washington made it impossible to travel the entire distance by boat. Just a few miles upstream from Washington, the Potomac cascades through two such barriers—the breathtakingly beautiful Great Falls and the less dramatic but equally impassable Little Falls.

To help traders move goods between the eastern markets and the western frontier more efficiently, 18th-century engineers proposed that a canal with a series of elevator locks be constructed parallel to the river. The first Potomac canal system was built at the urging of George Washington, who helped found the Patowmack Company for this purpose.

Not unlike modern construction projects like Boston's "Big Dig," cost overruns plagued the builders of the C&O Canal, which began to be built in 1828. What was supposed to cost only $3 million and stretch 460 mi (all the way to Pittsburgh) instead became a $13 million project that ended in Cumberland.

Eclipsed by the progress of the railroad, which had arrived in Cumberland eight years earlier, the canal was already obsolete by the time construction halted in 1850. Nevertheless, the canal remained in operation for over 70 years. Boats pulled by mules floated tons of cargo—coal, hay, hydraulic cement, fertilizer, anything that could be put on a boat—from Cumberland to Georgetown. The canal finally closed in 1924 after several devastating floods sent the canal owners into bankruptcy.

The Eastern Panhandle of West Virginia faces the canal and has several enticing towns where you can learn about history and "take the waters." At the canal's

6oth mi is Harpers Ferry—the most visited site in the state. The entire town is a historic district, much of it in a national park of the same name. Here you can learn about John Brown's attack on a federal arsenal, the coming of the railroad, and the area's African-American heritage. Harpers Ferry National Historical Park take you even further back in time—to the colonial period, when George Washington and Thomas Jefferson frequented this region and where Lewis and Clark got provisions before their historic expedition.

Also in the area is Charles Town, a center for thoroughbred racing; Martinsburg, the home of the most celebrated female spy of the Civil War; and the town of Berkeley Springs, known for its hot mineral baths and spas. Nearby is Cumberland, Maryland, the terminus of the C&O Canal and of interest in its own right to railroad fans.

Named after George Washington's youngest brother, who plotted out the town in 1786 and named several streets after family members, Charles Town is rich in history. Abolitionist John Brown was tried for treason and hanged here. The town of 3,100 is the county seat of Jefferson County, known for its fruit orchards and beef and dairy cattle as well as industries such as textiles and quarrying. Martinsburg was laid out by General Adam Stephen in 1773. With the arrival of the railroad, the town became an important rail and shipping point. In the 19th century, orchards were planted around Martinsburg, transforming it into a distribution center for apples and peaches. In fall, you can watch fruit being prepared for shipment.

Hot mineral waters have drawn people to Berkeley Springs for centuries. Native Americans traveled here for the healing powers of the "medicine waters," and wealthy colonials discovered the area later. George Washington helped establish the town as a health resort in 1776 and owned property nearby. The town of 700 still caters to those who come to enjoy the 74°F spring waters. Prospect Peak, a popular vantage point overlooking the Potomac River, is 3 mi west of the city.

The canal terminus in Cumberland, Maryland, is cradled in the Allegheny Mountains. Here a 1-mi natural pass in the mountains—the Narrows—was the young nation's gateway to the West. It allowed wagon trains, later locomotives, and eventually motorists to make their way westward. The National Pike (the first federally funded highway), the Baltimore & Ohio Railroad, and the canal all converged here. The National Park Service has a wonderful canal museum within the reconstructed 19th-century railroad station, which is also where the Western Maryland Scenic Railroad departs for excursions.

WHAT TO SEE & DO

BERKELEY SPRINGS, WV

Berkeley Springs State Park This 4-acre park near the center of town has a spring-fed pool and contains the famous mineral baths, which have been used by the public since 1776. The Roman Bath House from 1815 still stands. Reservations for minerals baths, massages, and other spa treatments are recommended. > 121 S. Washington St., Berkeley Springs, tel. 304/258–2711 or 800/225–5982, www.wvparks.com/berkeleysprings. Park free, baths and massages $10–$65. Park: daily dawn–10 PM; baths: daily 10–4:30.
Cacapon Resort State Park At 2,300 feet, Cacapon Mountain dominates this narrow 6,000-acre park, which is run through with 27 mi of hiking and bridle trails. The 18-hole Robert Trent Jones golf course surrounds a nearby lodge, 10 mi south of Berke-

The Canal's Brief Heyday

FOLKS CAME FROM FAR AND NEAR to celebrate the long-awaited opening of the C&O Canal. It was October 10, 1850, and the first five coal boats waited to start the run down the Potomac from Cumberland to Georgetown, a journey that would take seven days. "Many of us were young when this great work commenced," said the spokesman for the town, referring to the 22 years it took to complete the 185-mi-long ditch and towpath, which includes 74 lift locks, 7 dams, 11 aqueducts, and a 3,118-foot tunnel.

As each dam was completed, water from the Potomac River was diverted into the canal, and boats began using the watered sections. The canal arrived opposite Harpers Ferry in 1833, and reached Hancock, Maryland, in 1839. The final 50 mi was stalled by the challenges of constructing the tunnel at Paw Paw, labor unrest, and financial troubles, but the canal turned Cumberland—a mountain city 605 feet above sea level—into a port. Boats carried as many as a million tons of merchandise a year: primarily coal but also tobacco, grain, whiskey, furs, iron ore, timber, and other commodities were sent down the Potomac to Georgetown and Alexandria, which served as major distribution points via the Chesapeake Bay.

Cumberland was a busy place. At its peak, boatyards turned out 170 new craft a year and repaired many others. As many as 500 boats a season plied the canal and waited their turn in the port to collect cargo. Downtown, the stores for provisions vied for space with pool parlors and "grogshops" with such colorful names as Aunt Susan's Rising Sun Saloon and Louise's Den of Iniquity.

Each boat would rest two mules in the stern of the boat while two other mules pulled the boat along from the towpath. There were living and cooking quarters on the boats to sustain the crew on its weeklong journey.

In the 1950s a proposal to build a highway over the canal near Washington was thwarted by residents of the Palisades (between Georgetown and the Great Falls Tavern) and others concerned with the canal's history and legacy. The canal is the finest relic of America's canal-building era, and its route and structures are still almost entirely intact. Since 1971 the canal has been a national park, providing a window into the past and a marvelous place to enjoy the outdoors.

ley Springs off U.S. 522. > U.S. 522, Berkeley Springs, tel. 304/258–1022 or 800/462–6963, www.cacaponresort.com. Free. Daily.

Sleepy Creek Wildlife Management Area Wild turkey, squirrel, and deer roam this forested 22,000-acre area, which has hunting, a rifle range, and a 200-acre lake for boating and fishing. It has approximately 70 mi of hiking trails and 75 primitive campsites. > Jones Spring Rd., 6 mi west of I–81 off Rte. 9, Berkeley Springs, tel. 304/822–3551. Free. Daily.

CHARLES TOWN, WV

Charles Town Races Horse racing here dates back to the 18th century. There's thoroughbred racing day and night, as well as video gambling on 1,500 machines. The races are 1 mi east of town on U.S. 340 North. > Flowing Springs Rd., Charles Town, tel. 304/725–7001 or 800/795–7001, www.ctownraces.com. Free. Thurs.–Sat. 7:15 PM, Sun. 1.

Jefferson County Courthouse John Brown's trial was held here in October 1859. He was convicted of treason and sentenced to death for raiding the U.S. Arsenal in Harpers Ferry. That era's one-room courthouse, built in 1803, is incorporated into the present courthouse. The room where John Brown was tried is open to the public. > 100 E. Washington St., Charles Town 25414, tel. 304/725–9761 or 800/848–8687. Free. Tours Mon.–Sat. 10–4.

Jefferson County Museum John Brown's gun and the wagon that carried him to his execution are displayed here, along with Washington family memorabilia and Civil War artifacts. > 200 E. Washington St., Charles Town, tel. 304/725–8628. Free. Tours Apr.–Nov., Mon.–Sat. 10–4.

Site of the John Brown Gallows At John Brown's hanging in December 1859, some 1,500 troops surrounded the scaffold erected next to the courthouse. The site is marked by stones reportedly taken from his jail cell. > 635 S. Samuel St., Charles Town, tel. 304/725–9761. Free. Daily.

CUMBERLAND, MD

Cumberland Visitor Center/Western Maryland Station Inside a restored 19th-century railroad station, this excellent center has exhibits and short films that interpret canal and local history as well as the geology of the Potomac's Great Falls. Also on display is a replica canal boat. Ranger-led programs are offered on many weekends and some weekdays. Rest rooms and a bookshop are inside. > Room 304, 13 Canal St., Cumberland 21502, tel. 301/722–8226, www.nps.gov/choh. Daily 9–5.

History House (Gordon–Roberts House) Judge Josiah Gordon, president of the C&O Canal, lived for 20 years in this large 18-room house. Today the Victorian house is the headquarters for the Allegany County Historical Society and is furnished with period pieces, antiques, and displays depicting life in the mid-1800s. Special collection rooms, a genealogy research room, and a carriage house are also here. Guided hourly tours with costumed guides are available. > 218 Washington St., Cumberland 21502, tel. 301/777–8678, www.historyhouse.allconet.org. $3. June–Oct., Tues.–Sun. 11–4.

Western Maryland Scenic Railroad This three-hour, 32-mi round-trip ride to the 1891 Old Depot in Frostburg delivers panoramic vistas and views of rugged mountains. A 1916 Baldwin steam locomotive once used in Michigan's Upper Peninsula does the heavy work on weekends, and a diesel engine pulls the train weekdays. Inside the 19th-century train station, your point of departure, are the National Park Service's Cumberland Visitor Center and exhibits on the history of the C&O. > 13 Canal

St., Cumberland, tel. 301/759–4400 or 800/872–4650, www.wmsr.com. $19.50.
May–Sept., Tues.–Sun. 11:30; Oct., Mon.–Thurs. 11, Fri.–Sun. 11 and 4.

HARPERS FERRY, WV

Appalachian National Scenic Trail Two-and-one-half miles of this 2,150-mi footpath,
which runs from Georgia to Maine, are in West Virginia. This segment extends
through lower Harpers Ferry, following the Stone Steps and crossing the footbridge
over the Potomac River. > Shenandoah St. and High St., Harpers Ferry, tel.
304/535–6298. Free. Daily.

Harpers Ferry Ghost Tours You can wander the streets of Harpers Ferry by lantern
light to gain a unique look at the town's history. Guide Shirley Dougherty will take
you to meet the spirits from John Brown's raid. Tours meet on the patio of Hot
Dog Haven, across from the railroad station. > Potomac St., Harpers Ferry, tel.
304/725–8019. $3. Apr., Sat. at 8 PM; May–mid-Nov., Fri.–Sun. at 8 PM.

Harpers Ferry National Historical Park This 2,300-acre park includes land in West
Virginia, Virginia, and Maryland. Six major historical themes relating to the area's
past are illuminated here through museum exhibits and scheduled activities: the natural environment, industry, John Brown, the Civil War, African-American history, and
transportation. The park, West Virginia's most-visited attraction, includes the fort in
which John Brown was captured. > Rte. 340, Harpers Ferry, tel. 304/535–6298,
www.nps.gov/hafe. $3, cars $5. May–Oct., daily 8–6; Nov.–Apr., daily 8–5.

Jefferson's Rock From this vantage point Thomas Jefferson sat in 1783 and observed
West Virginia, Virginia, and Maryland. He wrote that the view was "well worth a trip
across the Atlantic." > Harpers Ferry National Historical Park, off Rte. 340. Free. Daily.

John Brown Museum Part of the Historical Park, this museum has exhibits and
artifacts from the Brown's 1859 raid of the U.S. Arsenal. > Shenandoah St., tel.
304/535–6298, www.nps.gov/hafe. Free with park admission. Daily.

John Brown's Fort Now a brick firehouse in Arsenal Square, this was where the
famed abolitionist was captured. The structure was dismantled in the early 1890s
and shipped to the World's Columbian Exposition in Chicago. It now stands near
its original site on Harpers Ferry park grounds. > Arsenal Sq., tel. 304/535–6298,
www.nps.gov/hafe. Free. Daily 8–5.

John Brown Wax Museum This privately owned facility contains life-size figures that
depict the life of abolitionist John Brown. > 168 High St., tel. 304/535–6342. $2.50.
Daily 9:30–4:30.

The Point At this gap in the Blue Ridge Mountains, you can get a panoramic view of
the town and surrounding area. It's in Harpers Ferry National Historical Park at the
southeast corner of town, at the convergence of the Potomac and Shenandoah rivers.
> Just off Shenandoah and Potomac Sts. Free. Daily.

MARTINSBURG, WV

Belle Boyd House The former home of the famous Confederate spy Belle Boyd was
built in 1853 in Greek-revival style. Today it houses Civil War antiquities and an
archives department with a focus on local history. There is period clothing on display
in the Corning Room. When only 17, Belle Boyd, known to her many admirers as "La
Belle Rebelle," shot a Union soldier in her parents' house after he threatened her
mother. > 126 E. Race St., Martinsburg, tel. 304/267–4713. Free. Wed.–Sat. 10–4.

General Adam Stephen House This limestone house was built 1772 and 1789 by
General Adam Stephen, a Revolutionary War officer and the founder of Martinsburg

(he named the town for a friend, Colonel Thomas B. Martin). The 1876 Triple Brick Museum, on the grounds, gets its name from the fact that it was built in three sections. It's now a museum devoted to local history. > 309 E. John St., Martinsburg, tel. 304/267–4434, www.travelwv.com. Free. May–Oct., Wed. and Fri. 10–2:30, weekends 2–5; tours by appointment.

Jefferson Orchards You can pick your own pumpkin in fall, or buy fresh-picked apples or baked goods at this 500-acre orchard. > Rte. 9, 7 mi east of Martinsburg, tel. 304/725–9149, www.jeffersonorchards.com. Free. Daily 8–4:30.

Paw Paw Tunnel Construction of this 3,118-foot tunnel took 14 years and was the final link in the Canal. Today you can hike 20 minutes through it or take a posted trail over the ridge above the tunnel, a strenuous, 2-mi pathway that takes about an hour to hike or to bike. > Mile 155 of the Canal, Rte. 9 (for information, contact 1850 Dual Hwy., Suite 100), Hagerstown, tel. 301/834–7100, www.nps.gov/choh. Daily; hrs vary.

Tours

Historical River Tours These raft trips ($40–$57) on the Potomac and Shenandoah are a good way to learn more about the history of the region. > 1257 Allstadts Hill Rd., Harpers Ferry, tel. 304/535–6649 or 800/988–4296, www.historicalrivertours.com. Tours Apr.–mid-June and early Sept.–mid-Nov., Wed.–Fri. 3, weekends 11, 1:30, and 3; mid-June–early Sept., Wed.–Fri. 11, 1:30, and 3, weekends 11, 1:30, 3, and 4:30.

National Park Service Canal Boats Narrated hour-long trips on replica, mule-drawn boats leave from the Great Falls Visitor Center. (Other boats also leave from Georgetown's Foundry Mall on Thomas Jefferson Street Northwest, half a block south of M Street in Georgetown). Reservations are not required; ticket sales begin two hours before each trip. Floods sometimes affect canal boat trips, so call the National Park Service office to check. > Tel. 202/653–5190 or 301/299–2026, www.nps.gov/choh. $8. Tours Apr.–mid-June and early Sept.–mid-Nov., Wed.–Fri. 3, weekends 11, 1:30, and 3; mid-June–early Sept., Wed.–Fri. 11, 1:30, and 3, weekends 11, 1:30, 3, and 4:30.

Sports

BOATING

West Virginia is renowned for its white-water rafting and its boating from spring to fall.

Blue Ridge Outfitters This company organizes excursions on Class II–III white-water rapids on the Potomac River, past Harpers Ferry. > Frontage Rd., Box 750, Harpers Ferry, WV 25425, tel. 304/725–3444 or 800/225–5982. $43–$68. Apr.–Oct.

River & Trail Outfitters White-water raft, canoe, kayak, and tube near Harpers Ferry. The company offers guided tours, lessons, biking and fishing trips, and gear rental and sales. From U.S. Highway 340, turn right on Valley Road at the yellow flashing lights just before the Potomac River Bridge. The building is immediately on the left. > 604 Valley Rd., Knoxville, MD, tel. 888/446–7529 or 301/695–5177, www.rivertrail.com.

River Riders, Inc. You can white-water raft, canoe, kayak, and tube near Harpers Ferry. Also available are guided tours, hiking, biking, lessons, and gear rental and sales. From Route 340, turn on Bloomery Road, go .3 mi and turn left onto the first hard paved road. > RR 5 Box 1260, Harpers Ferry, WV, tel. 304/535–2663 or 800/326–7238, www.riverriders.com.

Save the Date

JULY

Freedom's Birth Come to see the Fourth of July fireworks bonanza at Harpers Ferry National Historical Park, one of the best shows around. Live music at this free event augments the pyrotechnics. > Tel. 304/535–2627.

AUGUST

Jefferson County Fair This traditional county fair, held in the middle of the month, includes livestock shows, carnival rides, and entertainment. > Tel. 304/725–2055, www.jeffersoncountyfairwv.org.

SEPTEMBER

Mountain Heritage Arts and Crafts Festival Bluegrass and country music as well as artisans from across the country contribute to this nationally known festival, held at the end of the month in Charles Town. > Tel. 304/725–2055, www.jeffersoncounty.com/festival.

OCTOBER

Apple Butter Festival You can see this concoction of apples and sugar cooking in open kettles—and buy some to take home—at this family festival in Berkeley Springs. Hog-calling contests and turtle races are also highlights, along with 200 arts-and-crafts booths. > Tel. 304/258–3738, www.berkeleysprings.com/apple.

Election Day 1860 The Civil War era comes to life with a mustering of troops and military encampments at Harpers Ferry National Historical Park. > Tel. 304/535–6748.

NOVEMBER–DECEMBER

Christmas in Shepherdstown Strolling carolers in turn-of-the-20th-century garb, carriage rides, and house tours highlight this celebration, which begins at the end of November and continues through early December. > Tel. 304/876–2786 visitors center.

DECEMBER

Old Tyme Christmas Concerts, caroling, and ghost tours are held throughout town and in the Harpers Ferry National Historical Park. > Harpers Ferry, tel. 304/725–8019 or 304/535–2511.

WHERE TO STAY

BERKELEY SPRINGS, WV

Best Western Berkeley Springs Inn This crisp and neat stone-and-half-timber hotel is set off the main highway against foothills. Along interior corridors, the spacious guest rooms have two queen beds and solid oak furniture made by local craftsmen. Coffeemakers, irons and ironing boards, and hair dryers are in every room, and local calls are free. > 1776 Valley Rd., Berkeley Springs, WV 25411, tel. 866/945–9400 or 304/258–9400, fax 304/258–9445, www.bestwestern.com. 50 rooms, 8 suites. Restaurant, in-room data ports, cable TV, pool, business services, meeting rooms, no-smoking rooms. AE, D, MC, V. CP. ¢

Cacapon Lodge The "new" lodge in Cacapon Resort State Park was completed in 1956 and has 48 rooms filled with locally made oak furniture; the main lounge, paneled in black walnut, has a wood-burning fireplace. The 11-room Old Inn, with hand-hewn log beams and stone chimneys, was built in the 1930s by the Civilian Conservation Corps. There are also 44 cabins, 13 of which come with fireplaces, furnaces, and kitchenettes, and which are available year-round. Cable TV is available in some rooms. The lodge is 10 mi south of Berkeley Springs. > Cacapon Resort State

Park, U.S. 522, Berkeley Springs, WV 25411, tel. 304/258–1022 or 800/225–5982, fax 304/258–5323, www.cacaponresort.com. 59 rooms, 44 cabins. Dining room, picnic area, cable TV in some rooms, some kitchenettes, driving range, 18-hole golf course, putting green, tennis courts. AE, DC, MC, V. ¢–$

Coolfont Resort On 1,350 wooded acres, this rustic resort, complete with rocking chairs and hanging quilts, emphasizes recreation and activities—from chamber concerts to watercolor workshops. The individually decorated rooms are in the stately 1912 Manor House and have fireplaces. The A-frame chalet-style cottages are in pine groves throughout the resort grounds. The resort is 4 mi west on Route 9. > 1777 Cold Run Valley Rd., Berkeley Springs, WV 25411, tel. 304/258–4500, 800/888–8768 outside WV, fax 304/258–5499, www.coolfont.com. 22 rooms, 34 cottages. Dining room, picnic area, some refrigerators, tennis courts, pool, exercise equipment, hot tub, massage, beach, boating, hiking, sleigh rides, bar, children's programs (ages 5–14), playground, laundry facilities. AE, D, MC, V. $$$$

Country Inn and Renaissance Spa The white-columned front porch, colonial furnishings, and English garden at this inn may make you feel as if you've gone back in time; the spa facility will make you want to never leave. There's a mineral whirlpool bath here as well as a staff who give invigorating massages and other spa services. The lavish rooms are filled with antiques, and many have four-poster canopy beds. The country inn is one block from downtown Berkeley Springs. > 207 S. Washington St., Berkeley Springs, WV 25411, tel. 304/258–2210 or 800/822–6630, fax 304/258–3986, www.countryinnwv.com. 67 rooms, 54 with bath. Dining room, cable TV, massage, spa, business services. AE, D, DC, MC, V. $–$$

Highlawn Inn Built in the 1890s by Algernon Unger as a gift for his bride, this restored home later served as a boardinghouse. The interior has ornate fireplaces and period furnishings. Rooms are furnished with antiques, and most have either a fireplace or hot tub. In addition to the six rooms in the main house, there are four in Aunt Pearl's Building and two bedrooms in the Bathkeeper's Quarters. Some have kitchens or butler's pantries. Complimentary snacks are served in the afternoon. > 304 Market St., Berkeley Springs, WV 25411, tel. 304/258–5700 or 888/290–4163, www.highlawninn.com. 12 rooms in 4 buildings, 2 cottages. Some kitchens, cable TV, some in-room hot tubs; no room phones, no kids. MC, V. ¢–$

CUMBERLAND, MD

Inn at Walnut Bottom Two buildings make up this country inn: the Georgian-style 1820 Cowden House and the Queen Anne–style 1890 Dent House. The father of President Ulysses S. Grant's wife, Julia Dent, was born in the previous house built on this site. Each house is accented by antiques, pine floors, and Oriental rugs. Area state parks and the town's historic center are a short drive away. > 120 Greene St., Cumberland, MD 21502, tel. 301/777–0003 or 800/286–9718, fax 301/777–8288, www.iwbinfo.com. 12 rooms, 8 with bath. Cable TV, bicycles, business services. AE, D, MC, V. BP. ¢–$

Rocky Gap Lodge & Golf Resort This lakeside resort on 243 acres is inside one of Maryland's most spectacular state parks. Its wood paneling and rustic furniture are reminiscent of a country cabin. Jack Nicklaus designed the golf course here. > 16701 Lakeview Rd. NE, Flintstone, MD 21530, tel. 301/784–8400 or 800/724–0828, www.rockygapresort.com. 218 rooms, 4 suites. 2 restaurants, in-room data ports, cable TV with video games, 18-hole golf course, 2 tennis courts, indoor pool, gym, hot tub, beach, boating, fishing, bicycles, volleyball, bar, business services. AE, D, DC, MC, V. $$–$$$$

CHARLES TOWN, WV

Hillbrook In a rural area 6 mi southwest of Charles Town, this rambling wood-and-stone Tudor-style country inn is surrounded by terraced gardens. You are required to have the seven-course prix-fixe dinner ($75) here at least one night during your stay. > Summit Point Rd., Charles Town 25414, tel. 304/725–4223 or 800/304–4223, fax 304/725–4455, www.hillbrookinn.com. 11 rooms. Dining room, some refrigerators, some in-room hot tubs, bar, library, business services; no TV in some rooms. AE, D, MC, V. BP. $$$$

Washington House Inn This 1899 Victorian house was built by descendants of George Washington's brothers, John Augustine and Samuel, and is filled with period furnishings and fireplaces with carved oak mantles. Extra niceties like fresh flowers and terry robes make the guest rooms homey. The inn is in the center of colonial Charles Town. Afternoon snacks are complimentary. > 216 S. George St., Charles Town, WV 25414, tel. 304/725–7923 or 800/297–6957, fax 304/728–5150, www.washingtonhouseinnwv.com. 6 rooms. In-room data ports, cable TV, business services, airport shuttle; no smoking. AE, D, MC, V. CP. $

HARPERS FERRY, WV

Harpers Ferry Guest House This building is intended to conform to the federal architecture of the rest of town. The main guest rooms each have a four-poster queen bed and high sloping ceilings with fans. The front porch has a wisteria vine, rocking chairs, and a swing; a small private parking lot and flower gardens are out back. > 800 Washington St., Harpers Ferry, WV 25425, tel. 304/535–6955, www.harpersferry-wv.com. 3 rooms. No a/c, no kids under 10. No credit cards. BP. ¢–$

Historic Hilltop House Hotel Near the site that Thomas Jefferson described as "worth a voyage across the Atlantic," this 1888 stone inn has rooms that are attractively decorated in Victorian style. Included in its guest list are Alexander Graham Bell, Mark Twain, Carl Sandburg, Pearl S. Buck, and presidents Woodrow Wilson and Bill Clinton. > 400 E. Ridge St., Harpers Ferry, WV 25425, tel. 304/535–2132 or 800/338–8319, fax 304/535–6322, www.hilltophousehotel.net. 62 rooms. Restaurant, cable TV, bar, business services, meeting rooms. AE, MC, V. $

MARTINSBURG, WV

Bavarian Inn and Lodge Above the Potomac, this property encompasses six buildings within walking distance: a 1930 grey-stone restaurant originally built as a private residence; a main lodge, in half-timber style (added in 1994); and four riverfront chalets. All chalet rooms have balconies overlooking the Potomac River bend. The luxurious guest rooms have European-style furnishings with antique German items and canopy beds reminiscent of old Bavarian inns. The inn is two blocks north of downtown. > Rte. 480 (R.R. 3 Box 30), Martinsburg 25443, tel. 304/876–2551, fax 304/876–9355, www.bavarianinnwv.com. 73 rooms (30 in lodge and 43 in 4 riverfront chalets). Dining room, in-room data ports, some in-room hot tubs, cable TV, pool, putting green, tennis court, exercise equipment, bar, business services, meeting rooms. AE, D, DC, MC, V. ¢–$$

Boydville—the Inn at Martinsburg Built in 1812, this manor house is on 10 wooded acres; 19th-century notables such as Stonewall Jackson and Henry Clay both stayed here. French chandeliers light the front parlors, and murals adorn the guest rooms. The shops and restaurants of Martinsburg are a five-minute drive away. > 601 S. Queen St., Martinsburg 25401, tel. 304/263–1448, lfrye@intrepid.net. 7 rooms. MC, V. Closed Aug. $–$$

Farmhouse on Tomahawk Run About 10 mi west of Martinsburg, this large Civil War–era farmhouse and carriage house are beside the Tomahawk Run stream. The walking paths that surround it wind through 280 acres of woods, hills, and meadows. Rooms are furnished with period antiques and have private balconies. You can relax in one of the rocking chairs on the wraparound porch. The farmhouse has two guest rooms and a suite; the carriage house has two guest rooms, a kitchen, and a family room with wood-burning fireplace, TV, and VCR. > 1828 Tomahawk Run Rd., Hedgesville 25427, tel. 304/754–7350 or 888/266–9516, www.tomahawkrun.com. 5 rooms. Outdoor hot tub; no room TVs. AE, D, DC, V. BP. $

Woods Resort and Conference Center Surrounded by 1,800 acres, mountain views, and a golf course, this resort is furnished with rustic items. The contemporary lodge guest rooms are large, with wood-paneled or painted interior walls, rustic pine furnishings, and a king-size bed. All have great views of the resort's pond and outdoor pool. The Woods is 12 mi off I–81 Exit 16 West, the exit for Hedgesville and Berkeley Springs. > Mountain Lake Rd., Hedgesville 25427, tel. 304/754–7977 or 800/248–2222, fax 304/754–8146, www.thewoodsresort.com. 60 rooms in 3 lodges, 14 cabins. Dining room, some kitchenettes, refrigerators, some in-room hot tubs, cable TV, 3 pools (1 indoor), wading pools, tennis courts, exercise equipment, hot tub, bar (with entertainment), children's programs (ages 5–12), laundry facilities, business services. AE, D, DC, MC, V. $–$$

WHERE TO EAT

CUMBERLAND, MD

Fred Warner's German Restaurant After enjoying some homemade bread and typical German fare that includes sauerbraten and Jagerschnitzel (cutlets in a mushroom sauce) try to save room for one of Fred's rich desserts, such as chocolate torte, German chocolate cake, or Black Forest cake. > Rte. 220, Cresaptown, tel. 301/729–2361. AE, MC, V. Closed Mon. $–$$

Uncle Tucker's Woodfired Pizza and Brew House Western Maryland's only microbrewery has a wood-fired oven for pizza. Uncle Tucker carries a complete menu of pub food that includes crab and artichoke dip, garlic-roasted shrimp, crab-cake sandwiches, and baby-back ribs. > the Inn At Folck's Mill, I–68, Exit 46, 1 mi east of Cumberland, tel. 301/777–7005, www.edmasons.com. AE, MC, V. ¢–$

When Pigs Fly Six blocks west of Baltimore Street, this restaurant and lounge is full of pig paraphernalia—flying pigs hanging from the ceiling, pig pictures, pig figurines. As you might guess, the place is famous for its barbecued ribs, but the menu has many other choices such as barbecued chicken, steaks, prime rib, crab cakes and other seafood, pasta dishes, and numerous sides. > 18 Valley St., Cumberland, tel. 301/722–7447, www.pigsonline.com. AE, MC, V. $–$$

HARPERS FERRY AND MARTINSBURG, WV

Anvil Restaurant The main themes of the menu are seafood and steak; an array of cheesecakes and pies awaits you for dessert. For a less-formal experience, eat in the pub; the drafts are only 50¢ during happy hour. > 1270 Washington St., Harpers Ferry, tel. 304/535–2582, www.anvilrestaurant.com. AE, MC, V. Closed Mon. and Tues. $–$$$

Cracker Barrel Old Country Store Filled with artifacts, genuine antiques, memorabilia, and old farm equipment, the Cracker Barrel chain serves big helpings of Southern fare: chicken and dumplings, sugar-cured ham, farm-raised catfish filets, grilled pork chops, and breaded fried okra. > 725 Foxcroft Ave., Martinsburg, tel. 304/262–3660. AE, D, DC, MC, V. $

El Ranchero Serving traditional fare like fajitas and enchiladas, this eatery is in one of Martinsburg's larger shopping malls. The interior is decorated with authentic Mexican ornaments that include figurines and designs pounded out of copper. > N. Mall Plaza on Foxcroft Dr., Martinsburg, tel. 304/262–4053. AE, D, DC, MC, V. $–$$

Fazoli's Italian music plays in the background all day long at this casual eatery in downtown Martinsburg. Squares of lasagna are served by the dozen, but the spaghetti, fettuccine, ravioli, and pizza are also favorites. Vintage pictures of Italy line the walls. > 775 Foxcroft Ave., Martinsburg, tel. 304/262–2822. MC, V. ¢–$

Heatherfield's Restaurant In downtown Martinsburg, this restaurant has linen tablecloths, fresh flowers, and local artwork on the walls. The most popular dishes are the prime rib and the grilled chicken. > 301 Foxcroft Ave., Martinsburg, tel. 304/267–8311. AE, D, DC, MC, V. Closed Sun. No lunch. $–$$

Historic Boomtown Restaurant Inside a restored Victorian, this restaurant has four dining rooms filled with period antiques; the walls are lined with Civil War–era paintings. Outdoor seating is available on the patio in the garden. You can choose from salads, steak, and pasta; the homemade crab cakes are popular. > 522 W. King St., Martinsburg, tel. 304/263–8840. AE, D, MC, V. Closed Sun. $$–$$$

ESSENTIALS

Getting Here

You need a car to explore the segments of the C&O Canal and the surrounding countryside.

BY CAR

The fastest way to get the C&O Canal's terminus, at Cumberland, is to take I–270 to I–70 and then I–68 East (U.S. 40 E.) to Cumberland, Maryland. There are exits along the interstate to reach sections at the C&O Canal as well as the visitor centers at Brunswick (via U.S. 340 at Frederick, MD), Williamsport (via I–81 at Hagerstown), and Hancock (off I–70 just before I–68 merge).

This route is also the fastest way to reach Harpers Ferry, Charles Town, Martinsburg, and Berkeley Springs. To reach Harpers Ferry, take U.S. Route 340 at Frederick past the Brunswick Visitor Center. Charles Town is also on Route 340, past Harpers Ferry. Martinsburg and Berkeley Springs are west of Charles Town on Route 9. Alternatively, you can reach Berkeley Springs by staying on the Maryland side of the Potomac on I–70 to Hancock, then taking U.S. 522 to Berkeley Springs. Return to the Maryland side of the Potomac to drive to Cumberland from here.

Unless you're driving during rush hour, expect to be able to drive the speed limit on the interstate highways.

Parking is free at all the sites mentioned in this chapter. When visiting Harpers Ferry, the National Park Service requests that you park at the visitor center and take the free shuttle bus into the congested historic town.

Visitor Information

CONTACTS **Brunswick Visitor Center** > 40 W. Potomac St., Brunswick, MD 21716, tel. 301/834–7100. Daily; hrs vary.**Chesapeake and Ohio Canal National Historic Park Headquarters** > 1850 Dual Hwy., Suite 100, Hagerstown MD 21740-6620, tel. 301/739–4200, fax 301/739–5275, www.nps.gov/choh.**Hancock Visitor Center** > 326 E. Main St., Hancock 21750, tel. 301/678–5463, www.nps.gov/choh.**Jefferson County Convention & Visitor Bureau** > Rte. 340, Box A, Harpers Ferry, WV 25425, tel. 304/535–2627 or 800/848–8687, fax 304/535–2131, www.jeffersoncountycvb.com. May–Oct, daily 9–6; Nov.–Apr., daily 9–5.**Martinsburg/Berkeley County Convention and Visitors Bureau** > 208 S. Queen St., Martinsburg, WV 25401, tel. 304/264–8801 or 800/498–2386, www.travelwv.com.**Travel Berkeley Springs** > 304 Fairfax St., Berkeley Springs, WV 25411, tel. 304/258–9147 or 800/447–8797, www.berkeleysprings.com. **Western Maryland Station Center** > 13 Canal St., Cumberland, MD, tel. 800/872–4650, www.wmsr.com. **Williamsport Visitor Center** > 205 W. Potomac St., Williamsport 21795, tel. 301/582–0813. Wed.–Sun. 9–4:30.

Hunt Country

Leesburg is 60 mi west of Washington, D.C.

WINERIES, HORSE FARMS, AND 18TH-CENTURY MANSIONS AND FARMS proliferate in Virginia's hunt country, which lies primarily in Loudoun and Fauquier counties. The area, once part of 5 million acres granted by the king of England to seven noblemen in 1649, lies between the Potomac and Rappahannock rivers, with grassy, tree-topped hills that extend west toward West Virginia and the Blue Ridge Mountains. When you've had enough of its major sights, you can head to one of the many reasonably priced golf courses, or go picnic or read a book near one of the area's beautiful views.

Loudoun County is bordered by the Potomac to the north and West Virginia to the west. Stables, barns, and stacked-stone fences are scattered throughout the countryside. For more than two centuries, agriculture was the dominant way of life here, which had a relatively constant population of about 20,000. That began to change in the early 1960s, when Dulles International Airport was built in the southeastern part of the county. The airport attracted new businesses, workers, and their families to the area. At the same time, metropolitan D.C. began a period of rapid growth. Major road improvements made commuting from Loudoun County much easier (the eastern part is just 35 mi northwest of Washington, D.C.), and over the next three decades, the population of Loudoun County nearly quadrupled. About 200,000 people live there today.

Nevertheless, in and around the county's major towns of Middleburg and Leesburg, old Virginia carries on its traditions. What's now the town of Middleburg was surveyed by George Washington in 1763, when it was known as Chinn's Crossroads. It was a strategic point, midway on the route between Winchester and Alexandria (roughly what is now U.S. 50). Attractive boutiques and other stores line U.S. 50, the main street, and polo matches are played on Sunday June through Labor Day. Many horse farms are nearby, and the area is known for its steeplechases and fox hunts in spring and fall.

Leesburg, the county seat 18 mi northeast of Middleburg, is one of the oldest towns in northern Virginia. Established in 1758, it grew up at the crossroads of two colonial roads, now Routes 7 and 15. Once named "George Town," not for Washington but for King George II, it changed its name to Leesburg to honor Virginia's illustrious Lee family—an early sign of shifting allegiances before the Revolutionary War.

Leesburg is associated with several military campaigns. First it was a staging area during George Washington's push to the Ohio Valley during the French and Indian War (1754–60). When the British burned Washington during the War of 1812, James and Dolley Madison fled there. They brought with them for safekeeping official copies of the Declaration of Independence, the U.S. Constitution, and other important papers. During the Civil War, Colonel John Mosby and his Rangers were active in Loudoun County. A national cemetery near Leesburg marks the site of the Battle of Balls Bluff, where Oliver Wendell Holmes Jr., then a young Union soldier, fought in

1861. Leesburg's numerous fine Georgian and federal buildings are now offices, shops, restaurants, and homes. In or near Leesburg are museums, mansions, several wineries, and golf courses.

About 6 mi northwest of Leesburg is Waterford, a small village of some 90 homes and buildings. A Quaker miller founded the historic community in 1733, and for many decades it has been synonymous with fine crafts. Many of Waterford's original buildings, constructed in the regional vernacular style, survive; the town and more than 1,400 acres around it were declared a National Historic Landmark in 1970. The Waterford Foundation provides brochures for self-guided walking tours. There are no restaurants in the village, but the Waterford Market will make you a sandwich and has beverages and other food items. The market also carries crafts made by local artisans.

Fauquier County, at the southern boundary of Loudoun, was once part of the hunting grounds of the Manahoac Indians; it was settled by German and English immigrants in the 1700s. Driving through the pastoral farmland that punctuates the over 200,000 acres of forest that remain, you can see herds of Black Angus and other cattle grazing. Area poultry farms produce specialty breeds and eggs that come in brown and blue as well as white. The orchards here are planted with apples, peaches, pears, and cherries.

Traditional foxhunting meets and point-to-point races have made the Fauquier county seat, Warrenton, a center for equestrian events. The state's biggest steeplechase race, the Virginia Gold Cup, is held in nearby Great Meadows every May. Warrenton is mostly residential, with a small retail and commercial district in the town center. Historic Old Town has antiques stores, clothiers, and specialty shops. Sky Meadows State Park, in Front Royal to the north, has facilities for horseback riding, hiking, and camping. May through October, people pack picnics and head to the Flying Circus Air Show in Bealeton, 14 mi south of Warrenton.

WHAT TO SEE & DO

LEESBURG

Hidden Brook At this rustic, log-house winery, you can taste wines near a cozy fireplace or on a deck overlooking vineyards and mountains. Their nine wines include vidal blanc, chardonnay, rosé, chambourcin, cabernet sauvignon, merlot, and sweet amber. Hidden Brook is 7 mi north of Leesburg, off Route 15. > 43301 Spinks Ferry Rd., Leesburg, tel. 703/737–3935, www.hiddenbrookwinery.com. Free. Wed.–Fri. 11–5, weekends 11–6.

Loudoun Museum The permanent exhibits of the museum begin with the area's Native Americans, who lived here primarily from 15,000 BC until the early 1700s. Original documents and artifacts from that century forward show how life in the county developed. Also on display are artifacts from the Civil War and the two world wars, and Victorian furniture and clothing. Short videos available in the "History Minute Kiosk" add still more information about Loudoun, including why the county was called the "breadbasket of the Revolution." > 16 W. Loudoun St. SW, Leesburg, tel. 703/777–7427, www.loudounmuseum.org. $3. Mon.–Sat. 10–5, Sun. 1–5.

Morven Park Within this site's 1,200 acres are the Westmoreland Davis Equestrian Institute, a private riding school, and two museums: Morven Park Carriage Museum and the Museum of Hounds and Hunting. The 1781 mansion, the work of three architects, is done in a Greek-revival style and served as the residence for two governors.

Virginia Thoroughbreds

WITHOUT HORSES, the Virginia Colony would have failed. "Sixe mares and a [male] horse" arrived at Jamestown in August 1610. Unfortunately, they were eaten during a famine. Later, more horses arrived to cultivate the fields and to provide transportation. Eventually workhorses gave ground to pleasure mounts when newly rich 18th-century planters began to import "blooded" horses. The first English thoroughbred to arrive in Virginia was Bulle Rock in 1730, and more imported horses with Arabian blood arrived after that. The stud services of these stallions made Virginia horses the premier breed in American racing at the beginning of the 1800s, and Virginia led in the creation of the American thoroughbred.

As racing and fox hunting became popular sports, red-coated riders flying over brush and fences became a recognizable sight in Virginia. Outstanding racing horses and steeplechase jumpers are bred at more than a dozen major horse breeding farms in Virginia and hundreds of small ones. Today more than 150,000 head of horses are on Virginia soil. The Hunt Country Stable Tour, held each Memorial Day weekend, is a good opportunity to get an up-close view of the show, training, and breeding facilities around Middleburg and Upperville.

Most weekends in spring and fall, you can observe hunts, point-to-point racing, and steeplechases in Loudoun, Fauquier, and other counties that make up "Virginia Hunt Country." The 23 steeplechases that are run each year often benefit local charities. The Virginia Gold Cup, held the same spring day as the Kentucky Derby, and the International Gold Cup, held at The Plains in fall, are the two largest steeplechase events in the state.

Some horse shows have been around since the 1850s. The Upperville Colt and Horse Show, begun in 1853, is the oldest in the United States, and the Warrenton Pony Show, established in 1920, is the oldest of its kind. Many shows include dressage, in which the horse is led through complex movements. There are also jumper courses, saddle horse competitions, and a hunter division that's conducted over a course that simulates a fox hunt.

The mansion bears such a striking resemblance to the White House (completed in 1800) that it's been used in movies as a stand-in. The price of admission includes entrance to the two museums and to 16 of the mansion's rooms. > Rte. 7, 1 mi north of Leesburg, tel. 703/777–2414, www.morvenpark.org. $6. Apr.–Oct., Tues.–Fri. noon–5, Sat. 10–5, Sun. 1–5; Nov., weekends noon–5; tours during the 1st 3 wks of Dec., Tues.–Sun. noon–5.

Oatlands What was once a 5,000-acre plantation was built by a great-grandson of Robert "King" Carter, one of the wealthiest pre-Revolution planters in Virginia. The Greek-revival manor house was built in 1803; a stately portico and half-octagonal stair wings were added in 1827. The house, a National Trust Historic Site, has been meticulously restored, and the manicured fields that remain host public and private equestrian events from spring to fall. The terraced walls here border a restored English garden of 4½ acres. Oatlands is 5 mi south of Leesburg on Route 15. > 20850

Oatlands Plantation La. (Rte. 15), Leesburg, tel. 703/777–3174, www.oatlands.org. $8 (additional fee for special events). Apr.–Dec., Mon.–Sat. 10–5, Sun. 1–5.

Tarara Vineyard & Winery A modern stone building houses the winery and gift shop here, but the wine-making facilities and cellars occupy a 6,000-square-foot man-made cave dug into the hillside. In addition to sampling this 475-acre winery's products, you can stroll through the vineyards, walk 6 mi of hiking trails, picnic on the grounds, and even stay overnight at the bed-and-breakfast. Tarara produces cabernet franc, cabernet sauvignon, meritage, merlot, chardonnay, pinot gris, viognier, cameo, Terra Rouge, Wild River Red, and Charval. > 13648 Tarara La., Leesburg, tel. 703/771–7100, www.tarara.com. $5 tasting fee. Daily 11–5.

Willowcroft Farm Vineyards These vineyards, high atop the Catoctin Ridge, have panoramic views of the Loudoun Valley. In the 1800s the slopes were planted with orchards. Today vineyards, which have replaced the fruit trees, yield superior grapes. The rustic beauty of the winery, housed in the old red barn, and the award-winning wines, will give you reason to return to this peaceful spot. Willowcroft Farm produces vidal, chardonnay, cabernet sauvignon, cabernet franc, merlot, traminette, Riesling-muscat, seyval, and apple wines. > 38906 Mt. Gilead Rd., Leesburg, tel. 703/777–8161, www.willowcroftwine.com. $2 tasting fee. Mar.–Dec., Fri.–Sun. 11–5:30; Feb., weekends 11–5:30.

MIDDLEBURG

National Sporting Library Over 12,000 volumes on horse racing, dressage, show jumping, breeding, veterinary care, foxhunting, polo, and related topics are contained in this handsome building. Some of the books date from the 1500s. > 102 The Plains Rd., Middleburg, tel. 540/687–6542, www.nsl.org. Free. Mon. 1–4, Tues.–Fri. 10–4, Sat. by appointment only.

Piedmont Vineyards and Winery Three miles south of Middleburg, Piedmont has 25 acres of vines. The winery specializes in chardonnay and sémillon, but also makes some red wine. Construction on the manor house began around 1740. > The Plains Rd., Middleburg, tel. 540/687–5528, www.piedmontwines.com. $3 tasting fee. Tours Apr.–Dec., daily 11–5; Jan.–Mar., Wed.–Sun. 11–5; tasting room year-round Mon.–Sat. 10–5, Sun. 11–5.

Swedenburg Estate Vineyard One mile east of Middleburg, the winery's modern building is part of the Valley View Farm, which raises Angus beef cattle and grows crops. The Bull Run mountains form a backdrop for the vineyards. Swedenburg makes chardonnay, cabernet sauvignon, pinot noir, and Riesling wines. > Rte. 50, Middleburg, tel. 540/687–5219, www.swedenburgwines.com. $1 tasting fee. Daily 10–4.

WARRENTON

Oasis Winery One of the oldest wineries operating in the state, Oasis planted some of the first chardonnay, cabernet sauvignon, and merlot vines in Virginia in 1977. Its 100 acres are at the foot of Skyline Drive. The Oasis visitor center encompasses a patio, a three-tiered deck, a pavilion with a fountain, and a trellised patio. Oasis, which produces sparkling wines as well as still wines, also organizes wine country tours via limousine that start at $50 per person. > 14141 Hume Rd. (Rte. 635), Hume, tel. 540/835–7627 or 800/304–7656, www.oasiswine.com. $5 tasting fee includes souvenir glass. Daily 10–5; tours at 1 and 3.

Old Jail Museum The museum's two buildings, constructed in 1808 and 1823, are some of the oldest surviving examples of jails in Virginia. They hold exhibits on local and Civil War history. > 10 Waterloo St., tel. 540/347–5525, www.fauquierchamber.org. Free. Tues.–Sun. 10–4.

Pearmund Cellars This winery, on a farm dating from 1783, produces chardonnay, viognier, Riesling, vidal, cabernet franc, merlot, and other varietals. You can have a picnic at Pearmund with the beautiful foothills in the background. Light fare, wine-related gifts, and local artwork are also available for purchase. > 6190 Georgetown Rd., Broad Run, tel. 540/347–3475, www.pearmundcellars.com. $2 tasting fee. Mar.–Dec., Thurs.–Mon. 11–5; Jan. and Feb., weekends 11–5.

WATERFORD

Breaux Vineyards This 400-acre estate has over 65 acres planted with cabernet sauvignon, merlot, vidal blanc, seyval blanc, chardonnay, and sauvignon blanc grapes. The vineyards extend up Short Hill Mountain, and long mountain vistas can be seen from the tasting room, the patio, and the landscaped terraces. Cheeses, meat, spreads, and breads are all available for sale. There's a patio area with tables and chairs where you can sit, sip wine, and eat your food purchases. > 36888 Breaux Vineyards La., Hillsboro, tel. 540/668–6299, www.breauxvineyards.com. $3 tasting fee. Daily 11–5.

Loudoun Valley Vineyards French, German, and Italian grapes have been propagated in this estate's grapevine nursery since 1978. Wine accompaniments that include imported cheese, freshly baked baguettes, and several varieties of pâté can also be bought here. The large glass-walled tasting room has spacious wraparound decks and outdoor seating with good views. > 38516 Charlestown Pike, Waterford, tel. 540/882–3375, www.loudounvalleyvineyards.com. Free. Jan.–Mar., weekends 11–5; Apr.–Dec., Fri.–Sun. 11–5.

Union Cemetery Although it might appear that this cemetery is for Union soldiers, it's actually operated by the Union of Churches, and veterans from both sides of the Civil War are buried here. The multidenominational burial ground was established in the early 1800s on a rise at the northeast end of the village. The cemetery is segregated, with the black section in the rear. Both sections contain fine marble monuments, but many African-Americans could afford no more than a roughly flat stone from a field, or just a wooden marker that quickly weathered away. The resulting gaps in the rows are testaments to the inequalities of the day. > Fairfax St., tel. 540/882–3018, www.waterfordva-wca.org. Free. Daily dawn–dusk.

Windham Winery This lovely 300-acre farm has a tree-lined pond. The owners, the Bazaco family, trace their origins to Greece, where their ancestors have made wine for centuries. Windham produced its first vintage in 1995. Hope Bazaco makes fresh baklava once a week for those in the tasting room. > 14727 Mountain Rd. (Rte. 690), Hillsboro, tel. 540/668–6464, www.windhamwinery.com. Free. Fri. and Sat., and Mon. holidays 11–5:30.

Sports

GOLF

Goose Creek Golf Club Among the area's best public golf courses, par-72 Goose Creek (6,400/5,235; 70.3/71.3) is also reasonably priced. The layout has three tee stations, winding fairways with strategically placed bunkers, ponds, creeks, and trees. Ben Hogan's legendary score of 59 was a course record. A spacious clubhouse and outdoor patio provide the perfect place for hosting an outing or just relaxing after a great round of golf. The green fee is $54. > 43001 Golf Club Rd., Leesburg, tel. 703/729–2500, www.goosecreekgolf.com.

Lansdowne Resort Near Leesburg is the only full-service resort in the Washington, D.C., area. Along the banks of the Potomac, Lansdowne's par-72 course (7,057/5,213; 74.6/70.6), designed by Robert Trent Jones Jr., blends beautiful scenery with challenging play. The Lansdowne Golf Shop is in the resort's main building, overlooking the 18th green. The green fee is $95. > 44050 Woodridge Pkwy., Leesburg, tel. 703/729–8400, www.lansdowneresort.com.

Raspberry Falls Golf & Hunt Club This championship golf course (7,191/4,854; 75.6/67.8) rambles through Raspberry Plain, an 18th-century plantation. The rolling terrain, native hardwood trees, meandering streams, natural rock outcroppings, and spectacular vistas were all incorporated into Gary Player's design. The most dramatic and formidable feature: the Scottish-style stacked-sod bunkers. The clubhouse is a Southern mansion. Monthly fox hunts are held in fall and winter. > 41601 Raspberry Dr., Leesburg, tel. 703/779–2555 or 703/589–1042, www.raspberryfalls.com.

Stoneleigh Golf Club Influenced by the golf courses of Scotland, Stoneleigh also retains some antebellum touches—many of the old barns and stone houses on the property date back as far as 1700. The front 9 of the 18-hole, par-72 course (6,709/4,837; 73.1/69.1) plays through apple orchards with views of the Snickersville Gap. In the back nine are meadows, an old toll road, and ruins with views of the Catoctin and Sugarloaf mountains. Stoneleigh's 18th-century manor house, which has fireplaces and views of the 18th green, now serves as the clubhouse. An old "bank barn," with earth banked against one side, now holds carts. > 35271 Prestwick Ct., Round Hill, tel. 540/338–4653 or 703/589–1402, www.stoneleighgolf.com.

Virginia National Golf Club At what was the battlefield of the Cool Springs Civil War battle is one of Virginia's premier golf courses. Virginia National has 3 mi of unobstructed Shenandoah River vistas on one side of the course and the tree-lined foothills of the Blue Ridge Mountains, natural waterfalls, and abundant wildlife along the other. The par-72 course (6,950/4,852; 73.0/68.3) ebbs and flows like the river it mirrors, and sycamores and natural stands of weeping willows surround the greens. Green fees are $70. > 1400 Parker La., Bluemont, tel. 888/283–4653, www.virginianational.com.

HORSEBACK RIDING

Kelly's Ford Equestrian Center Horseback riding and lessons for all levels of experience are offered here. You can ride through miles of scenic country trails and back roads. The adjoining clubhouse is designed with two viewing levels to observe events inside. The center is on the site of a Civil War battlefield; nearby is the Chester Phelps Wildlife Management area, which is abundant with wildlife and scenic trails. Canoeing, biking, and fishing are also available. To get here, take U.S. 29 South 15 mi, take a left on 674, and then drive 5½ mi to Edwards Shop Road. > 16589 Edwards Shop Rd., Remington, tel. 540/399–1800 or 540/399–1779, www.innatkellysford.com. Daily 9–5.

Marriott Ranch You can take guided scenic trail rides of 1½ hours at this beautiful cattle ranch in the foothills of the Blue Ridge Mountains. In 1951, hotelier J. Willard Marriott Sr. came upon this piece of property, which reminded him of his boyhood days on the family farm in Utah. With over 1,500 head of cattle, the working farm continues to serve as a respite to Marriott family, friends, and associates. The ranch is 45 mi west of the Beltway; take I-66 West to Exit 18 and drive west on Route 55. Turn left on Route 726 to the entrance on the left. > 5305 Marriott La., Hume, tel. 540/364–2627, 540/364–3741, or 877/278–4574, www.marriottranch.com. Trail rides Tues.–Sun. at 10, noon, and 2.

Save the Date

MAY

Hunt Country Stable Tour Trinity Episcopal Church has hosted this popular annual viewing of area horse stables since 1960. Proceeds from the self-driven auto tour support church programs. > Box 127, Upperville, tel. 540/592–3711, www.middleburgonline.com/stabletour.

Virginia Gold Cup Held since 1922, this granddaddy of all steeplechases is held the first Saturday in May. To get to the racetrack, follow I–66 West to the Gainesville exit, and then take U.S. Route 29 (Route 211) to Warrenton. > 5089 Old Tavern Rd., The Plains 20198-2552, tel. 540/253–5001, www.greatmeadow.org.

Virginia Wine Festival The Virginia Wine Growers Association holds its East Coast wine festival at Great Meadows. The festivities include the fruits of 45 Virginia wineries, food and wine tastings, seminars, arts and crafts, and live entertainment. > 5089 Old Tavern Rd., The Plains 20198-2552, tel. 800/520–9670, www.showsinc.com.

MAY–OCTOBER

Flying Circus Air Show The Sunday shows at the Flying Circus Airfield include feats of daring and skill, skydiving, and formations. You can even take a ride in an open-cockpit biplane. > U.S. Rte. 17 at Rte. 644, Bealeton, tel. 540/439–8661, www.flyingcircusairshow.com.

JUNE

Upperville Colt and Horse Show Founded in 1853, Upperville is the oldest horse show in the United States. This weeklong hunter-and-jumper show begins the first Monday of June, and involves over 2,000 horse-and-rider combinations, from young children on ponies to leading Olympic and World Cup riders and horses. The show grounds are on Route 50, 1 mi east of Upperville. > Rte. 50 (Box 317), The Plains 20198, tel. 540/592–3858 or 540/253–5760, www.upperville.com.

Vintage Virginia Tastings of 350 vintages from over 45 Virginia wineries make up this giant festival held at Great Meadows. Wine seminars, arts-and-crafts displays, musical entertainment, and children's events such as grape stomping are also part of the fun. > 5089 Old Tavern Rd., The Plains, tel. 800/277–2675, www.vintagevirginia.org.

Warrenton Pony Show This show, considered the oldest in America, includes the finest showing of ponies in classes for jumpers, hunters, and sidesaddle. There are also showings of broodmares, foals, and yearlings. > Warrenton Horse Show Grounds, Shirley Ave., U.S. Hwy. 29 Bus., Warrenton, tel. 540/253–5593, 540/347–9442, or 540/364–4345.

JUNE–SEPTEMBER

Great Meadows Polo Twilight Polo matches with two full teams of four players each are played at 7:30 on Friday night in Great Meadow Stadium. Sunday-afternoon matches are played with only three men per team. Like soccer, the object is to score as many goals as possible in six 7-minute periods, called chukkers. The match is very fast and exciting, and each player uses up to six horses during one match, which lasts one to two hours. > 5089 Old Tavern Rd., The Plains 20198-2552, tel. 540/253–5156 or 540/253–5001, www.greatmeadow.org.

AUGUST

Prince William County Fair This 10-day fair includes agricultural exhibits, a truck and tractor pull, drag racing, a midway, and live musical entertainment. It's the largest county fair in the state. > Prince William County Fairgrounds, Business Rte. 234, Manassas, tel. 703/368–0173, www.pwcfair.com.

SEPTEMBER

Warrenton Horse Show Founded in 1899, the Labor Day Warrenton Horse Show is one of the few major horse shows to use only one ring. Find a seat, stay put, and let the action unfold before you. > U.S. Business Hwy. 29, Warrenton, tel. 540/347–9442, www.warrentonhorseshow.com.

OCTOBER

International Gold Cup Races The seven steeplechases that make up this event are held at a time when autumn leaves are at their peak. Crisp air, country tweeds, and elegant surroundings attract an audience of 25,000. > 5089 Old Tavern Rd., The Plains, tel. 540/253–5001, www.greatmeadow.org.

Morven Park Races Steeplechases take place all day long at this annual event. Pony rides, children's games, and crafts are also on offer. > Tel. 703/777–2414.

Waterford Homes Tour and Crafts Exhibit Demonstrations of traditional crafts, tours of historic homes, military reenactments, art exhibits, and music, dance, and food are all part of this three-day event, the oldest juried crafts fair in the state. Many of the crafts are available for sale. > Rte. 662 (Clarkes Gap Rd.), Waterford, tel. 540/882–3018, www.waterfordva-wca.org.

NOVEMBER–DECEMBER

Christmas at Oatlands The special holiday events at the Oatlands mansion include living-history demonstrations on weekends. > Oatlands Plantation, 28050 Oatlands Plantation La., tel. 703/777–3174.

WHERE TO STAY

LEESBURG

Holiday Inn–Leesburg at Carradoc Hall This hotel sits on 5 landscaped acres, with a gazebo and duck pond. Rooms re-create the late 1700s through antique reproduction furnishings and paintings. The main building is next to Carradoc Hall, a 1773 colonial mansion. > 1500 E. Market St. (Rte. 7), 20175, tel. 703/771–9200, fax 703/771–1575. 126 rooms, 4 suites. Restaurant, bar, cable TV, pool, exercise equipment, laundry facilities, business services, airport shuttle. AE, D, DC, MC, V. $

Lansdowne Conference Resort This modern resort sits on 205 acres of hills and tall trees bordered by the Potomac River. Lansdowne specializes in outdoor activities and has miles of hiking and jogging trails. Polished wood furniture, carpets, handsome wall decorations, and marble-accented bathrooms help make the property elegant. The golf course was designed by Robert Trent Jones Jr. > 44050 Woodridge Pkwy., off Rte. 7, 22075, tel. 703/729–8400 or 800/541–4801, fax 703/729–4096, www.lansdowneresort.com. 291 rooms, 14 suites. Restaurant, 2 cafés, 18-hole golf course, tennis court, pool, indoor pool, gym, billiards, racquetball, volleyball, bar. AE, D, DC, MC, V. $$$–$$$$

Leesburg Colonial Inn An 1806 redbrick hotel, this B&B is in the heart of the downtown historic district. The rooms are furnished with antiques, early-American furniture, and hardwood floors. Some also have original working fireplaces and canopy or four-poster beds. The inn is close to excellent golf courses, abundant Civil War history, and dozens of antique shops, and is only an 18-minute drive from Dulles Airport. > 19 S. King St., 20175, tel. 703/777–5000 or 800/392–1332, fax 703/777–7000, www.leesburgcolonialinn.com. 10 rooms. Restaurant, picnic area, room service, some in-room hot tubs, cable TV, library, airport shuttle, some pets allowed. AE, D, DC, MC, V. BP. ¢–$

Little River The rooms and cottages in this 1820 inn are furnished with antiques; some of the lodgings have fireplaces. A path leads from the inn to the restored Aldie Mill, now a gallery where local artists show their work. Antiques shops and a bakery are also within walking distance. > 39307 John Mosby Hwy., Aldie 22001, tel. 703/327–6742, www.aldie.com. 9 rooms, 6 with bath; 3 cottages. Picnic area; no phones in some rooms, no kids under 10 (in cottages). AE, MC, V. BP. ¢–$

Norris House The parlor, library, and dining room in this 1760 inn are furnished with elegant period pieces and antiques. Guest rooms have canopy, brass, or feather beds, and some rooms overlook the lovely garden. > 108 Loudoun St. SW, 20175, tel. 703/777–1806 or 800/644–1806, fax 703/771–8051, www.norrishouse.com. 6 rooms without bath. Picnic area, business services, airport shuttle; no phones in some rooms, no kids (weekends), no smoking. AE, D, DC, MC, V. BP. $

Tarara Vineyard Bed & Breakfast This contemporary stone-and-glass house sits on a 475-acre vineyard on a bluff above the Potomac River. Oriental rugs blanket the granite floors in the living room, where there's also a stone fireplace, a baby grand, and a wet bar. You can play tennis, go hiking, wander through the apple and pear orchards, or go fishing in the lake. You get a complimentary bottle of wine and two etched glasses with your room. > 13648 Tarara La., 20176, tel. 703/771–7100, fax 703/771–8443, www.tarara.com. 3 rooms, 1 suite. Dining room, some microwaves, some refrigerators, tennis court, lake, hiking, fishing; no room TVs, no kids, no smoking. AE, D, MC, V. CP. $

MIDDLEBURG

Middleburg Country Inn This three-story structure, built in 1820 and enlarged in 1858, was the rectory of St. John's Parish Episcopal Church until 1907. Its medium-size rooms are furnished with antiques and period reproductions and have working fireplaces. When weather permits, you can eat your full country breakfast alfresco. > 209 E. Washington St., Box 2065, 22117, tel. 540/687–6082 or 800/262–6082, fax 540/687–5603, www.midcountryinn.com. 5 rooms, 3 suites. Hot tub. AE, D, MC, V. BP. $$

WARRENTON

Black Horse Inn This antebellum estate served as a hospital during the Civil War. The rooms are furnished with antiques and have fireplaces. Afternoon tea is served, and box lunches are available. > 8393 Meetze Rd., 20187, tel. 540/349–4020, fax 540/349–4242, www.blackhorseinn.com. 6 rooms, 2 suites. Some in-room hot tubs, business services; no smoking. AE, MC, V. BP. $–$$

1763 Inn Called the Greystone House when it was built in 1763, this country inn on 50 acres was the site of considerable fighting during the Civil War. The individually decorated guest rooms have fireplaces. > 10087 John Mosby Hwy. (U.S. 50), Upperville 20184, tel. 540/592–3848, fax 540/592–3208, www.1763inn.com. 14 rooms, 4 cabins. Restaurant, some in-room hot tubs, cable TV, tennis court, pool, pond, fishing. AE, D, DC, MC, V. BP. $–$$

WATERFORD

George's Mill Farm Bed and Breakfast This massive stone house, dating from the 1860s, is run by descendants of the original owners. The floors are pine, and some of the antiques have been here since the place was built. The 200-acre property lies between the Shenandoah and Potomac rivers, in the Short Hill Mountains. It's 10 mi north of Waterford off Route 287. > 11867 Georges Mill Rd., Lovettsville 20180, tel. 540/822–5224, www.georgesmill.com. 4 rooms. Pond, fishing, some pets allowed; no room phones, no smoking. No credit cards. BP. ¢–$

Milltown Farms Inn The common areas in this 1765 log-and-stone home tend toward colonial elegance, but the private rooms are more spare, with exposed log walls and four-poster beds. You'll find this B&B at the end of a dirt road in the middle of 300 acres of rolling countryside. Children are allowed to stay here with advance notice. > 14163 Milltown Rd., 20197, tel. 540/882–4470 or 888/747–3942. 5 rooms. Some pets allowed; no room phones, no room TVs, no smoking. AE, D, DC, MC, V. BP. $

Poor House Farm Bed and Breakfast This 1814 brick building is much more cheerful than when it really was a poorhouse. The rooms include four-poster beds and wicker furniture, and the front porch is a lovely place to gaze across the 13 acres of pastures. > 35304 Poor House La., Round Hill 20141, tel. 540/554–2511, fax 540/554–8512, www.poorhousefarm.com. 3 rooms, 1 cottage. Some kitchenettes, cable TV, pond, fishing; no smoking. AE, MC, V. BP. $–$$

CAMPING

Sky Meadows State Park The 1,862 acres that make up this park on the eastern side of the Blue Ridge Mountains have been developed into an equestrian staging and bridle trail area. Rich in history, the park has rolling pastures and woodlands and some great views. The park also has interpretive programs and a visitor center in the historic Mount Bleak House, and freshwater fishing in a 1-acre pond. Hike-in campsites are ¾ mi from the parking lot. Campers must arrive before dusk, when the park closes. Sky Meadows has more than 6 mi of challenging and scenic riding trails on two loop trails. From the park, there's access to the Appalachian Trail. The park is a three-day hike from Harper's Ferry, West Virginia, and two days from Shenandoah National Park. Sky Meadows is 7 mi north of I-66. Take Exit 23 on Route 17 North. The park entrance is on State Route 710. > 11012 Edmonds La., Delaplane 20144, tel. 540/592–3556 or 800/933–7275, fax 540/592–3617, www.dcr.state.va.us/parks/skymeado.htm. 12 hike-in primitive campsites; 1 group campsite for up to 36 people. Pit toilets, running water (nonpotable), fire grates, picnic tables (3 under shelter), snack bar. Reservations essential. MC, V. ¢

WHERE TO EAT

LEESBURG

Green Tree Once a wayside inn, the Green Tree retains much of its original flavor—with just a few changes for the better. The taproom, for example, is no longer for men only, and women don't have to take dinner alone upstairs. There's a walk-in fireplace large enough to roast a pig on a spit, and the dining room has long wooden tables, tall wicker chairs, wide-plank flooring, and tin ceilings. The dishes are prepared according to authentic 18th-century recipes, and seasonal drinks are made from original recipes researched in the National Archives. A strolling musician plays on weekends. > 15 S. King St., 20175, tel. 703/777–7246. AE, D, DC, MC, V. $$$–$$$$

Laurel Brigade Inn History lovers congregate at this inn, the site of lot No. 30 in the original Leesburg plan from 1759. The original log house served travelers between Winchester and Alexandria; it later became a tavern and then a private house. The Laurel Brigade was a famous Confederate Cavalry unit commanded by Elijah V. White of Leesburg. In 1945, the building was restored, and in 1949 it became a six-room B&B inn. It retains a quiet 18th-century aura, with authentic period furnishings, marble mantel tops from France, Swiss door fixtures, and a gazebo in the garden. Baked scallops, filet mignon, and crab imperial are specialties. Outside seating is available, and there's a breakfast served on Sunday. > 20 W. Market St., 20175, tel. 703/777–1010. AE, D, MC, V. Closed Mon. **$$–$$$$**

Lightfoot Restaurant This Romanesque-revival building from 1888 was the Peoples National Bank for more than 50 years. Restored to its original grandeur, the restaurant was named in honor of Francis Lightfoot Lee, a signer of the Declaration of Independence. The wine "cellar" is actually the bank's vault. The seasonal American cuisine, based on local ingredients, includes Blue Ridge spinach salad, a variation on oysters Rockefeller, lamb T-bones marinated in garlic, and many kinds of seafood. > 11 N. King St., tel. 703/771–2233, www.lightfootrestaurant.com. AE, D, DC, MC, V. **$$$–$$$$**

Tuscarora Mill Named after an Indian tribe, this bar, restaurant, and bakery is in an 1898 mill. The 25-foot ceilings in the main dining room reveal mill workings and statues of griffons, the insignia of the Mill. The wine list includes 320 wines, some of which are carted around on an old grain scale. Try the roasted rack of lamb or the Alaskan halibut, both rotating house specials, or choose the sesame roasted salmon. The sautéed medallions of lobster is a favorite appetizer. > 203 Harrison St., tel. 703/771–9300. AE, D, DC, MC, V. **$–$$$$**

MIDDLEBURG

Black Coffee Bistro Comfort food with a contemporary twist highlights the menu at this small, family-run restaurant in a 1790s colonial house. The several small dining rooms have light blond-wood furnishings with large windows and lots of natural light. Toward the rear of the house is a cozy little room with sofas and a fireplace, the waiting area for a table on a busy night. The frequently changing menu reflects seasonal local products as well as herbs and flowers from the chef's garden next to the house. During the summer, the menu includes ginger-lime pork with pickled vegetables, and pan-seared breast of duck. Other seasons, you might find main dishes including a ragout of littleneck clams and mussels, grilled skirt steak with roasted corn, tenderloin, or grilled trout with asparagus. Desserts are house-made, and in summer include warm, fresh peach pie. > 101 S. Madison St., tel. 540/687–3632. Reservations essential. AE, MC, V. **$–$$$**

Coach Stop Restaurant Open since 1958 for breakfast, lunch, and dinner, this friendly restaurant is casual and comfortable. The Coach Stop is known for its homemade breakfast sausage, onion rings, soft-shell crabs and crab cakes, prime rib, roast turkey with stuffing, tender liver smothered with bacon and onions, and steaks. > 9 E. Washington St., tel. 540/687–5515, www.coachstop.com. AE, D, DC, MC, V. **$–$$**

Red Fox Inn George Washington once ate at this former tavern, built in 1728. There are two main dining rooms and a large terrace upstairs. The menu includes beef barbecue, filet mignon with blue cheese–walnut butter, and pork chops with fried apples. For dessert, there's rich bread pudding with a bourbon sauce. > 2 E. Washington St., tel. 540/478–1808. Reservations essential. AE, D, DC, MC, V. **$$–$$$**

WARRENTON

Depot Restaurant An architecturally intriguing late-19th-century train depot that was reconstructed indoors, the Depot contains a wealth of local history along with an excellent sampling of Mediterranean and American dishes. A chalkboard menu lists seasonal entrées and desserts. The Middle Eastern eggplant and main dish salads are standouts. The "Paris" room has a fireplace and 14 French doors, and there is seating in the garden. > 65 3rd St. S, 20186, tel. 540/347–1212. Reservations essential. MC, V. Closed Mon. $–$$

Fantastico Ristorante Italiano Inside a 14-room stone inn with a copper steeple and weather vane is this white-tablecloth restaurant with wooden beams and stucco walls. Seasonally you can dine in the garden. Fantastico is known for its fine northern Italian cuisine and menu of over 50 items, which includes homemade pastas, veal scallopini, osso buco, trout with almonds, salmon, and calamari. > 280 Broad View Ave., tel. 540/349–2575, fax 540/341–4658, www.fantastico-inn.com. AE, D, DC, MC, V. Closed Sun. No lunch Sat. $–$$$

Napoleon's A lovely 19th-century house is now a restaurant with two seating areas and flower gardens. There's a formal, romantic terrace upstairs where you can dine alfresco and a casual café downstairs. Specialties include dishes that employ fresh fish, Black Angus beef, and veal. There's a children's menu, and brunch is served on Sunday. The menu changes at least twice a year to take advantage of seasonal produce, meats, and seafoods, and the restaurant is known for its daily specials along with Wellington's mixed grill, venison steak, Virginia brook trout with lump crabmeat, and Fruits de Mer Provençal. > 67 Waterloo St., tel. 540/347–1200, fax 540/347–1661, www.napoleonsrestaurant.com. D, MC, V. $$$–$$$$

ESSENTIALS

Getting Here

Virginia's hunt country is rural, so a car is a must for seeing the sights. A bus goes to Leesburg, but you won't be able to head to any places outside the city.

BY CAR

From Washington, D.C., I–66 is the fastest route to Middleburg and Warrenton—except during high traffic times. The trip can take as little as an hour. The alternate route west is U.S. Highway 50. However, it has numerous stoplights until you get about 30 mi outside metropolitan Washington.

To get to Leesburg from U.S. Highway 50, go north on U.S. Route 15 at Gilbert's Corner. A faster route to Leesburg from the I–495 Capital Beltway is the limited-access Dulles Toll Road, connecting to the Greenway Toll Road at Dulles Airport. A slower, shorter, but free and more attractive road to Leesburg is State Route 7.

Once you are in Loudoun or Fauquier county, there are many routes that undulate past tidy, expansive horse farms. Many are close to Exits 31 and 28 off I–66. From Exit 31, drive State Route 626 between The Plains and Middleburg. You can also drive west on State Route 55 at The Plains and turn right on State Route 709 toward Middleburg. From Exit 28, drive north through Marshall on State Route 710 (Rectortown Road) and turn right on State Route 713, which will dead-end at U.S. Route 50 near Middleburg.

A scenic loop near Leesburg is off of U.S. Route 7 about 3 mi past the city center. At Clark's Gap, turn right on State Route 662 to Waterford and drive past Taylorstown until the road ends at U.S. Route 15. If leaving the area, you can cross the Potomac into Maryland via the Point of Rocks Bridge. Return to Leesburg by taking U.S. Route 15.

Parking at every site in this chapter is free.

Visitor Information

Most visitor centers are open 9–5 daily.

CONTACTS **Loudoun Tourism Council** > 108D South St. SE, Leesburg 22075, tel. 703/771–2617 or 800/752–6118, www.visitloudoun.org. **Warrenton–Fauquier County Visitors Center** > 183A Keith St., Warrenton 20186, tel. 540/347–4414, www.fauquierchamber.org. Daily 9–5. **Waterford Foundation** > Main and 2nd Sts., tel. 540/882–3018, www.waterfordva.org.

Potomac Highlands

10

Updated by CiCi Williamson

THE RIVER THAT GAINED ITS FAME by flowing past Mount Vernon and the nation's capital originates high in the mountains of West Virginia. The mighty Potomac officially begins at the Fairfax Stone, which once marked the western boundary of the land granted Lord Fairfax by the King of England. At this point, now inside a state park near Davis, the river is called the North Branch Potomac. It soon joins the South Branch, the Cacapon, and the beautiful Shenandoah before heading toward Washington and the Chesapeake Bay, 350 mi away.

En route, the Potomac crosses a mountainous landscape of imposing ridges, caves, and towering rock cliffs known as the Potomac Highlands. Dominated by the craggy peaks of the Allegheny Mountains, part of the Appalachian chain, the Potomac Highlands run north to south along the spine of the mountains. Ski resorts, hiking trails, caves, and rivers dot the region, which is dominated by the 900,000-acre Monongahela National Forest, with everything from skiing to spelunking, trout fishing to rock climbing. Spruce Knob, at 4,861 feet the highest point in West Virginia, is here.

As you might expect in a place called the "Mountaineer State," West Virginia has some of the nation's most beautiful scenery. If you're interested in camping, keep in mind that all of its 50 state forests and parks have campsites, and many have cabins. Area rivers are renowned for their roiling white-water rapids, and dozens of outfitters guide boatloads of people down these raging rivers each year. The Canaan Valley and Snowshoe/Silver Creek Mountain Resort are popular winter destinations for downhill and cross-country skiers and snowboarders. Rock climbers scale the vertical faces of the Spruce Knob–Seneca Rocks National Recreation Area, and lakes throughout the state draw boaters and anglers.

Only a few small towns are scattered among the forested mountains and river valleys. The oldest is Petersburg, settled by German colonists in 1745; it was named for Jacob Peterson, who opened its first store. Because of its location on the South Branch of the Potomac River, the town served as a Union outpost during the Civil War. Today, Petersburg is a convenient gateway to the Monongahela National Forest, Spruce Knob, and Petersburg Gap. The town of Davis, at the northern end of the Monongahela National Forest, is the product of a lumber boom. The town of 800 is a popular stopover for skiers, mountain bikers, and white-water rafters.

Marlinton is known as "the birthplace of rivers" because eight major waterways—the Cheat, Cranberry, Elk, Greenbrier, Shaver's Fork, Williams, Tygart, and Gauley—all begin there. The first settlers were Stephen Sewell and Jacob Marlin, the town's namesake. The two men came here in 1749 and built themselves a log cabin, thus establishing the first English settlement west of the Alleghenies. One night they had a serious quarrel, apparently over a religious question, and Sewell stormed out of the cabin and took up temporary residence in a hollow tree that stood until 1930 near the railroad station. The area's biggest draw now are its wonderful scenic railroads.

Moorefield, with a population of 2,148, is listed on the National Register of Historic Places. It was established in 1777 and named after Conrad Moore, who owned the land on which the town was laid out. Its historic district includes a tavern, theater, museum, and doctor's home.

It's no area for theme parks, grand opera, or 300-store shopping malls, but if you're in search of spectacular scenery and a great selection of things to do outside, the Highlands are a great escape from urban living.

WHAT TO SEE & DO

DAVIS

Blackwater Falls State Park Three miles southwest of Davis off Route 32, this densely wooded park is crowned by Blackwater Falls, a 50-foot-high waterfall on the Blackwater River. Tannic acid, dissolved from evergreen needles, accounts for the tea-color water. Bikes are available for rent here, and there are 10 mi of hiking trails. The park includes a 55-room lodge at the canyon rim, 26 cabins, and a 65-site campground. > County Rte. 29, tel. 304/259–5216 or 800/225–5982, www.blackwaterfalls.com. Free. Daily.

Canaan Valley National Wildlife Refuge Sitting 3,200 feet above sea level, the Canaan is the highest valley of its size east of the Rockies. There is a rich and unusual diversity in this wetland valley, where high altitude and a cold, humid climate have produced 40 types of ecological communities. The refuge supports 580 plant and 280 animal species, including the endangered Cheat Mountain salamander and the Virginia northern flying squirrel. The U.S. Fish and Wildlife Service purchased the land and established this refuge in 1994. > HC 70, Box 200, tel. 304/866–3858, northeast.fws.gov/wv/can_cd.htm.

Fairfax Stone State Park This 4-acre day-use area preserves the Fairfax Stone, a colonial property marker placed in 1746 at the headspring of the North Branch of the Potomac River. Originally the stone marked the western edge of the 6-million-acre tract of land between the Rappahannock and Potomac rivers that was given to Thomas, Lord Fairfax. No facilities are available here. > U.S. 219, north of Thomas, tel. 304/259–5216, www.wvparks.com/fairfaxstone.

MARLINTON

Cass Scenic Railroad State Park This state park encompasses an authentic turn-of-the-20th-century lumber-company town and allows you the chance to ride up to the second-highest peak in West Virginia in open railcars once used to haul logs off the mountain. Trains are drawn by geared Shay steam locomotives, built to negotiate steep terrain. Trips from 1½ hours up to 7 hours are available. > Off Rte. 92, on Rte. 66, Main St., Cass, tel. 304/456–4300, www.cassrailroad.com. Train trips $13–$45. Mid-May–Oct., daily; after Labor Day, weekends only; fall schedule varies.

Cranberry Glades Botanical Area The largest bogs in West Virginia encompass 750 acres and include plant and animal species that are common to the tundra but rare in Appalachia. A ½-mi boardwalk winds through parts of 35,600 acres. Bogs—acidic, spongy peat wetlands more common up north and in Canada—provide habitat for some unusual plants, including carnivorous ones. > Rte. 150, on Rtes. 39 and 55, 14 mi west of Marlinton, tel. 304/653–4826 or 304/846–2695, www.fs.fed.us/r9/mnf/sp/cranberry_glades.html. Free. Apr.–Nov., daily 9–5.

Durbin & Greenbrier Valley Railroad This 100-mi scenic train company travels through the most remote mountain country in the eastern United States. Three trains, one a steam engine built in 1910, can take you on various routes along the Greenbrier and Tygart rivers and through the Cheat Mountain wilderness. Trips last from two hours to all day. > Box 44, Durbin, tel. 304/686–7245 or 877/686–7245, www.mountainrail.com. $12–$34. Mid-May–Oct., Wed.–Sun.; mid-Apr.–mid-May and Nov., weekends only.

Greenbrier River Trail Once part of the Chesapeake & Ohio Railroad, this 76-mi trail is a place for hiking, biking, horseback riding, and cross-country skiing trail. Running from North Caldwell to 1 mi south of Cass Scenic Railroad State Park, the abandoned grade passes over 35 bridges and through two tunnels. There are a dozen cabins along the trail. Motorized vehicles are not permitted. > County Rd. 21 (Beaver Creek Rd.), off Rte. 9, tel. 304/799–4087, www.greenbrierrivertrail.com. Free. Daily.

National Radio Astronomy Observatory Jutting from the landscape 25 mi north of Marlinton proper, huge radio telescopes listen for life in outer space. The Robert C. Byrd Green Bank Telescope, completed in 1998, is the world's largest fully steerable single-aperture antenna. In addition to the GBT, several other telescopes are in service at the same site. > Rtes. 28 and 92, Green Bank 24944, tel. 304/456–2209, www.gb.nrao.edu. Free. Daily 9–4; tours by appointment on the hr.

Seneca State Forest The 11,684-acre state forest, bordering the Greenbrier River, is West Virginia's oldest. It has rental cabins, 23 mi of hiking trails, 40 mi or trails and roads for biking, and a small fishing lake. You can also swim or go tubing in the Greenbrier. > Rte. 28, 4 mi south of Dunmore, tel. 304/799–6213, www.senecastateforest.com. Free. Daily.

MOOREFIELD

Lost River State Park and Stables Part of this 3,712-acre park remains virgin forest. It was once owned by the illustrious Lee family of Virginia, who used it as a summer retreat in the early 1800s: a cabin from that era has been restored as a museum. You can come here to swim, fish, hike, and ride horses. Among the abundant wildlife are deer, raccoon, opossum, groundhogs, red and gray squirrels, numerous songbirds, wild turkey, and grouse. Standard log and year-round modern cabins are available for overnight or extended visits. A restaurant, swimming pool, nature and recreation program, and many other facilities are available in summer season. > Rte. 2, Box 24 (4 mi west of Rte. 259, on Rte. 12), Mathias, tel. 304/897–5372 or 800/225–5982, www.wvparks.com/lostriver. Free. Daily 6 AM–10 PM.

McCoy-McMechen Theatre Museum Eunice McCoy built this theater in 1928 and showed plays and movies there until her death in the 1980s, when she left most of her estate to the community to renovate the theater. Today, two museum rooms display items from her estate, and the 248-seat theater resembles its appearance in the Roaring '20s. Theatrical and musical groups perform here throughout the year. > 111 N. Main St., tel. 304/538–6560. $10. Tours by appointment only.

Nan & Pap's Flea Market This small, family-run flea market is a palace of second-hand goods, antiques, and other items. > 59 Jenkins Run Rd., tel. 304/538–6505. Closed Sun.

Old Stone Tavern The first section of this, the oldest home in town, was built in 1788, and two more sections were built in the mid-19th century and at the turn of the 20th century. Dark woodwork and leaded-glass bay windows accent the most recent section of the house. On the National Register of Historic Places, the home is occupied and only open to the public during Heritage Weekend. > 117 S. Main St., 26836, tel. 304/636–8400. Free. Private residence; open to public last weekend in Sept.

PETERSBURG

Monongahela National Forest Covering 909,000 acres in the heart of the Allegheny Mountains, the Monongahela includes the state's tallest mountain (Spruce Knob, at 4,861 feet), rock formations (Seneca Rocks), five wilderness areas, and hiking trails (including 124 mi of the Appalachian Trail). Here you can go hunting, fishing, rock climbing, spelunking, skiing, boating, swimming, camping, and more. Northern and southern plant zones overlap here, resulting in an abundance of tree, plant, and flower species; bear, deer, and wild turkey roam the woodlands. The main park headquarters is east of Elkins on U.S. 33. > 200 Sycamore St., Elkins 26241, tel. 304/636–1800, www.fs.fed.us/r9/mnf. Free. Daily.

Old Mill Listed on the National Register of Historic Places, this working gristmill still grinds corn, wheat, buckwheat, and rye. There is also a museum and an outlet for local craftspeople. The mill is 34 mi west of Petersburg off U.S. 33. > Rte. 32 N, Harman 26270, tel. 304/227–4598. Donations accepted. Memorial Day–Labor Day, daily 10–5.

Petersburg Gap On U.S. 220 and Route 55, Petersburg Gap rises to 800 feet, creating the Pictured Rocks, where figures of a fox and an ox, or buffalo, appear to have been carved into the cliffs. The trout fishing and canoeing between the tall rock walls draw people from all over the East Coast. > Tel. 304/636–8400. Free. Daily.

Seneca Caverns Spectacular stalactite and stalagmite formations adorn this 165-foot-deep cave, the state's largest. Seneca Indians took refuge from winter storms here, and legend has it that Princess Snow Bird married a young brave in the Grand Ballroom, a subterranean chamber 60 feet long, 30 feet wide, and 70 feet high. Guided tours are available. The site is about 30 mi southwest of Petersburg via Routes 28 and 55 near Riverton. > On Rte. 9, tel. 304/567–2691, www.senecacaverns.com. $8. June–Aug., daily 9–6:45; Sept.–Oct and Apr.-May, daily 10–4:45; Nov.–Mar., daily 10–4.

Smoke Hole Caverns Reportedly used by native tribes to smoke meat and by early white settlers to make moonshine, the caverns have several unusual rock formations, including one of the world's longest ribbon stalactites. > Rtes. 25 N and 55 E, tel. 304/257–4442, www.smokehole.com. $7.50. Daily 9–5.

Spruce Knob–Seneca Rocks National Recreation Area These 100,000 acres of the Monongahela National Forest, with rock climbing and mountain views, were designated in 1965 as the first National Recreation Area. > Junction of Hwys. 28 and 33, Seneca Rocks 26884, tel. 304/567–2827. Free. Park daily; visitor center Apr.–Oct., daily 9–5:30; Nov.–Mar., weekends 9–4:30.

Sports

FISHING

Most of West Virginia's trout streams are in the Potomac Highlands, and dozens of waterways dear to anglers originate here. Five fish hatcheries keep local streams stocked with bass, trout, and other game fish. Temporary and yearlong West Virginia fishing and hunting licenses are available at most local sporting goods stores. The U.S. Forest Service requires that stamps for hunting and fishing be purchased before doing either activity within national forest boundaries.

Buckhorn Trout Farm There's no license required for fishing for rainbow trout in one of this farm's three spring-fed ponds. You pay only for the fish you catch. > Rte. 3, Box 2, Fort Seybert, tel. 304/249–5253.

EQUIPMENT & TOURS **D and A Outfitters LLC** > 406 9th St., Belle, tel. 304/949–3339, www.dandaoutfitters.com. **Eagle's Nest Outfitters** > Rte. 220, Box 731, Petersburg, tel.

304/257–2393, www.wvweb.com/eaglesnest. **Smoke Hole Outfitters** > Rte. 28, Seneca Rocks, tel. 304/257–4442, 304/257–1705, or 800/828–8478, www.smokehole.com.

MOUNTAIN BIKING

Highland Scene Tours This group of guides specializes in adventure trips that include flat-water kayaking as well as mountain biking in the Canaan Valley area. > HC 70, Box 291, Davis 26260, tel. 304/866–4455 or 877/223–5388, www.highlandscenetours.com. *EQUIPMENT* **Blackwater Bikes** > Rte. 32, Box 190, Davis, tel. 304/159–5286, www.blackwaterbikes.com. **Fat Tire Cycle** > Rte. 20 S, Box 550, Buckhannon, tel. 304/472–5882, www.fattirecycle.com.

SKIING

There's terrific skiing in the Potomac Highlands. Downhill and cross-country skiing are available at several resorts near Davis, including Canaan Valley, Timberline Four Seasons Resort, and White Grass Ski Touring Center.

Canaan Valley Thirty-four slopes and a vertical drop of 850 feet make the Canaan Valley a popular winter destination. Snowboarding, snow tubing, night skiing, ice-skating, and 18 mi of cross-country ski trails are all available here. The resort is 10 mi south of Davis. > Rte. 32, Davis 26260, tel. 304/866–4121 or 800/622–4121, www.canaanresort.com. Lift tickets $43. Dec.–Mar.

Snowshoe/Silver Creek Mountain Resort Fifty-three slopes and trails make this the state's largest developed skiing and snowboarding operation. It has 125 mountain bike trails, a golf course, tennis courts, and swimming for year-round recreation. > 10 Snowshoe Dr., Rte. 66, Snowshoe, tel. 304/572–1000 or 304/572–4636, www.snowshoemtn.com. Lift tickets $29–$57. Daily.

Timberline Four Seasons Resort One of the longest ski trails south of New England, the 2-mi Salamander Run is one the highlights of this 55-acre resort, which has 35 slopes, a 1,000-foot vertical drop, and 150 inches of snow per year. Ten miles south of Davis, the resort also has snowboarding, night skiing, and cross-country trails. > 488 Timberline Rd., Davis 26260, tel. 304/866–4801 or 800/766–9464, www.timberlineresort.com. $39 (day only). Dec.–Mar.

White Grass Ski Touring Center There are 30 mi worth of cross-country skiing on the 45 trails here, as well as telemark glades and snowshoeing. The ski area is 8 mi south of Davis, off Route 32 South. > Freeland Run Rd., Davis 26260, tel. 304/866–4114, www.whitegrass.com. $15. Dec.–Mar. *EQUIPMENT & TOURS* **Elk River Touring Center** > U.S. 219, Slatyfork 26291, tel. 304/572–3771, www.ertc.com. **Ski Barn** > U.S. 219 and Snowshoe Rd., Slatyfork, tel. 304/572–1234, www.skibarn.net.

WHITE-WATER RAFTING

The same rivers that are good for fishing in their calmer stretches are often also good for white-water rafting in wilder sections. Both the north and south branches of the Potomac wind through the region, passing through some beautiful country on their way. The Greenbrier, the longest free-flowing river in the East, runs southward through more spectacular scenery. Some of the companies listed are in counties near the Potomac Highlands, but they all tours in the area. For those not familiar with West Virginia's stretches of white water, rafting with a guide is wise. *EQUIPMENT & TOURS* **ACE Adventure Center** > Box 1168, Oak Hill, WV 25901, tel. 304/469–2651 or 888/223–7238, www.aceraft.com. **Blackwater Outdoor Adventures** > Rte. 1, St. George, WV 26290, tel. 304/478–3775 or 800/225–5982, www.raftboc.com. Wed.–Sat. 10–5. **Drift-A-Bit Whitewater Rafting** > Box 885, Fayetteville, WV 25840, tel. 304/574–3282 or 800/633–7238, www.driftabit.com. **North**

American River Runners, Inc. > U.S. Rte. 60 W, Box 81, Hico, WV 25854, tel. 304/658–5276 or 800/950–2585, www.narr.com. **River Riders** > R. R. 5, Box 1260, Harpers Ferry, WV 25425, tel. 304/535–2663 or 800/326–7238, www.riverriders.com. **River & Trail Outfitters** > 604 Valley Rd., Knoxville, MD 21758, tel. 301/695–5177 or 888/446–7529, www.rivertrail.com.

Save the Date

MARCH

Governor's Cup Ski Race Watch top skiers compete in what is the oldest ski race in the South. The two-day downhill event, held in early March, takes place 10 mi south of Davis. > Timberline Four Seasons Resort, 488 Timberline Rd., Davis, tel. 800/782–2775, www.timberlineresort.com.

APRIL

Spring Mountain Festival Trout fishing contests, a catch and fry, a trout supper, local music, gospel singing, cloggers, wine tasting, antique cars, a 10K run, a parade, turkey calling, and owl-hooting contests are among the many events at this country extravaganza. > Petersburg, tel. 304/257–2722, www.gowv.com/special_events.htm.

JULY

West Virginia Poultry Convention and Festival Watch a reenactment of the Civil War or hunker down with some barbecued chicken at this summer festival. Events take place throughout the community the third week of the month. > Moorefield, tel. 304/538–2725.

SEPTEMBER

Autumn Harvest Festival and Roadkill Cook-Off The major ingredients for this cooking contest must be animals prone to becoming roadkill. Music and arts and crafts are also part of the event. > Marlinton, tel. 800/336–7009.

Hardy County Heritage and Harvest Weekend Held the last weekend of the month, this annual event is a chance to tour historic buildings that are often closed the rest of the year. The weekend festival also includes walking tours, a parade, a Civil War encampment, and an antique auto show. > Moorefield, tel. 304/538–6560 or 304/538–8080.

WHERE TO STAY

DAVIS

Blackwater Lodge Made of stone and wood, this lodge is in Blackwater Falls State Park, 3 mi southwest of Davis off Route 32. It's on a pine-studded rim of Blackwater Canyon; rooms in the front of the hotel overlook the canyon. > County Rte. 29, 26260, tel. 304/259–5216, fax 304/259–5881, www.blackwaterfalls.com. 54 rooms, 26 cabins. Dining room, picnic area, some kitchenettes, cable TV, indoor pool, lake, gym, hot tub, fishing, cross-country skiing, playground, shops, laundry facilities, business services, meeting rooms, no-smoking rooms. AE, DC, MC, V. ¢

Canaan Valley Resort and Conference Center This state-run recreational resort is in a 6,000-acre wooded area in the Allegheny Mountains; golfing, skiing, and hiking are all within 2 mi of the lodge. Rooms are in the lodge and in cabins and cottages tucked away in the forest. Guest rooms have traditional furniture and quilted bed-spreads. Cabins, available with two to four bedrooms, are completely furnished with kitchens, fireplaces, and baseboard heating. The deluxe four-bedroom cottages have TVs, phones, microwave ovens, and dishwashers. The inn is 10 mi south of Davis.

> Rte. 32, 26260, tel. 304/866–4121 or 800/622–4121, fax 304/866–2172, www.canaanresort.com. 250 rooms, 23 cabins, 4 cottages. Dining room, picnic area, some refrigerators, cable TV, driving range, 18-hole golf course, miniature golf, putting green, tennis courts, 2 pools (1 indoor), exercise equipment, hot tub, bicycles, cross-country skiing, downhill skiing, children's programs (ages 5–12), playground, laundry facilities, business services, meeting rooms. AE, D, DC, MC, V. ¢–$

MARLINTON

Marlinton Motor Inn This property, composed of two brick buildings in a rural area just outside Marlinton, is in the Allegheny Mountains, and surrounded by fields and woods. There are restaurants ½ mi away. > Rte. 219, North Marlinton 24954, tel. 304/799–4711 or 800/354–0821. 70 rooms. Restaurant, room service, pool, bar, some pets allowed. AE, D, DC, MC, V. ¢

River Place Built in 1994, this hotel is on the edge of town on the banks of the scenic Greenbrier River. The wraparound deck overlooks the river. In addition to the five large guest rooms, there is a three-bedroom cottage with a full kitchen available for use. Rooms have contemporary furnishings. The River Place restaurant offers daily specials and homemade desserts. > 814 1st Ave., 24954, tel. 304/799–7233, fax 304/799–4465, www.neumedia.net/~melriver. 8 rooms. Restaurant, cable TV; no pets. AE, MC, V. $

PETERSBURG

Hermitage Motor Inn There's a crafts shop and bookstore in this 1840s inn, which melds Victorian furnishings with modern facilities. The inn is in a commercial area, surrounded by several popular chain restaurants and stores. > 203 Virginia Ave., 26847, tel. 304/257–1711 or 800/437–6482, fax 304/257–4330, www.ohwy.com/wv/h/hermpete.htm. 38 rooms. Restaurant, in-room data ports, cable TV, pool, hot tub, business services. AE, D, DC, MC, V. ¢

Homestead Inn Motel On the edge of the city limits, this two-story brick motel has a small cattle and sheep farm out back; check out the arts-and-crafts gift shop for a souvenir. All rooms are accessible from outdoors, and each one has its own wall-length hand-painted mural. The inn is approximately 1 mi west of Petersburg and 20 mi east of Seneca Rocks. > Rtes. 55 and 28, 26847, tel. 304/257–1049. 12 rooms. Refrigerators, cable TV. AE, D, DC, MC, V. CP. ¢

North Fork Mountain Inn A rustic log inn nestled on a hilltop 15 mi west of Petersburg, the North Fork and its adjoining cottage are in the mountains, with scenic wilderness views. > Off Rte. 55, Box 114, 26201, tel. 304/257–1108. 6 rooms, 1 cottage. Some in-room hot tubs; no room phones. MC, V. CP. ¢–$

Smoke Hole Caverns Motel Next to Smoke Hole Caverns, just outside Petersburg, the motel and cabins are made of logs, and the beautiful wood finish is visible from both inside and out. Some rooms have fireplaces and hot tubs. > Rtes. 28 N and 55 E, HC 59, Seneca Rocks 26884, tel. 304/257–4442 or 800/828–8478, fax 304/257–2745. 13 rooms, 25 cabins, 18 log cabins. Some refrigerators, some in-room hot tubs, cable TV, pool, playground. AE, D, MC, V. ¢

Smoke Hole Lodge Bed & Breakfast The hotel is in a remote 1,500-acre area in West Virginia's famed Smoke Hole Gorge. Each of the guest rooms is unique, though all have a rustic country appeal, with antiques, handmade quilts, and some four-poster beds. > Rte. 28 S, 26847, tel. 304/242–8377 or 304/257–1539. 7 rooms. Cable TV, some pets allowed. No credit cards. CP. $–$$

CAMPING

Big Ridge Campgrounds One of the closest campgrounds to Virginia, Big Ridge is northwest of New Market near Lost River State Park. > HC 67, Box 78, Mathias 26812, tel. 304/897–6404. 50 campsites, 15 with partial hookups. Portable toilets, partial hookups (electric and water), dump station, showers. AE, D, DC, MC, V. Mid-May–early Oct. ¢

Blackwater Falls State Park These completely furnished cabins are in an attractive wooded area. They have wood-paneled walls, stone fireplaces, forced-air furnaces, and a bathroom with shower. Pets are not permitted in cabins but are allowed in the 65 campsites. The park is 3 mi southwest of Davis. > County Rte. 29 (Drawer 490), Davis 26260, tel. 304/259–5216 or 800/225–5982, www.blackwaterfalls.com. 25 cabins, 65 campsites, 32 with with partial hookups. Portable toilets, partial hookups (electric and water), dump station, showers, laundry facilities, play area. AE, D, DC, MC, V. Cabins yr-round; campsites late Apr.–Oct. ¢–$

Cheat River Campground Surrounded by the Monongahela National Forest, this is a great place to fish, swim, explore, or hike the many trails. In addition to campsites, there's a two-bedroom cabin with a sleeping loft and stone fireplace. The cabin has satellite TV, a hot tub, and a deck. The campground is on the Shavers Fork of the Cheat River a few miles from stores in Elkins. > 172 High St., Faulkner Rd., Bowden 26254, tel. 304/636–3624, www.cheatrivercamp.com. 30 campsites, 1 cabin. Flush toilets, pit toilets, full hookups, dump station, drinking water (Apr.–Oct.), showers, grills, picnic tables, electricity, swimming (river). AE, D, DC, MC, V. ¢

Kumbrabow State Forest Campsites, five cabins, and a three-bedroom cottage are near a fishing stream. Lodgings here have stone fireplaces, stoves, gaslights, and refrigerators but no running water. The cottage has gas heat. Kumbrabow is 24 mi south of Elkins and 7 mi south of Huttonsville. > Rtes. 219 and 16, Box 65, Huttonsville 26273, tel. 304/335–2219 or 800/225–5983, www.kumbrabow.com. 13 tent or RV sites, 1 cottage, 6 cabins. Flush toilets, pit toilets, partial hookups (electric and water), dump station, drinking water, laundry facilities, showers, refrigerators, stoves, grills, picnic tables, electricity. MC, V. Mid-Mar.–mid-Dec. $

Revelle's Family Campground This extensive property has 2 mi of riverfront campsites, cabins and cottages. The cottages and the 24-foot Pacific yurt (dome structure) each sleep six and have Franklin stoves, wraparound porches, hot tubs, showers, and fully equipped kitchens. Revelle's is on the banks of Shavers Fork of the Cheat River, 9 mi east of Elkins. > Faulkner Rd., Box 96, Bowden 26254, tel. 304/636–0023 or 877/988–2267, fax 304/636–0316, www.revelles.com. 4 cabins, 4 cottages, 1 yurt, 300 campsites. Flush toilets, partial hookups (electric and water), dump station, drinking water, laundry facilities, showers, grills, picnic tables, electricity, public telephone, general store, swimming (river), tubing, horseback riding. Reservations accepted. MC, V. ¢–$

Seneca State Forest Named after the tribe that once roamed the area, this forest has cabins with fireplaces, gaslights, wood-burning cookstoves, and gas refrigerator-freezers but no running water or electricity. They do come with linens, utensils, cleaning supplies, firewood, kindling, and matches. > Rte. 1, Box 140, Dunmore 24934, tel. 304/799–6213 or 800/225–5983, www.senecastateforest.com. 8 cabins, 10 campsites. Portable toilets, drinking water, laundry facilities, showers, fire grates, grills, picnic tables, electricity, public telephone, swimming (river/lake). MC, V. Apr.–Dec. ¢–$

Watoga State Park A sprawling wooded area laced with hiking and horseback-riding trails, the park has two campgrounds. Beaver Creek Campground is 8 mi south of Huntersville, near the park's north entrance. Riverside Campground, along the Greenbrier River, is near the western entrance of the park. > Rte. 27, 10 mi east of Hillsboro off Rte. 219, Marlinton 24954, tel. 304/799–4087, www.watoga.com. 31 partial hookups, 88 tent sites, 34 cabins (10 open yr-round). Flush toilets, partial hookups (electric), drinking water, laundry facilities, showers, grills, picnic tables, electricity, public telephone, swimming (lake). Reservations taken for some sites in summer. MC, V. $

WHERE TO EAT

ELKINS
Cheat River Lodge and Inn Audubon-inspired bird prints adorn this rustic inn, known for its fresh rainbow trout and farm-raised fish entrées. Outdoor deck seating overlooks the Cheat River. > Rte. 1, Box 115, 26241, tel. 304/636–6265. MC, V. Closed Mon. No lunch. $–$$$

MARLINTON
River Place This family-owned and -operated eater serves daily specials that include rainbow trout served with potatoes, salad, and dinner rolls. The dining room displays local artwork, honey and syrup containers, weavings, candles, and other handcrafted gifts. You can eat at the Amish oak tables, or sit outside on a deck overlooking the Greenbrier River. The desserts are very homey. > 814 1st Ave., 24954, tel. 304/799–7233, fax 304/799–4465. AE, MC, V. ¢–$$

MOOREFIELD
Colts Restaurant & Pizza Park Eatery The draw here is the country cooking—from grilled steaks and pizzas to homemade cobblers, apple dumplings, and pies. The eclectic dining room, covered in flowered wallpaper and hung with mounted deer heads and paintings by the owner's daughter, draws locals as well as tourists. It's just outside of Moorefield. > 425 S. Main St., 26836, tel. 304/538–2523. No credit cards. ¢–$$

PETERSBURG
Foxes Pizza Den Serving pizza, sandwiches, and salads, this is one of the town's oldest eateries. The house special is the Chester chicken, breaded and served with potatoes and vegetables. A huge painting of a fox is the only indication of this restaurant's namesake. > 508 Keyser Ave., tel. 304/257–4342. No credit cards. $
Sites Restaurant Established in 1915, the eatery serves everything from grilled cheese sandwiches to T-bone steaks; the peanut-butter pie is a popular dessert. A portrait of "Granddaddy" Dennis Sites, the restaurant's founder, peers over the cash register. > 35 S. Main St. 26847, tel. 304/257–1088. No credit cards. ¢–$

ESSENTIALS

Getting Here
A mountainous nature area, the Potomac Highlands are not served by any regular bus or train passenger service. The best way to visit is by car.
BY CAR
Leaving from Washington, D.C., take I–66 to Strasburg, Virginia, a trip of 78 mi. At Strasburg, take Route 55 about 50 mi to Moorefield. Continuing along

Route 55 will take you to Petersburg and the edge of the Monongahela National Forest.

Well worth a drive farther southwest in this region is the Highland Scenic Highway. From Marlinton, travel north on U.S. 219 to Edray and go west on Route 150 and Route 55, ending in Richwood. Allow two to four hours to enjoy this wild and undeveloped portion of the Monongahela National Forest. The mountainous terrain is covered by hardwood forests and capped by dark spruce at high elevations. You can cross a narrow and steep-walled valley where views of clear mountain streams are common. As you go, you pass through Cranberry Glades Botanical Area, Summit Lake, and the Falls of Hills Creek. Part of the byway follows the Williams River.

Visitor Information

CONTACTS **Pendleton County Visitors Commission** > Box 602, Franklin, WV 26807, tel. 304/358–7573, www.visitpendleton.com. **Pocahontas County Tourism Commission** > Box 275, Marlinton 24954, tel. 304/799–4636 or 800/336–7009, www.pocahontas.org. **Potomac Highlands Travel Council** > Box 1456, Elkins 26241, tel. 304/636–8400, www.mountainhighlands.com. **Randolph County Convention and Visitors Bureau** > 315 Railroad Ave., Suite 1, Elkins, WV 26241, tel. 304/636–2717 or 800/422–3304, www.randolphcountywv.com. **Tucker County Convention and Visitors Bureau** > William Ave., Box 565 Davis, WV 26260, tel. 304/259–5315 or 800/782–2775, www.canaanvalley.org.

Northern
Shenandoah Valley

Front Royal is 90 mi southwest of Washington, D.C.

11

Revised by Kristi Delovitch

EVERY YEAR WASHINGTONIANS head to Shenandoah National Park to drive along Skyline Drive, the park's main artery, for its 105 mi of awe-inspiring views. Fall is the most popular time to come; cars transform the two-lane road into a miniature Beltway as the foliage changes around them. The Virginia creeper, a vine that covers the trees, turns first, in September, followed by thousands of oak and hickory. The landscape along the drive turns an unforgettable shade of crimson speckled with orange and yellow.

The park's nearly 200,000 acres stretch more than 80 mi along the Blue Ridge mountain range. Inside are stunning vistas, more than 500 mi of hiking trails (including a section of the Appalachian Trail), and trout fishing in rushing streams. From the roads and trails, you might see wild turkeys, white-tailed deer, and sometimes even a black bear.

The Blue Ridge Mountains, like the Alleghenies to the west, are part of the Appalachian mountain system. In between the two ranges is the Shenandoah Valley, which parallels Virginia's western edge. Today, most of the valley is still relatively undeveloped. Farms outnumber strip malls, making it perfect for rest and relaxation. Isolated inns, many with fine restaurants, attract well-heeled patrons. The fancier restaurants here emphasize organic ingredients, many of which are locally grown. And the vineyards, creameries, and orchards that dot the landscape are often open for tours and tastings.

Winchester, 25 mi north of the Skyline Drive's northernmost entrance at Front Royal, is small, but this belies its historical importance. Established in 1752, it served as a headquarters for Colonel George Washington during the French and Indian War, which began two years later. During the Civil War, it was an important crossroads near the front line (it changed hands 72 times during the war) and was General Stonewall Jackson's headquarters for nearly two years.

Things are more peaceful today; the biggest attraction is the Shenandoah Apple Blossom Festival in May. Many boutiques, regional art galleries, and antiques stores are found within the town's 45-block historic district, especially near the six-block pedestrian mall. Winchester's also has a musical claim to fame as the birthplace of honky-tonk angel Patsy Cline; thousands visit her grave site each year at the Shenandoah Memorial Park cemetery, where a bell tower memorializes her.

New Market, 50 mi southwest of Winchester, has a small town center that makes a great afternoon stop. Civil War buffs should head to the New Market Battlefield, home of an infamous Confederate victory. Just outside of town are several impressive caves, formed by water eroding the primarily limestone base of the valley.

Though Harrisonburg, 20 mi down the road from Winchester, is often bypassed for the many antiques store and the rich farmlands that surround it, the town itself is worth a visit. Settled in 1739, it's a stronghold of Mennonites, who wear plain clothes and use horse-drawn buggies. The city is also a center of higher education, with James Madison University and Eastern Mennonite College in town and Bridgewater College nearby.

Staunton (pronounced *stan*-ton) is near Waynesboro, where Skyline Drive ends and the Blue Ridge Parkway begins. It's a town with a distinguished past. This was once the seat of government for Augusta County, which formed in 1738 and encompassed present-day West Virginia, Kentucky, Ohio, Illinois, Indiana, and the Pittsburgh area. After the state's General Assembly fled here from the British in 1781, Staunton was briefly the state's capital. Woodrow Wilson (1856–1924), the nation's 27th president and the 8th president from Virginia, is a native son. If you prefer a bit of culture with your past, be sure to visit the town's impressive reproduction of Shakespeare's Globe Theatre.

Just past the edge of the valley is Washington, often called "Little" Washington to differentiate it from its big sister. This tiny town of five blocks is the home of the much-lauded Inn at Little Washington as well as antiques shops, galleries, custom jewelry shops, and theaters.

WHAT TO SEE & DO

Shenandoah National Park Established in 1936, Shenandoah National Park follows the Blue Ridge Mountains for almost 80 mi, from Front Royal south to Waynesboro, and its 196,466 acres encompass some of the highest peaks in northern Virginia. Its Native American name has been variously translated as "Daughter of the Stars" and "River of High Mountains." A fairly narrow band of hardwood forests, the park climbs from the Shenandoah Valley floor to more than 4,000 feet high. Shenandoah is one of the most popular parks in the national park system, with many varied species of animal and plant life, trout streams, campgrounds, gorgeous views, and hundreds of miles of hiking trails, including a stretch of the Appalachian Trail. In summer and fall, rangers lead hikes, field seminars, evening campfire programs, and trips to Camp Hoover, which has special programs for children. You can rent horses for wilderness rides, and there is trout fishing in nearly three dozen streams. Some 200 species of birds make their home here, from ruffed grouse to barred owl, along with white-tailed deer, woodchuck, gray fox, and black bear. The **Harry F. Byrd Visitor Center** (Skyline Dr., Milepost 51, tel. 540/999–3283, Mar.–Oct., daily 9–5) is near the park's largest and most popular campground, Big Meadows. In April and May the area fills with blooming wildflowers. The **Dickey Ridge Visitor Center** (Skyline Dr., Milepost 4.6, tel. 540/635–3566, Mar.–Oct., daily 9–5) is near the Front Royal entrance to Skyline Drive. > Luray, tel. 540/999–3500, 540/999–3489 for interpretive programs, www.nps.gov/shen. $10 car, annual pass $20.

Skyline Drive The most popular way to see Shenandoah National Park is by driving the spectacular, 105-mi route that winds south from Front Royal to Waynesboro. To the west is the Shenandoah Valley; to the east, the rolling farmland of the Piedmont region. The fame of Skyline Drive has its drawbacks: holiday and weekend crowds in spring and fall, its most popular seasons, can slow traffic to far below the maximum speed of 35 mph. In winter, treacherous road conditions can cause the closing of parts of the drive. Nevertheless, for easily accessible wilderness and exciting views, few routes can compete with this one. Just come during the fine weather. > Entrances: southeast of Front Royal (via Rte. 340 at Milepost 0.6); Thornton Gap (via

U.S. 211 near Luray at Milepost 31.5); Swift Run Gap (U.S. Rte. 33 near Elkton at Milepost 65.7); Rockfish Gap (via I–64 near Waynesboro at Milepost 105.4). $10 per car.

NEAR THE PARK

Luray Caverns The largest caverns in the state are 9 mi west of Skyline Drive on U.S. 211. For millions of years, water has seeped through the limestone and clay to create rock and mineral formations. The world's only "stalacpipe organ" is composed of stalactites (calcite formations hanging from the ceilings of the caverns) that have been tuned to concert pitch and are tapped by rubber-tip plungers. The organ is played electronically for every tour and is played manually on special occasions. A one-hour tour begins every 20 minutes. > U.S. 211, Luray, tel. 540/743–6551, www.luraycaverns.com. $16. Mid-Mar.–mid-June, daily 9–6; mid-June–Labor Day, daily 9–7; Labor Day–Oct., daily 9–6; Nov.–mid-Mar., daily 9–4.

Skyline Caverns Two miles west of the northern entrance to Skyline Drive, this cavern is known for the anthodites, or spiked nodes, growing from its ceilings at an estimated rate of 1 inch every 7,000 years, and for its chambers with names that include Capital Dome, Rainbow Trail, Fairytale Lake, and Cathedral Hall. > U.S. 340 S, Front Royal, tel. 540/635–4545 or 800/296–4545, www.skylinecaverns.com. $14. Mid-June–Labor Day, daily 9–6:30; Labor Day–mid-Nov. and mid-Mar.–mid-June, weekdays 9–5, weekends 9–6; mid-Nov.–mid-Mar., daily 9–4.

Sharp Rock Vineyards This winery, at the base of Old Rag Mountain, is a perfect stop after a long day's hike. You can taste Sharp Rock's wines, which includes a reserve chardonnay, in a barn that's been refurbished as a tasting room. > 5 Sharp Rock Rd., Sperryville, tel. 540/987–9700, www.sharprockvineyards.com. Tour free, tastings $2. Mar.–Dec., Fri. 1–5, Sat. noon–5, Sun. 1–5.

HARRISONBURG

Green Valley Book Fair Six times a year in spring through fall, for several weeks at a time, liquidators sell a half million books at up to 90% off their retail cost in warehouses just off the stretch of I–81 between Staunton and Harrisonburg. The massive selection usually includes children's books, poetry, and science fiction, and nearly every other sort of genre. > 2192 Green Valley La., Mt. Crawford, tel. 540/434–0309, www.gvbookfair.com. 9–7 daily at designated times.

Natural Chimneys Regional Park In Mount Solon, 23 mi south of Harrisonburg, these seven freestanding limestone pylons stand from 65 to 120 feet tall and resemble the slender pillars of an Egyptian temple ruin. The exact geologic process that created these 500-million-year-old formations is unknown. Park facilities include connecting nature trails and a swimming pool. Every June and August a jousting tournament is held at the site. > I–81, Exit 240 W, Mount Solon, tel. 540/350–2510. $4 per person, $8 maximum fee per car. Daily 9–dusk.

Virginia Quilt Museum Examples of quilts made throughout the mid-Atlantic region are on view here. Though there are three rotating exhibits a year you can always expect to see a room of antique sewing machines and Women of the Civil War, an exhibit focusing on the stories behind the women and their quilts. Some of the unconventional quilts are in the shape of a fish or a small doll. > 301 S. Main St., tel. 540/433–3818. $5. Mon. and Thurs.–Sat. 10–4, Sun. 1–4.

NEW MARKET

Endless Caverns Discovered in 1879 by two boys and a dog chasing a rabbit, Endless Caverns were opened to the public in 1920. The caverns really do seemed endless, baffling numerous explorers. The tour is enhanced by lighting effects. > 3 mi south of New Market on Rte. 11 (Exit 264 or 257 off I-81), tel. 540/896-2283, www.endlesscaverns.com. $14. Mid-Mar.–mid-June and Labor Day–early Nov., daily 9–5; mid-June–Labor Day, daily 9–6; early Nov.–mid-Mar., daily 9–4.

New Market Battlefield Historical Park New Market was the site of a Confederate victory at the late date of 1864. Inside the 260-acre battlefield's Hall of Valor, a stained-glass window commemorates the battle, in which 257 Virginia Military Institute cadets, some as young as 15, were mobilized to improve the odds against superior Union numbers; 10 were killed. This circular building contains a chronology of the war, and a short film screened here covers Stonewall Jackson's legendary campaign in the Shenandoah Valley. The battle is reenacted at the park each May. > I-81, Exit 264, tel. 540/740-3101. $8. Daily 9–5.

Shenandoah Caverns The spectacular calcite formations found here, including a series resembling strips of bacon, were formed by water dripping through long, narrow cracks in the limestone. The colored lighting effects help differentiate the sparkling calcite crystals. The caverns are accessible to those in wheelchairs. Also on the grounds is American Celebration on Parade, an exhibit of floats from parades from throughout the last 50 years. > 261 Caverns Rd. (I-81, Exit 269), tel. 540/477-3115 or 888/422-8376, www.shenandoahcaverns.com. $13 for caverns only, $8 for float exhibit only, $17.50 for both. Mid-June–Labor Day, daily 9–6:15; Labor Day–Oct., daily 9–5:15; Nov.–mid-Apr., daily 9–4:15; mid-Apr.–mid-June, daily 9–5:15.

Shenville Creamery & Garden Market Besides being an active creamery, Shenville also includes a 50-acre vegetable farm and a garden market, deli, bakery, and ice cream parlor. After learning a little about agriculture, you can head for a large helping of freshly made ice cream. > 16094 Evergreen Valley Rd., Timberville, tel. 540/896-6357 or 877/600-7440. Mon.–Sat. 9–6.

STAUNTON

Blackfriars Playhouse Experience Shakespeare's plays the way the Elizabethans did. This near-duplicate of the Globe Theatre has gained worldwide acclaim for its attention to detail. Like those in 17th-century London, most of the seating here consists of benches (modern seat backs and cushions are available), with some stools right on stage. The interactive shows encourage audience participation by leaving lights on for the entire performance. > 10 S. Market St., tel. 540/885-5588, www.shenandoahshakespeare.com. $10–$26.

Frontier Culture Museum The four illustrative farmsteads at this agrarian museum, American, Scotch-Irish, German, and English, were painstakingly moved from their original sites and reassembled here. Livestock and plants resemble the historic breeds and varieties as closely as possible. The seasonal programs and activities include soap and broom making, cornhusking bees, and supper and barn dances. > 1250 Richmond Rd. (off I-81, Exit 222 to Rte. 250 W), tel. 540/332-7850, www.frontiermuseum.org. $10. Dec.–mid-Mar., daily 10–4; mid-Mar.–Nov., daily 9–5.

Grand Caverns Discovered in 1804 and opened to the public just two years later, Augusta County's Grand Caverns is America's oldest show cave. Thomas Jefferson paid an early visit, and Civil War troops from both sides were among those who descended into the subterranean wonderland. One highlight: an underground room that's one of the largest of its kind in the East. > I–81, Exit 235, 20 mi from Staunton, Grottoes, tel. 540/249–5705. $13.50. Apr.–Oct., daily 9–5; Mar., weekends 9–5.

Woodrow Wilson Birthplace and Museum This beautiful structure in the heart of downtown Staunton has period antiques, items from Wilson's political career, and some original pieces from when this museum was the residence of Wilson's father, a Presbyterian minister. Wilson's presidential limousine, a 1919 Pierce-Arrow sedan, is on display in the garage. > 24 N. Coalter St., tel. 540/885–0897 or 888/496–6376. $7. Mon.–Sat. 10–5, Sun. noon–5.

WINCHESTER

Glen Burnie Manor House and Gardens Colonel James Wood, Winchester's founder, named his estate a "glen of streams." A self-guided tour lets you meander through the 25 acres, which include beautifully designed rose, pattern, and perennial gardens; a Chinese garden stocked with koi; and even a water garden trickling with waterfalls over mossy rocks. Inside the 1736 Georgian house are fine antiques, paintings, and decorative objects collected by the last family member to live here, who died in 1992. > 100 W. Piccadilly St., tel. 540/662–1473. $8. Apr.–Oct., Tues.–Sat. 10–4, Sun. noon–4.

State Arboretum of Virginia A great place to bird-watch or to have a picnic, this 130-acre arboretum 9 mi east of Winchester has over 8,000 trees, including the most extensive collection of boxwoods in North America. Hands-on workshops and tours are available throughout the spring, summer, and fall. The perennial and herb gardens here are perfect for a stroll. > Rte. 50 E, Boyce, tel. 540/837–1758, www.virginia.edu/blandy. Free. Daily dawn–dusk.

Stonewall Jackson's Headquarters Museum Jackson used this restored 1854 home as his base of operations during the Valley Campaign in 1861–62. Among the artifacts on display are his prayer book and camp table. The reproduction wallpaper was a gift from the actress Mary Tyler Moore; it was her great-grandfather Lieutenant Colonel Lewis T. Moore who lent Jackson the use of the house. A $10 block ticket purchased at the museum also includes entry to two nearby historical attractions: **George Washington's Office Museum**, a preserved log cabin where Washington briefly lived during the French and Indian War; and **Abram's Delight Museum**, the oldest residence in Winchester. The stone house was owned by Isaac Hollingsworth, a prominent Quaker. > 415 N. Braddock St., tel. 540/667–3242, www.winchesterhistory.org. $5. Apr.–Oct., Mon.–Sat. 10–4, Sun. noon–4; Nov.–Mar., Fri. and Sat. 10–4, Sun. noon–4.

Sports

CANOEING

Downriver Canoe Day and overnight trips through Downriver Canoe start at $29 per canoe, $32 per kayak, $14 per tube, and $59 per raft. > Rte. 613, near Front Royal, Bentonville, tel. 540/635–5526 or 800/338–1963, www.downriver.com.

Front Royal Canoe This outfitter specializes in trips on the South Fork of Shenandoah River. A tube trip costs $14, and canoe, kayak, and raft trips, ranging from one hour to three days, cost from $30–$116. The company also rents boats, sells fishing accessories, and organizes guided horseback rides through Shenandoah River State Park. > U.S. 340, near Front Royal, 8567 Stonewall Jackson Hwy., tel. 540/635–5440 or 800/270–8808, www.frontroyalcanoe.com.

EQUIPMENT **Shenandoah River Outfitters** > Rte. 684, 6502 S. Page Valley Rd., Luray, tel. 540/743–4159 or 800/622–6632, www.shenandoahriver.com.

FISHING

To take advantage of the trout that abound in the 50 streams of Shenandoah National Park, you need a Virginia fishing license; a five-day license costs $5 ($12 for a year) and it's available in season (early April to mid-October) at concession stands along Skyline Drive.

Murray's Fly Shop This is the place for advice on fishing the Shenandoah or local trout and smallmouth bass streams. The store sells more than 30,000 flies annually and has hundreds of rods and reels for sale. The owner, an excellent fisherman himself, gives fly-fishing lessons and classes. Edinburg is 15 mi north of New Market. > 121 Main St., Edinburg, tel. 540/984–4212.

HIKING

Appalachian Trail Zigzagging across Skyline Drive, the Appalachian Trail can be easily reached by car. Its trails have many connections to the more than 500 mi of the Shenandoah Park's own network. Volunteers assist the National Park Service in upkeep of the AT, which generally has a smooth surface and gentle grade through the park. Three-sided shelters provide places for long-distance hikers to sleep overnight—or for day hikers to dodge a rain shower. If you're here in May or June, expect to see "thru-hikers" with heavy backpacks trudging on their 2,000-mi journey from Georgia to Maine. But you don't have to hike 2,000 mi, or even 2,000 feet, to experience the joyous sights of the wilderness—glorious foliage, rock formations, vistas, and perhaps a deer or even a bear.

Old Rag Mountain One of the most popular hikes in the region, Old Rag attracts tens of thousands each year. Strenuous switchbacks and challenging rock scrambles challenge adventurers during the 7-mi loop. Successful hikers are rewarded with magnificent 360-degree views of the valley from the top of the mountain. The Park Service limits the number people on the trial, so get there early. Park entrance fees apply. > Tel. 540/999–3500.

Shenandoah National Park Some 100 mi of the Appalachian Trail run through the park, along with 500 mi of other footpaths of varying length and difficulty; some lead to waterfalls, canyons, old-growth forests, and rocky outcrops with sweeping views of the Piedmont and the Shenandoah Valley. Maps are available at visitor centers and entrances. Many trails are accessible from Skyline Drive. > Tel. 540/999–3500.

White Oak Canyon and Dark Hollow Falls There are six waterfalls at White Oak Canyon, at Milepost 51.5. Dark Hollow Falls, 77 feet tall, is a mile from Big Meadows Lodge, at Milepost 50.5. > Mileposts 50.5 and 51.5, Skyline Dr., tel. 540/999–3283. Free with park admission. Park daily 24 hrs (closed at night in inclement weather and hunting season).

Save the Date

MAY

Shenandoah Apple Blossom Festival This week of activities includes parades, a carnival, circus, a 10K run, a bluegrass festival, and athletic and music competitions. > Winchester, tel. 540/662–3863 or 800/230–2139.

MAY–SEPTEMBER

Shenandoah Valley Music Festival Weekends from May to September this festival brings classical, jazz, big band, Celtic, and folk music to the Allegheny Mountains. The events are held at the Shrinemont Hotel, an early-19th-century spa that's now an Episcopal retreat. Arts-and-crafts displays and an ice cream social precede each concert. Concertgoers can sit on the lawn for $16 or in one of two pavilions for around $28; call ahead to reserve tickets. A bus to the festival from Woodstock (Exit 283 on

I–81) costs $5. > Rte. 263, 2 mi south of Bryce Resort, Orkney Springs, tel. 540/459–3396 or 800/459–3396, www.musicfest.org.

JUNE–AUGUST

Jousting Tournaments Natural Chimneys Regional Park plays host to tournaments on the third Saturday in June and a month later. > I–81, Exit 240 W, Mount Solon, tel. 540/350–2510, www.nationaljousting.com.

WHERE TO STAY

NEAR THE PARK

Big Meadows Lodge The smaller of two lodges in the park, this timber-and-stone building from 1939 is just steps from Skyline Drive and hiking trails. You can stay in the lodge's rustic rooms, the small motel, or in basic cabins. > Milepost 51.2 on Skyline Dr., Luray 22835, tel. 540/999–2221 or 800/999–4714, fax 540/999–2011, www.visitshenandoah.com. 39 lodge rooms, 58 motel rooms, 5 cabins. Restaurant, lounge, shop. AE, D, MC, V. Closed Nov.–Apr. ¢–$

Mimslyn Inn Nicknamed the "Grand Old Inn of Virginia," this magnificent antebellum-style hotel 9 mi west of the park is the place for those who wish to mix their wilderness fun with elegant lodging and dining, at relatively inexpensive rates. Soak in the Blue Ridge scenery while sitting on the column-graced veranda, which has its own bar. Or keep an eye on the gardens from inside the solarium. All rooms are furnished in a traditional manner and have plush beds. The restaurant ($–$$) serves classical American cuisine with a Virginia flair, such as venison, seared quail, and smoked apple pheasant sausage served on steamed red cabbage. > 401 W. Main St., Luray 22835, tel. 540/743–5105 or 800/296–5105, fax 540/743–2632, www.mimslyninn.com. 40 rooms, 9 suites. Restaurant, cable TV, lounge, shop, meeting rooms, some pets allowed (fee). AE, D, DC, V, MC. Closed weekdays Jan. and Feb. ¢–$

Skyland Lodge At 3,680 feet, the highest point on Skyline Drive, with views across the valley, Skyland has lodging that ranges from rustic cabins and motel-style rooms to suites. Days above 80° are rare at these heights. White-tailed deer come right up to the balcony of the cabins that are in grassy areas. > Milepost 41.7 on Skyline Dr., 22835, tel. 540/999–2211 or 800/999–4714, fax 540/999–2231, www.visitshenandoah.com. 176 rooms. Restaurant, bar, meeting rooms; no a/c, no room phones, no TV in some rooms. AE, D, MC, V. Closed Dec.–mid-Mar. $

HARRISONBURG

By the Side of the Road Tucked in a residential neighborhood, this large brick B&B (circa 1790) served as a Civil War hospital and later the home of a Mennonite bishop. Though the interior has been largely renovated, the wide planked wood floors and exposed brick walls in some rooms are original. The circa-1840 Fitzgerald Cottage, adjacent to the main house in the middle of an apple orchard, is a gem. You enter the bedroom on the main level and take a spiral staircase to the massive bathroom, where a Jacuzzi is in front of a huge, stone fireplace. For breakfast, dishes like waffles with fresh whipped cream are served on fine china. > 491 Garbers Church Rd., 22801, tel. 540/801–0430, www.bythesideoftheroad.com. 4 suites, 1 cottage. In-room data ports, hot tub. MC, V. BP. $–$$

Joshua Wilton House A row of trees guards the privacy of this circa-1888 B&B, decorated in a Victorian style and set on a large yard at the edge of the "Old Town" district. The sunroom and back patio are built for relaxation. Ask for Room 4; it has a lace-draped canopy bed and a turreted sitting area with a view of the Blue Ridge Mountains looming over Main Street. Room 2 has a fireplace. > 412 S. Main St., 22801, tel. 540/434–4464, fax 540/432–9525. 5 rooms. Restaurant, café, some in-room data ports; no room TVs, no kids under 8, no smoking. AE, DC, MC, V. BP. $

STAUNTON

Belle Grae Inn Rooms in this restored 1870 Victorian in the oldest part of town are furnished with antique rocking chairs and canopied or brass beds; a complimentary snifter of brandy awaits in each room. You can claim one of the rocking chairs in the huge, wraparound porch. The Continental food served here has many local touches. > 515 W. Frederick St., 24401, tel. 540/886–5151 or 888/541–5151, fax 540/886–6641, www.bellegrae.com. 8 rooms, 7 suites, 2 cottages. Restaurant, some microwaves, Internet; no smoking. AE, D, MC, V. MAP. $–$$$$

Frederick House Historic houses and restored town houses dating from 1810 make up this inn in the center of the historic district. All rooms are decorated with antiques, and some have fireplaces and private decks. A pub and a restaurant are nearby. > 28 N. New St., 24401, tel. 540/885–4220 or 800/334–5575, fax 540/885–5180, www.frederickhouse.com. 12 rooms, 11 suites. Cable TV, meeting rooms; no smoking. AE, D, DC, MC, V. ¢–$$

Sampson Eagon Inn Across the street from Woodrow Wilson's birthplace in the Gospel Hill section of town, this restored Greek revival (circa 1840) has a lot of period charm. In the spacious guest rooms are antique canopy beds, cozy sitting areas, and modern amenities. Don't miss the Kahlúa Belgian waffles for breakfast. > 238 E. Beverley St., 24401, tel. 540/886–8200 or 800/597–9722, www.eagoninn.com. 5 rooms. Cable TV with movies; no kids under 12, no smoking. AE, MC, V. BP. $

WASHINGTON

Bleu Rock Inn A former farmhouse on 80 acres with the mountains as a backdrop, Bleu Rock has a fishing pond, rolling pastures, and some vineyards. The equestrian center here boards horses (you may bring your own) and trains them for riders; there's also a polo arena and steeplechase course. Two on-site pros are available for polo and riding lessons. The guest rooms, simply furnished with light woods and lace curtains, are pleasing; the four upstairs have private balconies. > 12567 Lee Hwy., 22747, tel. 540/987–3190, fax 540/987–3193, www.bleurockinn.com. 5 rooms. Restaurant, fishing, hiking, horseback riding, pub, some pets allowed; no room phones, no room TVs. AE, D, DC, MC, V. BP. $–$$

Heritage House One block from the Inn at Little Washington, this circa-1837 manor house is now an affordable B&B. This little inn offers an affordable base from which to enjoy the town and the many stores, shops, and restaurants in the surrounding countryside. Ask for the garden suite, which has a great view of a blooming garden from its sunroom. Complimentary port and tea are served daily. > 291 Main St., 22747, tel. 540/675–3207, fax 540/675–2004 or 888/819–8280, www.heritagehousebb.com. 4 rooms, 1 suite. No room phones, no room TVs. MC, V. BP. $–$$

Inn at Little Washington The rich interior of the three-story white-frame inn is the work of Joyce Conway-Evans, who has designed theatrical sets and rooms in English royal houses. Plush canopy beds, marble bathrooms, and fresh flowers make the rooms sumptuous. Although most people visit for the food, staying here is an equally indulgent act. > Middle and Main Sts., 22747, tel. 540/675–3800, fax 540/675–3100. 10 rooms, 4 suites. Restaurant, in-room safes, bicycles. MC, V. Hotel and restaurant closed Tues., except in May and Oct. $$$$

WINCHESTER

Inn at Narrow Passage The 5 acres that contain this 250-year-old property hug the shore of the Shenandoah. Most rooms have views of the river or Massanutten Mountain. In winter, breakfast is served in front of the fire. You can fish for smallmouth bass in the river, just steps from your room. > 30 Chapman Landing Rd., at the corner of Rte. 11 and Chapman Rd., Edinburg 22664, tel. 540/459–8000 or 800/459–8002, fax 540/459–8001, www.narrowpassage.com. 12 rooms. No smoking. D, MC, V. BP. $

Inn at Vaucluse Spring On 100 rural acres this isolated 1785 manor house is decorated in federal-style antiques. Small country charms abound like the rocking chairs on the large porch and fireplaces in each room. A limestone spring and pond are on the property, as are numerous walking trails. Ask for the 1850 log cabin. > 231 Vaucluse Spring La., Stephens City 22655, tel. 540/869–0200 or 800/869–0525, fax 540/869–9546, www.vauclusespring.com. 12 rooms, 3 guest houses. Pool; no room phones, no room TVs, no children under 10. MC, V. BP. $–$$$$

L'Auberge Provençale Chef-owner Alain Borel and his wife, Celeste, of Avignon, France, bring the warm elegance of the south of France to this 1750s country inn, originally a sheep farm owned by Lord Fairfax. Rooms are eclectically decorated with French art and fabrics, and Victorian wicker and antiques; some have fireplaces. Breakfast includes fresh homemade croissants and apple crepes with maple syrup. > Rte. 340, White Post 22663, tel. 540/837–1375 or 800/638–1702, fax 540/837–2004, www.laubergeprovencale.com. 10 rooms, 4 suites. Restaurant, pool; no room phones, no room TVs, no kids under 10, no smoking. AE, D, MC, V, DC. Closed Jan. BP. $$–$$$$

River'd Inn To get here you first drive along a winding country road that's parallel to the Shenandoah River, and then over a low-water bridge to get to the 25-acre peninsula that holds this isolated inn. Many of the massive rooms are decorated with Victorian furnishings, and all of them have fireplaces. The restaurant, known as one of the best in the area, serves regional American cuisine. Don't miss the Sunday brunch. > 1972 Artz Rd., Woodstock 22664, tel. 540/459–5369 or 800/637–4561, fax 540/459–8241, www.riverdinn.com. 6 rooms, 2 suites. Restaurant, pool, hot tub. AE, D, DC, MC, V. Closed part of Jan. BP. $$–$$$$

CAMPING

Shenandoah National Park The park's more than 600 sites are spread over four campgrounds, with a fifth primitive campground, Dundo, set aside for large educational groups. The Big Meadows Campground, at the approximate midpoint of the park, accepts reservations; other campsites are available on a first-come, first-served basis. > Shenandoah National Park, Box 727, Luray 22835, tel. 540/999–3231, 800/365–2267 for Big Meadows and Dundo Reservations, fax 540/999–3623, www.nps.gov/shen. 53 tent-only sites, 164 RV or tent sites, 7 sites for educational groups. Flush toilets, dump station, drinking water, laundry facilities, showers. D, MC, V. Closed Dec.–Feb. ¢

WHERE TO EAT

NEAR THE PARK

Skyland Lodge Comfort food reigns at this lodge eatery, which serves popular country favorites like chicken potpie and pork chops with mashed potatoes. Fish, chicken, and pasta dishes are common. Try to grab a spot near the massive window; the views of the valley are unique. > Skyland Lodge, Milepost 41.7, near Luray, tel. 540/999–2211. AE, D, MC, V. Closed Dec.–Feb. ¢–$$$

HARRISONBURG

Calhoun's This restaurant-brewery is a popular hangout for locals and college students. Favorite beers, all made in-house, include honey blond, plowman porter, and the Smokin' Scottish. There's a seafood and steak special every night, and you can always count on a good burger. It's one of the few casual restaurants in town that has very late hours, with live jazz on Friday nights. > 41 Court Sq., tel. 540/434–8777. MC, V. $–$$$

Joshua Wilton House This B&B's restaurant is the most popular fine-dining place to eat in town. The menu changes daily, its components supplied by many small, local organic farmers. As an appetizer, try the smoked salmon on apple potato cake with dill crème fraîche; for a main course try the oven roasted duck or the filet mignon with garlic mashed potatoes. The dining room sprawls over the first floor of this massive Victorian. More casual dining is offered in the café. > 412 S. Main St., tel. 540/434–4464. AE, DC, MC, V. $$–$$$

Little Grill Collective This restaurant packs in the college students, especially Sunday brunch and Monday, where "the world eats free" and the restaurant becomes a sort of soup kitchen. Breakfast is served all day. The menu has a strong vegetarian focus, with a number of vegan (dishes made with no animal products) options available. Most everything, including the wonderful biscuits and pancakes, is homemade daily, with a strong emphasis on organic ingredients. No smoking is allowed in the restaurant. > 621 N. Main St., tel. 540/434–3594. No credit cards. Closed Tues.–Fri. 2:30–5. ¢

STAUNTON

Belle Grae Inn The sitting room and music room of this restored 1870 Victorian house have been converted into formal dining rooms, with brass wall sconces, Oriental rugs, and candles at the tables. The menu, which changes weekly, has Continental cuisine with a Southern flair. Homemade soups such as shiitake mushroom and smoked Gouda are served daily. Expect entrées like roast loin of pork served with apple-cranberry chutney or a pecan-encrusted tilapia. > 515 W. Frederick St., tel. 540/886–5151, www.bellegrae.com. AE, D, MC, V. $$$$

Mrs. Rowe's Restaurant A homey restaurant with plenty of booths, Rowe's has been operated by the same family since 1947 and enjoys a rock-solid reputation for inexpensive and delicious Southern meals. The fried chicken—skillet-cooked to order—is a standout. A local breakfast favorite is oven-hot biscuits topped with gravy (your choice of sausage, tenderloin, or creamy chipped beef). For dessert, try the rhubarb cobbler or lemon meringue in summer or the mincemeat pie, served with a rum-cream sauce, in fall. > I–81, Exit 222, tel. 540/886–1833. D, MC, V. ¢–$$

WASHINGTON

Bleu Rock Inn When dining at this inn, start with the marinated sushi-grade tuna, topped with cilantro, onions, and jalapeño and served over raw cucumber "noodles." For entrées, try the salmon that's engulfed with fresh crabmeat, or the fillet filled with Boursin cheese. The signature dessert, a banana chimichanga, has the fruit dusted with cinnamon and sugar, wrapped in a deep-fried tortilla, and topped with caramel, vanilla ice cream, and chocolate syrup. > 12567 Lee Hwy., tel. 540/987–3190, www.bleurockinn.com. AE, D, DC, MC, V. Closed Mon. and Tues. $$–$$$

Inn at Little Washington What began as a small-town eatery in 1978 has grown into a legend. Chef Patrick O'Connell's much-loved New American food is served in a slate-floor dining room with William Morris wallpaper. The seven-course dinner costs $148 per person on Saturday, $118 on Friday and Sunday, and $108 on weekdays, not including wine and drinks. > Middle and Main Sts., tel. 540/675–3800. MC, V. Hotel and restaurant closed Tues., except in May and Oct. $$$$

WINCHESTER

Four and Twenty Blackbirds This restaurant, once a general store, cooks eclectic New American fare and has quirky furnishings that include mismatched salt and pepper shakers shaped like blackbirds. The inventive menu changes every three weeks and always focuses on local, seasonal ingredients. Expect dishes like Tuscan halibut prepared with a black olive rub or the popular Portuguese seafood stew, with spicy chorizo (a Spanish sausage) and clams, mussels, calamari, and shrimp. The Sunday brunch is very popular. > 650 Zachary Taylor Hwy., Flint Hill, tel. 540/675–1111. MC, V. Closed Mon. and Tues. No lunch. $$$–$$$$

L'Auberge Provençale The acclaimed restaurant at this inn serves authentic Provençale cuisine ($72; reservations essential on weekends). Memorable entrées include foie gras with mango and ginger, and lobster in a vanilla butter sauce. Chef-owner Alain Borel and his wife, Celeste, hail from Avignon, France; they've brought south France's warm elegance here. Sunday brunch is served from 11:30 to 2:30. > Rte. 340, White Post, tel. 540/837–1375 or 800/638–1702, www.laubergeprovencale.com. AE, D, MC, V, DC. Closed Mon. and Tues. No lunch. $$$$

Sweet Caroline At the center of this dining room is a stage. Every Thursday through Sunday live regional and national musicians, mostly bluesmen, play until the wee hours of the night. Even the actor Dan Aykroyd has shown up, harmonica in hand, to reprise his role as a Blues Brother with the evening's scheduled band. For dinner, start with the calamari or crab-stuffed Portobellos and move on to entrées that include rack of lamb and pork medallions. > 29 W. Cork St., tel. 540/723–8805. Reservations essential. AE, MC, V. No lunch weekends. $–$$$

Violino Ristorante Italiano Homemade pasta—about 20 different kinds—fills the menu in this cheery, yellow-stucco restaurant in the city's Old Town. Owners Franco and Marcella Stocco and their son Riccardo (the men are chefs; Marcella manages the dining room) serve up their native northern Italian cuisine, including lobster *pansotti* (lobster-filled ravioli in a sauce of white wine and lemon sauce). A strolling violinist entertains diners on the weekends. The outdoor patio, enclosed by potted plants, is a quiet spot in the midst of street bustle. > 181 N. Loudoun St., tel. 540/667–8006. Reservations essential. AE, D, DC, MC, V. Closed Sun. $$–$$$$

ESSENTIALS

Getting Here

A car is the best way to get to and visit the area.

BY CAR

The many pleasant highways and routes that snake through western Virginia's rolling countryside make driving a particularly good way to travel. The region's interstates (I–64, I–81, and I–77) are scenic, but the same mountainous terrain that contributes to their beauty can also make them treacherous. Dense valley fog, mountain-shrouding clouds, and gusty ridgetop winds are concerns at any time of the year, and winter brings ice and snow conditions that can change dramatically in a few miles when the elevation changes.

Interstate 81 and Route 11 run north–south the length of the Shenandoah Valley and continue south into Tennessee. Interstate 66 West from Washington, D.C., which is 90 mi to the east, passes through Front Royal to meet I–81 and Route 11 at the northern end of the valley.

BY TRAIN

Amtrak has service three days to Staunton, en route from New York and Chicago.

LINE **Amtrak** > Tel. 800/872–7245, www.amtrak.com.
STATION **Staunton** > 1 Middlebrook Ave., Staunton.

Visitor Information

Staunton's tourist center has a walking tour guide of the town as well as information on the free trolley that makes numerous stops around town.

CONTACTS **Front Royal/Warren County Chamber of Commerce and Visitors Center** > 414 E. Main St., Front Royal 22630, tel. 540/635–3185, www.frontroyalchamber.com. **Harrisonburg-Rockingham Convention and Visitors Bureau** > 800 Country Club Rd., Harrisonburg 22801, tel. 540/434–3862, www.hrchamber.org. **Harry F. Byrd Visitor Center** > Skyline Dr., Milepost 51, Luray 22835, tel. 540/999–3283. **Shenandoah Valley Travel Association** > Box 1040, New Market 22844, tel. 540/740–3132 or 877/847–4878, www.shenandoah.org. **Staunton/Augusta Travel Information Center** > Box 810, Staunton 24401, tel. 540/332–3972 or 800/342–7982, www.stauntonva.org. **Winchester–Frederick County Convention and Visitors Bureau** > 1360 S. Pleasant Valley Rd., Winchester 22601, tel. 540/662–4135 or 800/662–1360, www.winchesterva.org.

Central Virginia Vineyards

Culpeper is 71 mi southwest of Washington, D.C.

12

Updated by CiCi Williamson

THOMAS JEFFERSON WOULD BE PLEASED. He was convinced that the Monticello area would be suitable for wine making, and now one-half of the wine grapes that go into the state's 300,000 annual cases of wine are grown in the three counties closest to Charlottesville: Albemarle, Orange, and Madison. Roaming around this beautiful part of the state—stopping here and there to taste wines or take in a museum or two—is a pleasant break from city life. Several wineries include fine restaurants, and a couple of them can even put you up for the night in luxurious rooms.

This area's wine-making roots predate the Republic—wineries were going strong until they were decimated first by the Civil War and then by Prohibition. But now, with the state's wine making on an upsurge, the area is central to the success of viticulture. The modern revival began with American hybrids, but shifted to French hybrids with a more sophisticated appeal. Major varietals grown here include chardonnay, cabernet sauvignon, and Riesling.

Of course, the area isn't given over entirely to the grape. Many people here live in sheltered valleys on small farms, where they retain traditional lifestyles. In addition, just as it has since the days of Thomas Jefferson, the beautiful countryside of rich, fertile meadows and gentle mountains has also enticed the gentry to grab great chunks of the land for their estates and horse farms. It all makes for a quirky union of old and new money, college students, farmers, and wineries.

Culpeper, founded in 1748, is the northernmost city covered in this chapter. George Washington was employed from 1749 to 1751 as the official county surveyor. Young George, 17 years old at the time, cited Culpeper County's "high and pleasant situation." Daniel Boone, famous American explorer, lived 5 mi away in Stevensburg for three years during the 1750s. Culpeper was at the forefront of the colonial rebellion against England. The citizens of the town were fierce patriots, protesting the Stamp Act, condemning the British Parliament, and pledging themselves to defend their rights with their "lives and fortunes." In 1777, the town's Minutemen marched to Williamsburg in answer to Governor Patrick Henry's call to arms.

During the Civil War, several large battles were fought in Culpeper's pastures and hillsides, and the wounded were treated in the town's churches and homes. Residents of this countryside experienced heavy fighting, but more often the area was the site of camps, cavalry action, hospitals, and Confederate supply. Brandy Station, north of Culpeper on Route 29, is the site of the largest cavalry battle in North America. An active and persistent preservation group has managed to save key sections. On the battlefield is the historic "Graffiti House," a two-story frame dwelling Brandy station that was used as a hospital by both the Union and the Confederate armies.

Today the downtown district has antiques stores, crafts shops, and a handful of eateries. An excellent small museum has exhibits on surveyor Washington, the Civil War, and some of the area's earliest inhabitants, the dinosaurs. A major north–south artery, U.S. Route 29, passes through Culpeper, making it a good stopover point on longer drives.

Farther south on U.S. Route 29 is Orange, a fertile agricultural area equally rich in history. Among the many estates dotting the countryside are Montpelier, the lifelong home of James Madison and his wife, Dolley. In Orange itself is the James Madison Museum, which contains artifacts from the Madison home as well as items from Orange's history. Orange's Exchange Hotel, strategically located on the Virginia Central Railway, became a Confederate military hospital; it now houses a Civil War museum. The Wilderness Battlefield, in the Spotsylvania National Military Park at the eastern end of the county (*see* Fredericksburg & the Northern Neck), was the scene of a May 1864 fight that left 26,000 soldiers dead.

WHAT TO SEE & DO

BARBOURSVILLE

Barboursville Vineyards This was the first vineyard in the state to grow only vinifera grapes (vinifera are of European origin; other vineyards were using American hybrids at the time). Barboursville, begun in 1976 by the sixth generation of an Italian viticultural dynasty, is on the former plantation of James Barbour, governor of the commonwealth from 1812 to 1814. The house, designed by Jefferson to resemble Monticello, was gutted by fire in 1884; the ruins remain. > 17655 Winery Rd. (near intersection of Rtes. 20 and 23), tel. 540/832–3824, www.barboursvillewine.com. Tastings $3, tours free. Tastings Mon.–Sat. 10–5, Sun. 11–5, tours weekends 10–4.

Burnley Vineyards & Daniel Cellars For more than 25 years, this small, family-owned winery has been making about a dozen different types of wine. The premises include a tasting room, guest house, banquet room, and a deck overlooking the vineyards and picnic area. > 4500 Winery La., 22923, tel. 540/832–2828, www.burnleywines.com. Tasting fee $2 (can be applied to your purchase). Jan.–Mar., Fri.–Mon. 11–5; Apr.–Dec., daily 11–5.

CULPEPER

Brandy Station On June 9, 1863 one of history's greatest cavalry engagements took place here, when over 20,000 troops, including 17,000 cavalry, engaged in battle. Confederate general J. E. B. Stuart got quite a scare: although the Union advance was repelled, the battle established that Union troops were strengthening and the dominance of the Confederate cavalry had been broken. On the battlefield is the "Graffiti House," used as a hospital by both armies. On the walls of the second floor, recuperating soldiers of both armies scrawled dozens of names and regimental identifications. It's one of the most concentrated and legible groupings of Civil War graffiti in existence. > Box 165 (off U.S. Rte. 29 near Culpeper), Brandy Station, tel. 703/403–1910, www.brandystation.org. Free. Wed. 11–4, Sun. noon–3; expanded hrs in summer.

Dominion Wine Cellars This winery makes specialty wines that include Blackberry and Raspberry Merlot, Lord Culpeper Seyval, and Filippo Mazzei Reserve. The Dominion label was launched in 1985 by a group of 20 growers, who formed the Virginia Wineries Cooperative. You can take a picnic on the grounds. > 1 Winery Ave., tel. 540/825–8772, www.williamsburgwineryltd.com. Tastings and tours free. Mon.–Sat. 10–4:30, Sun. noon–4:30.

Virginia's Vines

HUMBLE IT MAY HAVE BEEN, but the English settlers of Jamestown managed to produce the first wine in America by 1609. In the centuries that have followed, it has been either sink or swim for the state's wine industry—mostly sink. But after numerous tries, Virginia can proudly claim some 80 wineries.

In 1611 the Virginia Company, eager to establish wine making in the colonies, sent over French winegrowers along with slips and seeds of European vine stocks. For the next two centuries, French viticulturists attempted but failed to transplant European rootstock to the New World. The problem lay with the harsher climate of cold winters and hot, humid summers.

Thomas Jefferson believed that successful wine making in America would depend on native varietals. He was anxious to promote grape growing, both to encourage wine drinking for itself and to create a cash-crop alternative to tobacco. By 1800, he and other Virginians had begun developing hybrids, resulting in grapes that combined American hardiness with European finesse and complexity. The most popular are still growing today: Alexander, Concord, Isabella, Niagara, and Norton. The Catawba and Delaware are used for many of the many sparkling wines made in the eastern United States.

A strong wine-making industry developed in Virginia between 1800 and the Civil War. However, the war's fierce battles destroyed many vineyards. Prohibition finished off what the war did not, and by 1950, only 15 acres of grapes were being grown. A decade later, a revival began, with the Virginia grape industry starting over with American hybrids but soon shifting to French hybrids. By 1982 there were 17 wineries.

Today, Virginia is the sixth-largest wine-producing state, and its wines have won national and international acclaim. The 400 wine festivals and events that take place each year here attract hundreds of thousands. The "Virginia Wineries Festival & Tour Guide," available from the Virginia Wine Marketing Program (tel. 800/828–4637, www.virginiawines.org), covers the state's wineries; most offer tastings and tours. The guide is available free at visitor centers and through the organization itself.

Museum of Culpeper History Exhibits about this area of the Piedmont are attractively arranged in a Colonial Williamsburg–style building with a slate mansard roof. From dinosaurs to human settlers (Indians, Germans, and Englishmen), you'll find a wide sweep of the town's rich history in this downtown museum. Of special interest are exhibits about George Washington's surveying of the area and the role played by residents during the Revolutionary War. One old speed-limit sign for horse traffic in Culpeper cautions "a moderate trot." Outside are an Indian village and **Burgandine House,** the oldest house in town. This charming little log house with a clapboard exterior was built in 1749. With the exception of a few "mended" places, the interior is original. When Burgandine House was used as an inn and tavern its "house rules" allowed for women to sleep inside, but they had to go outside and be served through the window if they wanted a drink. > 803 S. Main St., tel. 540/829–1749. Free. Mon.–Sat. 11–5.

Old House Vineyards A renovated 1820s farmhouse serves as the winery in this mountain foothills area. Wines produced on the 24 acres include Vidal Blanc, Vidal Blanc Ice Wine, chardonnay, and merlot. > 18351 Corky's La., tel. 540/423–1032, www.oldhousevineyards.com. Free. Sat. 11–5, Sun. 1–5.

Prince Michel Winery Jean Leducq created this winery in the foothills of the Blue Ridge Mountains, 10 mi southwest of Culpeper, in 1982. The wine-tasting room is in a small museum dedicated to the history of wine making. You can take a free, self-guided tour of the production facility. An excellent restaurant is on the premises, and three elegant suites are available if you'd like to stay overnight. > HCR 4, Box 77, Leon, tel. 540/547–3707 or 800/800–9463, www.princemichel.com. Tastings $2 for 6 wines. Daily 10–5.

Rose River Vineyards & Trout Farm Within the Blue Ridge Mountains, the vines here share the grounds with apples, peaches, and beehives. You can fish for rainbow trout in the ponds: no license is required, but you do need your own fishing pole. Call ahead for pond hours. > Rte. 648, Syria, tel. 540/923–4050, www.roseriverwine.com. Free. Apr.–Dec., weekends 11–5.

ORANGE

Christensen Ridge One of Virginia's oldest wineries produces red and white wines on 200 acres that overlook the Blue Ridge Mountains. A log cabin and a five-bedroom house with pool can be rented from the winery. > HCR 02, Box 459, Madison 22727, tel. 540/923–4800, 800/660–3368 lodging reservations, www.christensenridge.com. Free. Oct., daily 11–5; Nov.–Sept., Fri.–Sun. 11–5.

Exchange Hotel and Civil War Museum During the Civil War, this Greek-revival hotel became a Confederate receiving hospital for wounded and dying soldiers, brought in by the trainload from nearby battlefields to the platform in front of the hotel. An estimated 70,000 soldiers were treated here between 1862 and 1865. One gallery in the museum is a re-creation of a military surgery room; another is a hospital ward. In addition to weapons, uniforms, and personal effects of both Union and Confederate soldiers, the museum displays the often crude medical equipment used for amputations, tooth extractions, and bloodletting. > 400 S. Main St., Gordonsville, tel. 540/832–2944, www.hgiexchange.org. $4. Mar. 15–May and Sept.–Dec., Tues.–Sat. 10–4; June–Aug., Tues.–Sat. 10–4, Sun. 1–4.

First Colony French-style wines are produced at this Charlottesville winery south of Monticello. Indoor and outdoor seating areas are available for picnics and private parties. > 1650 Harris Creek Rd., Charlottesville 22902, tel. 877/979–7105 or 434/979–7105, www.firstcolonywinery.com. Tastings and tours free. Daily 11–5.

Horton Cellars Winery Stunning stone underground cellars, views of the Blue Ridge Mountains, and a wonderful vaulted-ceiling tasting room are the highlights of this beautiful winery. The vineyards produce syrah, viognier, malbec, and other standard grape wines. Horton also makes wine from pears, peaches, raspberries, blueberries, and blackberries. > 6399 Spotswood Trail, Gordonsville 22942, tel. 540/832–7440 or 800/829–4633, www.hvwine.com. Tastings and tours free. Daily 10–5.

James Madison Museum James Madison's Campeachy chair, an 18th-century piece made for him by his friend Thomas Jefferson, is featured in this museum, which celebrates the fourth U.S. president. Other artifacts include furnishings from his nearby home, Montpelier; presidential correspondence; and china and glassware recovered from the White House before the British torched it during the War of 1812. Another permanent exhibit details the history of Orange. > 129 Caroline St., Orange, tel.

540/672–1776, fax 540/672–0231, www.jamesmadisonmuseum.org. $4. Mar.–Nov., weekdays 9–4, Sat. 10–4, Sun. 1–4; Dec.–Feb., weekdays 9–4.

Jefferson Vineyards In 1773 Jefferson gave this land to Filippo Mazzei, an Italian winegrower. His mission was to establish a European-style vineyard; Mazzei claimed that the soil and climate of Virginia were better than Italy's. The modern-day operation, begun in 1981, has produced some widely appreciated wines. The winery is open daily for tastings, and the free tours are conducted on the hour. > 1353 Thomas Jefferson Pkwy., Charlottesville, tel. 434/977–3042 or 800/272–3042, www.jeffersonvineyards.com. Free. Daily 11–5.

King Family Vineyards The tasting room in the large, white winery building has rustic wood floors and a stone fireplace. Lodging is available in a log cabin, built in the 1840s and later moved to its present location at Roseland Farm. The two-story cabin ($119 per night) has a sitting room with a stone fireplace, a full bath, and a front porch overlooking the lake. > 6550 Roseland Farm, Crozet 22932, tel. 434/823–7800, www.kingfamilyvineyards.com. Tastings $1, tours free. Daily 11–5; tours hourly noon–4.

Kluge Estate Winery & Vineyard Overlooking Monticello and Thomas Jefferson's first vineyards, the Kluge Estate's 50 acres are planted with cabernet sauvignon, cabernet franc, merlot, and chardonnay. > 100 Grand Cru Dr., Charlottesville 22902, tel. 434/977–3895, www.klugeestate.com. Tastings $5, tours free. Tastings Tues.–Sun., 10–5, tours by appt.

Montpelier The Madison family lived here from 1723 to 1844, when the estate was sold. The property changed hands six times before William duPont bought it in 1900. Today, the estate includes 2,700 acres, more than 130 buildings, extensive gardens and forests, and a steeplechase course. The duPonts enlarged and redecorated the house, so it only vaguely resembles its looks in Madison's day; historical analysis and restoration efforts are ongoing. The visitor center has an exhibit and video detailing the life and times of James and Dolley Madison. From there, you are given headphones for an audio tour around the property, which provides descriptions of historical and natural features. The main house exhibit does not attempt to re-create Madison's home but uses the mostly empty rooms as evocative spaces to weave a story of plantation life. The landscape walking tour includes a stop at the family cemetery where Madison and his wife are buried. > 11407 Constitution Hwy., Orange, tel. 540/672–2728 or 540/672–0003, www.montpelier.org. $7.50. Apr.–Nov., daily 10–4; Dec.–Mar., daily 11–3.

Oakencroft Vineyard & Winery With the Blue Ridge Mountains and a lake in the background, Oakencroft is in a beautiful locale. Chardonnays, cabernet sauvignons, and clarets are all made here. Free tours are offered during open hours; tastings are $1. > 1486 Oakencroft La., Charlottesville, tel. 434/296–4188, www.oakencroft.com. Free; tastings $1. Apr.–Dec., daily 11–4:30; Mar., weekends 11–4:30.

St. Thomas's Episcopal Church This 1833 church is believed to be the lone surviving example of Jeffersonian church architecture. It was modeled after Charlottesville's demolished Christ Church, which Thomas Jefferson designed. During the Civil War, the building served as a hospital following four different battles; Robert E. Lee worshiped here in the winter of 1863–64. > 119 Caroline St., Orange, tel. 540/672–3761. Donations accepted. Daily; tours by appointment.

Stone Mountain Vineyards Placed atop the Blue Ridge Mountains in Greene County, the vineyards ages its wine in a natural cave. There's an area set aside for picnicking. > 1376 Wyatt Mountain Rd. (Box 7), Dyke 22935, tel. 434/990–9463, www.stonemountainvineyards.com. Tastings $1, tours free. Mar., Sat. and Sun. 11–5; Apr.–Dec., Fri.–Sun. and federal holiday Mon. 11–5.

White Hall Vineyards Chardonnay, cabernet sauvignon, cabernet franc, merlot, muscat, gewürztraminer, touriga, and pinot gris are produced at this farm winery, 13 mi from Charlottesville. The winery has lovely grounds, a pleasantly shaded picnic area, and views of the Blue Ridge Mountains. > 5184 Sugar Ridge Rd., White Hall, tel. 434/823–8615, www.whitehallvineyards.com. Free. Mar.–mid-Dec., daily 11–5.

Save the Date

APRIL

Graves Mountain Spring Fling This weekend celebration, held at the end of the month 6 mi west of Culpeper, includes bluegrass music, cloggers, fly-fishing demonstrations, arts and crafts, hayrides, and horseback riding. > Graves Mountain Lodge, Rte. 670, Syria, tel. 540/923–4231, www.gravesmountain.com/springfling.htm.

MAY

Culpeper Day This early-May festival along Davis Street includes regional crafts, bluegrass and country music, and food vendors. > Tel. 540/825–7768.

AUGUST

Shakespeare in the Ruins For the first three weekends in August, the Bard reigns at the ruins of Governor Barbour's house at Barboursville Vineyards. The plays are put on by the longest-running community theater in Central Virginia. > Rte. 777, Barboursville, tel. 540/832–5355, www.shakespeareintheruins.com.

OCTOBER

Fall Fiber Festival and Sheepdog Trials Spinning, weaving, and shearing are demonstrated at this event, and vendors display fiber crafts and the animals that supplied the raw materials: sheep, llamas, alpacas, cashmere goats, and angora rabbits. The sheepdog trials are held on both days of the festival. There are children's programs, too. > Montpelier, Rte. 20, Orange, tel. 540/672–2935, www.fallfiberfestival.org.

WHERE TO STAY

CULPEPER

Fountain Hall Bed and Breakfast The basic structure of this stately bed-and-breakfast dates from 1859. In 1923, the building's front facade was remodeled in a colonial-revival style. Each room is plush with period antiques and reproductions, and decorated in a different style: 1920s art deco, Victorian, and early American. > 609 S. East St., 22701, tel. 540/825–8200, 800/298–4748 outside VA, fax 540/825–7716, www.fountainhall.com. 4 rooms, 2 suites. Picnic area, in-room data ports, some in-room hot tubs, some refrigerators, library, business services; no smoking. AE, D, DC, MC, V. CP. $–$$

Graves' Mountain Lodge This family-run resort lodge is on a peaceful, 135-year-old working farm with apple orchards and cattle, 6 mi west of Culpeper and next to Shenandoah National Park. You can stay in anything from a motel-like room to a rustic log cabin by a running river, to a one-room schoolhouse. Box lunches are available. > Rte. 670, 22743, tel. 540/923–4231, fax 540/923–4312, www.gravesmountain.com. 48 rooms, 13 cottages. Dining room, picnic area, tennis court, pool, playground, laundry facilities, business services, some pets allowed. D, MC, V. AP. Closed Dec.–mid-Mar. $–$$$

Hazel River Inn Peer out the windows of this 1880s home, which is surrounded by 5 acres of informal gardens and rambling hardwood forest. In the evening, you can take in views of the Blue Ridge Mountains while surrounded by an eclectic mix of antiques. Sip a complimentary glass of local wine or beer, and listen to the logs crackle in living- and dining-room fireplaces. The inn is a 15-minute drive northwest of Culpeper. > 11227 Eggsbornsville Rd., 22701, tel. 540/937–5854, www.hazelriverinn.com. 3 rooms. Pool; no room phones, no room TVs, no smoking. AE, MC, V. BP. $

Suites at Prince Michel This winery's gorgeous one-bedroom suites are luxuriously designed in French Provincial style along different themes. All suites have beautiful views, private garden patios, separate living rooms, and fireplaces. > HCR 4, Box 77, U.S. 29 S, Leon 22725, tel. 540/547–9720 or 800/800–9463, www.princemichel.com. 4 suites. Restaurant, room service, in-room data ports, in-room hot tubs, cable TV, in-room VCRs, business services. AE, MC, V. BP. $$$$

ORANGE

Hidden Inn This B&B was built in the late 1800s by descendents of Thomas Jefferson. In addition to the main house, a carriage house, a garden cottage, and a 1940s house also serve as lodgings. Rooms, furnished in period pieces or reproductions, come with handmade quilts and wingback chairs. > 249 Caroline St., 22960, tel. 540/672–3625 or 800/841–1253, fax 540/672–5029. 10 rooms. Dining room, some in-room hot tubs, some kitchenettes, some refrigerators; no TV in some rooms, no smoking. AE, MC, V. BP. $–$$

Holladay House Flower and herb gardens surround this 1830s, federal-style home, which has Victorian and colonial antiques as furnishings, rocking chairs in all rooms, and fireplaces in two of the guest rooms. The inn also has a parlor and a veranda. > 155 W. Main St., 22960, tel. 540/672–4893 or 800/358–4422, fax 540/672–3028, www.vawinetoursbandb.com. 6 rooms, 2 suites. Some in-room hot tubs, cable TV in some rooms; no smoking. AE, D, MC, V. BP. $

Inn at Meander Plantation Now a beloved landmark, this beautiful inn and horse farm was once part of the first plantation to be established in Madison County. Its owner, Colonel Joshua Fry, was the partner of Thomas Jefferson's father, who surveyed and drew the first official map of the State of Virginia. (A French copy of the map hangs in the living room.) > HCR 5 Box 460A (James Madison Hwy. 15), Locust Dale 22948, tel. 540/672–4912, fax 540/672–0405, www.meander.net. 6 rooms, 2 suites. AE, D, MC, V. BP. $–$$

Mayhurst Inn This Italianate Victorian mansion, built in 1859, is on 37 wooded acres. Filled with antiques, the B&B has a parlor and a spiral staircase reaching up four floors. Most guest rooms have fireplaces, and all have period furnishings. > 12460 Mayhurst La., 22960, tel. 540/672–5597 or 888/672–5597, fax 540/672–7447, www.mayhurstinn.com. 8 rooms, 1 suite. Some in-room hot tubs, pond, fishing, business services; no room TVs. AE, D, MC, V. BP. $

Willow Grove Inn An encampment site during the Revolutionary War, this restored plantation house, built in 1778, sits on 37 acres. Antiques and heirloom furnishings are throughout, and there's a piano in the parlor. Some guest rooms have fireplaces and private verandas. Box lunches are available. > 14079 Plantation Way, 22960, tel. 540/672–5982 or 800/949–1778, fax 540/672–3674, www.willowgroveinn.com. 5 rooms, 5 cottages. Restaurant, some in-room hot tubs, bar, business services, some pets allowed; no room TVs, no smoking. AE, D, MC, V. MAP. $$$–$$$$

WHERE TO EAT

CULPEPER

Hazel River Restaurant It's in one of the oldest buildings in downtown Culpeper (it served as a jail in the Civil War), so it's not surprising to find wide plank floors and hand-hewn beams in this candlelit restaurant. The steak, duck, and chicken dishes all have a twist—grilled chicken breast, for example, is marinated in blackberry vinaigrette and served with wild mushrooms. The home-smoked salmon and organic trout are also standouts. Many of the herbs and vegetables are grown at Culpeper's Hazel River Inn. > 195 E. Davis St., tel. 540/825–7148. AE, MC, V. Closed Wed. **$$–$$$**

Lord Culpeper Restaurant Local legend says the ghost of Culpeper's former mayor hangs out in this downtown building, built in 1933. If so, he's not going hungry, with choices including lemon-ginger chicken, salmon with sour cream dill sauce, and pork loin with caramelized apples and onions. Burgers, grilled fish, and steaks round out the menu. > 401 S. Main St., tel. 540/829–6445, www.lordculpeper.8m.com. AE, D, DC, MC, V. **$–$$$**

Pancho Villa's Mexican Family Restaurant Murals of the Mexican liberator are on the walls of this informal restaurant. The usual assortment of burritos, fajitas, enchiladas, and quesadillas show up on the menu, but so do more innovative specialties, such as bacon-wrapped shrimp stuffed with crabmeat. > 910 S. Main St., tel. 540/825–5268. AE, D, MC, V. **¢–$**

Prince Michel This restaurant, 10 mi southwest of Culpeper, is on the grounds of the Prince Michel winery. You can dine casually in the bistro area, which has a trellised booth alcove, or in a more elegant dining room, which has a view of the vineyards. The soft peach and blue-green of the table linen accents the European-style place settings, and the service is as dazzling as the crystal. Chef Alain Lecomte is committed to using local and fresh foods in his updated French dishes, such as the fillet of sole, stuffed with lobster and served on a bed of spinach with a lobster butter sauce, or the roasted duck breast with a cherry sauce and served with potatoes and turnips. A fixed-price menu ($70–$80) is available. > HCR 4, Box 77, U.S. 29 S, Leon 22725, tel. 540/547–9720 or 800/800–9463, www.princemichel.com/diningmain.htm. Jacket required. AE, MC, V. **$$$–$$$$**

ORANGE

Clark's Tavern This rustic tavern specializes in dressed-up versions of Southern classics. Maple-grilled breast of duck, pan-seared salmon wrapped in thin slices of country ham, and Carolina shrimp creole are house specialties. > 14079 Plantation Way, Orange, tel. 540/672–5982. AE, D, MC, V. **$$–$$$$**

Firehouse Cafe Local artwork, sculpture, and a small stage for live music on Friday nights fill this former firehouse in downtown Orange. The menu offers basic American fare, with emphasis on meat-and-potatoes entrées and generous sides. If you want a sure bet, go with the hand-patted hamburger and fresh fries. > 137 W. Main St. Orange, tel. 540/672–9001. MC, V. **¢–$**

Tolliver House Polished wood and captain's chairs are the order of the day in this former 1787 tavern, 9 mi south of Orange on Route 15. The dining area is like that of an English hunt club, and the menu includes steak and seafood dishes. The prime rib, served with new potatoes and steamed vegetables on the side, is popular for dinner. > 209 N. Main St., Gordonsville, tel. 540/832–3485. Reservations essential. AE, D, MC, V. **$$–$$$**

ESSENTIALS

Getting Here

You need a car to visit the wineries and other attractions of central Virginia. All the sights in this chapter are 2 to 2½ hours away from D.C.

BY CAR

From Washington, D.C., head west on I–66. (During Friday rush hour, traffic in this direction can be horrendous: if possible, leave town mid-morning to early afternoon.) Go past Manassas to Exit 43 (Rte. 29 S) and stay on Route 29 past Warrenton, where it's joined by Highway 15. Take Business 15 to downtown Culpeper. Continue on Route 15. Until this point, the roads have little allure, bordered as they are with strip malls and gas stations. But from now on, you will be traveling on "byways," Virginia's designations for its most scenic roads.

An especially beautiful drive is on U.S. Highway 15, between Culpeper and Gordonsville, and then via Route 231 to Shadwell. Another scenic road is U.S. Highway 20 between Orange and Charlottesville, passing Montpelier en route. The two-lane undulating roads go through old-growth forests that are little changed from colonial days. The hundred-foot hardwoods of sycamore, sweet gum, black walnut, ash, and maple shade both sides of the the asphalt like an awning.

Between Orange and Shadwell, Route 231 is bordered with handsome horse farms with names like Fox Meadow and Tally Ho. Mile after mile, the fences vary from painted white to ebony to split rail, but all are perfectly kept up, a sign that the gentry are in residence and have the money for the upkeep. The pastoral beauty along Route 231 ends in Shadwell, a blip in the road where Jefferson was born.

Visitor Information

CONTACTS **Culpeper County Chamber of Commerce** > 133 W. Davis St., Culpeper, VA 22701-3017, tel. 540/825–8628, www.co.culpeper.va.us. **Orange County Visitors Bureau** > 122 E. Main St. (Box 133), Orange 22960, tel. 540/672–1653, www.visitocva.com.

Hot Springs & White Sulphur Springs

Hot Springs is 210 mi southwest of Washington, D.C.

13

Updated by Kevin Myatt

LIKE TWO FORTRESSES standing sentinel over the dramatic Allegheny Mountains landscape, two sprawling resorts some 38 mi apart stand out from their rural surroundings. In fact, they also stand out from other major resorts throughout the world for their level of service, number of amenities, and the remote beauty of their surroundings. The two resorts, the Greenbrier in White Sulphur Springs, West Virginia, and the Homestead in Hot Springs, Virginia, are the last and grandest of their kind.

At one time, before the turn of the 20th century, the deep valleys of the Alleghenies, spa-centered resorts. But these days, many of the towns with "Springs" in their name—Sweet Chalybeate Springs, Healing Springs, Salt Sulphur Spring, among others—are just nondescript dots on a road map.

Although the Greenbrier and the Homestead have both had their setbacks throughout the years, they have in the end managed to not only survive, but thrive. Today, just as in decades and centuries past, they attract the rich and powerful as well as ordinary visitors, who often outnumber the locals in the lovely little towns near the resorts.

The Greenbrier, established in 1780, was rebuilt in 1858 and in 1930. It served as an army hospital during World War II; after the war, it was again renovated, reopening as a grand hotel in 1948. The six-story white columns are reminiscent of the White House. (In fact, if the Cold War had ever turned hot, that's what it might have become: in 1960, a complex of bunkers was secretly constructed underneath a new wing of the hotel to house government officials in the event of a nuclear war.) The resort's plushly carpeted, chandelier-graced main building is full of mazy hallways filled with antiques, exhibits, shops and other attractions.

The Homestead's origins go back to the 1750s, when early settlers built guest inns near the area's warm mineral springs. George Washington, at the time a 23-year-old commander of the Virginia militia, visited the area's springs around this time. The site became known as the Homestead in 1766, when a wooden lodge was built. Interest dwindled during the Civil War and Reconstruction, but by 1892, the banker J. Pierpont Morgan had begun a major upgrade of the resort. The redbrick structure, with a tower in the center, went up in the early 1900s. Golf arrived in 1892 with the building of the Old Course, and the South's first ski slope was constructed in 1959. Another face-lift, done in the 1990s, helped preserve the buildings' and grounds' early-1900s majesty.

An entire week's vacation, and certainly a weekend's worth, could be occupied without leaving the grounds of either resort. With a total of six 18-hole golf courses, miles of trails, outdoor sports that include croquet and horseback riding, many choices for food and shopping, as well as the spas themselves, the resorts are destinations in their own right. But the surrounding countryside offers its share of gems as well, and the mountains and surrounding country make driving almost any highway in the area a jaw-dropping experience. The principal communities include Hot Springs and Warm Springs near the Homestead; Covington and Clifton Forge, industrial Virginia towns along I–64 south of the Homestead; and White Sulphur Springs and its historic neighbor, Lewisburg, along I–64 in West Virginia.

WHAT TO SEE & DO

Douthat State Park More than 40 mi of trails crisscross this rugged, deeply wooded park 7 mi north of Clifton Forge. The trails are exceptionally groomed, and clear signs make it easy to avoid getting lost. The trails lead from a deep creek valley up past rushing waterfalls and on to majestic overlooks. > I–64, Exit 27 on Rte. 629, Clifton Forge, tel. 540/862–8100. $3, www.dcr.state.va.us/parks/douthat.htm.

Falling Spring At this overlook, you can see a 200-foot waterfall tumbling over a cliff. It's a pleasing stop on the way to or from the Homestead, 10 mi to the north. > U.S. 220, 6 mi north of Covington, www.covington.va.us.

Garth Newel Music Center Classical musical performances, lectures, and other cultural events take place at this 114-acre, wooded former estate 3 mi north of the Homestead. You can make reservations for a show and then picnic on the grounds. The Manor House has 10 rooms where you can stay; a five-course dinner is included as part of the rates. > U.S. 220, Warm Springs, tel. 540/839–5018 or 877/558–1689, www.garthnewel.org.

The Greenbrier Although it takes up half as much space as the Homestead, the Greenbrier has a similarly impressive list of possible activities, with golf, tennis, spa facilities, excellent restaurants, and shops. You can even take a new Land Rover off for a spin on one of two off-road courses (it costs $185 for the first hour and $100 for each hour after). The once-secret bunkers built by the U.S. government in 1960 are now on display, also. The 90-minute tour, which must be reserved in advance, costs $27. Kids under 10 are not permitted. > 300 W. Main St., White Sulphur Springs, tel. 304/536–1110 or 800/624–6070, www.greenbrier.com.

Greenbrier State Forest Just south of White Sulphur Springs, this outdoor area is made up of 5,130 acres. The 13 mi of hiking trails include one section that takes you up the 3,300-foot Kate's Mountain. You can also camp or go swimming here, and rental cabins are available. > Old Rte 60; take Exit 175 off I–64, White Sulphur Springs, tel. 304/536–1944, www.greenbriersf.com. Free. Daily 6 AM–10 PM.

The Homestead When you're on the 15,000 acres that make up the Homestead, it might seem as if the question is what *not* to do, rather than what to do. At the resort's on-site spa, the water bubbling up is 104°F. The extensive outdoor activities include downhill skiing in winter, hiking along mountain trails, fishing in mountain streams, and golfing on three courses. You might just want to wander through the grand, neoclassic interior, which is full of Roman columns and plush carpets. The Homestead draws many people just passing through or driving up for the day, so don't feel out of place if you just want to have a look around. > U.S. 220, Hot Springs, tel. 540/839–1766 or 800/838–1766, www.thehomestead.com.

Humpback Bridge On U.S. 60 about 3 mi west of Covington, a restored covered bridge originally built in 1835 is now a historic landmark. There are no central beams or other supports in the center; it's the bulging arch there that keeps things structurally sound. It's the only one of its kind in the United States. > U.S. 60, 3 mi west of Covington, www.covington.va.us.

Jefferson Pools Our third president did indeed soak in the mineral-rich hot springs here back in 1818 (Native Americans had been doing it long before him). Reservations are recommended for the baths, which start at $12. More information is avail-

The Bunker

AROUND WHITE SULPHUR SPRINGS *folks knew that the new addition to the Greenbrier hotel had a fallout shelter with it. And they knew the builders were pouring an awful lot of concrete. But no one knew the full scope of what had been built under the famous resort until a 1992 Washington Post article revealed the truth.*

That bunker was 112,000 square feet and nearly 70 stories underground. It had been built between 1959 and 1962 to house Congress in the event of a nuclear attack on the United States. For more than three decades, few knew about the bunker, and thankfully, it was never needed. It was only put on full alert once, shortly after its completion, during the Cuban Missile Crisis.

The government quickly decommissioned the bunker after the Post article, and three years later, the Greenbrier opened it up as a tourist attraction. But how did something that big stay a secret so long? The small team assigned to maintain the facility was called "Forsythe Associates," and

also performed audio and video work for the Greenbrier. Members of the top-secret team lived in area towns and blended into daily life, telling people they were TV repairmen at the massive resort.

The Greenbrier got an enormous windfall out of what was dubbed "Project Greek Island": a massive addition entirely at government expense, and now an extra attraction. You can now take a a tour of the subterranean labyrinth, heading into its dormitories, decontamination chambers, eating areas, and massive power plant.

able from the Homestead. > U.S. 220, Warm Springs, tel. 540/839–5346, www.thehomestead.com/spa/pools.asp. Daily 10–6.

Lake Moomaw A reservoir of 2,530-acres, Moomaw is surrounded by the George Washington National Forest, so there are no houses or other developments on its shore. People use the lake and the forest for swimming, boating, fishing, camping, and hiking. The lake has numerous access points around the lake, and 11 campgrounds, including 4 primitive ones. The Lake Moomaw Visitors Center is at Gathright Dam on State Route 605. Follow State Route 687 West from U.S. 220 north of Covington and follow the signs to the visitor center and other recreation areas. > Covington, tel. 540/862–8100, www.bathcountyva.org/recreation/GWNF.htm.

Lewisburg Historic District Sixty homes and other buildings from the 18th and 19th centuries make up this 235-acre historic district. The **Old Stone Church** (200 Church St., tel. 304/645–2676) is the centerpiece; it is believed this church was built in 1796 by women from the congregation: they carried the limestone blocks from the Greenbrier River, 4 mi away. Its slave balcony (from which slaves heard the service) and hand-hewn woodwork are still intact. > Tel. 304/645–1000 visitor center.

Lost World Caverns This cave's main room is 1,000 feet long and 75 feet wide. Stalactites, stalagmites, and flowstone (waterfall-like formations) fill this and other subterranean chambers. > HC34 Fairview Rd.; Rte. 60, 2 mi west of Lewisburg, tel. 304/645–6677, www.lostworldcaverns.com. $8. Mid-May–Labor Day, daily 9–7.

North House Museum Inside a restored house from 1820, this museum has antiques and artifacts dating from the early 1700s to the late 1800s. > 301 Washington St., Lewisburg, tel. 304/645–3398, www.greenbrierhistorical.org. $3. Mon.–Sat. 10–4.

Sports

Both the Greenbrier and the Homestead have scores of options for those with an avid taste for sports, including tennis, horseback riding, hiking, fly-fishing, and mountain biking.

GOLF

Few other places pack as much golf quantity and quality into such a relatively small area. The Homestead and the Greenbrier each have three 18-hole golf courses, and all six were influenced, designed, and played by some of the game's greatest names.

American golf's first organized play was at Oakhurst Links in 1884, a distinction that has led to White Sulphur Springs being dubbed the "Cooperstown of Golf." Golf came to the Homestead eight years later, and still three years before the first U.S. Open. The late golf legend Sam Snead, who lived most of his life near the Homestead, has left his imprint on both resorts' fine courses.

Greens fees for guests at the Greenbrier are $175 from April to October, $100 from November 1 through Thanksgiving. Rounds are free for guests from December through mid-March. The only course open to nonguests is the Old White Course; greens fees are $325.

Golf packages are available at both resorts. A golf package at the Homestead ranges from $251 off-season to $397 on in-season weekends. This includes room, meals, unlimited golf on the three courses below, golf cart, and use of the driving range and fitness center. Reservations should be made at least six months before; tee times fill up quickly.

Golf packages at the Greenbrier run from $272 off-season to $480 on in-season weekends. They include room, meals, unlimited play with a golf cart, preferred starting times, daily club cleaning and storage, unlimited use of the practice range, and a golf clinic. Caddies are not included.

Cascades Course In the years since its 1923 opening, this challenging par-70, 18-hole course (6,679/4,967; 73.0/70.3) has hosted seven USGA championships and two PGA events. Designed by William S. Flynn, the Cascade has sloping fairways that can be a challenge. Some say that it was Sam Snead's favorite course. Greens fees are $60 for the general public and $40 for resort guests. > The Homestead, tel. 540/839–1766 or 800/838–1766.

Cliff View Golf Club This semiprivate course grew from just a driving range in 1993 to an 18-hole, par-72 course in 1998. It's a much more inexpensive option for everyday golfers than the major resorts, with playing fees often less than half that at Greenbrier or Homestead (18-hole rates run no higher than $33). The scenery remains every bit as stunning. > 400 Friels Dr. (off Rte. 687, which is left off U.S. 200 between Covington and Hot Springs), Covington, tel. 540/962–2200 or 888/849–2200, www.cliffviewgolf.com.

1884 Oakhurst Links For a unique experience, try playing with 1800s-style hickory shaft clubs in costume at this 9-hole course manicured by grazing sheep. Built in 1884, this is the nation's oldest golf club. A tour of the property is included in the greens fee ($50), as are, if you like, period costumes. > 1 Montague St., White Sulphur Springs, tel. 304/536–1884, www.oakhurstlinks.com.

Greenbrier Course Jack Nicklaus redesigned this 18-hole, par-72 course (6,675/5.095; 73.1/69.8), originally built in 1924, in preparation for the 1979 Ryder Cup. It hosted the 1994 Solheim Cup as well. Bunkers surround the greens here, placing a premium on irons play and putting. > The Greenbrier, tel. 304/536–1110 or 800/624–6070.

Lower Cascades Course Built in 1963 by Robert Trent Jones, the par-72/70 Lower Cascades (6,619/4,726; 72.2/65.5) is known for maddening breaks and bunkers. Several top national amateur events have been run at this 18-hole course. > The Homestead, tel. 540/839–1766 or 800/838–1766.

Meadows Course The former Lakeside Course was given a new name after its 1999 renovation. The water hazards and bunkers of this par-71 course (6,807/5,001; 72.4/68.5) are frustrating, and the mountain views are lovely. > The Greenbrier, tel. 304/536–1110 or 800/624–6070.

Old Course A 6-hole course when it opened in 1892, the Old Course has been much altered over the years, although its first tee is still in the same spot. The par-72 course (6,211/4,952; 69.0/67.7) has an abundance of unusually angled fairways and small greens, with six par-3 holes. > The Homestead, tel. 540/839–1766 or 800/838–1766.

Old White Course With open fairways and sloping greens, Old White (6,652/5,179; 72.2/69.7) was built in 1913 to resemble Scottish links. Sam Snead and Ben Hogan are among the greats who have loved playing this par-70 course; golf course architect Robert Trent Jones once chose its first hole as the one for his own personal dream course. > The Greenbrier, tel. 304/536–1110 or 800/624–6070.

EQUIPMENT **Greenbrier Golf Club** > Tel. 304/536–1110 or 800/624–6070. **Homestead Golf Club** > Tel. 540/839–1766 or 800/838–1766.

Save the Date

FEBRUARY

Archduke Music Holiday The fine food and wine are as elegant as the chamber music this black-tie dinner celebrates. Named for Archduke Rudolph, Beethoven's patron and student, the benefit is held at the Garth Newel Music Center. > Rte. 220, Hot Springs, tel. 540/839–5018, www.garthnewel.org.

MAY

Show-Me Hike Through the month, wildflowers decorate Greenbrier State Forest and the Greenbrier Trail on hikes hosted by the White Sulphur Springs Garden Club. > Rte. 220, Hot Springs, tel. 304/536–1944 or 304/536–2500.

West Virginia Dandelion Festival Taste the greens and wine made from this yellow flower—and infamous weed. During this weekend-long festival you can also browse through locally made arts and crafts. > White Sulphur Springs, tel. 304/536–4007.

OCTOBER

Fall Foliage Festival Autumn's multihue robes of foliage in the Allegheny Mountains are celebrated with an arts-and-crafts festival and live music in early October. > Clifton Forge, tel. 540/862–4969.

WHERE TO STAY

The Greenbrier Built in 1760 and surrounded by 6,500 acres, the resort has a grand turn-of-the-20th-century style. Enter between its massive columns and walk through a colorfully carpeted lobby area with nine spacious chandeliered chambers. Every guest room is different and decorated in Dorothy Draper pastel prints. There is a tea and concert each afternoon in the lobby, and live music with dinner in the dining room. It is true elegance amid rustic surroundings. > 300 W. Main St., White Sulphur Springs 24986, tel. 304/536–1110 or 800/624–6070, fax 304/536–7854, www.greenbrier.com. 443 rooms, 32 suites, 67 cottages, 4 estate houses. 4 restaurants, dining room, room service, in-room data ports, some refrigerators, cable TV, driving range, 3 18-hole golf courses, 2 putting greens, 20 tennis courts, pro shop, 2 pools (1 indoor), wading pool, gym, hot tub, spa, boating, fishing, bicycles, bowling, croquet, hiking, ice-skating, sleigh rides, bar, theater, shops, Internet, meeting rooms, airport shuttle. AE, D, DC, MC, V. MAP. $$$$

The Homestead Host to a prestigious clientele since 1766, the Homestead has evolved from a country spa to a 15,000-acre resort and conference facility. From the glorious columns of the entry hall to the stunning views of the Allegheny Mountains, magnificence constantly surrounds those who stay here. Rooms in the sprawling red-brick building, built in 1891, have Georgian-style furnishings; some have fireplaces. An orchestra plays nightly in the formal dining room (dinner is included in the room rate), where Continental cuisine and regional specialties are served during six-course extravaganzas. > Rte. 220, Hot Springs 24445, tel. 540/839–1766 or 800/838–1766, fax 540/839–7670, www.thehomestead.com. 429 rooms, 77 suites. 6 restaurants, cable TV with movies and video games, 3 18-hole golf courses, 8 tennis courts, 2 pools (1 indoor), spa, bicycles, bowling, horseback riding, downhill skiing, ice-skating, cinema, video game room, Internet, meeting rooms, airport shuttle. AE, D, DC, MC, V. MAP. $–$$$$

NEAR THE GREENBRIER

General Lewis Country Inn The brick building is furnished with 19th-century pieces and antiques collected in the area. Every room has china, glass, prints, and other memorabilia; you can be sure the bed you sleep in is at least a century old. Downstairs is the inn's popular restaurant; Lewisburg historical sites are three blocks away. > 301 E. Washington St., Lewisburg 24901, tel. 800/628–4454. 24 rooms, 2 suites. Restaurant, dining room, room service, cable TV, bar; no smoking. AE, D, MC, V. $$

Lillian's Antique Shop and Bed & Breakfast Just a block from the Greenbrier, all the antiques in this 1905 Queen Anne–style cottage are for sale. One guest room is the servant's outbuilding. The three-course breakfast is served in the dining room. > 204 W. Main St., White Sulphur Springs 24986, tel. 877/536–1048, www.lilliansbedandbreakfast.com. 4 rooms. Cable TV, dining room; no smoking. AE, MC, V. BP. $$

Minnie Manor Inn This 1830s brick two-story house on a hill presents views over the historic town of Lewisburg. Fireplaces and floral Laura Ashley furnishings enhance the accommodations. > 403 E. Washington St., Lewisburg 24901, tel. 304/647–4096. 8 rooms. Cable TV, outdoor hot tub. No credit cards. BP. ¢

NEAR THE HOMESTEAD

Cliff View Golf Club Less expensive but with the same beautiful mountain surroundings of the large resorts, Cliff View has a package that includes an overnight stay, breakfast, and a round of golf for $80. The rooms, remarkably elegant for the cost, have an Appalachian theme and come with quilts that could have been sewn by grandma. Each of the rooms has access to a balcony with a view over the golf course and toward the bluffs over the Jackson River. > 400 Friels Dr. (off Rte. 687, which is left off U.S. 220 between Covington and Hot Springs), Covington 24426, tel. 540/962–2200 or 888/849–2200, www.cliffviewgolf.com. 8 rooms. Dining room, conference rooms, fishing, 18-hole golf course, pro shop, lounge; no room TVs. AE, MC, V. ¢

Inn at Gristmill Square Occupying five restored buildings at the same site as the Waterwheel Restaurant, the rooms inside this state historical landmark are in a colonial Virginia style. Four units are in the original miller's house; others occupy the former blacksmith's shop, hardware store, gristmill, and cottage. Some rooms have fireplaces and patios. > Rte. 645, Box 359, Warm Springs 24484, tel. 540/839–2231, fax 540/839–5770, www.gristmillsquare.com. 12 rooms, 5 suites, 1 apartment. Restaurant, cable TV, 3 tennis courts, pool, sauna, bar, meeting rooms. D, MC, V. BP. **$–$$**

Milton Hall This 1874 Gothic brick house, built as an elegant country retreat by English nobility, is on 44 acres. It's close to the George Washington National Forest and its abundant outdoor activities. The spacious rooms have Victorian furnishings and large beds. Box lunches can be ordered in advance. > 207 Thorny La. (I–64 [Exit 10] at Callaghan), Covington 24426, tel. 540/965–0196 or 877/764–5866, www.milton-hall.com. 6 rooms, 1 suite. Cable TV with movies, hiking; no smoking. D, MC, V. BP. **$$–$$$**

Roseloe Motel If the opulence of the Homestead is too much for you, the modest, homey, conventionally decorated rooms in this 1950s motel might be more your style. Six of the fourteen rooms provide kitchens or kitchenettes. Located near the Garth Newel Music Center, the Roseloe is halfway between Warm Springs and Hot Springs, where the fresh mountain air is bracing. > Rte. 1 (Box 590), Hot Springs 24445, tel. 540/839–5373. 14 rooms. Some kitchenettes, refrigerators, cable TV, some pets allowed. AE, D, MC, V. **¢**

WHERE TO EAT

THE GREENBRIER

Draper's Cafe This pleasant lunch spot is near many of Greenbrier's shops. You can eat inside or under an umbrella on the patio. Try the blackened salmon wrap or the fried green tomato sandwich for a West Virginia treat; you might want to save a little room for one of Draper's famous banana splits. > The Greenbrier, tel. 304/536–1110 or 800/624–6070. AE, D, DC, MC, V. No dinner. **$$–$$$**

Greenbrier Main Dining Room Included in the price of a daily stay at the Greenbrier is breakfast and dinner in the thickly carpeted dining room, which has thick chandeliers. The five-course dinner, prix fixe ($67) for those not staying here, changes daily; dishes have included grilled halibut with an eggplant salad and a mixed lamb grill with marinated lamb loin and mountain leek sausage. Before you even get to the main course, appetizers such as pan-roasted quail breast, chicken liver parfait, and duck with port wine jelly get you in the mood. For dessert, try Greenbrier's freestone peaches with whipped cream. > 300 W. Main St., White Sulphur Springs, tel. 304/536–1110 or 800/624–6070, www.greenbrier.com. AE, D, DC, MC, V. Reservations essential. **$$$$**

THE HOMESTEAD

Homestead Dining Room The traditional menu at the Homestead mixes Continental delicacies and regional specialties, such as Virginia smoked trout and Maryland soft-shell crab. Appetizers include items as varied as Hawaiian papaya with berries and lump crab meat with Gulf Coast shrimp. The dining room is included in rates if you're staying at the Homestead, but the bill can easily top $100 if you're not. The wine list is extensive and well chosen. An orchestra performs nightly. > The Homestead, tel. 540/839–1766 or 800/838–1766. AE, D, DC, MC, V. **$$$$**

Sam Snead's Tavern Across the street from the main Homestead property, this is a casual choice for times when you're looking for good food without dressing up. A creek runs under the old bank building that houses the tavern. The fare includes fresh trout and smoked ribs. The tavern's namesake frequented the tavern until his death in 2002. As you might expect from a place named for a golfing legend, the sports bar that's also here displays a great deal of PGA memorabilia. > U.S. 220, Hot Springs, tel. 540/839–7666. AE, MC, V. $–$$$

NEAR THE GREENBRIER

Trails Inn Restaurant Pull into the parking lot and give a honk to signal you're ready to order at this 1950s-style restaurant. The daily specials are delivered right to your car; there are also a few tables. Regular specials include panfried chicken, country-fried steak, spaghetti, meat loaf, and baked fish dishes. > Rte. 92, Neola, tel. 304/536–1900. No credit cards. $

Washington Street Inn The varied menu changes frequently in this restaurant, housed in a building from 1800. Marinated shrimp, mussels with penne pasta, and fillet of beef are among the highlights. Dine in the main room, decorated with Civil War memorabilia, or on the porch. > 208 W. Washington St., Lewisburg, tel. 304/645–1744. AE, D, DC, MC, V. Closed Sun. and Mon. $–$$

NEAR THE HOMESTEAD

Country Cafe A dining room with blue-checked tablecloths on each table provides down-home appeal for the country cooking here. Crafts and antiques line the walls, and a cast-iron stove sits in the corner. The Friday-night special is steamed shrimp, Saturday is prime rib night, and steaks and fried chicken are available every night. > U.S. 220, Hot Springs, tel. 540/839–2111. MC, V. Closed Mon. $$–$$$

Waterwheel Restaurant Part of a complex of five historic buildings, this restaurant is in a gristmill from 1700. A walk-in wine cellar, set among the gears of the original waterwheel, has 100 wine selections; you can step right in and choose a bottle for yourself. The dining area is decorated with Currier & Ives and Audubon prints. Menu favorites include fresh smoked trout and breast of chicken stuffed with wild rice, sausage, apples, and pecans. For dessert are such Old Virginny favorites as deep-dish apple pie, flavored with bourbon. Sunday brunch is both hearty and affordable. > Grist Mill Sq., Warm Springs, tel. 540/839–2231. D, MC, V. Closed Tues. Nov.–May. $$–$$$

ESSENTIALS

Getting Here

The best way to reach the Greenbrier and the Homestead is by car.

BY CAR

It's about a four-hour drive to either resort from Washington. The drive to the Greenbrier is almost entirely on interstate highways (you can even see the resort from a rest stop overlook on I–64). To get to the Greenbrier, take I–66 West to I–81, travel south to I–64 at Lexington (I–64 and I–81 share the same route between Staunton and Lexington), then go west on I–64, crossing into West Virginia. Take Exit 181, White Sulphur Springs. From there, the Greenbrier entrance is only 2 mi away on U.S. 60, which heads through the heart of the village.

One way to get to the Homestead is to take I–64 to Covington and then head 16 mi north on U.S. 220. For an alternate route that's shorter but also makes less use of interstates, first take I–66 West to I–81. Head south to Exit 240, toward Bridgewater, and then take Route 257 West to Route 42 heading south.

13

From Route 42 take Route 39 West to U.S. 220. Following Route 39 West from Lexington will take you through the dramatic Maury River gorge at Goshen Pass. The sight is worth a side trip, even if it's not directly on your route.

The drive to either resort is very scenic in good weather, but it can be hazardous in poor conditions. The winding, rugged roads, at much higher elevations that those in and near Washington, may be covered with ice and snow when temperatures are still well above freezing farther east. Fog, rain, and wind are other mountain hazards to look out for.

BY TRAIN
An Amtrak station is directly across from the Greenbrier's main gate. The Homestead is served by a station at Clifton Forge, 25 mi south. Neither station is staffed.
LINE **Amtrak** > Tel. 800/872–7245, www.amtrak.com.
STATIONS **Clifton Forge** > 400 S. Ridgeway St. **White Sulphur Springs** > 315 W. Main St.

Visitor Information

CONTACTS **Bath County Chamber of Commerce** > Rte 220, Box 718, Hot Springs 24445, tel. 540/839–5409 or 800/628–8092, www.bathcountyva.org. **Lewisburg Visitor Center** > 105 Church St., Lewisburg 24901, tel. 304/645–1000. **White Sulphur Springs Convention and Visitors Bureau** > 34 W. Main St., White Sulphur Springs 24986, tel. 304/536–3590 or 800/284–9440.

Southern Shenandoah Valley

Roanoke is 240 mi southwest of Washington, D.C.

14

Updated by Kevin Myatt

THE VERDANT PASTURES HERE, wedged between hazy blue ridgelines to the west and east, may seem to embody peacefulness itself. But many of the Southern Shenandoah Valley's most important sites deal with war. This is especially true in Lexington, where Robert E. Lee and Stonewall Jackson still evoke deep reverence a century and a half after their Confederate exploits. Just beyond the Blue Ridge on the eastern skyline is Bedford, the home of the National D-Day Memorial; farther east, in the Piedmont region, is Appomattox, where the Civil War ended.

Lexington and Roanoke, some 45 mi apart, are the focal points of the Southern Shenandoah, and a contrast in personalities. Lexington is the genteel small town, Roanoke the metropolitan hub. Lexington tends to be younger due to its two famous colleges; Roanoke is frequently recognized as one of the nation's best retirement cities. Lexington was founded during the Revolutionary War; Roanoke didn't start up until the 1870s, when it was a railroad town.

History and tradition are highly honored here. Country drives winding off from I–81 reveal columned mansions, tidy farmhouses, and red barns that suggest another era. At the time of the American Revolution, the Southern Shenandoah was the nation's frontier; sites such as Natural Bridge and the Peaks of Otter, explored by few settlers, seemed like legendary wild lands to colonists living in Eastern Seaboard cities. Today, what's been preserved of the wilderness allows for some great hiking, bicycling, and other recreation.

At the southern end of the Shenandoah Valley, in its own nearly contained bowl-shape valley, is Roanoke. Dubbed the "Star City of the South" for the 100-foot red-, white-, and blue-lighted star that's on a mountain above downtown, Roanoke is Virginia's largest city west of Richmond. The metropolitan area of 230,000 has enough city flavor to provide a degree of culture and elegance, but its location between the Blue Ridge Parkway and Appalachian Trail means that the wilds aren't too far away either; mountains dominate its horizons in all directions.

The Parkway begins at Waynesboro and snakes just east of the Shenandoah Valley, riding atop the Blue Ridge Mountains on its way south to Great Smoky Mountains National Park some 471 mi south in North Carolina. Roanoke is the largest city along its entire route. With the exception of Asheville, North Carolina, the rest of the parkway bypasses populated areas, as its New Deal–era designers intended. In Virginia, the parkway is especially scenic between Waynesboro and Roanoke, winding through the George Washington National Forest, near ridgetop views of crumpled-looking mountains and patchwork valleys.

From the parkway you can get a commanding view west across the valley and east across the Piedmont. In the Piedmont is Lynchburg, another metropolitan center for the region. It was here that Jefferson built his retreat, the octagonal Poplar Forest. Although the city's founder, John Lynch, was a Quaker pacifist, its most prominent

National D-Day Memorial

A HILLTOP IN VIRGINIA may seem like an odd choice for a memorial dedicated to those who gave their lives in the Invasion of Normandy, an ocean and more than half a century removed. So why was Bedford selected as the site?

On June 6, 1944—D-Day—Bedford lost 19 men in a single company of 30 soldiers. In proportion to its population of about 3,200, Bedford's losses were the highest of any community in the nation. Congress, recognizing the town as symbolic of all who suffered losses on that day, chose it as the site of the memorial.

The memorial's centerpiece is a granite arch engraved with the word "Overlord," the code name for D-Day. A flag plaza carries the standards of the 12 nations that contributed personnel and equipment to the massive operation. From the hill you can get a commanding view of Bedford, not much larger than it was in World War II. As President Bush said when dedicating the memorial on June 6, 2001, "This was

the place they left behind. And here was the life they dreamed of returning to." The most impressive part of the monument is the detailed iron sculptures of those soldiers. Sculpted by the Kansas artist Jim Brothers, they are scattered along a wall and in a pool beneath the arch.

The D-Day Memorial (tel. 540/586–3329, www.dday.org), just off U.S. 460 in Bedford, is open from 10 to 5 daily.

landmark is Monument Terrace, a war memorial: at the foot and head of the 139 limestone and granite steps that ascend to the Old City Courthouse are statues honoring a World War I doughboy and a Confederate soldier.

WHAT TO SEE & DO

BLUE RIDGE PARKWAY

Explore Park A 1,100-acre site near Roanoke, Explore Park depicts life in Virginia from three distinct periods between 1671 and 1850. Costumed interpreters represent early Native American life, the colonial frontier experience, and the life of a 19th-century settlement, with a schoolhouse and a blacksmith's shop. The park has 6 mi of hiking trails along the Roanoke River gorge as well as good places for mountain biking, fishing, canoeing, and kayaking. > 1½ mi north of Milepost 115 on the Blue Ridge Pkwy., tel. 540/427–1800 or 800/842–9163, www.explorepark.org. $8. May–Oct., Wed.–Sat. 10–5, Sun. noon–5.

James River Visitor Center This center occupies a natural water gap in the Blue Ridge. A footbridge over the James River leads to the Kanawha Canal Lock. The restored lock was once part of a 200-mi canal system that ran from Richmond across the Blue Ridge to Buchanan. > Milepost 63, Blue Ridge Pkwy., www.blueridgeparkway.org. Free. May–Oct., daily 9–5.

Peaks of Otter Recreation Area At this park you can get a close-up view of cone-shape Sharp Top Mountain (3,875 feet) and its twin, Flat Top (4,004 feet). Hiking trails lead to both peaks, as well as Harkening Hill, the restored Johnson homestead, to the Fallingwater Cascades, or around Abbott Lake in the shadow of the mountains. A pleasant lakeside lodge and campground along the placid lake below are an ideal base for local trekking. > Blue Ridge Pkwy., Milepost 86, tel. 540/586–4357, www.peaksofotter.com. Free.

LEXINGTON

Cyrus McCormick Museum The inventor of the first mechanical wheat reaper is honored here. Now a livestock research center, this mill farmstead is where Mc-Cormick did his work. In addition to the museum and family home, you can tour a blacksmith shop and gristmill. All are registered as National Historic Landmarks. > State Rte. 606, 5 mi north of Lexington, tel. 540/377–2255. Free. Daily 8:30–5.

George C. Marshall Museum Exhibits preserve the memory of the World War II army chief of staff, tracing his career from when he was aide-de-camp to John "Black Jack" Pershing in World War I to when, as secretary of state, he devised the Marshall Plan, a strategy for reviving postwar Western Europe. Marshall's Nobel peace prize is on display; so is the Oscar won by his aide Frank McCarthy, who produced the Best Picture of 1970, *Patton*. An electronically narrated map tells the story of World War II. > Virginia Military Institute campus, Letcher Ave., tel. 540/463–7103. $3. Daily 9–5.

Lexington Carriage Company Horse-drawn carriages from this company can take you for 50-minute rides through the historic town streets. > Lexington, tel. 540/463–5647. $16. Tours Apr.–Oct.

Natural Bridge of Virginia This impressive limestone arch, which supports Route 11, has been gradually carved out by Cedar Creek, now rushing 215 feet below. The Monacan Native American tribe called it the Bridge of God. George Washington carved his own initials in the stone when he surveyed the structure for Lord Halifax; Thomas Jefferson bought it from King George III. Also on the property are dizzying caverns that descend 34 stories, a wax museum, and an 18th-century village constructed by the Monacan Indian Nation. > I–81 S, Exit 180; I–81 N, Exit 175; 20 mi south of Lexington, tel. 540/291–2121 or 800/533–1410, www.naturalbridgeva.com. Bridge $10, all attractions $17. Mar.–Nov., daily 8 AM–dark.

Stonewall Jackson House Confederate General Jackson's private life is on display at the house he lived in for two years while teaching physics and military tactics to the cadets, before leaving for his command in the Civil War. He is revealed as a dedicated Presbyterian devoted to physical fitness, careful with money, musically inclined, and fond of gardening. This is the only house he ever owned; it is furnished now with period pieces and some of his belongings. > 8 E. Washington St., tel. 540/463–2552, www.stonewalljackson.org. $5. Mon.–Sat. 9–5; Sun. 1–5.

Theater at Lime Kiln The Kiln's solid rock walls create a dramatic backdrop for musicals, concerts, and performances as varied as Russian clowns and Vietnamese puppeteers. Original musicals are staged Tuesday through Saturday, and contemporary music concerts are given on Sunday throughout summer. > Lime Kiln Rd., tel. 540/463–7088, www.theateratlimekiln.com.

Virginia Military Institute The nation's oldest state-supported military college, VMI was founded in 1839. With an enrollment of about 1,300 cadets, the institute has admitted women since 1997. The Virginia Military Institute Museum in the lower level of Jackson Memorial Hall displays 15,000 artifacts, including Stonewall Jackson's stuffed and mounted horse, Little Sorrel, and the general's coat, pierced by the bullet that killed him at Chancellorsville. > Letcher Ave., tel. 540/464–7232, www.vmi.edu. Free. Daily 9–5.

Washington and Lee University Founded in 1749, W & L, as alums and students fondly call it, is named in gratitude for a large financial gift from our nation's first president and for the Confederate general who served as its president for five years after the Civil War. Today, with an enrollment of 2,000, the university occupies a campus of white-column, redbrick buildings around a central colonnade. The campus's Lee Chapel and Museum contains many relics of Robert E. Lee's family, including Edward Valentine's statue of the recumbent general. Here one can sense the affection and reverence that Lee inspired. > Jefferson St. (Rte. 11), tel. 540/463–8768, www2.wlu.edu. Free. Chapel Apr.–Oct., Mon.–Sat. 9–5, Sun. 1–5; Nov.–Mar., Mon.–Sat. 9–4, Sun. 1–4; campus tours Apr.–Oct., weekdays 10–4, Sat. 9:45–noon; Jan.–Mar., weekdays 10 and noon, Sat. 11.

LYNCHBURG

Anne Spencer House You can step into "Edankraal," the studio of this late poet of the Harlem Renaissance. Hers is the only work of a Virginian to appear in the *Norton Anthology of Modern American and English Poetry*. A librarian at one of Lynchburg's segregated black schools, Spencer (1882–1975) penned most of her work in this backgarden sanctuary, which has been left completely intact with her writing desk, bookcases, mementos, and walls tacked with photos and news clippings. > 1313 Pierce St., tel. 434/847–1459. $5. Tours by appointment.

Appomattox Court House This important site 25 mi east of Lynchburg has been restored to its appearance of April 9, 1865, when Confederate General Lee surrendered the Army of Northern Virginia to General Grant, ending the Civil War. There are 27 structures in the national historical park; most can be entered. A highlight is the reconstructed McLean House's parlor, where the articles of surrender were signed. > 3 mi north of Appomattox, on State Rte. 24, tel. 434/352–8987. $4. June–Aug., daily 9–5:30; Sept.–May, daily 8:30–5.

Pest House Medical Museum On the grounds of the Confederate Cemetery, the museum provides a brief but informative look into medical practices and instruments at the time of the Civil War and later. This 1840s frame building was the office of Dr. John Jay Terrell. (The actual Pest House, or House of Pestilence, was the city's first hospital. Those with infectious diseases were quarantined there.) > 4th and Taylor Sts., tel. 434/847–1465. Free. Daily dawn–dusk.

Point of Honor This mansion on Daniel's Hill was built in 1815 on the site of a duel. Once part of a 900-acre estate, this redbrick house surrounded by lawns retains a commanding view of the James River. The facade is elegantly symmetrical, with two octagonal bays joined by a balustrade on each of the building's two stories. The interiors have been restored and furnished with pieces authentic to the early-19th-century federal period, including wallpaper whose pattern is in the permanent collection of New York's Metropolitan Museum of Art. > 112 Cabell St., tel. 434/847–1459, www.pointofhonor.org. $5. Daily 10–4.

Thomas Jefferson's Poplar Forest Built by Jefferson as his "occasional retreat," this octagonal structure is erected on a slope 5 mi southwest of Lynchburg. The octagon's center is a square, skylighted dining room flanked by two smaller octagons. Restoration work continues to return the building to Jefferson's original design. > Rte. 661, Forest, tel. 434/525–1806, www.poplarforest.org. $7. Apr.–Nov., daily 10–4.

ROANOKE

Booker T. Washington National Monument Washington (1856–1915), born into slavery on this farm 25 mi southeast of Roanoke, was a remarkable educator and author who went on to advise Presidents McKinley, Roosevelt, and Taft and to take tea with Queen Victoria. More important, he started Tuskegee Institute in Alabama and inspired generations of African-Americans. Covering 224 acres, the farm's restored buildings; tools; crops; animals; and, in summer, interpreters in period costume all help show what life during slavery was like. > Rte. 122 (21 mi south of Bedford), tel. 540/721–2094, www.nps.gov/bowa. Free. Daily 9–5.

Dixie Caverns Rather than descending into the cave, you first must walk upstairs into the heart of a mountain. The spacious Cathedral Room, formations dubbed Turkey Wing and Wedding Bell, and an earthquake fault line are among the sights. There's also a mineral and fossil shop attached to the caverns. > 5753 W. Main St. (take I–81 to Exit 132, which links up with Rte. 11 [Rte. 460], Salem, tel. 540/380–2085. $7.50. May–Sept., daily 9:30–6; Oct.–Apr., daily 9:30–5.

Market Square The heart of Roanoke is Market Square, with Virginia's oldest continuous farmer's market, a multiethnic food court inside the restored City Market Building, and several restaurants, shops, and bars. A restored warehouse called Center in the Square contains the Mill Mountain Theatre and three museums, devoted to art, science, and history. The science museum has a planetarium and MegaDome theater. > 1 Market Sq. SE, tel. 540/342–5700, www.centerinthesquare.org. Science museum $6, with planetarium $8, with MegaDome $9; history museum $2; art museum $3. Museums closed Mon.

Mill Mountain Star The 100-foot-tall star, which is lit a patriotic red, white, and blue at night, is in a city park 1,000 feet above the Roanoke Valley. From either of the park's two overlooks, Roanoke, the "Star City of the South," looks like a scale model of a city. From the overlooks you can also see wave after wave of Appalachian ridgelines. > Mill Mountain Park, follow Walnut St. south 2 mi from downtown Roanoke; or take Parkway Spur Rd. 3 mi north from Blue Ridge Pkwy. at Milepost 120.3.

Mill Mountain Zoo Sharing the mountaintop with the star is one of only two nationally accredited zoos in Virginia. Though Asian animals like a rare Siberian tiger, snow leopards, and red pandas are the main attractions in this small zoo, many find the prairie dog exhibit the most entertaining. > Mill Mountain Park, follow Walnut St. south 2 mi from downtown Roanoke; or take Parkway Spur Rd. 3 mi north from Blue Ridge Pkwy. at Milepost 120.3, tel. 540/343–3241, www.mmzoo.org. $6. Daily 10–5 (gate closes at 4:30).

Virginia Museum of Transportation The largest collection of diesel and steam locomotives in the country is found in this downtown museum. On exhibit are a 1940s "highway post office" bus, a Ford/American LaFrance fire engine, and a large-model train layout. Roanoke got its start as a railroad town and was once the headquarters of the Norfolk & Western railroad. Many of the dozens of original train cars and engines were built in town. > 303 Norfolk Ave., tel. 540/342–5670, www.vmt.org. $6.30. Wed.–Sat. 10–5, Sun. noon–5.

Sports

BIKING

Blackwater Creek Natural Area More than 12 mi of trails, mostly level and paved, wind through deeply forested ribbons in Lynchburg, often making it hard to believe that you are just blocks from houses, fast-food restaurants, and banks. One trail goes through a 500-foot tunnel. The Percival's Island Trail extends more than a mile along a narrow strip of land in the middle of the James River near downtown. > www.lynchburgva.gov/parksandrec/blackwtr.htm.

Carvins Cove For a fairly rugged mountain bike experience, look to the network of dirt trails that cover the forested hillsides around this valley-tucked reservoir just west of Roanoke.
EQUIPMENT **Blackwater Creek Bike Rental** > 1611 Concord Tpke., Lynchburg, tel. 434/845–4030. **East Coasters Cycling and Fitness** > 4341 Starkey Rd. SW, Roanoke, tel. 540/774–7933. **Roanoke Parks and Recreation Department** > 210 Reserve Ave., Roanoke, tel. 540/563–9170 or 540/853–2236.

HIKING
Appalachian Trail The world-famous footpath crosses the area from southwest to northeast, crossing the Shenandoah Valley at Troutville, northwest of Roanoke. Two of the most photographed formations on the entire 2,000-mi route from Georgia to Maine, McAfee Knob and Dragon's Tooth, are accessible from trailheads on the Virginia 311 highway west of Roanoke. The trail crisscrosses the Blue Ridge Parkway between Roanoke and the Peaks of Otter, with several access points.
EQUIPMENT **Blue Ridge Outdoors** > Valley View Mall and Tanglewood Mall, Roanoke, tel. 540/777–2110 or 540/777–4311. **CMT Sporting Goods** > 3473 Brandon Ave., Roanoke, tel. 540/343–5533. **Outdoor Trails Co.** > Botetourt Commons, Daleville, tel. 540/992–5850.

Save the Date

APRIL
Vinton Dogwood Festival The small town of Vinton, just east of Roanoke, welcomes the blooming trees of spring each year with arts and crafts, a parade, and country music performances. > Tel. 540/983–0613, www.vintondogwoodfestival.org.

MAY
Strawberry Festival Thousands come to downtown Roanoke for fresh strawberry shortcake and ice cream, sold to support a local private school. > Crestar Plaza, Roanoke, tel. 540/563–5036.

MAY–JUNE
Festival in the Park May in Roanoke concludes with a two-week celebration of music, food, and crafts. Big-name entertainment is often on the bill for Memorial Day weekend, as are a fireworks display and a huge sidewalk art show. > Tel. 540/342–2640, www.roanokefestival.org.

JUNE
Miss Virginia Pageant The Roanoke Civic Center is the site of the annual event that determines who will represent Virginia in the Miss America pageant. > 710 Williamson Rd., Roanoke, tel. 540/981–1201, www.missva.com.
Roanoke Valley Horse Show Nearly 1,000 entries from across the country compete for prizes in this all-breed horse show at the Salem Civic Center. > 1001 Roanoke Rd., Salem, tel. 540/375–4013, www.roanokevalleyhorseshow.com.

JULY
Fourth of July Hot Air Balloon Rally As many as 20 balloons are launched from the grounds of Virginia Military Institute in Lexington on the morning of July 4. The balloon rally is followed by a day of music and food, and an evening fireworks show. > Tel. 540/463–8719.
Independence Celebration Interpreters in period dress act out the lives of local settlers during Thomas Jefferson's time, when Poplar Forest was still his retreat. Wagon rides and 19th-century crafts are also part of the Fourth of July event. > Poplar Forest, tel. 804/525–1806.

Music for Americans Fireworks and patriotic music reverberate off the Blue Ridge Mountains from Roanoke's Victory Stadium each Fourth of July. > Tel. 540/343–9127.
Virginia Commonwealth Games The competitors for this event come from around Virginia for sports ranging from basketball to chess at sites around the Roanoke Valley. > Tel. 540/343–0987 or 800/333–8274.

AUGUST
Thomas Jefferson's Tomato Faire Competitions centering around tomatoes and canned goods begin at sunrise in Lynchburg's Community Market. > Main and 12th Sts., Lynchburg, tel. 804/847–1499.
Vinton Old-Time Bluegrass Festival Hundreds of bands and individual pickers compete for prizes, and some more famous musicians give concerts as well. Crafts and a carnival are also on hand. > Vinton Farmers Market, tel. 540/983–0613 or 540/345–8545.

SEPTEMBER
Henry Street Heritage Festival This celebration of African-American culture takes place in a historically black neighborhood near downtown Roanoke. > Tel. 540/345–4818.
Kaleidoscope A monthlong celebration welcomes fall to Lynchburg, with events that include antiques shows, riverside music, and a teddy bear parade. > Tel. 804/847–1811 or 800/732–5821.
Olde Salem Days Some festivalgoers don 19th-century attire as Salem's frontier days are celebrated with antiques, crafts, music, and children's events. > Main St., Salem, tel. 540/772–8871.
Rockbridge Food and Wine Festival Enjoy wine tastings and food along with music and performances by the Lime Kiln players. > Theater at Lime Kiln, Lime Kiln Rd., Lexington, tel. 540/463–5375.
Rockbridge Mountain Music and Dance Festival Join the fun of old-time country music performances and dancing under the pavilion in Glen Maury Park, east of Lexington. > Glen Maury Park, 10th Ave., Buena Vista, tel. 540/261–7321 or 540/261–2880, www.rockbridgefestival.org.

SEPTEMBER–OCTOBER
Affair in the Square This huge formal party at Center in the Square includes dinner and dancing. > 1 Market Sq. SE, Roanoke, tel. 540/342–5700.

NOVEMBER
Christmas at the Market Lynchburg kicks off the holiday season with handcrafted Christmas items and a visit from Mr. and Mrs. Santa Claus. > Main St., Lynchburg, tel. 804 847–1499 or 800/732–5821.

NOVEMBER–DECEMBER
Festival of Trees Local businesses compete in decorating Christmas trees each Thanksgiving weekend in Roanoke. The trees remain on display through the Christmas season. > Tel. 540/344–0931.

WHERE TO STAY

BLUE RIDGE PARKWAY
Peaks of Otter Lodge This unpretentious, peaceful lodge is so popular that reservations are accepted beginning October for the following year. Every room looks out on Abbott Lake from a private terrace or balcony, and the interiors have a folksy quality. The restaurant's big draw is the Friday-night seafood buffet for $22. > Milepost 86,

Rte. 664, Box 489, Bedford 24523, tel. 540/586–1081 or 800/542–5927, fax 540/586–4420, www.peaksofotter.com. 63 rooms. Restaurant, fishing, hiking, bar, pub, meeting rooms; no room phones, no room TVs. MC, V. ¢

LEXINGTON

Maple Hall For a taste of the past, spend a night at this country inn of 1850. Once a plantation house, it's on 56 acres 6 mi north of Lexington. All rooms have period antiques and modern amenities; most have gas fireplaces as well. > Rte. 11, 24450, tel. 540/463–6693 or 877/463–2044, fax 540/463–7262, www.lexingtonhistoricinns.com/maplehall.htm. 17 rooms, 4 suites. Restaurant, tennis court, pool, fishing, hiking, meeting rooms. D, MC, V. BP. $–$$

Natural Bridge Hotel Within walking distance of the spectacular rock arch (there's also a shuttle bus), the colonial-style brick hotel has a beautiful location as well as numerous recreational facilities. Long porches with rocking chairs allow for leisurely appreciation of the Blue Ridge Mountains. Rooms are done in a colonial Virginia style. > Rte. 11, Box 57, Natural Bridge 24578, tel. 540/291–2121 or 800/533–1410, fax 540/291–1896, www.naturalbridgeva.com. 180 rooms. Restaurant, snack bar, some microwaves, cable TV with movies and video games, miniature golf, 2 tennis courts, pool, hiking, bar, meeting rooms. AE, D, DC, MC, V. ¢

ROANOKE

Bernard's Landing This resort on Smith Mountain Lake 45 minutes southeast of Roanoke rents one- to three-bedroom condominiums with water views and two- to five-bedroom town houses (all waterfront) for periods of up to two weeks. The units are separately owned, so furnishings vary widely, but all units have full kitchen facilities and private decks. > 775 Ashmeade Rd., Moneta 24121, tel. 540/721–8870 or 800/572–2048, fax 540/721–8383, www.bernardslanding.com. 60 units. Restaurant, kitchens, microwaves, cable TV, 6 tennis courts, 2 pools, gym, sauna, boating, fishing, racquetball, playground, Internet, meeting rooms. AE, D, MC, V. $–$$$

Hotel Roanoke and Conference Center This elegant Tudor-revival building was built in 1882 by the Norfolk & Western Railroad. The richly paneled lobby has Florentine marble floors and ceiling frescos, and guest room are furnished very traditionally. The Market Square Bridge, a glassed-in walkway, goes from the hotel across railroad tracks to downtown attractions. > 110 Shenandoah Ave., 24016, tel. 540/985–5900, fax 540/345–2890, www.hotelroanoke.com. 313 rooms, 19 suites. 2 restaurants, cable TV with movies and video games, pool, gym, bar, Internet, convention center, meeting rooms, airport shuttle, no-smoking rooms. AE, D, DC, MC, V. $$

Mountain Lake Centered around the highest natural lake east of the Mississippi, this resort has more than 20 different types of accommodations, including spartan cottages and plush suites in a majestic sandstone hotel from 1930 (the resort itself predates the Civil War). Atop 4,000-foot Salt Pond Mountain, Mountain Lake resort has an overwhelming number of outdoor activities available: you can hike, mountain bike, ride horses, swim, and boat within the 2,500-acre Mountain Lake Wilderness, which surrounds the hotel and is operated by a nonprofit organization. Nearby are the Jefferson National Forest and the Appalachian Trail. Pembroke is 50 mi west of Roanoke. > 115 Hotel Circle, 7 mi north of U.S. 460 on Rte. 700, Pembroke 24136, tel. 540/626–7121, www.mountainlakehotel.com. 28 cottages, 16 lodge rooms, 43 hotel rooms. Dining room, some microwaves, some refrigerators, pool, hot tub, bicycles, archery, hiking, video game room, shop, meeting rooms, Internet; no a/c, no room TVs. AE, D, MC, V. MAP. Closed Dec.–Apr. $$$–$$$$

CAMPING

Roanoke Mountain Campground You can camp amid forested hills just off the Blue Ridge Parkway only 5 mi from downtown Roanoke. A 5-mi hiking trail encircles the campground, and a scenic road leads to the vistas atop nearby Roanoke Mountain nearby. > Blue Ridge Pkwy., Milepost 120.5, Roanoke 24014, tel. 540/857–2491. 74 tent sites, 30 partial hookups. Flush toilets, partial hookups (electric and water), dump station, drinking water, grills, picnic tables, electricity, public telephone. No credit cards. Closed Nov.–Apr. ¢

WHERE TO EAT

LEXINGTON

Maple Hall At this former plantation house, dinner is served in three ground-floor rooms and on a glassed-in patio; the main dining room has a large decorative fireplace. Among notable entrées on the seasonal menu are beef fillet with green peppercorn sauce; veal sautéed with mushrooms in hollandaise sauce; and chicken Chesapeake, a chicken breast stuffed with spinach and crabmeat. > Rte. 11, tel. 540/463–6693 or 877/463–2044, fax 540/463–7262, www.lexingtonhistoricinns.com/maplehall.htm. D, MC, V. BP. $–$$$

The Palms Once a Victorian ice cream parlor, this full-service restaurant in an 1890 building has indoor and outdoor dining. Wood booths line the walls of the plant-filled room: the pressed-metal ceiling is original. Specialties include broccoli-cheese soup, charbroiled meats, and teriyaki chicken. > 101 W. Nelson St., tel. 540/463–7911. Reservations not accepted. D, MC, V. $

Wilson-Walker House This stately 1820 Greek-revival house serves some elegant regional dishes. Seafood is a specialty—try the pan-seared, potato-encrusted trout or the crab and shrimp cakes. The restaurant is not as expensive as one might expect, and is particularly affordable during the $5 chef's-special luncheon. > 30 N. Main St., tel. 540/463–3020. Reservations essential. AE, MC, V. Closed Sun. and Mon. $$$

ROANOKE

Carlos Brazilian International Cuisine You can watch the auburn sun set behind the mountain-rimmed western horizon from this restaurant, which serves French, Italian, Spanish, and Brazilian dishes. Try the *porco reacheado* (pork tenderloin stuffed with spinach and feta cheese) or the *moqueca mineira* (shrimp, clams, and whitefish in a Brazilian sauce). Brazilian radio often accompanies the meal. > 4167 Electric Rd., tel. 540/345–7661. AE, MC, V. Closed Sun. $–$$$

The Homeplace Inside an early-20th-century farm home in the valley hamlet of Catawba, grimy Appalachian Trail hikers, sharply dressed Sunday churchgoers, and Beltway weekenders are all greeted with equal warmth and served an all-you-can-eat selection of home-cooked country fare. Fried chicken, mashed potatoes, green beans, pinto beans, and hot biscuits are served to each table for $11 a person; add a dollar for a second meat selection. No alcohol is served, but the lemonade is delicious. > 7 mi west of Salem on Rte. 311 N (Exit 141 off I–81), Catawba, tel. 540/384–7252. Reservations not accepted. MC, V. No lunch Thurs.–Sat., no dinner Sun. $

The Library This quiet, elegant restaurant in a shopping center is decorated with shelves of books. Its frequently changing menu specializes in seafood dishes. Expect dishes such as sautéed Dover sole with almonds, fillet of beef with béarnaise sauce, and lobster tail. > Piccadilly Sq., 3117 Franklin Rd. SW, tel. 540/985–0811. Reservations essential. AE, DC, MC, V. Closed Sun. and Mon. No lunch. $$–$$$

Regency Dining Room This formal restaurant serves regional Southern cuisine; perennial favorites include peanut soup and steak Diane, prepared table-side. There's a good brunch here on Sunday. > Hotel Roanoke and Conference Center, 110 Shenandoah Ave., 24016, tel. 540/985–5900, fax 540/345–2890, www.hotelroanoke.com. AE, D, DC, MC, V. $$$$

ESSENTIALS

Getting Here

By far the simplest way to visit the Southern Shenandoah Valley is to jump in a car, head west on I–66 and then south on I–81. You can arrive at the region's major destinations in three to four hours of driving.

A flight from Dulles International to Roanoke is a relatively painless affair, and an Amtrak train trip to Lynchburg or a Greyhound bus trip to Roanoke can add a different flavor to the adventure. Except for city bus services in the Roanoke and Lynchburg areas, don't expect to find public transit systems in this mostly rural region.

BY BUS

Greyhound goes from Washington and to Roanoke up to six times daily. Buena Vista, just east of Lexington, has limited service, with two or three stops daily. Since the bus route to these locations takes five to seven hours from Washington and can cost $75 or more round-trip, you're better off driving if you have only a two- or three-day weekend planned.

DEPOTS **Buena Vista** > 211 W. 21st St., tel. 800/231–2222. **Roanoke** > 26 Salem Ave., tel. 540/343–5436.

LINE **Greyhound Lines** > Tel. 800/231–2222, www.greyhound.com.

BY CAR

Scenic drives are abundant in the Southern Shenandoah Valley, making car travel a particularly enticing way to enjoy the region. Interstate 81, the main thoroughfare through the area, is surrounded by emerald mountains and undulating pastures. Although scenic, I–81 can sometimes become hectic, since it's a north–south artery for truck traffic. Access to Roanoke is via I–581, a short spur from I–81, and U.S. 460 leads from Roanoke east to Bedford, Lynchburg, and Appomattox.

For a more serene drive, U.S. 11 roughly parallels I–81, connecting off-the-beaten-path towns like Buchanan and Troutville that retain much of yesteryear's charm. The ultimate driving experience in the region is the Blue Ridge Parkway, which begins near Waynesville and weaves south to Roanoke on its way to North Carolina.

The same mountainous terrain that contributes to the area's beauty can also make for treacherous travel. Dense valley fog banks, mountain-shrouding clouds, and gusty ridgetop winds are concerns at any time of the year, and winter brings ice and snow conditions that can change dramatically in a few miles when the elevation changes. I–81 has been the scene of many multicar fatal pileups caused by fog or snow, so always be cautious and try to avoid lengthy interstate travel during times of inclement weather.

BY PLANE

United Express connects Dulles International Airport and Roanoke Regional Airport with a one-hour turboprop or small jet flight each day. All other connections between Washington's airports and the regional airports at Roanoke and Lynchburg require plane changes, so that traveling by car or bus would generally be easier and much less expensive.

Both regional airports are relatively hassle-free and even cozy, but large enough for you to find a bite to eat or a bookstore to browse while awaiting a flight. Except during peak holiday periods, an hour is enough time to arrive in advance of your flight's departure time.

AIRPORTS **Lynchburg Regional Airport** > Rte. 29 S, Lynchburg, tel. 434/582–1150, www.ci.lynchburg.va.us/airport. **Roanoke Regional Airport** > 5202 Aviation Dr. NW (off I–581), Roanoke, tel. 540/362–1999, www.roanokeairport.com. *CARRIER* **United Express** > Tel. 800/241–6522 or 800/824–6200, www.ual.com.

BY TRAIN

Passenger train service in the southern Shenandoah Valley area is limited to Amtrak. Amtrak's *Crescent* runs between New York City and New Orleans and stops daily in Lynchburg. A complimentary shuttle bus on Sunday, Wednesday, and Friday connects Roanoke (Campbell Court and Roanoke Airport Sheraton) with an Amtrak station at Clifton Forge, 50 mi northwest. The Amtrak line through Clifton Forge connects Chicago and Washington.

LINE **Amtrak** > Tel. 800/872–7245, www.amtrak.com. *STATION* **Kemper Street Station** > 825 Kemper St., Lynchburg, tel. 434/847–8247.

Visitor Information

The National Park Service's office in Vinton has information on Virginia's section of the Blue Ridge Parkway, and the Lynchburg Parks and Recreation Department covers the Blackwater Creek Natural Area.

Roanoke Parks and Recreation Department can tell you more about the bike trails on Carvins Cove.

CONTACTS **Blue Ridge Parkway Visitors Center** > Explore Park, 1½ mi north of Milepost 115 on the Blue Ridge Pkwy., tel. 540/427–1800 or 800/842–9163, www.explorepark.org. **Lexington Visitor Center** > 106 E. Washington St., Lexington 24450, tel. 540/463–3777 or 877/453–9822, www.lexingtonvirginia.com. **Lynchburg Parks and Recreation Department** > 301 Grove St., Lynchburg 24501, tel. 434/847–1650, www.lynchburgva.gov/parksandrec/blackwtr.htm. **Lynchburg Regional Convention and Visitors Bureau** > 216 12th St., Lynchburg 24504, tel. 434/847–1811 or 800/732–5821. **National Park Service** > 2551 Mountain View Rd., Vinton, tel. 540/857–2490. **New River Valley Visitors Alliance** > 7502 Lee Hwy., Radford 24141, tel. 540/633–6788 or 888/398–8988. **Roanoke Parks and Recreation Department** > 210 Reserve Ave., Roanoke 24016, tel. 540/563–9170 or 540/853–2236. **Roanoke Valley Convention and Visitors Bureau** > 114 Market St., Roanoke 24011, tel. 540/342–6025 or 800/635–5535, www.visitroanokeva.com. **Shenandoah Valley Travel Association** > Box 1040, New Market 22844, tel. 540/740–3132 or 877/847–4878, www.shenandoah.org.

Charlottesville

100 mi southwest of Washington, D.C.

15

Revised by Karyn-Siobhan Robinson

THOSE WHO LOVE HISTORY FLOCK to Charlottesville primarily because it's at the core of what Virginians call "Mr. Jefferson's country." Although the third president's influence is inescapable throughout the Commonwealth (and far beyond its borders), Jefferson's legacy is especially strong in Charlottesville and in other parts of Albemarle and Orange counties. It's here that you find a concentration of buildings and sites associated with him and the giants among his contemporaries.

In the center of the state, Charlottesville has been an important crossroads since colonial times. Main Street follows one of the first trails from the Tidewater area to the west. Named in 1762 for Queen Charlotte, wife of George III, the town today is a cosmopolitan college known for its fine buildings as well as its lush countryside. Just 2 mi to the southeast is the area's leading attraction: Monticello, the distinguished home that Thomas Jefferson designed and built for himself. Both it and the enterprise of his last years, the University of Virginia, are musts for appreciators of architecture as well as those who want to know their history.

But Charlottesville is interesting for much more than just its past. One of America's best small arts towns, it nurtures a thriving arts community, many of whose painters, printmakers, and sculptors have studios in the McGuffey Art Center. ArtInPlace, a program that brings works to public places throughout town, is a great way to glimpse a bit of the homegrown talent. Check the Web site (www.artinplace.org) to find out the locations of the outdoor sculptures, which change on an annual basis. Several annual festivals have also added to the city's luster, among them the Virginia Film Festival and the Virginia Festival of the Book.

For listings of cultural events, music, and movies, and a guide to restaurants, pick up a free copy of the *C-Ville Weekly* (www.c-ville.com), an arts-and-entertainment newspaper available in restaurants and hotels throughout the city. If you are near the University of Virginia campus, consult the student newspaper the *Cavalier Daily* (www.cavalierdaily.com) for the latest on college sports and events.

The city's six-block downtown pedestrian mall, a brick-paved street of restored buildings that stretches along Main Street, is its legal and financial hub as well as a big entertainment draw: outdoor restaurants and cafés, concerts, and impromptu theatrical events keep things hopping here.

For many, Charlottesville's natural beauty is reason enough to visit the area. The Blue Ridge Mountains and rolling countryside are the backdrop here, and azaleas and dogwoods are abundant throughout the region. In recent years the countryside has been discovered by celebrities, including the actress Sissy Spacek, best-selling author John Grisham, and musician Dave Matthews, as well as a growing community of writers, artists, and musicians.

WHAT TO SEE & DO

Ash Lawn–Highland Two miles from the much grander Monticello, this more modest home is every bit as marked by the personality of the president who lived in it. The building is no longer the simple farmhouse that James Monroe had built in 1799: he just lived in the L-shape single story at the rear. It was a later owner who added on a more prominent two-story section. (The furniture, however, is mostly original.) The small rooms inside are crowded with gifts from notables and with souvenirs from Monroe's time as envoy to France. Such coziness befits the fifth U.S. president, the first to come from the middle class. The Ash Lawn–Highland of today is a 535-acre farm where peacocks and sheep roam. > 1000 James Monroe Pkwy., tel. 434/293–9539, www.ashlawnhighland.org. $8. Apr.–Oct., daily 9–6; Nov.–Mar., daily 10–5.

Downtown Mall This six-block brick pedestrian mall is filled with specialty stores, cinemas, art galleries, restaurants, and coffeehouses. The restored buildings are from the 1800s and early 1900s. > Main St.

McGuffey Art Center Housed in a converted school building from 1916, the McGuffey contains the Second Street Gallery and studios of painters, printmakers, metalworkers, and sculptors. All the studios are open the public, and dance performances are occasionally put on here. > 201 2nd St. NW, tel. 434/295–7973, avenue.org/Arts/McGuffey. Free. Sept.–mid.-Aug., Tues.–Sat. 10–5, Sun. noon–5.

Michie Tavern Close to both Monticello and Ash Lawn–Highland, this tavern is popular with visitors. Most of the complex was built 17 mi away at Earlysville, in 1784, and moved here piece by piece in 1927. Costumed hostesses lead your party into a series of rooms, where historically based skits are performed and recorded historical narrations are played. The restaurant's "Colonial" lunch is fried chicken. The old gristmill has been converted into a gift shop. > 683 Thomas Jefferson Pkwy. (Rte. 53), tel. 434/977–1234, www.michietavern.com. $8. Daily 9–5.

Miller's At this large, comfortable bar, blues, folk, and jazz musicians all perform. Rock musician Dave Matthews used to tend bar here. The Downtown Mall's brick streets will lead you to one of the large outdoor cafés. The bar has three floors, with eight pool tables on the third floor. > Downtown Mall, 109 W. Main St., tel. 434/971–8511.

Monticello The most famous of Jefferson's homes was a sort of monument to himself. Monticello, constructed from 1769 to 1809, is typical of no single architectural style, but instead is primarily a neoclassical repudiation of the prevalent English Georgian style and the colonial mentality behind it. As you might expect of Jefferson, every detail in the house makes a statement. The staircases are narrow and hidden because he considered them unsightly and a waste of space, and contrary to plantation tradition, his outbuildings are in the back and not on the east side (the direction from which his guests would arrive). Throughout the house are Jefferson's inventions, including a seven-day clock and a two-pen contraption that allowed him to make a copy of his correspondence as he wrote it—without having to show it to a copyist. On site are re-created gardens, the plantation street where his slaves lived, and a gift shop. Arrive early to avoid a long wait for a tour of the house, and don't plan on seeing everything in one visit. > Rte. 53, tel. 434/984–9800, www.monticello.org. $11. Mar.–Oct., daily 8–5; Nov.–Feb., daily 9–4:30.

Monticello Visitors Center Much of the history of Monticello is not explained on the house tour itself, so plan on making a stop at the visitor center as well. A wide assortment of personal memorabilia and artifacts recovered during recent archaeological excavations at Monticello is on display. The free, 35-minute film delves into Jefferson's political career. > Rte. 20 S from Charlottesville (I–64 Monticello, Exit 121A), tel. 434/977–1783, www.monticello.org. Mar.–Oct., daily 9–5:30; Nov.–Feb., daily 9–5.

Prism Coffeehouse This space has been a great place to hear folk music ever since a group of UVA students opened it in 1966. The acoustic acts here tend to play blues, bluegrass, and Irish music. No smoking or alcohol is allowed. > 214 Rugby Rd., tel. 434/977–7476, www.theprism.org. Late Sept.–mid-May.

University of Virginia One of the nation's most notable public universities was founded and designed by a 76-year-old Thomas Jefferson, who called himself its "father" in his own epitaph. A poll of experts at the time of the U.S. bicentennial designated this complex "the proudest achievement of American architecture in the past 200 years." Only the most outstanding students qualify for the coveted rooms that flank the Lawn, a green, terraced expanse that flows down from the Rotunda, a half-scale replica of the Pantheon in Rome. Behind the Pavilions, where senior faculty live, serpentine walls surround small, flowering gardens. Edgar Allan Poe's room—where he spent one year as a student until debts forced him to leave—is preserved on the West Range at No. 13. Tours begin indoors in the Rotunda, whose entrance is on the Lawn side. The **Bayly Art Museum** (155 Rugby Rd., tel. 434/924–3592, free, Tues.–Sun. 1–5), one block north of the Rotunda, exhibits art from around the world from ancient times to the present day. > Ivy and Emmet Sts., tel. 434/924–3239, www.virginia.edu. Free. 30-min to 1-hr historic tours daily at 10, 11, 2, 3, and 4. Rotunda daily 9–4:45. University closed during winter break Dec. and Jan. and during spring exams the 1st 3 wks of May.

Virginia Discovery Museum The hands-on exhibits at this museum are meant to interest children in science, the arts, history, and the humanities. Children can step inside a giant kaleidoscope or watch bees in action in a real hive. The big attractions here are the computer lab and "make-it-and-take-it" art studio for kids ages 2–10. The projects change each week. The on-site log cabin is equipped with a sleeping loft, a fireplace, and a crib with dolls and play food. > 524 E. Main St., tel. 434/977–1025, www.vadm.org. $4. Tues.–Sat. 10–5, Sun. 1–5.

Walton's Mountain Museum This one-of-a-kind museum in the hills of Schuyler is dedicated to the hit 1970s television series *The Waltons*. Earl Hamner Jr., the series' creator, grew up in this rural hamlet and attended school in the building that now houses the museum. Some of the original sets are here, including the kitchen and Ike Godsey's store, as well as memorabilia and photo displays that let you compare Hamner's real family with his TV creation. At least once a year, former cast members gather here for a "reunion" and are invariably mobbed by fans. > Schuyler Community Center, Rte. 617, Schuyler, tel. 434/831–2000, www.waltonmuseum.org. $5. Mar.–Nov., daily 10–4.

Tours

Albemarle County Historical Society The group's walking tours, which depart Saturday at 10 AM April–October, cover all the major historical sights in downtown. > McIntire Bldg. 200 2nd St., NE, tel. 434/296–1492, avenue.org/achs/Walkingtour/home.html.

Shopping

Charlottesville ranks as one of the top 10 book markets nationally. The city's independent bookstores, especially those that specialize in used and antiquarian books, are great for a visit.

Blue Whale Books Run by an antiquarian-book dealer, Blue Whale has thousands of books in all categories and price ranges, from one dollar to several hundred. > 115 W. Main St., tel. 434/296–4646.

Daedalus Bookshop This bookstore's three floors have books crammed into every nook and cranny. The fiction selection here is impressive. > 123 4th St. NE, tel. 434/293–7595.

Heartwood Books Close to the university campus, Heartwood specializes in scholarly works, including a good collection of theology and philosophy. > 5 Elliewood Ave., tel. 434/295–7083.

New Dominion Bookshop Open since 1924, New Dominion is the oldest independent bookseller in Virginia. John Grisham kicks off his book tours here. > 404 E. Main St., tel. 434/295–2552, www.newdominionbookshop.com.

Save the Date

MARCH

Virginia Festival of the Book Writers, editors, book agents, and those who just love books come to town for this festival. The events include readings, book signings, and panel discussions. > Tel. 804/924–3296, www.vabook.org.

JUNE–JULY

Ash Lawn Opera Festival Music aficionados come to the Ash Lawn–Highland's gardens where one of the country's top-ranked summer opera companies mount pieces drawn from musical theater and the classic repertoire. > www.ashlawnopera.org.

OCTOBER

Virginia Film Festival Charlottesville's film festival includes screenings of important new movies, panel discussions, and appearances by celebrities. The movies are shown at four sites around the university and downtown. > Tel. 800/882–3378, www.vafilm.com.

WHERE TO STAY

Boar's Head Inn Set on 55 acres in west Charlottesville, this local landmark resembles an English country inn, with flower gardens, ponds, and a gristmill from 1834. The rooms have king-size four-poster beds and Italian Anichini linens; many have balconies. Some suites have fireplaces. In addition to many other activities, even hot-air ballooning is available, through a nearby outfitter. > U.S. 250 W, Box 5307, 22905, tel. 434/296–2181 or 800/476–1988, fax 434/972–6019, www.boarsheadinn.com. 171 rooms, 11 suites. 3 restaurants, cable TV with movies and video games, 18-hole golf course, 20 tennis courts, 4 pools, health club, spa, fishing, racquetball, squash, shop, Internet, meeting rooms. AE, D, DC, MC, V. $$–$$$$

Clifton, the Country Inn In this circa-1800 manor house lived Thomas Mann Randolph, a son-in-law of Thomas Jefferson who served as governor of Virginia and as a member of the U.S. Congress. Each guest room retains its original fireplace (plentifully stocked with firewood), and down comforters cover the antique beds, making the quarters cozy. The former livery and carriage houses have been converted into rustic hideaways, as has Randolph's law office, which overlooks the Rivanna River and is now the honeymoon cottage. The dining room's menu changes nightly. A five- or six-course prix-fixe meal costs $55 on weekdays and $65 on Friday and Saturday. > 1296 Clifton Inn Dr., 7 mi east of Charlottesville on U.S. 250, 22911, tel. 434/971–1800 or 888/971–1800, fax 434/971–7098, www.timeandplacehomes.com. 7

rooms, 7 suites. Restaurant, tennis court, pool, lake, hot tub, fishing, croquet, hiking, volleyball; no room TVs, no smoking. MC, V. BP. $$$–$$$$

English Inn A version of the B&B theme on a large but comfortable scale, the English Inn has a three-story atrium lobby with cascading plants. The suites have a sitting room, wet bar, king-size bed, and reproduction antiques; other rooms have modern furnishings. Each morning a full hot buffet is set out. The management here prides itself on keeping things a bit more cozy than what you might find at an average hotel. > 2000 Morton Dr., 22901, tel. 434/971–9900 or 800/786–5400, fax 434/977–8008, www.wytestone.com. 67 rooms, 21 suites. Cable TV, indoor pool, gym, sauna. AE, DC, MC, V. BP. ¢

Hampton Inn & Suites This downtown hotel is just five blocks from the grounds of the University of Virginia and within walking distance of "The Corner," a hub of restaurants and boutiques. Suites here have kitchenettes with refrigerators. Rates include a deluxe Continental breakfast—waffles and French toast in addition to the usual muffins and cereal. > 900 W. Main St. 22903, tel. 434/923–8600 or 800/426–7866, fax 434/923–8601, www.hampsuites.com. 75 rooms, 25 suites. In-room data ports, kitchenettes, refrigerators, cable TV, gym, laundry service, Internet, meeting rooms, airport shuttle. AE, DC, MC, V. CP. ¢–$

High Meadows Vineyard Inn Two styles of architecture are joined by a hall in this bed-and-breakfast (and working vineyard). Listed on the National Register of Historic Places, the inn is 15 mi south of Monticello. There are five rooms in the Victorian section and two rooms in the federal section: all have curtains and bed hangings with a handcrafted look. Monday through Wednesday, the kitchen prepares hot take-out meals that include dishes such as crepes and quiche. Dinner is served in the dining room by reservation Thursday through Sunday. Hors d'oeuvres and samples of Virginia wines are available on the weekend. > 55 High Meadows La., Scottsville 24590, tel. 434/286–2218 or 800/232–1832, fax 434/286–2124, www.highmeadows.com. 7 rooms, 5 suites. Dining room, some in-room VCRs, some pets allowed (fee); no room phones; no TV in some rooms, no smoking. AE, D, MC, V. BP. $–$$

Keswick Hall at Monticello This 1912 Tuscan villa is on 600 lush acres that are 5 mi east of Charlottesville. At this luxurious, cosmopolitan retreat, the guest rooms and common areas are decorated in Laura Ashley fabrics and wallpapers, and each room is furnished with English and American antiques. Some have whirlpool baths and balconies. The 18-hole golf course, designed by Arnold Palmer, spreads across the rear of the estate. There is no check-in desk here; you are welcomed inside as if you are entering someone's home. The facilities of the private Keswick Club are open to those staying overnight. > 701 Club Dr., Keswick 22947, tel. 434/979–3440 or 800/274–5391, fax 434/977–4171, www.keswick.com. 44 rooms, 4 suites. 2 restaurants, dining room, some in-room hot tubs, cable TV with movies, 18-hole golf course, 5 tennis courts, 2 pools (1 indoor), health club, spa, fishing, bicycles, croquet, meeting rooms, some pets allowed (fee). AE, DC, MC, V. $$$$

Omni Charlottesville This attractive member of the luxury chain looms over one end of the Downtown Mall. The triangular rooms at the point of the wedge-shape building get light from two sides. Rooms are done in a mixture of modern and colonial styles and use blond wood and maroon fabrics; the seven-story atrium lobby is bright and is decorated with potted plants. > 235 W. Main St., 22902, tel. 434/971–5500 or 800/843–6664, fax 434/979–4456, www.omnihotels.com. 204 rooms, 7 suites. Restaurant, cable TV with movies and video games, 2 pools (1 indoor), gym, hot tub, sauna, bar, Internet. AE, DC, MC, V. $–$$

Prospect Hill Plantation Inn The columns and decorative cornice borders of this 1732 plantation house were added in Victorian times, when it was rebuilt. Four furnished rooms and one suite are in the main house, where dinner (one seating) is a leisurely production by the family of innkeepers and chefs. But the prize quarters are the eight refurbished rooms and suites in the outbuildings: one is a cottage, one a carriage house, and several have whirlpools. The inn is 15 mi east of Charlottesville. > 2887 Poindexter Rd., Trevilians 23093, tel. 800/277–0844, www.prospecthill.com. 10 rooms, 3 suites. Restaurant, some in-room hot tubs, pool, meeting rooms; no room TVs. AE, D, MC, V. MAP. $$$$

Silver Thatch Inn Four-poster beds and period antiques are just part of what give charm to this 1780 white-clapboard colonial farmhouse, 8 mi north of town. Part of the inn was built in the late 1700s, with a president's cottage built in the 1980s. The friendly hosts can help you arrange outdoor activities at nearby locations. > 3001 Hollymead Dr., 22911, tel. 434/978–4686 or 800/261–0720, fax 434/973–6156, www.silverthatch.com. 7 rooms. Restaurant, pool; no room phones, no room TVs, no kids under 14, no smoking. AE, DC, MC, V. BP. $–$$

200 South Street Inn Two houses, one of them a former brothel, have been combined and restored to create this old-fashioned inn in the historic district, one block from the Downtown Mall. Furnishings throughout are English and Belgian antiques. Several rooms come with a canopy bed, sitting room, fireplace, and whirlpool. > 200 South St., 22901, tel. 434/979–0200 or 800/964–7008, fax 434/979–4403, www.southstreetinn.com. 17 rooms, 3 suites. Some in-room hot tubs, cable TV, Internet; no smoking. AE, MC, V. BP. $–$$$

WHERE TO EAT

C&O Restaurant Behind a boarded-up storefront adorned with a lighted-up Pepsi sign is one of the best restaurants in town. The formal dining room upstairs (seatings begin at 6:30), the lively bistro downstairs, and the cozy mezzanine in between share a French-influenced menu that has Pacific Rim and American Southwest touches. For a starter try the veal sweetbreads simmered in cream; the entrées include steak *chinois* (flank steak panfried with soy sauce and fresh ginger cream). There's a wine list of 300 bottles. > 515 E. Water St., tel. 434/971–7044, www.candorestaurant.com. AE, MC, V. $$–$$$

Continental Divide A neon sign in the window of this local favorite says "Get in here"—you might miss the small storefront restaurant otherwise. The Southwestern menu includes quesadillas, burritos, spicy pork tacos, and enchiladas. The margaritas are potent. Cactus plants decorate the front window, and the booths have funky lights. It can get crowded and convivial, but customers like it that way. > 811 W. Main St., tel. 434/984–0143. Reservations not accepted. MC, V. No lunch. $

Crozet Pizza With up to 35 possible toppings available, including unusual, seasonal items such as snow peas and asparagus spears, this out-of-the-way parlor 12 mi west of Charlottesville makes some of Virginia's best pizza. On the weekend, takeout must be ordered hours in advance. The red clapboard restaurant has a down-home interior, with portraits of the owners' forebears and one wall covered with business cards from around the world. > Rte. 240, Crozet, tel. 434/823–2132. No credit cards. Closed Sun. and Mon. ¢–$$

Duner's This former motel diner 5 mi west of Charlottesville fills up early. The fanciful menu, which changes daily, emphasizes fresh, seasonal fare in its seafood and pasta dishes. Appetizers may include lamb and green peppercorn pâté with grilled bread. For an entrée, try morel-mushroom risotto cakes or shrimp in lemongrass and coconut milk over linguine. The red-tile floor and decorative copper pots on the walls keep things bright and warm. The Sunday brunch is an equally big draw. > U.S. 250 W, Ivy, tel. 434/293–8352. Reservations not accepted. MC, V. No lunch Mon.–Sat. $$–$$$$

Eastern Standard Chef Janet Jospe's fusion cuisine incorporates the cooking of many cultures, especially those in and around Asia. Specialties in the formal dining room upstairs include pan-seared duck breast in a barbecue glaze and loin of lamb with mint pesto. Curries and stir-fry Asian dishes are also available. Escafé, a popular bistro downstairs with a big bar and hip furnishings, serves pastas and light fare. > Downtown Mall, 102 Old Preston Ave., tel. 434/295–8668. AE, D, DC, MC, V. Closed Sun.–Tues. No lunch. $$–$$$

Hamilton's at First and Main A local favorite, this Downtown Mall eatery has a warm terra-cotta interior and an eclectic cuisine. Try the pan-roasted halibut on a Cuban black-bean cake with a citrus salsa, or, if you're a pasta lover, the farfalle tossed with shrimp, country ham, sweet peppers, shiitake, and asparagus. In warmer weather, the outdoor patio doubles as a great perch to people-watch. > 101 W. Main St., tel. 434/295–6649. MC, V. Closed Sun. $–$$$

Hardware Store Deli sandwiches, burgers, crepes, salads, seafood, and ice cream from the soda fountain are what's on sale today in this former Victorian hardware store. Some of the wood paneling and brick walls have been here since 1890. > 316 E. Main St., tel. 434/977–1518 or 800/426–6001. AE, DC, MC, V. Closed Sun. ¢–$

Métropolitain The kitchen is in the middle of this airy restaurant, where diners can watch their meal take shape from a distance. The French-American cuisine reflects the diverse tastes of the restaurant's two owners—one hails from the mountains of West Virginia, the other from Burgundy, France. Especially popular dishes include shrimp cakes with Thai sauce and salmon "filet mignon" with horseradish crust, potato risotto, spinach, and cabernet glaze. Fried grits are also available. > 214 W. Water St., tel. 434/977–1043. AE, D, MC, V. No lunch. $$$–$$$$

OXO Just off the Downtown Mall, this chic restaurant has created a gastronomic fervor among diners since it opened in 1999. Chef-owner John Haywood puts a modern twist on classic French cuisine and changes the menu every few weeks. Notable entrées include oven-roasted beef tenderloin with truffles, mashed potatoes, and sautéed spinach, and pan-seared snapper wrapped in potato crepes. The extensive wine list is mostly Californian. > 215 W. Water St., tel. 434/977–8111. AE, D, MC, V. No lunch. $$$–$$$$

ESSENTIALS

Getting Here

It's good to have a car in Charlottesville in order to explore some of the outlying areas. To explore downtown, park in one of the many lots nearby.

BY BUS

Greyhound Lines serves Charlottesville. It also schedules several trips daily to and from Abingdon and Roanoke on its transcontinental routes between major U.S. cities. Buena Vista, just east of Lexington, and Staunton have daily service to and from New York City and points south.

DEPOT **Charlottesville** > 310 W. Main St., tel. 434/295–5131.

LINE **Greyhound Lines** > Tel. 800/231–2222, www.greyhound.com.

BY CAR

The many pleasant highways and routes that snake through western Virginia's rolling countryside make driving a particularly good way to travel. The region's interstates (I–64, I–81, and I–77) are remarkably scenic, but the same mountainous terrain that contributes to their beauty can also make them treacherous. Dense valley fog banks, mountain-shrouding clouds, and gusty ridgetop winds are concerns at any time of the year, and winter brings ice and snow conditions that can change dramatically in a few miles when the elevation changes.

From Washington, get on I–66 and head west through Front Royal and take either I–81 or U.S. 11 South to Staunton. From there take I–64 East to Charlottesville, 30 mi away.

Bumper-to-bumper traffic jams are rare in Charlottesville and every other city in the region. The major exception: autumn Saturdays when the University of Virginia has a home football game. Virginia Tech games can similarly snarl traffic in the Roanoke–New River Valley area, including on I–81.

On-street parking in Charlottesville is tight and often hard to come by in downtown and near the University of Virginia. There are several pay parking lots and parking garages on Water Street and on the corner of Market Street and 5th Street Northeast.

BY TRAIN

Union Station is a stop on Amtrak's thrice-weekly runs between Washington, D.C., and Chicago and its daily trips between New York City and New Orleans.
LINE **Amtrak** > Tel. 800/872–7245, www.amtrak.com.
STATION **Union Station** > 810 W. Main St., Charlottesville, tel. 434/296–4559.

Visitor Information

CONTACT **Charlottesville/Albemarle Convention and Visitors Bureau** > Rte. 20 S, Box 178, Charlottesville 22902, tel. 434/977–1783 or 877/386–1102, www.charlottesvilletourism.org.

Fredericksburg & the Northern Neck

Fredericksburg is 50 mi south of Washington, D.C.

16

Updated by CiCi Williamson

THE BIRTHPLACES OF THREE PRESIDENTS and several famous patriots are in the Northern Neck, a tranquil peninsula surrounded by the Potomac and Rappahannock rivers and the Chesapeake Bay. George Washington, James Monroe, John Tyler, and the Lee brothers and their nephew Robert E. Lee were born here, and the nearby city of Fredericksburg has many associations with these and other leaders, including Thomas Jefferson.

With numerous Revolutionary War and Civil War sites, Fredericksburg is tailored to history buffs. Halfway between Washington and Richmond, near the falls of the Rappahannock River, the town's 40-block National Historic District contains more than 350 original 18th- and 19th-century buildings. George Washington knew Fredericksburg well, having grown up just across the Rappahannock on Ferry Farm. (The myths about chopping down a cherry tree and throwing a coin across the Rappahannock—later described as the Potomac—refer to this period of his life.)

In later years Washington often visited his mother in the home he purchased for her on Charles Street. The magnificent home of his sister as well as President Monroe's office are also open to the public. The town is a favorite with antiques collectors, who cruise the dealers' shops along Caroline Street.

Although the area was visited by explorer Captain John Smith as early as 1608, Fredericksburg wasn't founded until 1728. Established as a frontier port to serve nearby tobacco farmers and iron miners, Fredericksburg took its name from England's crown prince at the time, Frederick Louis, the eldest son of King George II. The streets still bear names of his family members: George, Caroline, Sophia, Princess Anne, William, and Amelia.

Fredericksburg prospered in the decades after independence, benefiting from its location midway along the route between Washington and Richmond—an important intersection of railroad lines and waterways. When the Civil War broke out, it became the linchpin of the Confederate defense of Richmond and therefore the target of Union assaults. In December 1862, Union forces attacked the town in what was to be the first of four major battles fought in and around Fredericksburg. In the battle of Sunken Road, Confederate defenders sheltered by a stone wall at the base of Marye's Heights mowed down thousands of Union soldiers who charged across the fields. The nearby Fredericksburg/Spotsylvania National Military Park presents the story of the area's role in the Civil War.

By the war's end, fighting in Fredericksburg and at the nearby Chancellorsville, Wilderness, and Spotsylvania Court House battlefields resulted in more than 100,000 dead or wounded. Fredericksburg's cemeteries hold the remains of 17,000 soldiers from both sides. Miraculously, despite heavy bombardment and house-to-house fighting, much of the city remained intact.

Today the city is being overrun for a different reason. The town appeals to commuters fleeing the Washington, D.C., area for kinder, less expensive environs. The railroad lines that were so crucial to transporting Civil War supplies now bring workers to and from the nation's capital an hour away, and the sacred Civil War battlegrounds share the area with legions of shopping centers.

The Northern Neck begins about 20 mi east of Fredericksburg. Peace and quiet reign in this 90-mi-long, million-acre peninsula. It's a rural land that still retains much of the same wildness it did when Captain John Smith first visited in 1608. Even at the peninsula's start, the area is forested and tranquil, making it a place to relax, enjoy nature, and explore. The wide rivers and the Chesapeake Bay entice water lovers and sports anglers as well.

If you plan to cook in or camp out, bring your favorite staples from home or stop in either Heathville, Kilmarnock, or Warsaw, where full-service supermarkets can be found. In summer, just-picked local produce is sold at numerous roadside stands and farmers' markets.

WHAT TO SEE & DO

FREDERICKSBURG

Belmont The last owner of this 1790s Georgian-style house was American artist Gari Melchers, who was chairman of the Smithsonian Commission to establish the National Gallery of Art in Washington; his wife, Corinne, deeded the 27-acre estate and its collections to Virginia. Belmont is now a public museum and a Virginia National Historic Landmark administered by Mary Washington College. You can take a one-hour tour of the spacious house, which is furnished with a rich collection of antiques. Galleries in the stone studio, built by Melchers in 1924, house the largest repository of his work. An orientation movie is shown in the reception area, the former carriage house. > 224 Washington St., Falmouth, tel. 540/654–1015. $6. Mar.–Nov., Mon.–Sat. 10–5, Sun. 1–5; Dec.–Feb., Mon.–Sat. 10–4, Sun. 1–4.

Chatham Manor A fine example of Georgian architecture, Chatham Manor was built between 1768 and 1771 by William Fitzhugh on a site overlooking the Rappahannock River and the town of Fredericksburg. Fitzhugh, a noted plantation owner, frequently hosted such luminaries as George Washington and Thomas Jefferson. During the Civil War, Union forces commandeered the house and converted it into a headquarters and hospital. President Abraham Lincoln conferred with his generals here; Clara Barton (founder of the American Red Cross) and poet Walt Whitman tended the wounded. After the war, the house and gardens were restored by private owners. The home itself is now a museum housing exhibits spanning several centuries. Concerts are often held here in summer. > Chatham La., Falmouth, tel. 540/371–0802. $4 (includes Fredericksburg/Spotsylvania National Military Park). Daily 9–5.

Fredericksburg Area Museum and Cultural Center In an 1816 building once used as a market and town hall, this museum's six permanent exhibits tell the story of the area from prehistoric times through the Revolutionary and Civil wars to the present. Displays include dinosaur footprints from a nearby quarry, Native American artifacts, an 18th-century plantation account book with an inventory of slaves, and Confederate memorabilia. > 907 Princess Anne St., Historic District, tel. 540/371–3037, www.famcc.org. $5. Apr.–Nov., Mon.–Sat. 9–5, Sun. 1–5; Dec.–Mar., Mon.–Sat. 10–4, Sun. 1–4.

Fredericksburg/Spotsylvania National Military Park The 9,000-acre park actually includes four battlefields and three historic buildings, all accessible for a single admission price. At the Fredericksburg and Chancellorsville visitor centers you can learn about the area's role in the Civil War by watching a 22-minute video at Fredericksburg and a 12-minute slide show at Spotsylvania, and by viewing displays of soldiers' art and battlefield relics. In season, park rangers lead walking tours. The centers' tour cassettes ($4.95 rental, $7.50 purchase) and maps show how to reach hiking trails at the Wilderness, Chancellorsville (where General Stonewall Jackson was mistakenly shot by his own troops), and Spotsylvania Court House battlefields, all within 15 mi of Fredericksburg.

Just outside the Fredericksburg Battlefield park visitor center is Sunken Road, where from December 11 to 13, 1862, General Robert E. Lee led his troops to a bloody but resounding victory over Union forces attacking across the Rappahannock. Total casualties reached 18,000. Much of the stone wall that protected Lee's sharpshooters is now a re-creation, but 100 yards from the visitor center, part of the original wall overlooks the statue *The Angel of Marye's Heights,* by Felix de Weldon. This memorial honors Sergeant Richard Kirkland, a South Carolinian who risked his life to bring water to wounded foes; he later died at the Battle of Chickamauga. > Fredericksburg Battlefield park visitor center, Lafayette Blvd. and Sunken Rd., tel. 540/373–6122; Chancellorsville Battlefield visitor center, Rte. 3 W, tel. 540/786–2880. $4 (includes all 4 battlefields, Chatham Manor, and other historic buildings). Visitor centers daily 9–5, driving and walking tours daily dawn–dusk.

George Washington's Ferry Farm Washington's boyhood home, once the site of a ferry crossing, is just across the Rappahannock River from downtown Fredericksburg. Living here from age 6 to 19, Washington received his formal education and taught himself surveying while *not* busy chopping a cherry tree or throwing a dollar across the Rappahannock—legends concocted by Parson Weems. The mainly archaeological site has an exhibit on "George Washington: Boy Before Legend," and ongoing excavations. Colonial games are held daily June through August. Ferry Farm, which once consisted of 600 acres, became a major artillery base and river-crossing site for Union forces during the Battle of Fredericksburg. > 268 Kings Hwy. (Rte. 3 E), at Ferry Rd., tel. 540/370–0732, www.kenmore.org. $3. Mid-Feb.–late May and early Sept.–Dec., daily 11–4; late May–early Sept., daily 10–5.

James Monroe Museum and Memorial Library This tiny one-story building—on the site where Monroe, who became the fifth president of the United States, practiced law from 1787 to 1789—contains many of Monroe's possessions, collected and preserved by his family. They include a mahogany dispatch box used during the negotiation of the 1803 Louisiana Purchase (Monroe was minister to France under Thomas Jefferson) and the desk on which Monroe signed the doctrine named for him. > 908 Charles St., tel. 540/654–2110. $4. Mar.–Nov., daily 9–5; Dec.–Feb., daily 10–4.

Kenmore Named Kenmore by a later owner, this house was built in 1775 on a 1,300-acre plantation owned by Colonel Fielding Lewis, a patriot, merchant, and brother-in-law of George Washington. Lewis sacrificed much of his fortune to operate a gun factory that supplied the American forces during the Revolutionary War. As a result, his debts forced his widow to sell the home after his death. Kenmore's plain exterior belies its lavish interior. The plaster ceiling moldings are outstanding and even more ornate than those at Mount Vernon. It's believed that the artisan responsible for the ceilings worked frequently in both homes, though his name is unknown, possibly because he was an indentured servant. Most of the lavish furnishings are in storage until about 2005 while the mansion undergoes a $5 million restoration. Guided 30-minute architectural tours of the home are conducted by docents, and the subterranean Crowningshield museum on the grounds displays some of the furniture, family portraits, and changing exhibits of Fredericksburg life. > 1201 Washington Ave., tel. 540/373-3381, www.kenmore.org. $6. Mar.-Nov., Mon.-Sat. 10-5, Sun. noon-5; Jan. and Feb., weekdays by reservation only, Sat. noon-4.

Mary Washington House George purchased a three-room cottage for his mother in 1772 for £225, renovated it, and more than doubled its size with additions. She spent the last 17 years of her life here, tending the garden where her original boxwoods still flourish today, and where many a bride and groom now exchange their vows. The home has been a museum since 1930. Inside, displays include Mrs. Washington's "best dressing glass," a silver-over-tin mirror in a Chippendale frame; her teapot; Washington family dinnerware; and period furniture. The kitchen and its spit are original. Tours begin on the back porch with a history of the house. From there you can see the brick sidewalk leading to Kenmore, the home of Mrs. Washington's only daughter, Betty Washington Lewis. > 1200 Charles St., tel. 540/373-1569. $5. Apr.-Nov., Mon.-Sat. 9-5, Sun. 11-5; Dec.-Mar., Mon.-Sat. 10-4, Sun. noon-4.

National Cemetery The National Cemetery is the final resting place of 15,000 Union dead, most of whom were never identified. > Lafayette Blvd. and Sunken Rd., tel. 540/373-6122. Daily sunrise-sunset.

Rising Sun Tavern In 1760 George Washington's brother Charles built as his home what later became the Rising Sun Tavern, a watering hole for such patriots as the Lee brothers (the only siblings to sign the Declaration of Independence); Patrick Henry, the five-term governor of Virginia who said, "Give me liberty or give me death"; and future presidents Washington and Jefferson. A "wench" in period costume leads a tour without stepping out of character. From her you hear how travelers slept and what they ate and drank at this busy institution. In the taproom you're served spiced tea. > 1304 Caroline St., tel. 540/371-1494. $5. Apr.-Nov., Mon.-Sat. 9-5, Sun. 11-5; Dec.-Mar., Mon.-Sat. 10-4, Sun. noon-4.

NORTHERN NECK

George Washington Birthplace National Monument Near the town of Oak Grove on Route 3, all signs point to the national park on the Potomac River. At Pope's Creek is a 550-acre park mirroring the peaceful rural life our first president preferred. The house in which Mary Ball Washington gave birth to George in 1732 burned in 1779, but native clay was used to make bricks for a representative 18th-century plantation home. Costumed interpreters lead tours through the Memorial House, which has items dating from the time of Washington's childhood. The grounds include a kitchen, garden, cemetery with 32 Washington family graves, and the Colonial Living Farm, worked by methods employed in colonial days. Picnic facilities are available year-round. > Rte. 3, Oak Grove, tel. 804/224-1732, www.nps.gov/gewa. $3. Daily 9-5.

Ingleside Plantation Vineyards One of Virginia's oldest and largest wineries, Ingleside produces one of the state's few sparkling wines. The vineyards cover about 50 acres of gently rolling countryside that, with its climate and sandy loam soil, is similar to that in Bordeaux, France. The winery has a tasting bar, a gift shop with grape-related gifts, a large outdoor patio with umbrella tables and a fountain, and a large indoor room for group tastings and buffet lunch. The winery is about 40 minutes east of Fredericksburg and only a few miles from the Washington Birthplace National

Monument. From Route 3, turn south on Rte. 638 at the winery's signpost. > 5872 Leedstown Rd., Oak Grove, tel. 804/224–8687. $2. Mon.–Sat. 10–5, Sun. noon–5.

Mary Ball Washington Museum and Library This four-building complex honors George Washington's mother, who was born in Lancaster County. Lancaster House, built about 1798, contains Washington family memorabilia and historic items related to the county and the Northern Neck. The Steuart-Blakemore Building houses a genealogical library, and the Old Jail is a lending library and archives. > 8346 Mary Ball Rd., Lancaster, tel. 804/462–7280, www.mbwm.org. Free. Dec.–Mar., Tues.–Fri. 9–5; Apr.–Nov., Tues.–Fri. 9–5, Sat. 10–3.

Stratford Hall Plantation Robert E. Lee, future commander of the Confederate Army, was born in the Great House, one of the country's finest examples of colonial architecture. Eight chimneys in two squares top the H-shape brick home, built in the 1730s by Lee's great-great-uncle, colonial governor Thomas Lee. The house contains Robert E. Lee's crib, original family pieces, and period furnishings. Two of Thomas Lee's sons, Richard Henry Lee and Francis Lightfoot Lee, were the only brothers to sign the the Declaration of Independence. The working colonial plantation covers 1,600 acres and has gardens, a kitchen, smokehouse, laundry, orangery, springhouses, coach house, stables, slave quarters, and a gristmill that operates Saturday May through October from 1:30 to 3:30. A plantation luncheon and à la carte items are served daily from 11:30 to 3 in a large log cabin restaurant. Its outdoor screened deck overlooks the woodlands. > Rte. 3, Stratford, tel. 804/493–8038. $7. Daily 9–5.

Tours

BOAT TOURS

Rappahannock River Cruises A cruise 20 mi up the river to the Ingleside winery leaves from Tappahannock. The *Capt. Thomas* takes passengers on the narrated day cruise. A buffet lunch is served at the winery ($10), or you can bring your own. To reach the dock, take U.S. 17 south from Tappahannock to Hoskins Creek. The cruise departs daily at 10, returning at 4. > Hoskins Creek, Tappahannock, tel. 804/453–2628, www.tangiercruise.com. $20. May–Oct., daily tour at 10.

Smith Island and Chesapeake Bay Cruises Popular cruises to Smith and Tangier islands in the Chesapeake Bay leave from Reedville. The 150-passenger ship *Captain Evans* sails from the KOA Kampground at Smith Point on Route 802, departing at 10 AM and returning at 3:45 PM daily. The 13½-mi trip takes 1½ hours and passes a 5,000-acre waterfowl and wildlife refuge. Now a part of Maryland, Smith Island—a Methodist colony settled by British colonists from Cornwall—can also be reached from Crisfield, on Maryland's Eastern Shore. Lunch is available at several restaurants on the island. Reservations are required. > 382 Campground Rd., behind the KOA Kampground, tel. 804/453–3430, www.eaglesnest.net/smithislandcruise. $18.50. May–mid-Oct.

Tangier Island and Chesapeake Cruises Tangier is a Virginia island in the Chesapeake Bay named by Captain John Smith. This largely unspoiled fishing village of narrow streets can be reached by the ship *Chesapeake Breeze*. The ship departs at 10 AM and returns at 3:45 PM daily, cruising 1½ hours each way. The island has several restaurants serving lunch. From the intersection of U.S. 360 and Route 646, drive 1½ mi; then turn left on Highway 656 (Buzzard's Point Rd.), which leads to the dock. Make a reservation in advance. > 468 Buzzard's Point Rd., Reedville, tel. 804/453–2628, www.tangiercruise.com. $20. May–Oct., daily tour at 10.

WALKING TOURS

The Fredericksburg Department of Tourism, in the visitor center, publishes a booklet that includes a short history of Fredericksburg and a self-guided tour covering 29 sights.

Living History Company of Fredericksburg This company's walking tours are tailored to the desires of those taking them. > Tel. 540/898–0737, www.historyexperiences.com.

Save the Date

First Friday The first Friday of each month brings special events to the Old Town sections of Fredericksburg. They might include a block party with live music, dancing, and food; outdoor concerts next to the visitor center (weather permitting); and show openings in galleries and studios. > Tel. 800/678–4748, www.fredericksburgvirginia.net.

FEBRUARY

George Washington Day and George Washington's Birthday Celebration George's birthday brings games, colonial-era activities, crafts, and a birthday cake at his boyhood home, Ferry Farm. Admission to six museums and historic attractions is reduced as part of the observance. > Tel. 800/678–4748, www.fredericksburgvirginia.net.

APRIL

Historic Garden Week The chance to tour historic homes and gardens in Fredericksburg and the surrounding countryside of Spotsylvania County is part of this impressive statewide house and garden tour event. > Tel. 540/373–1776 or 800/678–4748, www.vagardenweek.org.

MAY

Fredericksburg Civil War Weekend One of the biggest Civil War–related events in the area, this Memorial Day weekend event is a mix of living history, children's activities, and concerts with period music and instruments. Ceremonies are held for the 15,000 soldiers buried here. Other events include a rollicking riverboat cruise, Civil War weapons demonstrations, and guided tours through the Fredericksburg, Spotsylvania, and Stafford countryside by some of the region's most knowledgeable historians. > Tel. 800/678–4748, www.fredericksburgvirginia.net.

Spring on the Plantation Costumed interpreters at the George Washington Birthplace National Monument reenact the lives of colonial gentry, indentured servants, and slaves. Sheep shearing and ox-driving demonstrations are two of the featured events. > Tel. 804/224–1732.

MAY–JUNE

Fredericksburg Music Festival This concert series brings chamber music and other kinds of music to locations around town, including St. George's Church and Mary Washington College's Dodd Auditorium. > Tel. 800/678–4748, www.fredericksburgvirginia.net.

JULY

Fourth of July Celebration at Stratford Hall Richard Henry Lee and Francis Lightfoot Lee, both signers of the Declaration of Independence, are honored through fireworks and music at Stratford Hall. Light refreshments are served, and admission is reduced. > Tel. 804/493–8038, www.stratfordhall.org.

SEPTEMBER

Great Rappahannock River Duck Race Come here for live music, food, and the race of as many 15,000 bright yellow ducks, which drive down the Rappahannock. Winning rubber fowl gain prizes for their owners. > Tel. 800/678–4748, www.fredericksburgvirginia.net.

Rappahannock Riverfest Fresh crabs and other food, music, and auctions are all part of the fun at George Washington's Ferry Farm. > Tel. 800/678–4748, www.fredericksburgvirginia.net. Donation requested.

NOVEMBER

Old Town Holiday Open House On two days in early November, businesses in Old Town begin the Christmas season with decorations, music and food, and extra hours. > Tel. 800/678–4748, www.fredericksburgvirginia.net. Free.

DECEMBER

Christmas Candlelight Tour A highlight of Fredericksburg's holiday season is this granddaddy of all holiday home tours, held in the middle of December. Some of the most historic and interesting private homes in Old Town are bedecked with Christmas decorations and open for tours by costumed hostesses. There's music, dancing, and food. > Tel. 800/678–4748, www.fredericksburgvirginia.net.

WHERE TO STAY

FREDERICKSBURG

Fredericksburg Colonial Inn This 1920s motel with moss-green siding and forest-green awnings conceals a center staircase popular for weddings. Rooms are furnished with authentic antiques and appointments from the Civil War period, and the lobby has an old-time upright piano. Breakfast includes beverages, cereal, and coffee cake. > 1707 Princess Anne St., 22401, tel. 540/371–5666, www.fci1.com. 30 rooms. Refrigerators, cable TV, piano, meeting rooms; no smoking. AE, MC, V. CP. ¢–$

Kenmore Inn The front porch seems to beckon you up to the door of this house, a few blocks from the visitor center downtown. Inside, antique furniture abounds. Four guest rooms have working fireplaces. On weekends, you can head to the English pub for live music. > 1200 Princess Anne St., 22401, tel. 540/371–7622, fax 540/371–5480, www.kenmoreinn.com. 9 rooms. Restaurant, pub; no room TVs. AE, D, DC, MC, V. CP. $–$$

Richard Johnston Inn This elegant B&B was constructed in the late 1700s and served as the home of Richard Johnston, mayor of Fredericksburg from March 1809 to March 1810. Guest rooms are decorated with period antiques and reproductions. The aroma of freshly baked breads and muffins entices you to breakfast in the large federal-style dining room set with fine china, silver, and linens. The inn is across from the visitor center and two blocks from the train station. > 711 Caroline St., 22401, tel. 540/899–7606. 6 rooms, 2 suites. Free parking, some pets allowed (fee); no room phones, no TV in some rooms, no kids under 12, no smoking. AE, MC, V. BP. ¢–$$

NORTHERN NECK

The Gables A four-story redbrick Victorian mansion from the 1890s, the Gables was built by Captain Albert Fisher, one of the founders of the local fishing industry. The lovingly restored house has period antiques throughout. There are two guest rooms in the main house and four more in the adjacent carriage house. The Gables has its own deep-water dock on Cockrell's Creek with easy access to the Chesapeake Bay.

> Main St., Reedville 22539, tel. 804/453–5209, www.thegablesbb.com. 6 rooms. Dining room, some fans, dock, billiards, piano; no kids, no smoking. AE, D, MC, V. BP. $

Heritage Park Resort On Menokin Bay, this campground has panoramic views overlooking the Rappahannock River and scenic wildlife settings. The rustic, wooden, two-bedroom cottages are heated and air-conditioned so they can be rented year-round. Each has a living room with navy plaid chairs and sofa, a dining room, and a fully equipped kitchen. With its banquet facilities for 300, the resort is a good place for picnics, receptions, and family reunions. There are also 78 campsites, some of which have full hookups or partial hookups. > 2570 Newland Rd. (Rte. 674, 2½ mi west of U.S. 360), Warsaw 22572, tel. 804/333–4038, fax 804/333–4039, www.heritagepark.com. 5 cottages. Kitchens, tennis court, pool, boating. AE, D, MC, V. $

Hope and Glory Inn A former schoolhouse built in 1890 is now a pale-honey-color Victorian B&B. The first-floor classrooms have been opened into an expansive, columned lobby with a painted checkerboard floor. The upstairs bedrooms and small cottages behind the inn are decorated in what might be called California romantic, with pastel painted floors and interesting (nonruffled) window treatments. > 634 King Carter Dr., Irvington 22480, tel. 804/438–6053 or 800/497–8228, fax 804/438–6053, www.hopeandglory.com. 6 rooms, 1 suite, 4 cottages. Dining room, some pets allowed (fee); no room phones, no room TVs, no kids under 12, no smoking. MC, V. BP. $$

Inn at Montross This rustic inn is very close to Stratford Hall and Washington's Birthplace. Damaged by fire in the mid-1700s, it was rebuilt with the original timbers in 1790. Five guest rooms on the second floor over the pub are furnished with colonial reproductions and tasteful watercolors. > 21 Polk St., Montross 22520, tel. 804/493–0573, fax 804/493–9118, www.innatmontross.com. 5 rooms. Dining room, restaurant; no room phones, no room TVs. AE, MC, V. $

Tides Inn This elegant inn's 18-hole "Golden Eagle" golf course is one of Virginia's best. The many amenities here include free use of bicycles, paddleboats, canoes, sailboats, daily yacht excursions, and water taxi service to the marina. Dinners are served in a plush room overlooking the yacht basin. All rooms come with DVD players as well as hair dryers and coffeemakers. There's dancing in the Chesapeake Club seven nights a week. > 480 King Carter Dr., Irvington 22480, tel. 804/438–5000 or 800/843–3746, fax 804/438–5222, www.tidesinn.com. 106 rooms. 5 restaurants, in-room data ports, room service, cable TV, in-room VCRs, 9-hole golf course, 18-hole golf course, 4 tennis courts, 3 pools, spa, gym, boating, bicycles, croquet, horseshoes, shuffleboard, lounge, dance club, shops, baby-sitting, children's programs (ages 4–12), laundry facilities, airport shuttle, some pets allowed. AE, D, DC, MC, V. $$$$

Westmoreland State Park One of Virginia's most beautiful campgrounds, the 1,300 acres that make up this park have hiking trails that wind through marshlands, woods, and meadows and along the Potomac River. You can fish, rent a boat or kayak, or simply picnic here. The comfortable, climate-controlled cabins have complete kitchens with microwave oven and toaster, dishes, silverware, and cooking utensils (bring your own dish-washing supplies). Living rooms have a sofa, dining table, and working fireplace. The basic furnishings include linens for four beds. > 1650 State Park Rd. (Rte. 1), Box 600, Montross 22520-9717, tel. 804/493–8821 or 800/933–7275, fax 804/493–8329, www.dcr.state.va.us/parks/westmore.htm. 27 cabins. Grocery, picnic area, kitchens, microwaves, pool, boating, fishing, hiking, laundry facilities; no phones, no TV. AE, MC, V. Closed Nov.–Apr. ¢

Windmill Point Resort & Marina This "last resort" on the Northern Neck is its easternmost point. The beachfront hotel has 1 mi of white-sand beach on the bay and 150 transient boat slips at its marina. The rooms are basic motel style. Drive east on

Route 695 to get here: it's 7 mi from White Stone. > 56 Windjammer La. (Rte. 695), Box 368, White Stone 22578, tel. 804/435–1166, fax 804/435–0789. 61 rooms. Restaurant, 9-hole golf course, 3 tennis courts, 2 pools, boating, marina, bicycles, meeting rooms. AE, MC, V. ¢–$

CAMPING

Cole's Point Plantation This 110-acre wooded campground on the Potomac River has a 575-foot fishing pier, a boat ramp, and a 120-slip full-service marina. The facility has four log cabins that can sleep 4–13 people. > Rte. 612, Coles Point 22442, tel. 804/472–3955, fax 804/472–4488, www.colespoint.com. 74 full hookups or tent sites, 35 partial hookups or tent sites, 1 tent site, 4 cabins. Flush toilets, full hookups, partial hookups (electric and water), pool, swimming (river), restaurant,boating, marina, fishing, bicycles. Reservations essential. AE, MC, V. May–Oct. ¢

Westmoreland State Park In addition to campsites, this full-service park also has six camping cabins that provide shelter but few other amenities. > 1650 State Park Rd. (Rte. 1), Box 600, Montross 22520-9717, tel. 804/493–8821 or 800/933–7275, fax 804/493–8329, www.dcr.state.va.us/parks/westmore.htm. 46 partial hookups, 74 without hookups, 6 cabins. Flush toilets, partial hookups (electric and water), drinking water, laundry facilities, showers, fire grates, grills, picnic tables, electricity, general store, swimming (river). AE, MC, V. Mar.–Nov. ¢

WHERE TO EAT

FREDERICKSBURG

Bistro 309 The windowed facade and vaulted ceiling beckon you into a colorful dining room with touches of copper, an old pine bar, and changing local art. Changing menus employ fresh fish, wild game, and vegetables of the season, with daily specials displayed on a chalkboard. Quail, rainbow trout, and lamb are specialties. > 309 William St., tel. 540/371–9999, fax 540/371–3756. AE, MC, V. $$$–$$$$

Claiborne's On the walls of this swank eatery in the 1910-era Fredericksburg train station are historic train photographs. The restaurant—decorated in a dark green-and-navy color scheme with mahogany-and-brass bars—specializes in low-country Southern cuisine. Accompanying the steaks, chops, and seafood are ample vegetable side dishes served family style. > 200 Lafayette Blvd., tel. 540/371–7080, www.claibornesrestaurant.com. AE, DC, MC, V. No lunch Mon.–Sat. No dinner Sun. $$–$$$$

La Petite Auberge Inside a pre-Revolutionary brick general store, this white-tablecloth restaurant actually has three dining rooms, as well as a small bar. Specialties such as house-cut beef, French onion soup, and seafood are all served with a Continental accent. A prix-fixe ($14) three-course dinner is served from 5:30 to 7 Monday through Thursday. > 311 William St., tel. 540/371–2727. AE, D, MC, V. Closed Sun. $$–$$$

Merriman's Restaurant & Bar Although it's in an old brick storefront, Merriman's serves its "fresh natural cuisine" in a dining room painted bright yellow. On the menu are Mediterranean dishes such as linguine Mykonos, Greek salad, and Middle Eastern hummus as well as classic Virginia meats and seafood. Desserts are made fresh daily. > 715 Caroline St., tel. 540/371–7723. AE, D, DC, MC, V. $–$$$$

Sammy T's A tin ceiling, high wooden booths, and wooden ceiling fans make things homey here. Tall chairs are at the bar, which is stocked with nearly 50 brands of beer. Vegetarian dishes, healthful foods, and homemade soups and breads share the menu with hamburgers and dinner platters. There's a separate no-smoking section around the corner, but the main dining room is much chummier and probably worth chancing the smoke. > 801 Caroline St., tel. 540/371–2008. D, MC, V. ¢–$$

Smythe's Cottage & Tavern Taking a step into this cozy little building of several small dining rooms—once a blacksmith's house—is like taking a step back in time. The surroundings are colonial; the lunch and dinner menus, classic Virginia: seafood pie, quail, stuffed flounder. > 303 Fauquier St., tel. 540/373–1645. MC, V. Closed Tues. $$–$$$

ESSENTIALS

Getting Here

Having a car is advisable in Fredericksburg. It's essential for touring the Northern Neck and the historic homes, battlefields, and other attractions.

BY BUS

Greyhound buses depart seven times a day from Washington to Fredericksburg between 7 AM and 5 PM. A round-trip ticket is $18.50 but a ticket doesn't guarantee a seat, so arrive early and get in line to board. Fredericksburg buses stop at a station on Alternate Route 1, about 2 mi from the center of town; cabs and a cheap regional bus service are available there.

DEPOT **Fredericksburg Greyhound** > 1400 Jefferson Davis Hwy., 22401, tel. 540/373–2103.

LINE **Greyhound** > Tel. 609/345–6617 or 800/231–2222, www.greyhound.com.

BY CAR

To drive to Fredericksburg from Washington, D.C., take I–95 South to Route 3 (Exit 130-A), turn left, and follow the signs. The drive takes about an hour one way; add 45 minutes during rush hour.

To reach the Northern Neck from Fredericksburg take either Route 3 South or U.S. 17 to Route 360, crossing the Rappahannock River at Tappahannock Bridge. Driving north from Williamsburg and Hampton roads, cross the river at Greys Point by driving north on Route 3. Access from Maryland and Washington, D.C., is over the Potomac River toll bridge on Route 301. Virginia's Potomac Gateway Visitors Center in King George is close by.

BY TRAIN

Amtrak trains operate between Washington's Union Station and Fredericksburg several times daily. A one-way ticket costs $14–$18 between Fredericksburg and Washington. The unmanned Fredericksburg station is two blocks from the historic district.

The Virginia Rail Express, which uses the same tracks and station as Amtrak, provides weekday commuter service between Fredericksburg and Washington's Union Station with additional stops near hotels in Crystal City, L'Enfant Plaza, and elsewhere. A round-trip ticket from Washington's Union Station to Fredericksburg costs $13.40.

There is no mass transit to the Northern Neck, but you can take the train to Fredericksburg and rent a car.

LINES **Amtrak** > Tel. 800/872–7245, www.amtrak.com. **Virginia Rail Express** > Tel. 703/658–6200 or 800/743–3873, www.vre.org.

STATION **Fredericksburg station** > Caroline St. and Lafayette Blvd.

Visitor Information

The Fredericksburg Visitor Center has passes that enable you to park for a whole day in what are usually two-hour zones as well as money-saving passes to city attractions ($24 for entry to nine sights; $16 for four sights). Before heading out on a tour, you may want to see the orientation slide show. The center building itself was constructed in 1824 as a residence and confectionery; during the Civil War it was used as a prison.

CONTACTS **Fredericksburg Visitor Center** > 706 Caroline St., Fredericksburg 22401, tel. 540/373–1776 or 800/678–4748, fax 540/372–6587, www.fredericksburgvirginia.net. **Potomac Gateway Visitor Center** > 3540 James Madison Pkwy., King George 22485, tel. 540/663–3205, www.northernneck.org. **Reedville Visitor Center** > Box 312, Reedville 22539, tel. 800/453–6167, www.northernneck.org.

Richmond

100 mi south of Washington, D.C.

17

Updated by Karyn-Siobhan Robinson

AT ROUGHLY THE CENTER OF VIRGINIA, the Commonwealth's capital is in many ways the state's historical center as well. Reminders of this legacy can be glimpsed around almost every city corner. Richmond was named by William Byrd II, who laid out the city at the base of the James River's falls in 1737; he probably named it after the English borough Richmond upon Thames. In 1780, it became the capital of Virginia, largely through the efforts of Thomas Jefferson, who also designed its lovely state capitol. By the time of the Civil War, when it became the Confederacy's capital, it was the most industrialized city in the South.

Although Richmond is only a two-hour drive from Washington, the culture and attitude of the two cities are much further apart than the distance might imply. Travel south to Richmond and you enter a world of Southern gentility. Time and life move more slowly in Richmond, where there's a Southern charm that endures. Standing in line for anything in the city can spark a conversation about the weather. If you have an accent that is not typically Central Virginian, you may be asked where you're from—and welcomed to the area.

Richmond's historic attractions lie north of the James River, which bisects the city with a sweeping curve. The heart of old Richmond is the Court End district downtown. Close to the capitol, this area contains seven National Historic Landmarks, three museums, and 11 additional buildings on the National Register of Historic Places—all within eight blocks. This area draws high-profile politicos and power brokers.

Running west from the Court End district is Main Street, which is lined with banks (banking has always been an important part of the city's economic vitality). Stores are concentrated along Grace Street. Cary Street, an east–west thoroughfare, becomes the cobblestone center of Shockoe Slip between 12th and 15th streets. This area, once the city's largest commercial trading district, and Shockoe Bottom, on land that was formerly a Native American trading post, are filled with trendy shops, restaurants, and nightlife. Some Shockoe Bottom landmarks are the 17th Street Farmers' Market, operating since 1775, and Main Street Station, Richmond's first train terminal, an elaborate Victorian structure capped by red tiles. To the east above the James River is Church Hill, a fashionable neighborhood of restored 18th- and 19th-century homes and churches. It was in St. John's Church that Patrick Henry delivered his famous battle cry, "Give me liberty or give me death!" Be sure to visit—the views from its grounds are not to be missed.

The city's most famous promenade, Monument Avenue, began in 1890 with a statue to commemorate Confederate general Robert E. Lee. Today it is graced with statues of other local luminaries, including generals Stonewall Jackson and J. E. B. Stuart, and tennis player Arthur Ashe.

As you might expect, Richmond is an important resource for those researching genealogy and history. City residents are proud of their history and often the average citizen is surprisingly knowledgeable about local history and family history. The following libraries or archives make interesting stops for the casual browser as well as for those in search of their roots: the Library of Virginia, Virginia Historical Society Museum of Virginia History, American Historical Foundation Museum, and Black History Museum & Cultural Center of Virginia. Another important repository, the Beth Ahabah Museum & Archives, chronicles the history of Richmond's Jewish community, which began in 1650.

It isn't all colonies and Confederates here, however. One of the South's preeminent art cities (the first state-supported art museum opened here in 1933), Richmond has more than just the surfeit of historic portraits you might expect. In addition to museums holding artifacts and traditional works, it's also a local center for avant-garde painting and sculpture. The art department at Virginia Commonwealth University has a strong influence on the city's art scene. VCU's professors and students bring a newness and vitality to Richmond, enlivening (and often shaking up) locals.

While you're in town, be sure to sample the food. Standbys like sweet tea, biscuits, fried chicken, and seasonal fruit cobblers are all tasty and authentic parts of Richmond.

WHAT TO SEE & DO

Agecroft Hall Built in Lancashire, England, during the reign of Henry VIII, Agecroft Hall was transported here in 1926. The finest Tudor manor house in the United States, it's set amid gardens with plantings typical of 1580–1640. Inside is an extensive assortment of Tudor and early-Stuart art and furniture as well as some priceless collector's items. > 4305 Sulgrave Rd., tel. 804/353–4241, www.agecrofthall.com. $7. Tues.–Sat. 10–4, Sun. 12:30–5.

Beth Ahabah Museum & Archives This repository contains articles and documents related to the Richmond and southern Jewish experience, including the records of two congregations. Beth Ahabah is the sixth-oldest synagogue in the United States. > 1109 W. Franklin St., tel. 804/353–2668, www.bethahabah.org. $3 suggested donation. Sun.–Thurs. 10–3.

Black History Museum & Cultural Center of Virginia The goal of this museum in the Jackson Ward is to gather visual, oral, and written records and artifacts of the African-American experience in Virginia. On display are 5,000 documents, pieces of art, artifacts, and textiles from ethnic groups throughout Africa, and artwork by artists Sam Gilliam, John Biggers, and P. H. Polk. > 00 Clay St., at Foushee St., tel. 804/780–9093, www.blackhistorymuseum.org. $4. Tues.–Sat. 10–5.

Canal Walk The 1¼-mi Canal Walk meanders through downtown Richmond along the James River following the Haxall and Kanawha canals. Along the way, look for the Flood Wall Gallery, with portraits of famous Virginians, and bronze medallions put up by the Richmond Historical Riverfront Foundation. The path intersects with many other places of interest, including the Richmond National Battlefield Park Civil War Visitor Center. **Richmond Canal Cruises** (139 Virginia St., Richmond, tel. 804/649–2800) operates a 35-minute ride on the canal in a 38-seat open boat. Tours, which cost $5, depart from the Turning Basin near 14th and Virginia streets. If you're in a car, try to find the site before parking. Lack of prominent signage makes it challenging to find, and parking lots are a few blocks away.

Children's Museum of Richmond A welcoming, hands-on place for children and other family members, the museum is a place to climb, explore, experiment, and play until every surface area is smudged with fingerprints. It's bright, colorful, and crowded.

How It Works lets children experiment with tools, materials, and their own endless energy. The Feeling Good Neighborhood has a functioning apple orchard as well as a monster-size digestive system. Our Great Outdoors houses the museum's most popular attraction, a 40-foot replica of a Virginia limestone cave that serves as an introduction to earth science, oceanography, and rock collecting. In the Art Studio, the paint gets on someone else's walls for a change. > 2626 W. Broad St., tel. 804/474–2667 or 877/295–2667, www.c-mor.org. $6.50. Mon.–Sat. 9:30–5, Sun. noon–5.

Edgar Allan Poe Museum Richmond's oldest residence, the Old Stone House in the Church Hill Historic District just east of downtown, now holds a museum honoring the famous writer. Poe grew up in Richmond, and although he never lived in this 1737 structure, his disciples have made it a shrine with some of the writer's possessions on display. The Raven Room has illustrations inspired by his most famous poem. > 1914 E. Main St., Richmond, tel. 804/648–5523 or 888/213–2763, www.poemuseum.org. $6. Tues.–Sat. 10–5, Sun. noon–5 (last tour departs at 4).

Hollywood Cemetery Many noted Virginians are buried here, including Presidents John Tyler and James Monroe; Confederate president Jefferson Davis; Generals Fitzhugh Lee, J. E. B. Stuart, and George E. Pickett; the statesman John Randolph; and Matthew Fontaine Maury, a naval scientist. > Cherry and Albemarle Sts., Richmond, tel. 804/648–8501. Free. Mon.–Sat. 7–5, Sun. 8–5.

John Marshall House John Marshall was chief justice of the U.S. Supreme Court for 34 years—longer than any other. He built his redbrick federal-style house with neoclassical motifs in 1790. Appointed to the court by President John Adams, Marshall also served as secretary of state and ambassador to France. The house, fully restored and furnished, has wood paneling and wainscoting, narrow arched passageways, and a mix of period pieces and heirlooms. The house has been a beautifully maintained museum since 1913. > 9th and Marshall Sts., Richmond, tel. 804/648–7998, www.apva.org/apva/marshall_house.php. $5. Tues.–Sat. 10–5, Sun. noon–5.

Lewis Ginter Botanical Garden Among the extensive gardens here are numerous specialty collections of ivy, narcissus, azaleas, rhododendrons, daylilies, and roses. Special areas include the Healing Garden (medicinal plants), the Children's Garden, Asian Valley, Flagler Perennial, English Cottage, and Tea House. The huge visitor center houses meeting facilities, gallery space for exhibitions, a gift shop, and a café open for lunch daily. In 2002, a spectacular glass conservatory with a 63-foot-tall dome opened. The garden is northwest of downtown. > 1800 Lakeside Ave., Richmond, tel. 804/262–9887, www.lewisginter.org. $8. Daily 9–5.

Maggie L. Walker National Historic Site From 1904 to 1934, this restored 25-room brick building was the home of a pioneering African-American businesswoman and educator whose endeavors included banking, insurance, and a newspaper. You can take a 30-minute tour of the house and see a movie about her accomplishments. > 110½ E. Leigh St., Richmond, tel. 804/771–2017, www.nps/gov.malw. Free. Wed.–Sun. 9–5.

Maymont On this 100-acre Victorian estate are the lavish Maymont House museum, a carriage collection, and elaborate Italian and Japanese gardens. The complex also includes the Nature and Visitor Center, exhibits on native wildlife, and a children's farm. A café is open for lunch, and tram tours and carriage rides are available. > 2201 Shields Lake Dr., Richmond, tel. 804/358–7166, www.maymont.org. Donations accepted. Grounds daily 10–7; mansion, nature center, and barn Tues.–Sun. noon–5.

Museum and White House of the Confederacy Come here for a good look at a crucial period in Richmond's history. Start at the museum, which has elaborate permanent exhibitions on the Civil War. The "world's largest collection of Confederate memorabilia" includes the sword Robert E. Lee wore to the surrender at Appomattox.

Next door is the "White House," which has in fact always been painted gray. Made of brick in 1818, the building was stuccoed to give the appearance of large stone blocks. Preservationists have painstakingly re-created the interior as it was during the Civil War, when Jefferson Davis lived in the house. During the 45-minute guided tour, you can see the entry hall's 9-foot-tall French rococo mirrors and its floorcloth, painted to resemble ceramic tiles. You can park free in the adjacent hospital parking garage; the museum will validate tickets. > 1201 E. Clay St., Richmond, tel. 804/649–1861, www.moc.org. Combination ticket $9.50; museum only, $6; White House only, $7. Mon.–Sat. 10–5, Sun. noon–5.

Paramount's Kings Dominion This amusement park 20 mi north of Richmond is great for children, but parents will need to bring lots of money and patience; lines often begin forming an hour before the park opens. The more than 100 rides include a roller coaster that's launched on compressed air and the "Xtreme SkyFlyer," a variation on the bungee-jumping theme. > I–95 (Doswell Exit 98), Doswell, tel. 804/876–5000, www.kingsdominion.com. $32, parking $5. June–Aug., daily 10 AM–10:30 PM; May and Sept., weekends (hrs vary, call ahead).

Richmond International Raceway What might arguably be the biggest sports attraction in the area is especially popular when the NASCAR circuit comes to town. Top racers who have made an appearance here include Jeff Burton, Jeff Gordon, Rusty Wallace, and Mark Martin. The facility seats over 10,000, but tickets sell out fast. > 602 E. Laburnum Ave., Richmond, tel. 804/345–7223, www.rir.com.

Richmond National Battlefield Park Visitor Center Inside what was once the Tredegar Iron Works, this is the best place to get maps and other materials on the Civil War battlefields and attractions in the Richmond area. A self-guided tour and optional tape tour for purchase covers the two major military threats to Richmond—the Peninsula Campaign of 1862 and the Overland Campaign of 1864—as well as the impact on Richmond's home front. Three floors of exhibits in the main building include unique artifacts on loan from other Civil War history institutions. Other original buildings on the site are a carpentry shop, gun foundry, office, and company store.

Built in 1837, the ironworks, along with smaller area iron foundries, made Richmond the center of iron manufacturing in the southern United States. When the Civil War began in 1861, the ironworks geared up to make the artillery, ammunition, and other matériel that sustained the Confederate war machine. Its rolling mills provided the armor plating for warships, including the ironclad CSS *Virginia*. The works, saved from burning in 1865, went on to play an important role in rebuilding the devastated South; it also produced munitions in both world wars. A bookstore and café are adjacent to the visitor center. If you're lucky, you may still find free on-street parking; a pay lot at the visitor center costs $4. > 5th and Tredegar Sts., Richmond, tel. 804/771–2145. Free. Daily 9–5.

St. John's Episcopal Church For security reasons, the rebellious Second Virginia Convention met in Richmond instead of at Williamsburg; it was in this 1741 church on March 23, 1775, that Patrick Henry delivered the speech in which he declared, "Give me liberty or give me death!" His argument persuaded the Second Virginia Convention to arm a Virginia militia. The speech is reenacted May–September on Sunday at 2 PM. The cemetery includes the graves of Edgar Allan Poe's mother, Elizabeth Arnold Poe, and many famous early Virginians, notably George Wythe, a signer of the Declaration of Independence. The chapel gift shop, in the old Victorian Gothic house on the grounds, has colonial crafts and and other items for sale. Guided tours are led on the half hour; those planning a Saturday visit should call ahead, especially in May and June; weddings often close the church to the public. > 2401 E. Broad St., at 24th St., tel. 804/648–5015. $3. Mon.–Sat. 10–4, Sun. 1–4.

Valentine Richmond History Center This center impressively documents the life and history of Richmond with exhibits that cover topics from architecture to race relations. Wickham House (1812), a part of the center, is more rightly a mansion; it was designed by architect Alexander Parris, the creator of Boston's Faneuil Hall. John Wickham was Richmond's wealthiest citizen of the time, and Daniel Webster and Zachary Taylor were frequent guests. The house interiors are stunning, but not everything is opulent: the slave quarters, also meticulously restored, provide a chilling contrast to the mansion's splendor. > 1015 E. Clay St., Richmond, tel. 804/649–0711, www.richmondhistorycenter.com. $7. Tues.–Sat. 10–5, Sun. noon–5.

Virginia Aviation Museum The legendary SR-71 Blackbird spy plane is the newest permanent addition to this hangar-style museum east of downtown. Able to travel faster than three times the speed of sound and at an elevation of more than 85,000 feet (near the edge of the earth's atmosphere), the U.S. Air Force's 32 Blackbirds were used on reconnaissance missions from 1964 to 1990. The museum also has Captain Dick Merrill's 1930s open-cockpit mail plane; airworthy replicas of the Wright brothers' 1900, 1901, and 1902 gliders; and a World War I SPAD VII in mint condition. Virginia's Aviation Hall of Fame is also housed at this branch of the Science Museum of Virginia. To get here, take Exit 197 off I–64 East and follow signs to the museum. > Richmond International Airport, 5701 Huntsman Rd., tel. 804/236–3622, www.smv.org. $4. Mon.–Sat. 9:30–5, Sun. noon–5.

Virginia Historical Society Museum of Virginia History With 7 million manuscripts and 125,000 books, the library here is a key stop for researchers and genealogists. The visitor-friendly museum mounts regularly changing exhibits and has permanent exhibitions that include an 800-piece collection of Confederate weapons and equipment and "The Story of Virginia, an American Experience," which covers 16,000 years of history and has galleries on topics such as Becoming Confederates and Becoming Equal Virginians. > 428 N. Boulevard, at Kensington Ave., Richmond, tel. 804/358–4901, www.vahistorical.org. $4. Mon.–Sat. 10–5; Sun., galleries only, 1–5.

Virginia House Built in 1119, this English monastery–turned–country house was saved from a 1925 demolition. Its new owners, Alexander and Virginia Weddell, had it dismantled stone by stone, and seven ships carried the components across the Atlantic and up the James River. After three years of reconstruction, the Weddells had their house (named for Mrs. Weddell, not the state), a re-creation of a European estate with lush gardens. After the couple's death in a train crash, the house was bequeathed to the Virginia Historical Society. The mansion is furnished with treasures acquired worldwide during Weddell's career in the diplomatic service. Mansion tours are given on the hour. Extensive gardens have seasonal flowerings year-round. > 4301 Sulgrave Rd., Richmond, tel. 804/353–4251. $5. Fri.–Sat. 10–4, Sun. 12:30–5; last tour begins 1 hr before closing.

Virginia State Capitol Thomas Jefferson designed this grand edifice in 1785, modeling it on a Roman temple—the Maison Carrée—in Nîmes, France. The capitol, the seat of the oldest lawmaking body in the United States, is still in use by the state government. It contains a wealth of sculpture: busts of each of the eight presidents that Virginia has given the nation, and a famous life-size—and lifelike—statue of George Washington by Houdon. In the old Hall of the House of Delegates, Robert E. Lee accepted the command of the Confederate forces in Virginia (a bronze statue marks the spot where he stood). Free guided tours of the capitol lasting 20–30 minutes are conducted weekdays 9 to 5. Elsewhere on the grounds, at the Old Bell Tower at 9th Street, you can get travel information for the entire state. > Capitol Sq., Richmond, tel. 804/698–1788. Free. Apr.–Nov., daily 9–5; Dec.–Mar., Mon.–Sat. 9–5, Sun. 1–5.

Wilton William Randolph III built this elegant Georgian house in 1753 on the only James River plantation in Richmond. Once 14 mi downriver, the home was moved brick by brick to its current site when industry encroached upon its former location. Wilton is the only house in Virginia with every room completely paneled from floor to ceiling: its pastel-painted panels and sunlit alcoves are part of its beauty. The home's 1815 period furnishings include the family's original desk bookcase and an original map of Virginia drawn by Thomas Jefferson's father. The Garden Club of Virginia landscaped the terraced lawns that overlook the James River. > 215 S. Wilton Rd., off Cary St., Richmond, tel. 804/282–5936, www.wiltonhousemuseum.org. $5. Mar.–Jan., Tues.–Sat. 10–4:30 (last tour at 3:45); Sun. 1:30–4:30.

NEARBY

Pamplin Historical Park This is the site of the April 2, 1865, Union attack on General Robert E. Lee's formerly impenetrable defense line. The Union troops forced Lee to abandon Petersburg. Today you are greeted by the 300-foot-long facade of the Battle-field Center, a concrete representation of the Confederate battle lines. Besides the center, which focuses on the April 2 battle, there's a 2-mi battle trail with 2,100 feet of 8-foot-high earthen fortifications, reconstructed soldier huts, and original picket posts. Also on the grounds is **Tudor Hall**, an 1812 plantation home that served as the 1864 headquarters for Confederate general Samuel McGowan. Costumed interpreters bring the era to life, and reconstructed outbuildings have exhibits and displays. The **National Museum of the Civil War Soldier** on the grounds has interactive displays and nearly 1,000 artifacts. You can select an audio guide that includes selections from the actual letters and diaries of a soldier. The park also has a café and a large store. Allow at least two hours to visit the park and museum. > 6125 Boydton Plank Rd., off U.S. 1 Petersburg, I–85 S, Exit 63A, tel. 804/861–2408 or 877/726–7546, www.pamplinpark.org. $10. Daily 9–5; call for extended summer hrs.

Petersburg National Battlefield On this battlefield more than 60,000 Union and Confederate soldiers died during the siege of the city. A pronounced depression in the ground is the eroded remnant of the Crater, the result of a 4-ton gunpowder ex-plosion set off by Union forces in one failed attack. The 1,500-acre park is laced with several miles of earthworks and includes two forts. In the visitor center, maps and models convey background information vital to the self-guided driving tour, during which you park at specified spots on the tour road and proceed on foot to points of interest. > Rte. 36, 2½ mi east of downtown, Petersburg, tel. 804/732–3531, www.nps.gov/pete. Car $4, cyclist or pedestrian $2. Park mid-June–Labor Day, daily 8:30–dusk; Labor Day–mid-June, daily 8–5. Visitor center daily 8:30–5:30.

Tours

Historic Richmond Tours Historic Richmond Tours organizes tours on subjects such as women of Richmond, architecture, the Civil War, the Revolution, homes and gardens, and battlefields, as well as walking tours ($5). It also runs daily two- to four-hour driving tours of the city in air-conditioned vans for $16–$22. Reservations are re-quired. > 1701 Williamsburg Rd., Richmond, tel. 804/222–8595, www.richmonddiscoveries.com.

Richmond Discoveries This private company offers area excursions, including trips that highlight Civil War history, horseback tours, and customized rambles for large groups or small families. > 1701 Williamsburg Rd., Richmond, tel. 804/222–8595, www.richmonddiscoveries.com.

Shopping

Carytown Richmond's largest and oldest outdoor shopping area takes place amid restored historic buildings. The locally owned retailers here sell wares that include clothing, antiques, flowers, and many different kinds of food. Originally a residential area called Westhampton Avenue, the area began to change into a commercial area when the Byrd Theater was built in 1928. Still operational and fully preserved, the Byrd screens movies at nostalgic discount prices. > W. Cary St. from Thompson St. to the Boulevard.

17th Street Farmers' Market Next to the old Main Street Station, this market is surrounded by art galleries, boutiques, and antiques shops, many in converted warehouses and factories. Look for vendors selling everything from knit scarves to flowers to free-range chicken. > 17th and Main Sts., tel. 804/646–0477, www.17thstreetfarmersmarket.com.

Shockoe Slip A neighborhood of tobacco warehouses during the 18th and 19th centuries, this trendy area is now full of boutiques and branches of upscale specialty stores. Look for "City Ambassadors," a contingent of citizens who can help you get acquainted with the area. They wear blue-and-yellow parkas in winter and red polo shirts in summer. > E. Cary St. between 12th and 15th Sts.

Save the Date

APRIL

Easter on Parade This street festival on historic Monument Avenue is Richmond's favorite spring celebration. The attractions include music, children's entertainment, delicious food, and first-rate people-watching. > Tel. 804/788–6466, www.citycelebrations.org.

Family Easter at Maymont At this Richmond Easter tradition, activities include egg hunts, "Best Bonnet" contests, a straw maze, pony rides, and live musical entertainment. > Tel. 804/358–7166, www.maymont.org.

Historic Garden Week in Virginia During this annual event, you can tour the Commonwealth's most beautiful and impressive properties. > Tel. 804/644–7776, vagardenweek.org.

MAY–AUGUST

Friday Cheers On Friday evenings in summer, Brown's Island is the place to hear some of the area's top bands perform. > Tel. 804/788–6466, www.citycelebrations.org.

JULY

Summer City Fest Music, arts, crafts, and carnival rides are all part of this festival, held during the first half of the month. > Brown's Island, tel. 804/788–6466, www.citycelebrations.org.

SEPTEMBER–OCTOBER

State Fair of Virginia This traditional state fair includes agricultural exhibits, animal contests, a carnival, entertainment, and a midway. > Tel. 804/228–3200 or 800/588–3247, www.statefair.com.

NOVEMBER–DECEMBER

GardenFest of Lights During the holiday season this 25-acre garden puts on more than 450,000 colorful lights and arranges them in botanical themes and beautiful botanical holiday decorations. > Lewis Ginter Botanical Garden, tel. 804/262–9887 Ext. 399, www.lewisginter.org.

WHERE TO STAY

Berkeley Hotel Built in 1995 to blend in with the rest of Richmond's buildings, this handsome, European-style hotel combines intimacy with the services of a much larger property—and it's just two blocks from the capitol. Each room has a coffeemaker, iron, ironing board, and hair dryer; passes to the Capitol Club health club are free. > 1200 E. Cary St., 23219, tel. 804/780–1300, fax 804/343–1885. 54 rooms, 1 suite. Restaurant, in-room data ports, gym, lobby lounge, dry cleaning, laundry service, concierge, meeting rooms; no-smoking rooms. AE, D, DC, MC, V. $–$$

Best Western Hanover House At this reasonably priced hotel, rooms are done in a pleasant pale blue and have balconies or patios. Some rooms have entrances on the parking lot. The in-room cable TV carries HBO and Disney channels. Two restaurants are within walking distance. Also nearby is the Virginia Center Commons shopping mall; Kings Dominion and Richmond are both about 10 mi away. > 10296 Sliding Hill Rd. (I–95, Exit 86), Ashland 23005, tel. 804/550–2805 or 800/528–1234, fax 804/550–2104, www.bestwestern.com. 93 rooms. Cable TV, pool, gym, laundry facilities, meeting rooms, free parking; no-smoking rooms. AE, D, DC, MC, V. CP. ¢

Commonwealth Park Suites Hotel Rub elbows with the senators and representatives who make this their home when the state legislature is in session. The original brick structure was established in 1846 primarily as a saloon that offered rooms for its drunk clientele. It burned during the Civil War battle for Richmond and was rebuilt around 1896 as a 10-story hotel. Across the street from the capitol and its magnolia-filled park, the hotel could be somewhere in Europe; still, its reproduction 18th-century mahogany furniture, museum prints, and brass chandeliers confirm that you are in a southern state. All suites are equipped with coffeemakers, hair dryers, irons, and ironing boards. A deluxe Continental breakfast is included weekdays. > 901 Bank St., 23219, tel. 804/343–7300 or 888/343–7301, fax 804/343–1025. 59 suites. In-room data ports, minibars, dry cleaning, laundry service, meeting rooms; no-smoking rooms. . AE, D, DC, MC, V. $$

Crowne Plaza Hotel Guest rooms in this wedge-shape hotel in the business district have views of the Richmond skyline or the James River; triangular rooms at the wedge's point have both. Transportation to area attractions is free on request. The lobby has a three-story atrium; the stylish, modern guest rooms are pink and burgundy. > 555 E. Canal St., Richmond 23219, tel. 804/788–0900 or 800/227–6963, fax 804/788–7087, www.crowneplaza.com. 296 rooms, 10 suites. Restaurant, indoor pool, health club, sauna, bar, nightclub, concierge floor. AE, D, DC, MC, V. $–$$

Jefferson Hotel The staircase of 36 steps in the lobby of this downtown beaux arts–style hotel resembles the one in *Gone with the Wind*. The Jefferson, built in 1895, has an opulent grand entrance and indoor swimming pool and terrace; the lobby courtyard is skylighted. Yellow, blues, mauves, and dark woods dominate in the guest rooms, which have reproduction 19th-century furnishings. The Lemaire restaurant is highly respected. > 101 W. Franklin St., at Adams St., 23220, tel. 804/788–8000 or 800/424–8014, fax 804/225–0334, www.jefferson-hotel.com. 275 rooms, 27 suites. 2 restaurants, room service, indoor pool, health club, bar. AE, D, DC, MC, V. $$$–$$$$

Linden Row Inn Edgar Allan Poe played in the garden that became the beautiful brick courtyards within this row of 1840s Greek-revival town houses. The main building is furnished in antiques and period reproductions; the carriage-house garden quarters are decorated in an old English style and have homemade quilts. Afternoons end with a wine-and-cheese reception in the beautiful parlor. Also complimentary are transportation to nearby historic attractions and passes to the YMCA's health club. The inn's dining room, open for breakfast, lunch, and dinner, is in the former stables. > 101 N. 1st St., at Franklin St., 23219, tel. 804/783–7000 or 800/348–7424, fax 804/648–7504, www.lindenrowinn.com. 60 rooms, 10 suites. Restaurant, in-room data ports, dry cleaning, laundry service; no-smoking rooms. AE, D, DC, MC, V. CP. $–$$$

Omni Richmond This luxury hotel in the James Center is next to Shockoe Slip and close to numerous small restaurants and shops. The impressive coral marble lobby has a mural of old Richmond along the river. The rooms are furnished in contemporary style with honey and peach tones. You may even want to bring binoculars to enjoy the spectacular view from the upper floors, particularly from rooms facing the James River. Guest privileges at the Capitol Club health club are available for a day fee. > 100 S. 12th St., 23219, tel. 804/344–7000, fax 804/648–6704, www.omnihotels.com. 361 rooms, 12 suites. 2 restaurants, room service, in-room data ports, indoor-outdoor pool, gym, sauna, bar, meeting rooms, parking (fee). AE, D, DC, MC, V. ¢–$$

WHERE TO EAT

Amici Ristorante Game dishes such as pheasant ravioli, stuffed quail, buffalo with Gorgonzola, and ostrich appear regularly on the menu along with osso buco and other northern Italian dishes. In the cozy first floor of this Carytown restaurant, the walls around the booths are adorned with flowered tapestries and oil paintings of Italy. The more formal second floor has white walls trimmed with stenciled grapes and vines. > 3343 W. Cary St., tel. 804/353–4700. AE, MC, V. $$$–$$$$

Europa At this Mediterranean café and tapas bar, there are plenty of enticing main dishes, but many diners opt to make a meal from the extensive list of tapas priced in the single digits: Spanish meats and cheeses, lamb meatballs, codfish fritters, and stewed squid. Housed in a former warehouse in Shockoe Bottom just a few blocks from the capitol, the lively restaurant has a quarry-tile floor and original brick walls. Paella fanciers can choose from three versions: "La Valencia" (the traditional meats, fish, and shellfish); "La Marinera" (fish and shellfish); or "La Barcelonesa" (chicken, chorizo, and lamb). > 1409 E. Cary St., tel. 804/643–0911, www.europarichmond.com. AE, MC, V. Closed Sun. $$–$$$

Joe's Inn Spaghetti is the specialty—especially the Greek version, with feta and provolone cheese baked on top—and sandwiches (around $5) are distinguished for their generous proportions. Regulars predominate at this local Fan District hangout, but they make newcomers feel right at home. Brunch is served on Sunday. > 205 N. Shields Ave., tel. 804/355–2282. AE, MC, V. $

Lemaire The formal rooms of the grandest restaurant in Richmond have an elegant glass conservatory highlighted with ornamental iron and a copper roof. Named for the maître d' Jefferson employed while president, Lemaire serves a seasonal menu with a French accent as well as a deep Virginia drawl. Local Virginia specialties and produce appear throughout: mainstays include Virginia peanut soup, smoked local trout, roasted boneless rack of Virginia lamb, and Chesapeake crab cakes. Three meals a day are served. > Jefferson Hotel, 101 W. Franklin St., at Adams St., tel. 804/788–8000, www.jefferson-hotel.com. AE, D, DC, MC, V. $$$$

Mamma Zu's Dine early to avoid a wait at this local favorite, a well-kept secret in the Oregon Hill neighborhood. Jaguars and BMWs stand out when parked alongside this worse-for-wear building. The shabbiness continues indoors with the peeling, painted concrete floor and artsy doodles on orange walls. There's only one menu—myriad hand-chalked items in Italian on a blackboard over the bar—and only one word for the authentic Italian food: outstanding. Service, however, can vary in quality. Dishes change, but pasta and seafood are always on the menu. > 501 Pine St., tel. 804/788–4205. Reservations not accepted. AE. Closed Sun. **$–$$**

Strawberry Street Cafe An unlimited salad bar ($5) in a claw-foot bathtub is this Fan District café's trademark. Homemade soups, unique sandwiches, and broiled crab cakes are among the offerings. Brunch is available on Sunday, and there's a Strawberry Street Market next door. > 421 Strawberry St., tel. 804/353–6860, www.strawberrystreetcafe.com. AE, MC, V. **¢–$$**

Tobacco Company A tobacco warehouse built in the 1860s houses this popular spot. Prime rib (seconds on the house), fresh seafood, and daily specials are the pride of the menu. Perennials include chicken Chesapeake (with crabmeat) and veal marsala. The Atrium has live music nightly. > 1201 E. Cary St., tel. 804/782–9431, www.thetobaccocompany.com. AE, D, MC, V. **$$$–$$$$**

ESSENTIALS

Getting Here

Travel to Richmond is quite easy from the metro D.C. area. Frequent arrival and departure times, combined with easy access from downtown D.C., make train and bus travel relatively effortless. It's also a quick drive down I–95.

However, although the city has a viable bus system, many of the area's attractions can only be reached by car.

BY BUS

Greyhound buses depart seven times a day from Washington to Richmond between 7 AM and 5 PM. A round-trip ticket is $37 to Richmond, but a ticket doesn't guarantee a seat, so arrive early and get in line to board.

Greater Richmond Transit operates bus service in Richmond. Buses run daily, 5 AM–12:30 AM; fares are $1.25–$1.50 (exact change required). Most buses are wheelchair accessible.

DEPOTS **Petersburg Greyhound** > 108 E. Washington St., tel. 804/732–2905. **Richmond Greyhound** > 2910 N. Boulevard, tel. 804/254–5910.
LINES **Greater Richmond Transit** > Tel. 804/358–4782, www.ridegrtc.com. **Greyhound Lines** > Tel. 800/231–2222, www.greyhound.com.

BY CAR

Richmond is at the intersection of Interstates 95 and 64, which run north–south and east–west, respectively.

Although the city has a viable bus system, many of the area's attractions can only be reached by car.

BY TRAIN

Amtrak trains operate between Washington's Union Station and Richmond daily. The train station is north of town. A one-way ticket costs $21–$26.
LINE **Amtrak** > Tel. 800/872–7245, www.amtrak.com.
STATION **Richmond station** > 7519 Staples Mill Rd., tel. 804/553–2903.

Visitor Information

CONTACTS **Richmond National Battlefield Park Civil War Visitor Center** > 5th and Tredegar Sts., tel. 804/771–2145. **Richmond Region Visitor Center,** > 405 N. 3rd St., Richmond 23219, tel. 804/783–7450, www.richmondva.org. **Virginia Tourism Corporation** > 901 E. Byrd St., Richmond, tel. 800/932–5827, www.richmondva.org; Bell Tower at Capitol Sq., 9th and Franklin Sts., Richmond, tel. 804/648–3146; information by mail: 403 N. 3rd St., 23219.

The Historic Triangle

Williamsburg is 150 mi south of Washington, D.C.

18

Updated by CiCi Williamson

JAMESTOWN, WILLIAMSBURG, AND YORKTOWN— they're three of the most significant sites in our nation's history. Remarkably, the decisive battle for the nation's independence took place just 20 mi away from where the first permanent English settlement was established 174 years earlier. Colonial Williamsburg lies between the other two towns.

Just like any good story, the Historic Triangle should be enjoyed in its proper sequence—from the beginning, through the middle, to the end. It's best to begin your visit on the marshy lowlands along the James River, where Jamestown stands, move inland to the vigorous colonial town of Williamsburg, and conclude your visit on the battlefields of Yorktown.

There are not one but two Jamestowns to visit on the peninsula: Jamestown, the Original Site, and the Jamestown Settlement re-creation. To reach them, you drive along the Colonial Parkway, a scenic 23-mi roadway that connects the three sites of the Historic Triangle. The parkway, mostly fronting the James River, winds through marshy areas, pine trees, and scrub that supplanted the original hardwood forests chopped down or shipped back to England by early colonists. Jamestown, the Original Site, an ongoing archaeological study of the first permanent English settlement in the New World, is at the parkway's terminus. Recent archaeological work has uncovered remains of the original 1607 James Fort.

Jamestown Settlement, operated by the Commonwealth of Virginia, is a living-history museum, with two elements: indoors, a theater and exhibition galleries; and outdoors, re-created, full-scale settings of life in 1610, and replicas of the pitifully small ships that delivered the first settlers in 1607. Jamestown was capital of the Virginia colony until it was moved to Williamsburg in 1699, partly to escape the unhealthy island. Williamsburg, named for King William III, already had the College of William and Mary, founded in 1693. At that time, the population of the Virginia colony had grown to include 58,000 of the 250,000 Anglos living in the colonies, and Williamsburg served as its cultural and political center.

Colonial Williamsburg—the largest and most visited attraction in Virginia today—was the capital from 1699 to 1780, before the seat of government was moved to Richmond for greater protection during the Revolutionary War. Covering 173 acres, this living-history museum on a colossal scale was reconstructed and built over a span of 40 years thanks to a bequest of $80 million by John D. Rockefeller, Jr. Work began in 1926, and by the 1930s buildings were being opened to the public. Roughly 600 post-colonial structures were demolished, more than 80 period buildings were restored, and 40 replicas were reconstructed over excavated foundations.

The streets may be unrealistically clean for that era, and hundreds of others will be exploring the buildings along with you, but the city's rich details as well as its sheer size could hold your attention for days. The College of William and Mary, America's second-oldest university, adjoins the reconstructed Williamsburg.

Completing the "historic triangle" is Yorktown, the site of the final major battle in the American Revolution. In spring of 1781, Continental troops commanded by the Marquis de Lafayette forced Cornwallis toward the Chesapeake Bay, and the British took defensive positions in Yorktown. When a French fleet prevented the British navy from entering the bay to help Cornwallis, Washington forced him to surrender on October 19, and the Peace of Paris was finally signed in 1783.

The battlefield is maintained today by the National Park Service. You may explore the battlefield by car, stopping at the site of Washington's headquarters. Close by is the excellent Yorktown Victory Center, run by the Jamestown-Yorktown Foundation. Like Colonial Williamsburg, these two sights re-create the buildings and activities of the 1700s, using interpreters in period dress.

In addition to the historic sites, amusement parks, golf courses, and many outlet shopping centers are also in the area. There is much more to see here than fits into a weekend. You might want to bolster your trip by adding a Friday and Monday, or return some other weekend to finish seeing it all.

WHAT TO SEE & DO

JAMESTOWN

Jamestown, the Original Site Since 1934, the National Park Service has been conducting archaeological explorations at what was the first permanent English settlement in the New World. Cooperative efforts by the NPS and the Association for the Preservation of Virginia Antiquities (which owns 22 acres of the island) have exposed foundations, streets, property ditches, fences, and the James Fort site. Markers, recorded messages, and paintings around the park supplement the tour. In addition to maps and information about special programs and ranger-led tours, the **Jamestown Visitor Center** contains one of the most extensive collections of 17th-century artifacts in the United States. A 15-minute film provides a perspective of the island's history. Audiotapes for self-guided tours can be rented here, and books and other educational materials are sold in the gift shop.

The **Jamestown Island Loop Drive** winds through Jamestown Island's woods and marshes for 5 mi and is posted with historically informative signs and interpretive paintings that show what a building might have looked like where only ruins or foundations now stand. The drive will introduce you to the natural environment that the English colonists encountered. The "Gallery in the Woods," a series of interpretive paintings, illustrates the earliest industries attempted by the settlers. At the reconstructed **Glasshouse**, artisans demonstrate glassblowing, an unsuccessful business venture of the early colonists. The original ruins of Jamestown's 1608 glass furnace are all that remain of their efforts.

New Towne contains the ruins of an early country house belonging to Henry Hartwell, a founder of the College of William and Mary. Other ruins include Ambler House and a part of the old James City, which dates to the 1620s. Foundations of several statehouses also are visible. A 1-mi self-guided walking tour takes you along the old streets, where markers indicate the sites of former structures. **Old Church Tower** is the only original structure on Jamestown Island. Dating from the 1640s, the tower was part of Jamestown's first brick church, which was used until about 1750 and then fell into ruin. The tower is now part of Memorial Church.

Dale House holds the laboratories and offices of the Jamestown Rediscovery Project, an ongoing archaeological investigation headed by the Association for the Preservation of Virginia Antiquities. A gallery allows you to observe the workings of an archaeological lab and see some of the items unearthed in recent digs. Archaeologists have found pieces of armor like those worn by soldiers in Europe in the late 16th and early 17th centuries, plus animal bones that indicate the early colonists survived on fish and turtles. Coins, tobacco pipes, ceramic fragments, and more are on display.
> Jamestown Island, tel. 757/229–1733, fax 757/898–6025, www.nps.gov/colo. $5 (includes admission to all sites on the island). Daily 9–5.

Jamestown Settlement Not to be confused with Jamestown Island, Jamestown Settlement is an adjacent living-history museum complex. Built in 1957 to celebrate the 350th anniversary of Jamestown's founding, the museum has several indoor exhibits as well as outdoor areas that provide a glimpse of life during the early 1600s. A 20-minute film and three permanent galleries—the English Gallery, the Powhatan Indian Gallery, and the Jamestown Gallery—focus on the conditions that led to the English colonization of America, the culture of its indigenous Native American tribes, and the development of Jamestown from an outpost into an economically secure entity. Artifacts from the period are used with reproductions, dioramas, and graphics to tell the Jamestown story. **James Fort,** a three-sided recreation of the first Jamestown settlers' home, is a living museum, with "colonists" cooking, making armor, and talking about their often difficult lives.

The **Powhatan Indian Village** is a re-creation of the Native American settlement that once existed between Jamestown and Richmond in Quanset huts. As you walk through this living-history village of huts, you can see people tanning furs, cooking, preserving food, and making tools. Down at the dock, on the James River, are full-size **replicas** of the three ships that brought the first settlers to the colonies: the *Susan Constant,* the *Discovery,* and the *Godspeed.* Except in those rare instances when she's out to sea, you can come aboard the *Susan Constant,* on which interpreters share stories about the 104 men and boys who landed here in 1607. Sometimes the other two ships are also open to the public. > Rte. 31 S at Colonial Pkwy., tel. 757/253–4838 or 888/593–4682, fax 757/253–5299, www.historyisfun.org. $10.25. Daily 9–5.

WILLIAMSBURG

Abby Aldrich Rockefeller Folk Art Museum Devoted to "decorative usefulware"—toys, furniture, weather vanes, coffeepots, and quilts—this museum displays objects within typical 19th-century domestic interiors. There are also folk paintings, rustic sculptures, and needlepoint pictures. Since the 1920s, the collection has grown five times from the original 400 pieces acquired by the wife of Colonial Williamsburg's first and principal benefactor. > S. England St.

Bruton Parish Church Although this church is within the historic area, the lovely brick Episcopal church is an active congregation independent of Colonial Williamsburg. Bruton Parish has served continuously as a house of worship since it was built in 1715. One of its 20th-century pastors, W. A. R. Goodwin, provided the impetus for Williamsburg's restoration. The church tower, topped by a beige wooden steeple, was added in 1769. During the Revolution its "liberty bell" was rung to summon people for announcements. The white pews, tall and boxed in, are characteristic of

The Colony Restored

WILLIAMSBURG HAS LONG CEASED TO BE POLITICALLY IMPORTANT, but now that it resembles itself in its era of glory, it's a jewel of the commonwealth. The restoration project, begun in 1926, was inspired by a Bruton Parish pastor, W. A. R. Goodwin, and financed by John D. Rockefeller Jr. The work of the archaeologists and historians of the Colonial Williamsburg Foundation continues to this day, and the restored area of the city is operated by the Foundation as a living-history museum.

In Colonial Williamsburg, 88 original 18th-century and early-19th-century structures have been meticulously restored, and another 40 have been reconstructed on their original sites. There is one slight anachronism here: a 19th-century federal house, privately owned and closed to the public. In all, 225 period rooms have been furnished from the Foundation's collection of more than 100,000 pieces of furniture, pottery, china, glass, silver, pewter, textiles, tools, and carpeting.

Period authenticity also governs the landscaping of the 90 acres of gardens and public greens. The restored area covers 173 acres; surrounded by another greenbelt, it's controlled by the Foundation, which guards against development that could mar the illusion of a colonial city.

Despite its large scale, Colonial Williamsburg can seem almost cozy. One million people come here annually, and all year long hundreds of costumed interpreters, wearing bonnets or three-corner hats, rove and ride through the streets (you can even rent outfits for your children). Dozens of skilled craftspeople, also in costume, demonstrate and explain their trades inside their workshops. They include the shoemaker, the cooper (he makes barrels), the gunsmith, the blacksmith, the musical instrument maker, the silversmith, and the wig maker. Their wares are for sale nearby.

Colonial Williamsburg makes an effort to not just represent the lives of a privileged few, and to not gloss over disturbing aspects of the country's history. Slavery, religious freedom, family life, commerce and trade, land acquisition, and the Revolution are portrayed in four living-history demonstrations. In the 1½-hour "About Town" walking tour, you can be personally escorted by such famous patriots as Thomas Jefferson or Martha Washington. In "Talk of the Town" you can get a firsthand account of the events that were important to the community, and the nation, in spring of 1774. Free black and enslaved men struggle with issues of identity and survival in "Among the Dipping Gourds." At the meetinghouse, you can step into the controversial world of the Reverend James Waddell, a "Licensed Dissenter."

The vignettes that are staged throughout the day take place in the streets and in public buildings. These may include dramatic afternoon court trials or fascinating estate appraisals. Depending on the days you visit, you may see the House of Burgesses dissolve, its members charging out to make revolutionary plans at the Raleigh Tavern. Food and drink are no longer served at the Raleigh, but the four taverns that do serve fare that approximates that of long ago.

the starkly graceful, colonial ecclesiastical architecture of the region. When sitting in a pew, listening to the history of the church, keep in mind that you could be sitting where Thomas Jefferson, Ben Franklin, or George Washington once listened to sermons. The stone baptismal font is believed to have come from an older Jamestown church. Many local eminences, including one royal governor, are interred in the graveyard. The fully operational church is open to the public. > Duke of Gloucester St., west of Palace St. (Box 3520), tel. 757/229–2891, www.brutonparish.org. Donations accepted. Daily dawn–dusk; Sun. services 7:30, 9, 11:15, 5:30; candelight concerts held many evenings.

Busch Gardens Williamsburg This theme park that covers 100 acres has more than 35 rides and nine re-creations of European and French-Canadian hamlets. In addition to roller coasters, bumper cars, and water rides, the park also has a small, walk-through nature preserve with gray wolves. Costumed actors add character to the theme areas, and two covered trains circle the park while cable-car gondolas pass overhead. > U.S. 60, 3 mi east of Williamsburg, tel. 757/253–3350 or 800/343–7946, www.buschgardens.com. $42.99, parking $7. Apr.–mid-May, Sat. 10–10, Sun. 10–7; mid-May–mid-June, Sun.–Fri. 10–7, Sat. 10–10; mid-June–July, daily 10–10; Aug., Sun.–Fri. 10–10, Sat. 10–midnight; Sept.–Oct., Fri. 10–6, weekends 10–7.

Carter's Grove Plantation Reconstructed after extensive archaeological investigation, this plantation examines 400 years of history, starting in 1619 with the fortified hamlet of Wolstenholme Towne. Exhibits in the Winthrop Rockefeller Archaeology Museum here provide further insight. The 18th century is represented by slave dwellings on their original foundations, where costumed interpreters explain the crucial role African-Americans played on plantations. Dramatic plays take place here during the evening. The mansion, built in 1755, was owned by Carter Burwell, grandson of "King" Carter, who made a fortune as one of Virginia's wealthiest landowners and greatest explorers. The mansion was extensively remodeled in 1919, and further additions were made in the 1930s. The interior is notable for the original wood paneling and elaborate carvings. A one-way scenic country road, also used for biking, leads from Carter's Grove through woods, meadows, marshes, and streams back to Williamsburg. > U.S. 60, 6 mi east of Colonial Williamsburg, tel. 757/229–1000. $18 (included in any regular Williamsburg pass), play $10. Mid-Mar.–Dec., Tues.–Sun. 9–5.

Colonial Williamsburg What's now a convincing re-creation of a late-18th-century city was in fact the capital of Virginia from 1699 to 1780. Now it's the top tourist attraction in the state. Its restored buildings and costumed interpreters help provide insight into the lifestyles and preoccupations of colonial America. Craftspeople here make rifles, wigs, wagon wheels, and other colonial necessities and extravagances. Up and down Duke of Gloucester Street the carriages roll as the bell clangs in Bruton Church's tower. Actors and musicians give performances, militiamen perform drills, and the tavern owners serve authentically colonial dishes. At the visitor center, your logical first stop, you can park for free, buy tickets, see a 35-minute introductory movie, and pick up the very useful visitors' guide, which has a list of regular events and special programs and a map of the Historic Area.

The spine of Colonial Williamsburg's restored area is the broad, 1-mi-long **Duke of Gloucester Street.** On Saturday at noon, from March to October, the Junior Fife and Drum Corps marches the length of the street and performs a stirring drill. Along this artery alone, or just off it, are two dozen attractions. West on Duke of Gloucester

Street from the Capitol are a dozen 18th-century shops—including those of the apothecary, the wig maker, the silversmith, and the milliner.

The **Capitol** (east end of Duke of Gloucester St.) is the building that made this town so important. It was here that the pre-Revolutionary House of Burgesses (dominated by up-and-coming gentry) challenged the royally appointed council (an almost medieval body made up of the bigger landowners). In 1765, the House eventually arrived at the resolutions, known as Henry's Resolves (after Patrick Henry), that amounted to rebellion. An informative tour explains the development, stage by stage, of American democracy from its English parliamentary roots. Occasional reenactments, including witch trials, dramatize the evolution of American jurisprudence. What stands on the site today is a reproduction of the 1705 structure that burned down in 1747. Darkwood wainscoting, pewter chandeliers, and towering ceilings contribute to a handsome impression.

His Majesty's Governor Alexander Spotswood built the original **Governor's Palace** (northern end of Palace Green) in 1720, and seven British viceroys, the last of them Lord Dunmore in 1775, lived in this appropriately showy mansion. The 800 guns and swords arrayed on the walls and ceilings of several rooms herald the power of the Crown. Some of the furnishings are original, and the rest are matched to an extraordinary inventory of 16,000 items. Lavishly appointed as it is, the palace is furnished to the time just before the Revolution. During the Revolution, it housed the commonwealth's first two governors, Patrick Henry and Thomas Jefferson. The original residence burned down in 1781, and today's reconstruction stands on the original foundation.

The **Public Hospital** (Francis St.), a reconstruction of a 1773 insane asylum, is an informative, shocking look at the treatment of the mentally ill in the 18th and 19th centuries. It also serves as cover for a modern edifice that houses very different exhibitions; entrance to the DeWitt Wallace Decorative Arts Museum, which holds English and American furniture, textiles, prints, metals, and ceramics of the 17th to the early 19th centuries, is through the hospital lobby.

Wetherburn's Tavern (Duke of Gloucester St., across from Raleigh Tavern), which offered refreshment, entertainment, and lodging beginning in 1743, may be the most accurately furnished building in Colonial Williamsburg, with contents that conform to a room-by-room inventory taken in 1760. Excavations at this site have yielded more than 200,000 artifacts. The outbuildings include the original dairy and a reconstructed kitchen. Vegetables are still grown in the small garden.

At the **military encampment,** on Nicholson Street, you can get a feeling for military life in the 1700s. During warm weather, "Join the Continental Army," an interactive theater performance, lets you experience military life on the eve of the Revolution. Under the guidance of costumed militiamen, drill and make camp in a 45-minute participatory program. If you want to join the ranks for a little while, you can volunteer at the site. The original **Courthouse** (north side of Duke of Gloucester St., west of Queen St.) of 1770 was used by municipal and county courts until 1932. Civil and minor criminal matters and cases involving slaves were adjudicated here; other trials were conducted at the Capitol. The stocks once used to punish misdemeanors are outside the building: they can make for a perverse photo opportunity. The courthouse's exterior has been restored to its original appearance. You might be able to participate in scheduled reenactments of court sessions. > 102 Information Center Dr., off U.S. 60, tel. 757/220–7645 or 800/447–8679, www.colonialwilliamsburg.com.

Annual passes $39–$59, good for 1 year, admit bearer to every Colonial Williamsburg–run site. General admission $33 for the 1st day, can be upgraded to annual pass and includes all museums and exhibitions. Tickets also sold at the Lumber House in historic area and at the Williamsburg Attraction Center. Daily 9–5.

Water Country USA The more than 30 water rides and attractions, live entertainment, shops, and restaurants here all have a colorful 1950s and '60s surf theme. The Meltdown is a four-person toboggan with 180-degree turns and a 76-foot drop. The Nitro Racer is a superspeed slide down a 382-foot drop into a big splash. The largest attraction here, a heated pool, is 4,500 square feet. > Rte. 199, 3 mi off I–64, Exit 242B, tel. 757/253–3350 or 800/343–7946, www.4adventure.com. $31.99. May, Fri.–Sun. 10–6; early to mid-June, daily 10–6; mid-June–July, daily 10–8; Aug., daily 10–7.

Williamsburg Winery Carrying on a Virginia tradition of wine making that began with early settlers, the winery offers guided tours, a well-stocked wineshop, a unique 17th-century tasting room, and a museum of wine-making artifacts. A casual luncheon is served in the Gabriel Archer Tavern. Be sure to give the cabernets and merlots a try. > 5800 Wessex Hundred, off Lake Powell Rd. and Rte. 199, Williamsburg, tel. 757/229–0999. $6 (includes tasting of 5–7 wines and a souvenir glass). Mid-Feb.–mid-Jan., Mon.–Sat. 10:30–5:30, Sun. 11–5:30.

Wren Building This 1695 structure, based on the work of the celebrated London architect Sir Christopher Wren, is part of the College of William and Mary, whose campus extends to the west. The Wren building's redbrick outer walls are original, but fire gutted the interiors several times, and the current quarters are largely reconstructions of the 20th century. The faculty common room, with a table covered with green felt and an antique globe, calls to mind Oxford and Cambridge universities, the models for this New World institution. Jefferson studied and later taught law here to James Monroe and others. Tours, led by undergraduates, include the chapel where colonial leader Peyton Randolph is buried. > West end of Duke of Gloucester St.

YORKTOWN

Yorktown Battlefield It was on this land in 1781 that the British surrendered to American and French forces. The museum in the visitor center has on exhibit part of General George Washington's original field tent. Dioramas, illuminated maps, and a short movie about the battle make the sobering point that Washington's victory was hardly inevitable. A look around from the roof's observation deck can help you visualize the events of the campaign. Guided by an audio tour ($2) rented from the gift shop, you may explore the battlefield by car, stopping at the site of Washington's headquarters, a couple of crucial redoubts (breastworks dug into the ground), and the field where surrender took place. > Rte. 238 off Colonial Pkwy., tel. 757/898–2410. $5. Visitor center daily 9–5 (extended hrs in summer).

Shopping

Shopping is such a large part of the Williamsburg area that many people travel here for that reason alone. Nine stores and shops in Colonial Williamsburg itself imitate those once run in the 1700s. Among the typical wares are silver tea services, jewelry, pottery, pewter and brass items, ironwork, tobacco and herbs, candles, hats, baskets, books, maps and prints, and baked goods.

Merchants Square Among stately trees, brick walks, and storefronts, this extraordinary colonial-revival village of 41 shops and restaurants is adjacent to Colonial Williamsburg. Merchants include Laura Ashley, the Porcelain Collector of Williamsburg, and the J. Fenton Gallery. Quilts Unlimited and the Campus Shop carry William and Mary gifts and clothing. Two crafts stores here sell approved reproductions of the antiques on display in the houses and museums. > West end Duke of Gloucester St., Williamsburg, tel. 757/220-7354. Daily.

OUTLETS

Less than 10 minutes west of Colonial Williamsburg, in the tiny town of Lightfoot, are many outlet malls. If you are driving from Richmond to Williamsburg on I-64, go west at Exit 234 to Lightfoot. When you reach U.S. 60 (Richmond Rd.), the outlets—both freestanding and in shopping centers—are on both sides of the road. Most outlet shops are open Monday–Saturday 10–9, Sunday 10–6. In January and February, some stores close weekdays at 6.

Prime Outlets at Williamsburg The largest of the outlets has more than 85 stores. Liz Claiborne, Jones New York, Royal Doulton, L. L. Bean, Waterford-Wedgwood, Mikasa, Eddie Bauer, Tommy Hilfiger, Brooks Brothers, Nike, Guess, Nautica, and Cole Haan are all here. It's also the country's only outlet for Lladro, known for its figurines. > U.S. 60, Lightfoot, tel. 757/565-0702.

Williamsburg Outlet Mall The more than 60 shops that make up this mall include the Jockey Store, Linens 'n Things, Farberware, Levi's, and Bass. > U.S. 60 W, Lightfoot, tel. 888/746-7333.

Williamsburg Pottery Factory An attraction in itself, this factory has a parking area that's usually crammed with tour buses. Covering 200 acres, this enormous outlet store sells luggage, clothing, furniture, food and wine, china, crystal, and—its original commodity—pottery. Individual stores such as Pfaltzgraff and Banister Shoes are within the compound. > U.S. 60 W, Lightfoot, tel. 757/564-3326.

Save the Date

APRIL

Historic Garden Week Symposium Colonial Williamsburg's longest-running symposium brings in speakers who can answer questions on practical gardening matters. It's a part of the Historic Garden Week, a statewide annual event that raises funds for the restoration of historic gardens and grounds. > Tel. 804/644-7776 or 800/603-0948, www.vagardenweek.org.

MAY

Jamestown Day An early-May encampment, tactical demonstrations, maritime demonstrations, and lectures commemorate the 1607 founding of Jamestown. > Tel. 757/898-2410.

OCTOBER

An Occasion for the Arts Usually held the first Sunday of October, Occasion includes a juried art competition and live Dixieland and rock music. Food is plentiful, and there are many activities for kids, too. > Merchants Sq., tel. 757/220-1736.

Yorktown Day and Victory Celebration Revolutionary War reenactors hold a mid-month weekend encampment and commemorate the war's end with a parade, demonstrations, and patriotic ceremonies. > Tel. 757/220-1736.

NOVEMBER
Foods and Feasts of Colonial Virginia At Jamestown, you can see "colonists" and Powhatan Indians gather, preserve, and prepare food. At Yorktown, you can see just what it was that the Revolutionaries were fed. > Tel. 757/253–4838 or 888/593–4682.

DECEMBER
Grand Illumination Special programs, tours, workshops, and concerts all take place during Colonial Williamsburg's Christmas season. A highlight is the Grand Illumination, when all the windows in the historic district are lit with candles; the event also includes fireworks, a military tattoo, and twilight entertainment. Separate celebrations are held at the plantations and at Yorktown. > Colonial Williamsburg, tel. 800/603–0948, www.colonialwilliamsburg.com.

WHERE TO STAY

COLONIAL WILLIAMSBURG AREA

Colonial Houses A stay at this inn seems particularly moving at night, when the town's historic area is quiet and you have Williamsburg pretty much to yourself. Five of the 25 homes and two of the taverns are 18th-century structures; the others have been rebuilt on their original foundations. Lodgings are furnished with antiques, period reproductions, and 20th-century amenities such as hair dryers, irons, ironing boards, and coffeemakers; the staff is costumed. A very hospitable touch is the complimentary fruit basket and bottle of wine delivered to each room. The Colonial Houses share the facilities of the adjacent Williamsburg Inn, and the Williamsburg Lodge. > 136 E. Francis St., Box 1776, 23187, tel. 757/229–1000 or 800/447–8679, fax 757/565–8444, www.colonialwilliamsburg.com. 77 rooms. Cable TV, room service, dry cleaning; no smoking. AE, D, DC, MC, V. $–$$

Governor Spottswood Motel This one-story redbrick motel has been extended gradually, section by section, since the 1950s. Furnishings reflect the influence of Colonial Williamsburg. In classic motel style, each room faces its parking space. There's lawn space and a sunken garden area for the swimming pool. Seven cottages sleep four to seven people, and 14 rooms have kitchens. It's a good value for the location. > 1508 Richmond Rd., 23185, tel. 757/229–6444 or 800/368–1244, fax 757/253–2410, www.govspottswood.com. 78 rooms. Some kitchens, cable TV, pool, playground. AE, DC, MC, V. ¢

Kingsmill Resort This manicured, 3,000-acre complex on the James River has everything, even a marina and boat ramp. The largest golf resort in Virginia, this is where the Michelob Championship on the PGA tour is held each year. You can play year-round on three championship courses; a fourth course—a par-3, 9-hole gem—is free if you stay here. The numerous brands of beer served at the property's Moody's Tavern are a clue to the acreage's owner: they're all Anheuser-Busch products. Accommodations include beautifully decorated guest rooms and one- to three-bedroom suites with fully equipped kitchens and washers and dryers. The menu at the expensive Bray Dining Room includes inventive dishes that employ seafood, game birds, and steak. A free shuttle bus travels several times daily to and from Williamsburg, Busch Gardens (another Anheuser-Busch holding), and Water Country USA. > 1010 Kingsmill Rd., 23185, tel. 757/253–1703 or 800/832–5665, fax 757/253–8246, www.kingsmill.com. 235 rooms, 175 suites. 5 restaurants, in-room data ports, 3 18-hole golf courses, 9-hole golf course, putting green, 15 tennis courts, 2 pools (1 indoor), wading pool, health club, sauna, spa, steam room, beach, boating, fishing, billiards, bar, baby-sitting, dry cleaning, laundry service, concierge, business services, meeting rooms. AE, D, DC, MC, V. **$$–$$$**

Quality Inn Lord Paget Tall white columns front this modern motel. Eight rooms are accessed via stairs off the spacious lobby, which has Oriental carpets; others have parking at the front door. Some rooms have canopy beds. Refrigerators and microwaves are available for a fee. The property has a 2½-acre lake and lovely gardens. > 901 Capitol Landing Rd., 23185, tel. 757/229–4444 or 800/537–2438. 94 rooms. Coffee shop, microwaves, refrigerators, putting green, pool, lake, dock, fishing, laundry service, free parking, no-smoking rooms. AE, D, DC, MC, V. CP. ¢

War Hill Inn This inn was designed by a Colonial Williamsburg architect to resemble a period structure: the two-story redbrick building at the center has two wood-frame wings. Inside are appropriate antiques and reproductions. The War Hill is inside a 32-acre operating cattle farm, 4 mi from the Colonial Williamsburg information center. Those in search of privacy will want one of the cottages or the first-floor suite (other rooms open onto a common hallway). > 4560 Long Hill Rd., 23188, tel. 757/565–0248 or 800/743–0248, www.warhillinn.com. 6 rooms, 2 cottages. Some in-room hot tubs, some kitchettes, cable TV. MC, V. **$–$$**

Williamsburg Inn This grand hotel from 1937 is owned and operated by Colonial Williamsburg. Rooms are beautifully and individually furnished with reproductions and antiques in the English Regency style, and genteel service and tradition reign. Rooms come with such perks as complimentary morning coffee and afternoon tea, a daily newspaper, turndown service, and bathrobes. The Providence Wings, adjacent to the inn, are less formal; rooms are in a contemporary style with Asian accents and overlook the tennis courts, a private pond, and a wooded area. > 136 E. Francis St., Box 1776, 23187-1776, tel. 757/229–1000 or 800/447–8679, fax 757/220–7096, www.colonialwilliamsburg.com. 62 rooms, 14 suites. Restaurant, room service, in-room VCRs, 2 18-hole golf courses, 9-hole golf course, tennis court, 2 pools (1 indoor), gym, spa, croquet, hiking, lawn bowling, bar, lounge, piano, children's programs (ages 5–12), dry cleaning, laundry service, concierge, meeting rooms, no-smoking rooms. AE, D, DC, MC, V. **$$$$**

Williamsburg Lodge At this larger establishment there's none of the formality of the Williamsburg Inn across the street, but the furnishings are just as interesting. Reproductions from the adjacent Abby Aldrich Rockefeller Folk Art Museum accent the rooms, which are getting a bit worn. The paneled lobby, where there's a fireplace, is cozy. The expansive health club is shared by those staying at the Williamsburg Inn and Colonial Houses. Every room has a hair dryer, iron, and ironing board; some rooms have coffeemakers. Nightly entertainment includes music or plays (free with special expanded passes) in the lobby lounge. > 310 S. England St., 23187, tel. 757/229–1000 or 800/447–8679, fax 757/220–7799, www.colonialwilliamsburg.com. 264 rooms, 2 suites. 2 restaurants, 2 18-hole golf courses, 9-hole golf course, 2 pools (1 indoor), health club, sauna, bicycles, lobby lounge, dry cleaning, laundry facilities, laundry service, concierge, business services, meeting rooms, no-smoking rooms. AE, D, DC, MC, V. **$–$$**

Williamsburg Sampler Bed & Breakfast Inn Charming and hospitable, this redbrick inn near the historic district is modeled after an 18th-century, plantation-style home. Rooms have 18th- and 19th-century antiques, pewter pieces, four-poster beds, and pleasant views of the city. The suites are particularly inviting: each has a separate sitting room, French doors, and a porch overlooking gardens. > 922 Jamestown Rd., 23185, tel. 757/253–0398 or 800/722–1169, fax 757/253–2669, www.williamsburgsampler.com. 4 rooms, 2 suites. Dining room, fans, cable TV, in-room VCRs; no smoking. AE, D, DC, MC, V. BP. **$–$$**

WHERE TO EAT

COLONIAL WILLIAMSBURG AREA

18th-century taverns The four authentic taverns in the Historic Area are outfitted with costumed waiters and oversize napkins and cutlery. The fare, all hearty early American, varies from tavern to tavern, and is served at lunch, dinner, and Sunday brunch. The dishes are a bit overpriced, but a meal at any tavern is a good way to get into the spirit of the era. Chownings, a reconstructed alehouse, serves casual meals that include Welsh rarebit, oyster fritters, and sandwiches, and heartier fare such as Brunswick stew, duckling, and prime rib. Christiana Campbell's was George Washington's favorite tavern; it looks out upon the Capitol just across the street. The specialty here is seafood. King's Arms, the most upscale of the colonial taverns, catered to the gentry in its day. As balladeers stroll about, diners eat dishes that include peanut soup and game pie. Shields Tavern serves 18th-century low-country cuisine in eight dining rooms and in the garden, which also has balladeers. These taverns help support the Colonial Williamsburg Foundation. All offer outdoor dining. > Tel. 800/447–8679. Reservations essential. AE, D, MC, V. No smoking. **$$–$$$$**

Aberdeen Barn Saws, pitchforks, oxen yokes, and the like hang on the barn walls, but the wood tables are lacquered, and the napkins are linen. Specialties include slow-roasted prime rib of beef; baby-back Danish pork ribs barbecued with a sauce of peach preserves and Southern Comfort; and shrimp Dijon. An ample but not esoteric wine list is dominated by California vintages (there are Virginia selections, too). > 1601 Richmond Rd., tel. 757/229–6661. AE, D, MC, V. No lunch. **$$–$$$$**

Berret's Restaurant and Raw Bar One of the most reliable seafood spots around, Berret's is in Merchants Square. Upscale but casual, the restaurant lights crackling fires during colder months and opens up its pleasant outdoor patio when it's warm. Entrées and appetizers employ fresh Chesapeake Bay seafood. It's usually a sure bet to try any of the nightly specials of fresh fish, which often include perfectly prepared tuna. The she-crab soup, a house favorite, is a blend of crabmeat, cream, and crab roe with just a hint of sherry. > 199 Boundary St., tel. 757/253–1847. AE, D, DC, MC, V. Closed Mon. Jan.–early Feb. **$$$–$$$$**

College Delly It's easy to forget that this is a college town, but this cheerful dive keeps up the school spirit. The white-brick eatery with forest-green canvas awnings is fairly dark and scruffy inside. Walls are hung with fraternity and sorority pictures, graduation snapshots, and sports-team photos. Booths and tables are in the William and Mary colors of green and gold. Deli sandwiches, pasta, stromboli, and Greek dishes are all prepared with fresh ingredients and are unfailingly delicious, and there is a wide selection of beers on tap. The Delly delivers orders free to nearby hotels from 6 PM to 1 AM. > 336 Richmond Rd., tel. 757/229–6627. MC, V. **¢–$**

Le Yaca A mall of small boutiques is the unlikely location for this French-country eatery. The dining room has soft pastel colors, hardwood floors, candlelight, and a central open fireplace. The menu is arranged in the French manner, with four prix-fixe menus and 10 entrées, including whole duck breast with black truffle sauce, leg of lamb with rosemary garlic sauce, and fresh scallops and shrimp with champagne sauce. The restaurant is in the Village Shops at Kingsmill, on U.S. 60 East, near Busch Gardens. > 1915 Pocahontas Trail, tel. 757/220–3616. AE, D, DC, MC, V. Closed Sun. and 1st 2 wks of Jan. **$$–$$$$**

Old Chickahominy House Reminiscent of old-fashioned Virginia tearooms, this colonial-style restaurant has delectable goodies served up by sweet, grandmotherly types. For breakfast there's Virginia ham and eggs, made-from-scratch biscuits, country bacon, sausage, and grits. Lunch brings Brunswick stew, Virginia ham biscuits, fruit salad, and homemade pie. > 1211 Jamestown Rd., tel. 757/229–4689. MC, V. No dinner. **$**

Peking You might not guess by its appearance, but this Chinese restaurant with a Mongolian grill is a treat. The daily buffet offers both stick-to-your-ribs Chinese and Mongolian dishes. At the grill, choose the ingredients you want in your entrée, and watch the cooks prepare it in front of you. The shopping center location is just outside the historic district. > 120 J. Waller Mill Rd., tel. 757/229–2288. AE, D, MC, V. **¢–$$**

Regency Room This restaurant in the Williamsburg Inn is known for its elegance, attentive service, and quality cuisine. Among crystal chandeliers, Asian silk-screen prints, and full silver service, you can sample chateaubriand carved table-side, as well as lobster bisque and rich ice cream desserts. It may almost seem as if you're treated like royalty. A jacket and tie are required at dinner and Sunday brunch. > Williamsburg Inn, 136 E. Francis St., tel. 757/229–1000. Reservations essential. AE, D, DC, MC, V. **$$$–$$$$**

The Trellis With vaulted ceilings and hardwood floors, the Trellis is an airy and pleasant place for romantic dinners. The imaginative lunch and dinner menus change with the seasons. A dazzling wine list complements such tasty morsels as homemade tomato bisque, wild boar, and soft-shell crabs. The seafood entrées are particularly good, and many patrons wouldn't leave without ordering the rich Death by Chocolate, the signature dessert. > Merchants Sq., tel. 757/229–8610. AE, MC, V. **$$–$$$$**

Whaling Company Fresh seafood is the drawing card at this large wooden building, which wouldn't look out of place in a New England fishing village. Despite its out-of-town look, the restaurant has an authenticity sometimes hard to find in touristy towns. Locals come in for the fresh scallops, fish, and other tasty morsels from the sea. Steaks are available, but no poultry or other meats are served. The restaurant is off U.S. 60 West just after the Route 199 interchange. > 494 McLaws Circle, tel. 757/229–0275. AE, DC, MC, V. No lunch. **$$**

ESSENTIALS

Getting Here

The most convenient way to visit the entire area is to drive your own car. However, bus and train services are frequent although more expensive—especially for a family. Williamsburg has a bus service, but it doesn't go to Jamestown or Yorktown. To get to those historic sites without a car, you would need to take a private tour or other transportation.

It's best to avoid visiting this popular area in the height of summer, when crowds are large and the temperature is frequently in the 90s. Spring and fall have better weather and fewer people; from January to the end of March and from mid-September through November the crowds are thinnest.

The height of spring bloom comes at the end of April, when Virginia celebrates Historic Garden Week and many old homes open to the public. As Christmas nears, many shoppers come to Merchants Square in town and the discount outlets on Richmond Road. Books rooms far in advance if you're coming during the "Grand Illumination," the opening festival of the December holiday season.

BY BUS

Greyhound runs about five buses a day from Washington to Williamsburg. A couple of the runs do not require changing buses in Richmond; most do. Reserved seats are not possible and purchasing a ticket does not guarantee a seat. Ticket in hand, you must get in line to board. If the bus has originated in another city, already-boarded passengers have preference for seats when re-boarding.

Once in Williamsburg, the city has local bus service that serves Colonial Williamsburg, Busch Gardens Williamsburg, the Williamsburg Pottery Factory, the Music Theatre, Prime Outlets, and the College of William and Mary. It operates Monday–Saturday from 6 AM to 10 PM from Memorial Day to Labor Day and from 6 AM to 8 PM in the off-season.

DEPOT **Williamsburg Transportation Center** > 468 N. Boundary St., Williamsburg, tel. 757/229–8750, www.ci.williamsburg.va.us/direct/train.html.
LINES **Greyhound Lines** > Tel. 800/231–2222, www.greyhound.com. **Williamsburg Area Transport** > Tel. 757/259–4093, www.williamsburgtransport.com.

BY CAR

A car is the most convenient way to travel to the Historic Triangle and see its sights. A nonstop trip from Washington to Williamsburg via I–95 and I–64 takes 3 to 3½ hours. To see Colonial Williamsburg, you can park free, purchase your tickets, and take the free shuttle bus into the Historic Area. A car is handy for driving to Jamestown and Yorktown, and driving between the two areas along the Colonial Parkway is a beautiful, scenic drive—a destination in itself.

If you have more leisure time and want to take a beautiful but slower road into the Historic Triangle off the Interstate, take the I–295 Richmond Bypass off I–95 and exit at Route 5, designated a Virginia Byway and one of the loveliest roads in the state. The two-lane road rambles between stands of pecan, hickory, cherry, and feathery cedar trees. In some places, the trees join over the road to make a shady umbrella, and in others, planted fields form a giant patchwork quilt.

While in Colonial Williamsburg, it's best to leave your car at your hotel or at one of the free lots near a transportation center or shopping area; cars are not allowed in the Historic Area.

BY FERRY

The Jamestown–Scotland Ferry takes vehicles across the James River. Operating since 1945, the free 15-minute ride across the river will give you a unique view of land the first colonists saw as they traveled on the same river almost 400 years ago. The ferry leaves from both sides of the river on Route 31 every 30 to 60 minutes. Contact the ferry company for schedules.

LINE **Jamestown–Scotland Ferry** > Tel. 800/823–3779, www.virginiadot.org/comtravel/ferry-jamestown.asp.

BY TRAIN

Amtrak has twice-daily service between Washington, D.C., and Williamsburg. The trip takes about 3½ hours and does not require a change of trains. The cost is about $80 per person.

The Williamsburg Transportation Center Amtrak Station is open daily from 7:30 AM to 10 PM.
LINE **Amtrak** > Tel. 800/872–7245, www.amtrak.com.
STATION **Williamsburg Transportation Center Amtrak Station** > 468 N. Boundary St., Williamsburg, tel. 757/229–8750, www.ci.williamsburg.va.us/direct/train.html.

Visitor Information

CONTACTS **Colonial National Historic Park** > Box 210, Yorktown 23690, tel. 757/898–3400 (Jamestown Interpretation 757/229–1733, Yorktown Interpretation 757/898–2410), www.nps.gov/colo. **Colonial Williamsburg Visitor Center** > Box 1776, Williamsburg 23187-1776, tel. 800/246–2099. **Williamsburg Area Convention and Visitors Bureau** > 421 N. Boundary St. (Box 3585), Williamsburg 23187, tel. 757/253–0192 or 800/368–6511, www.visitwilliamsburg.com.

Hampton Roads

Norfolk is 190 mi southeast of Washington, D.C.

19

By CiCi Williamson

WATER, WATER EVERYWHERE: it's the reason that the world's largest naval base is in the area known collectively as Hampton Roads, the harbor at the end of Virginia's southernmost peninsula, Here the James, Elizabeth, and Nansemond rivers flow together into the Chesapeake Bay and Atlantic Ocean. A quintet of major waterside cites—Norfolk, Newport News, Portsmouth, Hampton, and Virginia Beach—played a crucial role in the discovery and settlement of the nation, its struggle for independence, and the conflict that nearly dissolved the Union.

The Hampton Roads area is made up of the large natural harbor, the peninsula to the north that extends southeast from Williamsburg, and the Tidewater area between the mouth of the harbor and the Atlantic Ocean. On the peninsula are the cities of Newport News and Hampton; to the south and east are Norfolk, Portsmouth, and Virginia Beach. These cities have been shaped by their proximity to the Chesapeake Bay and the rivers that empty into it, either as ports and shipbuilding centers or, in the case of Virginia Beach, as a hugely popular beach town. Newport News, Hampton, Norfolk, and Portsmouth are the "old" cities of this area; recent development and revival efforts have made them worthy of more than just a quick look. Virginia Beach, although the first area encountered by the first colonists, is the newest of the five and now the most populous in the state.

When traveling to the area from Washington, D.C., via I–95 and I–64, the first city you reach is Newport News, which stretches for almost 35 mi along the James River from near Williamsburg to the mouth of Hampton Roads harbor. Origins of the city's name are uncertain, but references to "Newportes Newes" are found as early as 1619 in the Virginia Company of London's records. The name may commemorate English mariner Captain Christopher Newport, who captained the *Susan Constant,* and the three ships that landed at Jamestown in 1607.

Newport News Shipbuilding is one of the largest privately owned shipyards in the world, and with approximately 18,000 employees, is probably the second-largest employer in Virginia. It is the only shipyard in the country capable of building nuclear aircraft carriers. Don't miss the excellent maritime museum here—it might be the very best museum in the state.

At the eastern end of the peninsula at the mouth of the Hampton Roads harbor is Hampton, founded in 1610 on a Kecoughtan Indian village. One of Virginia's major colonial cities and a bustling seaport, Hampton is the oldest continuously existing English-speaking settlement in the United States. The city has been partially destroyed three times: by the British during the Revolution and again during the War of 1812, then by Confederates preempting Union invaders during the Civil War.

Since the mid-1990s, Hampton has been undergoing a face-lift. It hosts many summer concerts and family festivals. It also holds the country's first aviation research facility, NASA Langley Research Center. The center was headquarters for the first manned space program in the United States: astronauts for the *Mercury* and *Apollo* missions trained here. It's fitting, then, that the city has an excellent air-and-space museum.

The site that eventually became the center of present-day Norfolk was either Indian corn land or primeval forest until the English took over. During the Revolutionary War, the British bombarded Norfolk and the city burned to the ground; only St. Paul's Church survived, and it remains in use today. Fighting again occurred during the Civil War.

There's plenty to see in this old navy town, including historic homes, botanical gardens, and even the resting place of a famous World War II general. The arts are also well represented with ballet, opera, symphony, and an excellent art museum. Like many other old Southern towns, Norfolk has undergone a renaissance, epitomized by the charming shops and cafés in the historic village of Ghent. More than three dozen cruise ships call yearly, and many sightseeing boats leave from Norfolk on harbor and naval base tours.

A five-minute pedestrian ferry across the Elizabeth River makes traveling to Portsmouth from Norfolk easy. Portsmouth has a well-maintained historic district of 18th-century homes. Near the district are several museums. This area was first explored by Captain John Smith from Jamestown in 1608, and was recognized early as a suitable shipbuilding location. Today it's the site of the Norfolk Naval Shipyard, the world's largest facility of its type.

The heart of Virginia Beach—a stretch of the Atlantic shore from Cape Henry south to Rudee Inlet—has been a popular summertime destination for years. With 6 mi of crowded public beach, high-rises, amusements, and a busy 40-block boardwalk, Virginia's most populated city is now a place for peaceful communion with nature. The Boardwalk and Atlantic Avenue have teak benches, an oceanfront park, and a 3-mi bike trail. As for getting into the water, there are plenty of places to sail, surf, and go scuba diving. The farther north you go, the more beach there is in proportion to bars, T-shirt parlors, and video arcades. Most activities and events in town are oriented toward families. Virginia Beach, which in the 1950s claimed to have the world's longest public beach, is now working hard to fight oceanfront erosion and rebuild its once showy boardwalk.

Hampton Roads is centered on the water, so it's not surprising that the most crowded time to visit is summer. If your plans are flexible, visit on the shoulder seasons of spring or fall. Even in winter, the weather tends to be temperate, and although ocean water will be too cold for swimming, it's fine weather for playing golf or taking boat tours on climate-controlled decks.

WHAT TO SEE & DO

HAMPTON

Ft. Monroe The channel between Chesapeake Bay and Hampton Roads is the "mouth" of Hampton Roads. On the north side of this passage, Hampton's Ft. Monroe, built in stages between 1819 and 1834, is the largest stone fort in the country and the only one on active duty to actually be enclosed by a moat. Robert E. Lee and Edgar Allan Poe served here in the antebellum years, and it remained a Union stronghold in Confederate territory throughout the Civil War. After the war, Confederate president Jefferson Davis was imprisoned for a time in one of the fort's casemates (a chamber in the wall); his cell and those adjacent to it now house the Casemate Museum. Exhibits of weapons, uniforms, models, drawings, and extensive Civil War relics retell the fort's history, depict coastal artillery activities, and describe the military lifestyle through the Civil War years. > Rte. 258 (Mercury Blvd.), tel. 757/788–3391. Free. Daily 10:30–4:30.

St. John's Church Little of early Hampton has survived the shellings and conflicts of the past, but St. John's brick walls, built in 1728, have. Today a stained-glass window honors Pocahontas, the Native American princess who is said to have saved the life of Captain John Smith in 1608. The communion silver on display, made in London in 1618, is the oldest such service still used in this country. The parish, founded in the same year as the city (1610), also claims to be the oldest in continuous service in America. You may listen to a taped interpretation or take a guided tour (by arrangement) and visit a small museum in the parish house. > 100 W. Queens Way, tel. 757/722–2567. Free. Weekdays 9–3, Sat. 9–noon.

Virginia Air and Space Center This nine-story, futuristic center is the official repository of the NASA Langley Research Center. Its space artifacts include a 3-billion-year-old moon rock, the *Apollo 12* command capsule, and a lunar lander. The center also holds a dozen full-size aircraft, southeast Virginia's only IMAX theater, and hands-on exhibits that let you see yourself as an astronaut. The Hampton Roads History Center, inside the museum and included in its admission charge, depicts the area's colorful history through archaeological and audiovisual exhibitions that include partial reproductions of colonial buildings. Full-scale reproductions of the gun turret of the USS *Monitor* and a portion of the CSS *Virginia* casemate show how the two ironclads changed the course of naval history at the start of the 1862 Peninsula Campaign in Hampton Roads. > Downtown Waterfront, 600 Settlers Landing Rd. (I–64, Exit 267), tel. 757/727–0800, www.vasc.org. Space Center $6.50, Space Center and 1 IMAX movie $9.50. Memorial Day–Labor Day, Mon.–Wed. 10–5, Thurs.–Sun. 10–7; Labor Day–Memorial Day, daily 10–5.

NEWPORT NEWS

Endview Plantation Built in 1769 and restored to its 1862 appearance, the two-story Georgian frame house with double chimneys retains a great deal of original wood flooring, doors, and windows. The farm was used by General Thomas Nelson's Virginia Militia on September 28, 1781 en route to Yorktown. During the 1862 Peninsula Campaign, both Confederate and Union troops used it as a field hospital, and it was Union general George B. McClellan's headquarters during the Battle of Williamsburg. > 362 Yorktown Rd. (Rte. 238 E; take Exit 247 from I–64), Newport News 23603, tel. 757/887–1862, www.endview.org. $5. Apr.–Dec., Mon. and Wed. 10–4, Sun. 1–5; Jan.–Mar. Mon. 10–4 and Sun. 1–5.

Lee Hall Mansion The only large antebellum plantation house remaining on the lower Virginia Peninsula was begun in 1848. Tours of the brick mansion progress through seven rooms beautifully decorated in the style of the mid-1800s, highlighting plantation life, furnishings, architecture, Richard D. Lee and his family, and the impact of the Civil War on local society. Used by Confederate generals as a command center, the house is also a museum documenting the 1862 Peninsula Campaign. > 163 Yorktown Rd. (Exit 247 from I–64), Newport News 23603, tel. 757/888–3371, www.leehall.org. $5. Apr.–Dec., Mon. and Wed.–Sat. 10–4, Sun. 1–5; Jan.–Mar., Mon. and Thurs.–Sat. 10–4, Sun. 1–5. Guided tours every ½ hr.

Mariners' Museum A world history of seagoing vessels and the people who sailed them is the concern of this outstanding museum in a 550-acre park. Among the more than 50 full-size craft on display are a Native American bark canoe, a sailing yacht, a speedboat, a gondola, a Coast Guard cutter, and a Chinese sampan. In separate galleries you can often watch the progress of a boat under construction; view ornate and sometimes huge figureheads; examine the watermen's culture of the Chesapeake Bay; and learn about the history of the U.S. Navy. Don't miss the scrimshaw or the authentic scale models hand-carved by August Crabtree: so tiny that you must view them through magnifying glasses, they portray shipbuilding accomplishments from those of ancient Egypt to 19th-century Britain. The museum also holds artifacts from the RMS *Titanic* and the ironclad USS *Monitor*, which served in the 1862 Peninsula Campaign and today lies off the coast of North Carolina. > 100 Museum Dr. (I–64, Exit 258A), tel. 757/595–0368 or 800/581–7245, www.mariner.org. $6. Daily 10–5.

Virginia Living Museum The indigenous animals that live here are in wild or simulated lakefront habitats that allow you to observe their natural behavior. A trail leads to the water's edge, where otters and blue herons can be spotted, then upland past de-scented skunks, lame bald eagles (wounded by hunters), and cute but unpettable bobcats. A 40-foot-tall outdoor aviary re-creates a wetlands habitat. Indoors, the Planetarium, for those three and up, offers more celestial sights; call for show times. The tacky Safari minigolf site may be fun for children and others, but it lessens the splendor of the environment. > 524 J. Clyde Morris Blvd., tel. 757/595–1900, www.valivingmuseum.org. Museum $9, planetarium $3, combination ticket $11. Memorial Day–Labor Day, daily 9–6; Labor Day–Memorial Day, Mon.–Sat. 9–5, Sun. noon–5.

Virginia War Museum The 60,000 artifacts here include a graffiti-covered section of the Berlin Wall, a Civil War blockade runner's uniform, weapons, uniforms, wartime posters, photographs, and other memorabilia. It traces military history from 1775 on through the Gulf War and includes an outdoor exhibition of seven tanks and cannons. > Huntington Park, 9285 Warwick Blvd. (Rte. 60), tel. 757/247–8523, www.warmuseum.org. $5. Mon.–Sat. 9–5, Sun. 1–5.

NORFOLK

Chrysler Museum of Art One of America's major art museums, the Chrysler has a broad permanent collection with works by Rubens, Gainsborough, Renoir, Picasso, van Gogh, Andy Warhol, and Pollock. Classical and pre-Columbian civilizations are also represented. The decorative-arts collection includes exquisite English porcelain and art nouveau furnishings. Every American glassmaker between 1825 and 1950 is represented in the glass collection, which has an extensive number of Tiffany pieces, as well as artifacts from ancient Rome and the Near and Far East. > 245 W. Olney Rd., tel. 757/664–6200, www.chrysler.org. $7. Wed. 10–9, Thurs.–Sat. 10–5, Sun. 1–5.

d'Art Center You can watch 30 painters, sculptors, glassworkers, quilters, and other artists at work in their studios here. > 125 College Pl., Norfolk, tel. 757/625–4211, www.d-artcenter.org.

Douglas MacArthur Memorial An "army brat" with no hometown, the controversial war hero General MacArthur (1880–1964) designated this navy town as his burial place and the site for a monument to himself because his mother was born here—and possibly because no one as well known as he had a monument nearby (MacArthur's ego was formidable). In the rotunda of the old City Hall, converted according to MacArthur's design, is the mausoleum; 11 adjoining galleries house mementos of MacArthur's career, such as his signature corncob pipe and the Japanese instruments of surrender that concluded World War II. Next door the general's staff car is on display, and a 24-minute biography is screened. > Bank St. and City Hall Ave., tel. 757/441–2965, sites.communitylink.org/mac. Donations accepted. Mon.–Sat. 10–5, Sun. 11–5.

Ghent A mix of chic shops, including antiques stores and upscale clothing and shoe boutiques and eateries, is in a turn-of-the-20th-century neighborhood that runs from the Elizabeth River to York Street, to West Olney Road and Llewellyn Avenue. Colley Avenue and 21st Street is the hub. The **Palace Shops** (21st St. and Llewellyn Ave., tel. 757/622–9999) will please shoppers looking for some finery. Antiques hunters should head to the **Ghent Market and Antique Center** (1400 Granby St., tel. 757/625–2897), where there's a city block full of goods. Fine kitchen equipment and accessories can be found at the lovely **Bouillabaisse** (1611 Colley Ave., Norfolk, tel. 757/627–7774).

Hermitage Foundation Museum Inside an English Tudor–style house that was built by a textile tycoon around 1900, the Hermitage contains the largest privately owned collection of Asian art in the United States—including ivory and jade carvings, ancient bronzes, and a 1,400-year-old marble Buddha from China. The decorative-art collections include Tiffany glass, Persian rugs, and furniture from the Middle East, India, Europe, and America. You may picnic on the 12-acre grounds along the Lafayette River. > 7637 N. Shore Rd., tel. 757/423–2052, www.hermitagefoundation.org. $5. Feb.–Dec., Mon., Tues., and Thurs.–Sat. 10–5, Sun. 1–5.

Moses Myers House The federal redbrick home, built by its namesake in 1792, is exceptional, and not just for its elegance. In the long Adam-style dining room, a wood writing desk holds a collection of fine china—and a set of silver kiddush cups (Moses Myers was Norfolk's first permanent Jewish resident). A transplanted New Yorker, Myers made his fortune in Norfolk in shipping, then served as a diplomat and a customhouse officer. His grandson married James Madison's grandniece, his great-grandson served as mayor, and the family kept the house for five generations. The furnishings, 70% of them original, include family portraits by Gilbert Stuart and Thomas Sully. > 331 Bank St., tel. 757/333–1085, www.chrysler.org/myers_house.html. $5; $10, combination ticket with Chrysler Museum. Wed.–Sat. 10–4, Sun. 1–4.

Nauticus A popular attraction on Norfolk's much-redeveloped waterfront, the National Maritime Center has more than 70 high-tech exhibits on three "decks." The site's exhibits on concepts as ancient as shipbuilding are right next to interactive displays that encompass the modern naval world. Weather satellites, underwater archaeology, and the Loch Ness Monster all come together here. There are additional fees for the AEGIS Theater and Virtual Adventures. Inside Nauticus, the free **Hampton Roads Naval Museum** (www.hrnm.navy.mil) interprets the history of the U.S. Navy in Hampton Roads. Outdoors is the battleship USS *Wisconsin*, which has enormous gun turrets and a conning tower that's impressive up close. > 1 Waterside Dr., tel. 757/664–1000, www.nauticus.org. $9.50, Hampton Roads Naval Museum and battleship free. Memorial Day–Labor Day, daily 10–6; Labor Day–Memorial Day, Tues.–Sat. 10–5, Sun. noon–5.

Norfolk Botanical Garden Besides growing an abundance of azaleas, rhododendrons, and camellias, this 175-acre garden also has a fragrance garden for the blind, with identification labels in Braille. A delicately landscaped Japanese garden has trees native to that country, including unusual strains of cherry and maple. From mid-March to October, boats and trams carry you along routes to view seasonal plants and flowers, including 4,000 varieties of roses on 3½ acres. Year-round you can stroll 12 mi of paths. Eleven marble statues of famous artists, carved in the late 19th century by Moses Ezekiel, enhance the natural beauty of the gardens. The lakeside is ideal for picnics. > 6700 Azalea Garden Rd., tel. 757/441–5831,

www.virginiagarden.org. Garden $6, boat tours $3. Mid-Apr.–mid-Oct., daily 9–7;
mid-Oct.–mid-Apr., daily 9–5.
Norfolk Naval Base On the northern edge of the city, this is an impressive sight,
holding as it does more than 100 ships of the Atlantic Fleet. Among them is the USS
Theodore Roosevelt, a nuclear-powered aircraft carrier with a crew of 6,300, one of the
largest warships in the world. The submarine piers and the heliport are also memorable. Tour buses operate year-round, departing from the naval-base tour office.
> 9079 Hampton Blvd., tel. 757/444–7955, 757/444–1577 visitors office,
www.navstanorva.navy.mil/tour. Tour $5: Tours daily 11, 12, 1, and 2.
Portsmouth Naval Shipyard Museum This waterfront museum has exhibits on
naval history that include models of 18th-century warships. You can board the retired
Coast Guard lightship (a floating lighthouse), whose quarters below deck have been
furnished authentically. The museum is close to the pedestrian ferry landing. > 2
High St., Portsmouth, tel. 757/393–8591, www.portsnavalmuseums.com. $3, includes
lightship museum. Tues.–Sat. 10–5, Sun. 1–5.
St. Paul's Church Constructed in 1739, St. Paul's was the only building in town to
survive the bombardment and conflagration of New Year's Day 1776; a cannonball
fired by the British fleet remains embedded in the southeastern wall. An earlier
church had been built on this site in 1641, and the churchyard contains graves dating
from the 1600s. > St. Paul's Blvd. and City Hall Ave., tel. 757/627–4353. Donations accepted. Tues.–Fri. 10–4.

VIRGINIA BEACH

Adam Thoroughgood House Inland from the shore is the late-17th-century house
named for a rich plantation owner who died in 1640. This little (45- by 22-feet) brick
house, probably constructed by a Thoroughgood grandson, recalls the English cottage architecture of the period, with a protruding chimney and a steeply pitched roof.
The four-room early plantation home has a 17th-century garden with characteristic
hedges. > 1636 Parish Rd., tel. 757/460–7588. $4. Tues.–Sat. 10–5, Sun. 1–5.
Atlantic Wildfowl Heritage Museum Sandwiched between high-rise hotels is this
cottage which holds fine waterfowl art and artifacts, including decoys (thousands of
waterfowl migrate through eastern Virginia on their way north and south). The building, a small cottage built in 1895 by Virginia Beach's first mayor and postmaster,
Bernard Holland, is the oldest building of its kind on the oceanfront. Purchased in
1909 by a Norfolk banker and cotton broker, it's also known as the de Witt Cottage.
> 1113 Atlantic Ave., tel. 757/437–8432, www.awhm.org. Free. Memorial Day–Sept.,
Mon.–Sat. 10–5, Sun. noon–5; Oct.–Memorial Day, Tues.–Sat. 10–5, Sun. noon–5.
First Landing State Park Spanish moss grows no farther north than this park,
and blue spruce appears no farther south. First Landing is also a haven for
red and gray foxes, raccoons, opossums, water snakes, and other denizens of
swamp and dune. Boardwalks built just above the water level let you get close to
flora and fauna while keeping your feet dry, and there are campgrounds and cabins,
picnic areas, and guided tours. > 2500 Shore Dr. (U.S. 60), tel. 757/412–2300,
www.dcr.state.va.us/parks/1stland.htm. Apr.–Oct., weekdays $3 per car, weekends
$4; Nov.–Mar., $2. Apr.–Oct., park daily 8 AM–dusk, visitor center weekdays 8–4,
weekends 9–4; Nov.–Mar., park Sun.–Fri. 8 AM–dusk, visitor center weekdays 8–4,
Sun. 9–4.
Francis Land House and Gardens A 200-year-old plantation home, beautiful gardens, flowers and trees, and a wooded wetland area with walking trails make up this
7-acre site. The gardens grow heirloom vegetables, herbs, and formal plantings. House

tours of furnished period rooms and special exhibits relate to Virginia Beach history, with particular emphasis on the colonial and federal eras. > 3131 Virginia Beach Blvd., Virginia Beach 23452, tel. 757/431–4000, www.vabeach.com/points/francisland.htm. $4. Tues.–Sat. 9–5, Sun. 11–5.

Harpoon Larry's This local watering hole with true character is no tourist trap. Don't be surprised to see a great white shark staring back at you as you eat a juicy piece of that shark's cousin (mahimahi) stuffed with fresh Chesapeake Bay crabmeat, or enjoy raw oysters and a cold Corona. Some come just for the pool table. > 24th and Pacific Sts., tel. 757/422–6000, www.harpoonlarryskillerseafood.com.

Old Cape Henry Lighthouse The northeastern tip of Virginia Beach, on the cape where the mouth of the bay meets the ocean, is near where the English landed on their way to Jamestown in 1607. This lighthouse, however, didn't light anyone's way until 1792. You can still climb to the top of the old lighthouse in summer; a new, working lighthouse is closed to visitors. > U.S. 60, tel. 757/422–9421, www.apva.org/apva/cape_henry.php. $3. Mid-Mar.–Oct., daily 10–5; Nov. and Jan.–mid-Mar., daily 10–4.

Virginia Marine Science Museum The sea is the subject at this popular facility, with more than 200 exhibits. This is no place to be passive; many exhibits require participation. You can use computers to predict the weather and solve the pollution crisis, watch the birds in the salt marsh through telescopes on a deck, handle horseshoe crabs, take a simulated journey to the bottom of the sea in a submarine, and study fish up close in tanks that re-create underwater environments. The museum is almost 2 mi inland from Rudee Inlet at the southern end of Virginia Beach. > 717 General Booth Blvd., tel. 757/425–3474, www.vmsm.com. $9.95. Daily 9–5 (until 7 Mon.–Sat., mid-June–Labor Day).

Tours

American Rover Sailing Tours Tours aboard a striking 135-foot topsail schooner take you around Hampton Roads' nautical historical landmarks and the Norfolk Naval Base. The majestic, three-masted tall ship, modeled after the cargo schooners that once sailed the Chesapeake Bay, leaves from the downtown Norfolk Waterfront for narrated harbor cruises of two and three hours. The trips cost $15–$22. > Waterside Festival Marketplace, Norfolk, tel. 757/627–7245, www.americanrover.com. Mid-May–mid-Sept.

Carrie B Riverboat A scaled-down reproduction of a Mississippi paddle-wheeler riverboat, the *Carrie B*, cruises Hampton Roads for 2 or 2½ hours to give you an unobstructed view of navy aircraft carriers, nuclear submarines, the nation's oldest dry dock, Fort Norfolk, and the site at which the USS *Monitor* encountered the CSS *Virginia* during the Civil War. > Waterside Festival Marketplace, Norfolk, tel. 757/393–4735, www.carriebcruises.com. $14–$16. Apr.–mid-Oct., daily noon, 2, and 6.

Norfolk Trolley This guided tour of the historic downtown area allows you to get on and off as you please. Tickets are available at the Hampton Roads Transit kiosk at Waterside Festival Marketplace. > 333 Waterside Dr., Norfolk, tel. 757/640–6300.

Olde Towne Trolley Tour Portsmouth's Olde Towne Trolley Tour gives you the inside story of major historical events. It departs from points in downtown on Sunday and Wednesday at 10:45. > 6 Crawford Pkwy., Portsmouth, tel. 757/393–5111.

Sports

Wild River Outfitters From kayaking to backpacking, rock climbing to car camping, Wild River Outfitters has 9,000 square feet of retail space and hundreds of canoes and kayaks in stock. Virginia Beach's oldest guide service, Wild River can also take you kayak and dolphin touring. > 3636 Virginia Beach Blvd., No. 108, Virginia Beach, tel. 757/431–8566 or 877/431–8566, www.wildriveroutfitters.com.

FISHING

Around Newport News you can expect excellent catches of striper, flounder, and the occasional catfish.

Mariners' Museum You can rent boats for use on Lake Maury, on the museum's grounds. The lake is open for fishing in spring and summer. Encircling the lake is the 5-mi Noland Trail. > 100 Museum Dr., Newport News, tel. 757/591–7799, www.mariner.org.

Venture Inn Charters Half- and full-day charter trips are available from April to December, leaving from the Hampton Downtown Public Piers. The fishing excursions turn up croaker, flounder, gray trout, and striped bass. > 766 Settlers Landing Rd., Hampton, tel. 757/850–8960 or 800/853–5002, www.ventureinncharters.com.

SCUBA DIVING

Lynnhaven Dive Center The staff at Lynnhaven lead dives and give scuba lessons. > 1413 N. Great Neck Rd., Virginia Beach, tel. 757/481–7949, www.ldcscuba.com. *EQUIPMENT* **Chick's Beach Sailing Center** > 3304 Shore Dr., Virginia Beach, tel. 757/460–2238 or 757/481–3067.

Save the Date

APRIL

International Azalea Festival This colorful event, the region's oldest festival, is packed with pomp and circumstance. Held in mid- to late April in Norfolk, the festival includes a grand parade that heads through downtown, the coronation of a queen and court chosen from a field of young women representing the NATO countries, an air show, a fashion show, a ball, and a weekend of live entertainment highlighted by the performance of a major recording artist. > Tel. 757/445–6647 Ext. 1, www.azaleafestival.org.

APRIL–MAY

Virginia Arts Festival Showcased at this two-week event are renowned artists from the worlds of classical, jazz, and world music, as well as dance and musical theater. > Tel. 757/664–6492, www.virginiaartsfest.com.

JUNE

Hampton Jazz Festival Some of the country's top blues, soul, pop, and jazz performers share the stage late in the month in Hampton. > Hampton Coliseum, 1000 Coliseum Dr., tel. 757/838–4203.

Harborfest This festival in Norfolk draws upwards of 250,000 people early every June. The waterfront celebration provides nonstop live entertainment, water and air shows, sailing ships, food, and fireworks. > Waterfront, between Nauticus and Waterside Festival Hall, tel. 757/441–2345.

AUGUST

East Coast Surfing Championship Top-notch surfers vie for the championship off the Virginia Beach coast in mid-August. > Tel. 757/499–8822.

Hampton Cup Regatta Mid-month, the oldest and largest powerboat race in the United States is held in Hampton. Live entertainment and children's activities are part of the fun. > Tel. 757/722–5343 or 800/487–8778.

SEPTEMBER

Neptune Festival This five-day family affair in Virginia Beach, held in the middle of the month, includes a sand castle competition, air show, live entertainment, fresh seafood, a gala ball, and fireworks. > Tel. 757/498–0215.

DECEMBER

Christmas in the Field The second weekend of December brings this Civil War reenactment to the Virginia War Museum. > Virginia War Museum, 9285 Warwick Blvd. (Rte. 60), tel. 757/247–8523, www.warmuseum.org.

WHERE TO STAY

HAMPTON

Arrow Inn Near Williamsburg and many of the places to golf and fish, this inexpensive hotel is a great place for an extended getaway. > 7 Semple Farm Rd. (off I–64 take Exit 261 B), 23666, tel. 757/865–0300 or 800/833–2520, www.arrowinn.com. 59 rooms. Some kitchenettes, some microwaves, refrigerators, cable TV, laundry facilities, some pets allowed (fee), no-smoking rooms. AE, D, DC, MC, V. ¢

Holiday Inn Hampton Halfway between Colonial Williamsburg and Virginia Beach, this complex of buildings stands on 13 beautifully landscaped acres. About half the rooms have a pink-and-green color scheme; others are darker, with cherrywood dressers and tables. Sofas convert into extra beds in many rooms. Some rooms overlook the indoor pool in the atrium, and others have doors that open, motel-style, directly onto the parking lot. > 1815 W. Mercury Blvd., 23666, tel. 757/838–0200 or 800/842–9370, fax 757/838–4964. 320 rooms. Restaurant, 2 pools (1 indoor), gym, sauna, bar. AE, D, DC, MC, V. $

Radisson Hotel Hampton The nine-story Radisson has the premier location in town, right at a marina and a block away from the Virginia Air and Space Center. Most rooms look over the harbor or the handsome plaza in front of the space center. > 700 Settlers Landing Rd., 23669, tel. 757/727–9700 or 800/333–3333, fax 757/722–4557, www.radisson.com. 172 rooms, Restaurant, café, pool, gym, bar. AE, D, DC, MC, V. $–$$

NORFOLK

Clarion James Madison Hotel In the early 1900s, this hotel was the skyscraper of Norfolk—coming in at eight stories. The hotel still maintains a domineering presence downtown. You can sip a microbrew on a leather seat in the lobby's lounge, where exquisite Tiffany chandeliers, mahogany wood pillars, and Oriental rugs recall the Jazz Age. Rooms, however, have ordinary traditional hotel furnishings, except for the original claw-foot sinks in the bathrooms. > 345 Granby St., Norfolk 23510, tel. 757/622–6682 or 888/402–6682, fax 757/683–5949. 127 rooms, 54 suites. Restaurant, in-room data ports, cable TV with video games, lobby lounge, dry cleaning, laundry facilities, concierge, meeting rooms, free parking. AE, D, MC, V. ¢–$

Holiday Inn Olde Towne With the Portsmouth waterfront just outside, and the historic district's attractions so nearby, this hotel is well situated. The undistinguished appearance of the building hides pleasant things inside: public and guest rooms vary in size, but all have a modern look, and some private guest rooms share water views from a balcony. The restaurant overlooks the Elizabeth River and Norfolk's downtown skyline on the opposite shore. > 8 Crawford Pkwy., Portsmouth 23704, tel.

757/393–2573 or 800/465–4329, fax 757/399–1248. 210 rooms, 5 suites. Restaurant, in-room data ports, pool, gym, lobby lounge, laundry facilities, laundry service, meeting rooms. AE, D, DC, MC, V. $

Norfolk Waterside Marriott This downtown hotel is connected to the Waterside Festival Hall shopping area by a ramp and is close to Town Point Park, site of many festivals. The handsome lobby, with wood paneling, a central staircase, silk tapestries, and federal-style furniture, sets a high standard that continues throughout the hotel. Rooms, it must be said, are somewhat small. > 235 E. Main St., Norfolk 23510, tel. 757/627–4200 or 800/228–9290, fax 757/628–6452, www.marriott.com. 396 rooms, 8 suites. 2 restaurants, in-room data ports, indoor pool, lobby lounge. AE, D, DC, MC, V. $–$$$

Sheraton Norfolk Waterside Hotel Modern is the word for the way this hotel is furnished, from the bright, spacious lobby to the ample rooms and large suites. A ground-floor bar with dramatic 30-foot windows overlooks the Elizabeth River—many rooms also have a beautiful view over the water. This Sheraton is close to the Waterside Festival Hall shopping area. > 777 Waterside Dr., Norfolk 23510, tel. 757/622–6664, fax 757/625–8271, www.sheraton.com. 426 rooms, 20 suites. Restaurant, pool, lounge. AE, D, DC, MC, V. $–$$

VIRGINIA BEACH

Cavalier Hotels In the quieter north end of town, this 18-acre resort complex combines the original Cavalier Hotel of 1927, a seven-story redbrick building on a hill, with an oceanfront high-rise built across the street in 1973. The clientele is about evenly divided between conventioneers and families. F. Scott and Zelda Fitzgerald stayed regularly in the older section (it has since been lavishly refurbished). If you stay on the hilltop, you can see the water—and get to it easily by shuttle van or a short walk. The newer building overlooks 600 feet of private beach. There is a fee for tennis, but the other athletic facilities are free. > Atlantic Ave. and 42nd St., 23451, tel. 757/425–8555 or 888/746–2327, fax 757/425–0629, www.cavalierhotel.com. 400 rooms. 5 restaurants, in-room data ports, putting green, 4 tennis courts, 2 pools (1 indoor), wading pool, gym, beach, croquet, volleyball, baby-sitting, playground, no-smoking rooms. AE, D, DC, MC, V. $$–$$$

Clarion Hotel Town Center Virginia Beach This sparkling white, modern hotel is midway between Norfolk and the beach and 15 mi from Norfolk International Airport. The skylighted lobby overlooks a glassed-in indoor pool. Rooms have a sitting area with sofa and desk; there are floral spreads and moss-color carpeting, with prints of flowers on the wall. Every room has a hair dryer, iron, ironing board, and coffeemaker. Coffee in the lobby is complimentary. > 4453 Bonney Rd., 23462, tel. 757/473–1700 or 800/847–5202, fax 757/552–0477, www.clarioninn.com. 149 rooms. Restaurant, in-room data ports, refrigerators, pool, gym, hot tub, lobby lounge, dry cleaning, laundry service, meeting rooms; no-smoking rooms. AE, D, DC, MC, V. ¢–$

Ramada Plaza Resort Oceanfront With its 17-story tower, this Ramada is the tallest hotel in the city. Rooms that do not face the ocean directly have either a partial view or overlook the swimming pool, where there's a summer swim-up bar. The modern lobby is dressed in mauve and emerald and has a skylighted atrium. Each guest room has a coffeemaker, iron, ironing board, and hair dryer. Beds have quilted spreads and striped draperies. Gus' Mariner Restaurant, a fancy restaurant with prices to match, serves good seafood. > 57th St. and Oceanfront, 23451, tel. 757/428–7025 or 800/365–3032, fax 757/428–2921, www.ramada.com. 247 rooms. 2 restaurants, mi-

crowaves, refrigerators, in-room safes, indoor-outdoor pool, gym, sauna, bar, dry
cleaning, laundry service, convention center, meeting rooms, no-smoking rooms. AE,
D, DC, MC, V. $–$$$

WHERE TO EAT

HAMPTON & NEWPORT NEWS

Captain George's Although there is an ample à la carte menu, the main pull here is
the 70-item, all-you-can-eat buffet of fried, steamed, and broiled seafood. Highlights
are steamed Alaskan crab legs, steamed shrimp with Old Bay seasoning (a locally
made favorite), broiled flounder, steamed mussels, and she-crab soup. Among the
15 desserts are baklava and five fruit cobblers. A mural of the Chesapeake Bay domi-
nates the largest of four dining rooms, which has tables with tops embedded with
seashells. > 2710 W. Mercury Blvd., Hampton, tel. 757/826–1435. AE, MC, V. No lunch
Mon.–Sat. $$$

Fisherman's Wharf Decorated with ship figureheads and other seagoing paraphernalia, this restaurant is on the second floor of a building on the working waterfront. A
seafood-heavy buffet of up to 75 items, including Dungeness or snow crab legs, mussels, cherrystone clams, fish, and prime rib, is set up nightly in a large boat in the dining room. > 14 Ivy Home Rd., Newport News, tel. 757/480–3113. AE, D, DC, MC, V.
Closed Mon. No lunch Tues.–Sat. $$$

Grate Steak Farm implements and unfinished pine walls decorate the four dining
rooms, which are casual and boisterous. You can choose your own steak and then
grill it yourself on a huge barbecue grill. The menu also includes fried shrimp, grilled
tuna, and salad bars. Prime rib, served on the bone if you like, is slowly roasted here.
> 1934 Coliseum Dr., Hampton, tel. 757/827–1886. AE, D, DC, MC, V. No lunch.
$$–$$$$

Grey Goose Tearoom An enticing aroma and a gift shop displaying tea-related items
greet patrons of this cozy tearoom decorated with Victorian tea-party prints, antique
teapots, and knickknacks. Brunswick stew, creamy Hampton blue-crab soup, and biscuits are permanent fixtures on the "everything homemade" menu, and daily specials
are posted on the wall. Desserts are especially good, but avoid the canned fruit salad
on iceberg lettuce. > 1101-A W. Queens Way, Hampton, tel. 757/723–7978. AE, D, DC,
MC, V. Closed Sun. $

Herman's Harbor House You may think you've gone off course as you drive through
this residential neighborhood, but just keep going. Herman's, at the end of Deep
Creek Road, serves the area's best crab cakes, accompanying them with ample portions of vegetables. The diverse menu also includes other Tidewater-style seafood
dishes as well as steak, veal, and pasta, and desserts made in-house. Expect crowds
even on weekday nights at this local favorite. > 663 Deep Creek Rd. (I–64, Exit 258A,
to Warwick Blvd. to Deep Creek Rd.), Newport News, tel. 757/930–1000. AE, D, MC,
V. $–$$$$

NORFOLK

Freemason Abbey Restaurant and Tavern This former church building has 40-foot-
high cathedral ceilings and large windows that look onto the business district.
There's intimate dining at the reconstructed-steel mezzanine; downstairs you can get
lighter fare. Regular appetizers include artichoke dip and ham-wrapped scallops. The

wild game nights are quite an occasion: wild boar, alligator, and any other type of meat you can think of is served. > 209 W. Freemason St., tel. 757/622–3966. AE, D, DC, MC, V. **$–$$$**

La Galleria The interior of this excellent restaurant, not done in the usual homey Southern style, may appear cold, but it is impressive. Decorations include Corinthian columns and large urns imported from Italy, and a pianist often plays soft music. Among the menu choices are the *vongole al casino* starter (baked clams sprinkled with herbs, garlic, and bread crumbs) and many excellent pastas and main courses, such as salmon sautéed in herbs, garlic, and white wine. > 120 College Pl., tel. 757/623–3939. AE, DC, MC, V. **$$–$$$**

Magnolia Steak Modestly upscale but casual, Magnolia exhibits Southern hospitality through its excellent, all-American fare. Steak is just the beginning. The restaurant does great things with seafood, hamburgers, salads, daily specials, and a delicious appetizer platter of onion rings (just $5) that feeds four. There are two dining rooms—one a bit more formal than the other, a wraparound patio festooned with flowers, a billiard parlor, and a bar that stays open until 2 AM. > 749 W Princess Anne Rd., at Colley Ave., tel. 757/625–0400. AE, D, MC, V. No lunch weekends. **¢–$**

Wild Monkey From its scrumptious $10 meat loaf to the smoked salmon with blue cheese, this restaurant wows to the last bite. Its ever-changing wine list is bountiful, and there's even a board with recommended wine and food pairings. For a starter, try the pork and ginger dumplings; end with the pecan pie. If you go for Sunday brunch, the Cuban is a fine sandwich, and the frittata is a unique take on a traditional Italian dish. Make sure to get here early. > Colley Ave., tel. 757/627–6462. Reservations not accepted. AE, MC, V. No dinner Sun. **$–$$**

VIRGINIA BEACH

Croaker's A great local favorite, Croaker's isn't a restaurant that many people passing through the area know about. Far from the crowds, it's at the north end of Shore Drive. Along with melt-in-your-mouth crab cakes, Croaker's serves a mean Oysters William (oysters with white wine, butter, and shallots). Another surprise is the excellent steaks, which are cut to order. > 3629 Shore Dr., tel. 757/363–2490. AE, D, DC, MC, V. No lunch. **$–$$$**

The Lighthouse Many oilcloth-covered tables in these six nautically themed dining rooms overlook the ocean or the inlet. The floors are red clay tile; the walls have dark-wood paneling. But the main attraction here is the seafood. If you can't decide whether you want Maine lobster, chicken, shrimp, or crab cakes, you can try the mixed grill, where you can mix and match any two items. > 1st St. and Atlantic Ave., tel. 757/428–7974. AE, D, DC, MC, V. **$$–$$$**

Rockafeller's The Down East architecture of this local favorite with double-deck porches hints at the seafood that's available. The restaurant has a bar, a raw bar, and alfresco dining in good weather (in cool weather, the large window wall still gives you a water view). Seafood, pasta, chicken, and beef share the menu with salads and sandwiches. Rockafeller's (and several other restaurants) are tucked away on Rudee Inlet. To get here, go south on Pacific Avenue and turn right on Winston-Salem immediately before the Rudee Inlet bridge. The street ends at Mediterranean Avenue. > 308 Mediterranean Ave., tel. 757/422–5654. AE, D, DC, MC, V. **$–$$**

ESSENTIALS

Getting Here

Unless you wish to confine your trip to one city in Hampton Roads, having a car in this area is a near necessity.

BY BUS

Greyhound Lines typically runs six or so departures daily from Hampton, Norfolk, and Virginia Beach to and from Washington, D.C. Most but not all require changing buses in Richmond. Reserved seats are not possible, and purchasing a ticket does not guarantee a seat. Ticket in hand, you must get in line to board. If the bus has originated in another city, already-boarded passengers have preference for existing seats when reboarding. It is possible to check your luggage, for which you receive a baggage claim ticket. However, although checked, if you must change buses, it's up to you to move your luggage to the next bus.

In Norfolk, the free NET (Norfolk Electric Transit) shuttle bus runs within downtown, making a total of 16 stops along a 2.2-mi route throughout the downtown every 6 to 18 minutes. NET service is weekdays 6:30 AM–11 PM, Saturday noon–midnight, and Sunday noon–8.

DEPOTS **Charles Carr/Hampton Depot** > 2 W. Pembrook Ave., Hampton, tel. 757/722–9861. **Greyhound Norfolk Depot** > 701 Monticello Ave., Norfolk, tel. 757/625–7500, www.greyhound.com. **Myles of Travel** > 1017 Laskin Rd., Virginia Beach, tel. 757/422–2998.

LINES **Greyhound Lines** > Tel. 800/231–2222. **Norfolk Electric Transit (NET)** > Tel. 757/222–6100.

BY CAR

To get to the Hampton Roads area, take I–95 South to Richmond, and then take I–295 to I–64 East to Newport News.

Interstate 664 creates a circular beltway through the Hampton Roads area, connecting Newport News and Norfolk, via Suffolk. Interstate 64 runs northwest through Norfolk to intersect with I–664 in Hampton and I–95 at Richmond. U.S. 58 and what was once I–44 is now just an extension of I–264 (part of I–64).

TRAFFIC The area is well served with expressways and interstate highways, but these routes are also used by a lot of local drivers. Because the ragged coastline is constantly interrupted by water, driving from one town to another usually means going through a tunnel or over a bridge, either one of which may create a traffic bottleneck. The entrance to the tunnel between Hampton and Norfolk can get very congested, especially on weekends, so listen to your car radio for updated traffic reports.

With a long list of tunnels and bridges connecting myriad waterways, it is easy to find yourself headed in the wrong direction. Highways have adequate signs, but sometimes it may be too late to merge before entering a tunnel or bridge. Traffic is highly congested during rush hour and in peak summer months, when the beach traffic can grind everything to a halt.

In congested periods, use the less-traveled I–664. The 17½-mi Chesapeake Bay Bridge-Tunnel is the only connection between the southern part of Virginia and the Eastern Shore; U.S. 13 is the main route up the spine of the Eastern Shore peninsula into Maryland.

BY TRAIN

Amtrak has service twice daily between Washington, D.C., and Newport News. The trip takes about four hours and does not require a change of trains. The cost is about $90 per person.

LINE **Amtrak** > Tel. 800/872–7245, www.amtrak.com.

STATION **Newport News Amtrak Station** > 9304 Warwick Blvd., Newport News, tel. 757/245–3589, www.amtrak.com.

Visitor Information

Many area visitor bureaus have self-guided walking or driving tours your can take. The Cannonball walking trail, for instance, connects historic sights in downtown Norfolk.

CONTACTS **Hampton Convention and Visitors Bureau** > 710 Settlers Landing Rd., Hampton 23669, tel. 757/727–1102 or 800/800–2202, www.hampton.va.us. **Hampton Roads Transit Kiosk** > Waterfront, 333 Waterside Dr., tel. 757/623–3222, www.watersidemarketplace.com. **Newport News Visitor Information Center** > 13560 Jefferson Ave. (1–64, Exit 250B), Newport News 23603, tel. 757/886–7777 or 888/493–7386, www.newport-news.org/visitorinfo. **Norfolk Convention and Visitors Bureau** > End of 4th View St., Norfolk 23503, tel. 757/441–1852 or 800/368–3097, www.norfolkcvb.com. **Portsmouth Convention and Visitors Bureau** > 505 Crawford St., Suite 2, Portsmouth 23704, tel. 757/393–5327 or 800/767–8782, www.ci.portsmouth.va.us. **Virginia Beach Visitor Information Center** > 2100 Parks Ave., Virginia Beach 23451, tel. 757/437–4888, www.vbfun.com.

Southern Maryland

St. Mary's City is 55 mi south of Washington, D.C.

20

Updated by Karyn-Siobhan Robinson

JUST AN HOUR from Washington, D.C., and from the Virginia state line, Southern Maryland has begun to gain new residents from the Annapolis-Baltimore-Washington triangle. Seeking cheaper housing, good schools, and a slower pace of life, the newcomers have also found a region with a great deal of lore and history—qualities that also make it an great option for a quick weekend trip.

From their very founding in the 1600s on through the present day, the counties of Calvert, Charles, and St. Mary's have had economies based on tobacco and fishing: waterways and the abundant seafood harvested from them are essential to the area, as are depot towns for shipping the tobacco and other crops.

About 35 mi southwest of Annapolis, the relatively rural Charles County is flanked on its west by the Potomac River, which bends as if flows south from Washington. Less-traveled county and state roads crisscross the pristine countryside. One of the communities here, Port Tobacco, is one of the oldest in the East. It first existed as the Native American settlement of "Potopaco." (The similarity between this Native American name—meaning "the jutting of water inland"—and the name for the plant that was to become a cornerstone of the region's economy—is purely coincidental.) Potopaco was colonized by the English in 1634, and later in the century emerged as a major seaport. The Historic District includes the reconstructed early-19th-century courthouse; Catslide House, one of the area's four surviving 18th-century homes; and a restored one-room schoolhouse, dating to 1876 and used as such until 1953.

In 2002, a tornado ripped through La Plata, a town a few miles west of Port Tobacco. Many of the burg's buildings were destroyed by the 24-mi path of destruction—downtown La Plata essentially disappeared. Town leaders used the opportunity to re-think its layout. Where there was once just a strip of unrelated stores on two sides of Route 301, this vision of a town center with sidewalks for outdoor cafés and strolling is now unfolding everywhere.

South of Charles County and forming a peninsula between the Chesapeake Bay and the Potomac River is St. Mary's County. As you travel the area, keep an eye out for road signs with silhouettes of a horse and buggy and the words "Stay Alert" and "Share the Road"—they hint at the Amish and other Mennonite groups that live here. They can often be seen at local farmer's markets selling homemade delicacies and fresh fruit and vegetables. Notable towns in St. Mary's include Lexington Park, Point Lookout, and Chapel Point.

Calvert County, the long, narrow peninsula between the Patuxent River and the Chesapeake Bay, is an area that remains largely undiscovered by many Washingtonians. The main route from Washington, Route 4, merges with Route 2 near Sunderland and continues on to the county's southern tip. Exploring the bay-side and riverside communities to either side of the highway, including Chesapeake Beach, Port Republic, and St. Leonard, is an immersion in the area's living heritage of agriculture and fishing.

Despite its subdivisions and the shopping centers that accompany them, Southern Maryland retains its rural character. In spring, summer, and fall, roadside stands burst with fresh produce here. (In season, look for Silver Queen corn, a tasty regional specialty.) Except for the fair-weather getaway of Solomons Island and Historic St. Mary's City, an archaeological site-in-progress, the region remains largely undiscovered by tourists. This makes it all the better for those who come for the water views, miles of scenic roads, and historic sites. You can stay here in inns and bed-and-breakfasts that are right on the water or in the fields and woodlands of the unspoiled countryside.

WHAT TO SEE & DO

CHESAPEAKE BEACH

All Saints Episcopal Church Built in the 1770s, the brick church replaced a log building that served as the sanctuary of a parish founded in 1692. The hilltop site seems farther than it really is from a busy junction nearby. A simple, classic look is evident inside and out. The church sits amid mature trees and wrought iron–fenced family grave sites dating to the 1700s. Indoors, the clay-tile floor, classic white box pews, and plain windows set off the subtle blue-and-rose stained-glass window over the altar. > Junction of Rtes. 2 and 4, Sunderland, tel. 410/257–6306, www.allsaintssunderland.ang-md.org. Daily 10–5. Services Sun. 8 AM and 10:30 AM.

Chesapeake Bay Railway Museum Inside the railroad's 1898 trackside terminus, this museum provides memorable glimpses of the onetime resort's turn-of-the-20th-century glory days. Among its exhibits are a glass-enclosed model of the town of Chesapeake Beach, a gleaming, black Ford Model T that once carried guests from the station to their hotels, a hand-carved horse from the magnificent carousel, and a slot machine as well as photos of early vacationers. One of the railroad's passenger cars rests nearby. > 4155 Mears Ave. (Rte. 261), tel. 410/257–3892. Free. May–Sept., daily 1–4; Apr. and Oct., weekends 1–4 and by appointment.

LA PLATA

African-American Heritage Society Museum The artifacts here allow you to learn about the lives of Charles County's African-Americans, from those who lived under slavery in the 1600s on through those living in the present. > 7485 Crain Hwy., tel. 301/843–0371, www.dnr.state.md.us. Donations accepted. By appointment only.

Mount Carmel Monastery The site of the first monastery of nuns in colonial America, Mount Carmel was founded in 1790 by four women, three from Southern Maryland. Two of the original convent buildings have been restored and are open for visits. > 5678 Mount Carmel Rd., tel. 301/934–1654, users.erols.com/carmel-of-port-tobacco. Daily mass: weekdays at 7:15 AM; weekends 8 AM. Grounds daily 9–5.

Thomas Stone National Historic Site The Charles County home of Thomas Stone, one of four Maryland signers of the Declaration of Independence, was built in the 1770s. Painstakingly rebuilt after a devastating fire left it a shell in the late 1970s, the building re-creates the distinctive five-part Georgian house inside and out. The two-story main plantation house is linked to the two wings and adjoining hallways in an arc rather than a straight line. All rooms have exquisite details, such as built-in cabinets, elaborate moldings, a table set with fine china, gilded mirrors, and a piano. The house overlooks terraced fields and the family grave site. > 6655 Rose Hill Rd., between Rtes. 6 and 225, 4 mi west of La Plata, tel. 301/392–1776, www.nps.gov/thst. Free. Mid-June–Aug., daily 9–5; Sept.–mid-June, Wed.–Sun. 9–5.

ST. LEONARD

Battle Creek Cypress Swamp Sanctuary With the northernmost naturally occurring stand of bald cypress trees in the United States, the 100-acre Battle Creek Cypress Swamp Sanctuary provides close-up looks at the forest primeval. A ¼-mi elevated boardwalk at the bottom of a steep but sturdy column of steps gives you a good vantage point to see the swamp, thick with 100-foot trees that are more than a thousand years old. Guides at the nature center can alert you to the seasonal changes in the vegetation and the doings of squirrels, owls, and other wildlife. Indoor exhibits focus on the area's natural and cultural history. > Sixes Rd. (Rte. 506), Battle Creek, tel. 410/535–5327, www.calvertparks.org. Free. Tues.–Sat. 10–4:30, Sun. 1–4:30.

Chesapeake MarketPlace Made up of 100 shops, 80 of which deal in antiques and collectibles, this is Southern Maryland's largest indoor market. The 20 other shops sell gifts, local crafts, custom sewing, ceramics, and more. > 5015 St. Leonard Rd., tel. 410/586–3725 or 410/586–1161, www.chesapeakemarketplace.com. Closed Mon. and Tues.

Christ Episcopal Church Calvert County's oldest continuously worshipping congregation, Christ Church traces its origins to 1672, when a log-cabin church stood at the site. Its 1772 brick replacement, coated with plaster, is notable for its biblical garden, planted with species mentioned in the scriptures. Port Republic School No. 7 is on the church's property. Since immediately after the Civil War the grounds have been a venue for jousting (Maryland's state sport) on the last Saturday in August. > 3100 Broomes Island Rd. (Rte. 264), Port Republic, tel. 410/586–0565. Free. Daily dawn–dusk.

Flag Ponds Nature Park On the forested heights of Calvert Cliffs overlooking the Chesapeake Bay, this park was a busy fishery until the 1950s. Today, it has one of Calvert County's few public bay beaches, a fishing pier, 3 mi of gently graded hiking trails, observation decks at two ponds, a boardwalk through wetlands, and indoor wildlife exhibits. Soaring cliffs, flat marshland, and wildflowers (including the Blue Flag Iris, for which the park is named) provide stunning contrasts, and the shoreline trail here is not seashells but abundant fossils dating to the Miocene age, 10–20 million years ago, when Southern Maryland was covered by ocean. > Rtes. 2 and 4, Lusby, tel. 410/586–1477, www.calvertparks.org. $6 per vehicle Apr.–Oct.; $3 per vehicle Nov.–Mar. Memorial Day–Labor Day, weekdays 9–6, weekends 9–8; Labor Day–Memorial Day, weekends 9–6.

Jefferson Patterson Park and Museum Behind 2½ mi of scenic Patuxent riverfront stretch 544 acres of woods and farmland. The 70-odd archaeological sites have yielded evidence of 9,000 years of human habitation—from prehistory through colonial times. You can follow an archaeology trail to inspect artifacts of the successive hunter-gatherer, early agricultural, and plantation societies that once roamed and settled this land. Displays include primitive knives and axes, fragments of Native American pottery, and colonial glassware. Stroll along the nature trails to take a look at wildlife, antique agricultural equipment, and fields of crops. > 10115 Mackall Rd. (Rte. 265), tel. 410/586–8500, www.jefpat.org. Free. Mid-Apr.–mid-Oct., Wed.–Sun. 10–5.

Port Republic School No. 7 A classic one-room schoolhouse built in the 1880s, the school looks for all the world as if today's lesson could begin any minute. The restored classroom comes with archetypal desks, inkwells, and a school bell. Until 1932 a single teacher taught children in seven grades here. > 3100 Broomes Island Rd. (Rte. 264), Port Republic, tel. 410/586–0482. Free. Memorial Day–Labor Day, Sun. 2–4 and by appointment.

Vera's White Sands For a taste of the tropics *and* the Far East along St. Leonard's Creek, wet your lips with an umbrella-topped cocktail at Vera's, a celebration of owner

Vera Freeman's world travels and exotic tastes. For years, clad in her trademark long gowns and feather boas, she's taken her place at the piano and entertained diners and bar patrons. Open May through October, Vera's maintains a swimming pool that is, as Vera says, "for all the fun times." There's a deepwater (15-feet) marina here with 84 slips. Lusby is 6 mi southeast of St. Leonard. > Rte. 4, Lusby, tel. 410/586–1182. May–Oct.

ST. MARY'S CITY

Cecil's Old Mill Local handmade crafts and original art are on sale in this building. Listed in the National Register of Historic Places, Great Mills was one of Maryland's first industrial districts. The mill itself dates from 1900. > Off Rte. 5 on Indian Bridge Rd., Great Mills, tel. 301/994–1510, users.erols.com/harperr/stmarysart/mill.htm. Mid-Mar.–Aug., Fri.–Sun. 10–5; Sept. and Oct., Thurs.–Sun. 10–5; Nov.–late Dec., daily 10–5.

Historic St. Mary's City In 1934, a first step in the rebirth of St. Mary's was taken. In commemoration of the 300th anniversary of Maryland, the colony's imposing State House, originally built in 1676, was reconstructed. In the early 1970s, a vast archaeo-logical-reconstruction program began in earnest, a project that has revealed nearly 200 individual sites. The entire 800-plus acres have become a living-history museum and archaeological park.

The historic complex includes several notable reconstructions and reproductions. The State House of 1676, like its larger and grander counterpart in Williamsburg, has an upper and a lower chamber for the corresponding houses of Parliament. This 1934 replica is based on court documents from the period; the original was dismantled in 1829 (many of the bricks were used for nearby Trinity Church). The small square-rigged ship docked behind the State House, the *Maryland Dove,* is an accurate replica of one of the two vessels that conveyed the original settlers from England. Nearby is Farthing's Ordinary, a reconstructed inn.

Godiah Spray Tobacco Plantation depicts life on a 17th-century tobacco farm in the Maryland wilderness. Interpreters portray the Spray family—the real family lived about 20 mi away—and its indentured servants, enlisting onlookers in such house-hold chores as cooking and gardening or in working the tobacco field. The buildings, including the main dwelling house and outbuildings, were built using period tools and techniques.

Throughout Historic St. Mary's City, you're encouraged to explore other sites and ex-hibits-in-progress: the town center, the location of the first Catholic church in the Eng-lish colonies, a "victualing" and lodging house, and the woodland Native American hamlet. Historic interpreters in costume—and in character—add realism to the expe-rience. > Rte. 5, tel. 240/895–4990 or 800/762–1634, www.stmaryscity.org. $7.50. Call for exhibit hrs.

Patuxent Naval Air Museum The museum houses items used for the research, de-velopment, and testing of naval aircraft. Seventeen vintage aircraft are displayed out-side. Inside, you may climb into a cockpit trainer and view some of the more improbable creations that never passed muster, such as the Goodyear "Inflatoplane" and a portable helicopter. > Patuxent River Naval Air Station, Rte. 235 (3 Notch Rd.), Lexington Park, tel. 301/863–7418, www.paxmuseum.com. Free. Tues.–Sun. 10–5.

Piney Point Lighthouse Museum The first permanent lighthouse constructed on the Potomac River is now the center of a small, 6-acre park. A museum includes lighthouse history and artifacts from Maryland's first historic shipwreck dive pre-serve—the remains of the U-1105 Black Panther German submarine. After the U.S. Navy tested the U-boat's capabilities, it was sunk here. > Lighthouse Rd., Piney Point, tel. 301/769–2222, www.stmarysmd.com/recreate/museums. Donation requested. May–Oct., Fri.–Mon. noon–5.

Point Lookout State Park Two memorial obelisks greet travelers to remind them of the dark history of this starkly alluring point of land. Beginning in 1863, a Union prison stood at the farthest tip of the peninsula, just across the Potomac from Con-federate Virginia. During the last two years of the conflict, nearly 4,000 of the 50,000 Confederate soldiers here died because of poor conditions. All that remains of the prison are some earthen fortifications, partially rebuilt and known as Fort Lincoln, with markers noting the sites of hospitals and other buildings. A small museum sup-plies some of the details. The 500-acre state park has boating facilities, nature trails, and a beach for swimming. The RV campground, with hookups, is open year-round; tent camping facilities close from early November through late March. > Rte. 5, tel. 301/872–5688, www.dnr.state.md.us. May–Sept., weekends and holidays $3; Oct.–Apr. free. Daily dawn–dusk.

St. Ignatius Church One of the oldest Catholic parishes in continuous service in the United States, the current church was built in 1798. It's all that survives of the pre-Revolutionary plantation of St. Inigoes. A church dating from the 1630s had stood where this church, named for the founder of the Jesuits, stands now. Several veterans of the Revolution are buried in the church graveyard, alongside Jesuit priests who served here. To see inside the church, ask for the key at the sentry box of the naval in-stallation next door. > 8855 Chapel Point Rd., Chapel Point. tel. 301/934–8245, www.chapelpoint.org. Donations accepted. By appointment.

St. Mary's College of Maryland An intimate, state-run liberal arts school, St. Mary's functions as the cultural center for the surrounding community. The student body of some 1,600 benefit from the academic rigors of an excellent private education, but at an open, affordable institution that dates back to 1840. Overlooking the St. Mary's River (which feeds into the Chesapeake Bay), the peaceful campus makes a delightful place for a picnic, especially in fall or spring, when the humidity level is low, the breeze blows off the water, and sailboarders catch crosswinds from the bay. Conces-sions in the college's Campus Center are open to the public. > Rte. 5, tel. 240/895–2000, www.smcm.edu.

Sotterley Plantation The distinguished house on the grounds of this 18th-century plantation is the earliest known (1717) post-in-ground structure in the United States: in place of a foundation, cedar timbers driven straight into the ground support it. The house is a sampler of architectural styles and interior design from the last two cen-turies. On the grounds of this National Historic Landmark are other buildings from the 18th through early-20th centuries, including a colonial customs warehouse, a smokehouse, a "necessary" (an outhouse), and a restored slave cabin. > Rte. 245, Hollywood, 12 mi north of Lexington Park via Rtes. 235 and 245, tel. 301/373–2280, www.sotterley.com. $7. May–Oct., Tues.–Sat. 10–4, Sun. noon–4.

SOLOMONS

Annmarie Garden on St. John The art placed on these 30 acres is designed to work with the plants that surround it. One of the more intriguing installations is "13 Talking Benches." Each tells an ecological story by depicting a plant that grows in Southern Maryland, including dogwood, loblolly pines, pawpaw trees, and tobacco. Smooth, friendly pathways curve through the grounds. Little here is off-limits, and picnickers are welcome to settle in virtually anywhere. Be sure to visit the mosaic-filled rest rooms. > Dowell Rd., tel. 410/326–4640, www.annmariegarden.org. Free. Daily 10–4.

Calvert Marine Museum Concerned with the history of both the river and the bay, the bright, spacious exhibition hall contains models and life-size examples of historically significant types of working and pleasure boats. A grouping of 15 tanks holds important examples of marine life; the river otters here are often at play. The jaws of a white shark open above an exhibit on fossils, and children can sift through sharks' teeth and other specimens and examine them under microscopes. Outside, small craft of different periods are on display in a waterside shed, and on many summer afternoons you can take a cruise aboard a converted 1899 bugeye sailboat, *William B. Tennison*. There's also a restored hexagonal lighthouse from 1883 that's perched like an insect on six slender legs. The **J. C. Lore & Sons Oyster House** (June–Aug., daily 1–4:30; May and Sept., weekends 1–4:30), built in 1934 and now part of the museum, was once a processing plant. This National Historic Landmark displays the tools used by oystermen, crabbers, and fishermen. > Rte. 2 at Solomons Island Rd., tel. 410/326–2042, 410/326–8217 weekends, www.calvertmarinemuseum.com. $5. Daily 10–5.

Solomons Walkabout This informal and friendly walk, run by longtime Calvert County residents Cindy and Mary, includes stops at area lighthouses and churches as well as the riverside. > 1701 Williamsburg Rd., tel. 410/394–0775, www.solomonswalkabout.com.

WALDORF

American Indian Cultural Center and Piscataway Indian Museum This museum emphasizes the life of Maryland's indigenous people prior to the 17th century and strives to be a source for information on the art and culture of the Piscataway Native Americans. Artifacts, tools, and weapons are on display, and there is a full-scale reproduction of a traditional longhouse. > 16816 Country La., tel. 301/372–1932. $3. By appointment.

Dr. Samuel A. Mudd House John Wilkes Booth ended up here at 4 AM on Good Friday, 1865, his leg broken after having leaped from the presidential box at Ford's Theater. Most likely, the 32-year-old Dr. Mudd had no idea his patient was wanted for the assassination of Abraham Lincoln. Nonetheless, Mudd was convicted of aiding a fugitive and sentenced to life in prison. (President Andrew Johnson pardoned him in 1869.) Today the two-story house set on 10 rolling acres in Charles County looks as if the doctor is still in. The dark purple couch where Mudd examined Booth remains in the downstairs parlor, 18th-century family pieces fill the rooms, and the doctor's crude instruments are displayed. There is a 30-minute guided tour of the house, an exhibit building, and Mudd's original tombstone. > 14940 Hoffman Rd., tel. 301/645–6870, www.somd.lib.md.us/MUSEUMS/Mudd.htm. $3. Apr.–late Nov., Wed. and weekends 11–4.

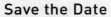

Save the Date

JUNE–JULY

St. Mary's College of Maryland River Concert Series These Friday-night concerts of classical music are performed riverside by Chesapeake Orchestra. They make frequent use of guest artists. > Rte. 5, tel. 240/895–4107, www.smcm.edu/rcs.

JULY

Solomons July 4 Fireworks You can come by boat as well as car to see the fireworks light up over the Patuxent River. > Tel. 410/326–4820.

AUGUST

Beach Party on the Square There are volleyball, dancing, an outdoor movie, and music at this Leonardtown festival. > Tel. 301/475–9791.

Calvert Co. Joust & Dinner The longest-running tournament of Maryland's state sport is held the last Saturday in August at Christ Episcopal Church. The National Jousting Association can also provide details on about 48 jousting tournaments and events that take place from April through November. > 3100 Broomes Island Rd. (Rte. 264), Port Republic, tel. 410/266–7304, www.nationaljousting.com.

St. Ignatius Summer Festival In addition to children's games, and bingo, there's also a fried-chicken and ham dinner with all the fixings. It's held at the church on the third Saturday in August. > 8855 Chapel Point Rd., Chapel Point, tel. 301/934–8245, www.chapelpoint.org.

Solomons Island Festival This festival includes a kid's fair, antiques, flea market, and live music. > Tel. 410/326–9474.

SEPTEMBER

Charles County Fair Livestock and produce shows, crafts, a midway, and live entertainment are all part of this traditional fair. > La Plata, tel. 301/932–1234.

St. Mary's County Fair Art and crafts and 4-H projects are all on display at this fair. There's also a carnival. > Leonardtown, tel. 301/475–8434.

OCTOBER

SMC Oyster Festival This mid-October event includes a shucking contest and oyster cook-off as well as seafood exhibits, arts and crafts, and live entertainment. > Leonardtown, tel. 301/863–5015.

WHERE TO STAY

PORT REPUBLIC

Serenity Acres B&B Set on 5 acres of wood, Serenity Acres is about 6 mi north of Prince Frederick. Its understated rooms, all with queen-size beds, are genuinely homey. The year-round, screened-in hot tub, sunk into a wooden deck, and the in-ground pool are refreshing after a long day of touring. > 4270 Hardesty Rd., Huntingtown 20639, tel. 410/535–3744 or 800/485–4251, fax 410/535–3835, www.bbonline.com/md/serenity. 4 rooms. In-room VCRs, pool, exercise equipment, hot tub, no-smoking rooms. MC, V. BP. $

ST. MARY'S CITY

Brome-Howard Inn On 30 acres of farmland, this 19th-century farmhouse was once part of a tobacco plantation. Rooms are decorated with the original family furnishings. You can relax on one of the big outdoor porches or patios and watch the lazy St. Mary's River nearby. In the evening, there are two candlelit dining rooms—the foyer and the formal parlor. Five miles of hiking trails lead to St. Mary's City, and the inn has bikes available for use. > 18281 Rosecroft Rd., 20686, tel. 301/866–0656, fax 301/866–9660, www.bromehowardinn.com. 3 rooms, 1 suite. Restaurant, bicycles, hiking, library. AE, MC, V. BP. $–$$

Potomac View Farm Bed & Breakfast Construction of this white wood-frame "telescope" farmhouse, built in progressively smaller sections, began in 1830. It's furnished with handsome, simple oak furniture and decorative quilts. The rooms have some elegant touches, such as 10-foot ceilings with crown moldings. One of the restored outbuildings, originally the gardener's cottage, is now a room with its own bath. A one-bedroom kitchenette apartment attached to the main house also has its own bath. The waterside inn sits on 120 acres of farmland planted with corn and soybeans. The proprietors also operate the marina, where charters can be arranged. > 44477 Tall Timbers Rd., Tall Timbers 20690, tel. 301/994–2311. 5 rooms without bath, 1 suite, 1 cottage. Restaurant, pool, beach, boating, marina, bar, laundry service. AE, D, MC, V. BP. ¢–$

St. Michael's Manor & Vineyard Joe and Nancy Dick have run their B&B on Long Neck Creek since the early 1980s—and they've harvested grapes from their 3 acres of vines nearly as long as that. Rooms overlook the water and are decorated with antiques and family heirlooms, the beds covered with hand-sewn quilts. There is a working fireplace at each end of the public space on the ground floor in the Georgian-style main building. Nancy's eggs Benedict are always popular, and her airy Austrian puff pancakes over fresh apples or peaches are delicious. > 50200 St. Michael's Manor Way, Scotland 20687, tel. 301/872–4025, www.stmichaels-manor.com. 4 rooms. Pool, bicycles, some pets allowed; no smoking. No credit cards. Closed Jan. and Feb. BP. ¢

SOLOMONS

Back Creek Inn Built as a waterman's home in 1880, this wood-frame house sits on well-tended grounds that lead to the edge of Back Creek. There's an outdoor deck next to a beautiful perennial garden, and you can soak in the open-air hot tub. Three rooms look out on the Patuxent River or Back Creek, and one opens onto the garden. Breakfast is served in the dining room or by the lily pond. > Calvert and Alexander Sts., 20688, tel. 410/326–2022, fax 410/326–2946, www.bbonline.com/md/backcreek. 4 rooms, 2 suites, 1 cottage. Dining room, cable TV, outdoor hot tub, bicycles, no-smoking rooms; no kids under 12. MC, V. Closed mid-Dec.–early Jan. BP. $–$$$

Holiday Inn Select Conference Center and Marina In this five-story waterfront hotel, every guest room has a water view (if you count the swimming pool); rooms look onto the cove, the open creek, or the courtyard. Whirlpools are available in some suites. Designed to accommodate convention and meeting business, the hotel is often heavily booked, so try to reserve early. > 155 Holiday Dr., Box 1099, 20688, tel. 410/326–6311 or 800/356–2009, fax 410/326–1069, solomonsmd.hiselect.com. 276 rooms, 50 suites. Restaurant, room service, in-room data ports, some kitchenettes, 2 tennis courts, pool, gym, sauna, volleyball, 2 bars, shop, laundry facilities, business services, meeting rooms, no-smoking rooms. AE, D, DC, MC, V. $

Solomons Victorian Inn On the Back Creek side of narrow Solomons Island this three-story, yellow frame house was built in 1906 by the foremost shipbuilder on the Chesapeake Bay. Six rooms look onto Solomons Harbor and two have garden views. All are furnished with roughly equal numbers of period antiques and reproductions, and every room has an ornate armoire. Afternoon refreshments and breakfast are served on an enclosed porch. > Charles and Maltby Sts., Box 759, 20688, tel.

410/326–4811, fax 410/326–0133, www.bbonline.com/md/solomons. 8 rooms. No smoking. AE, MC, V. BP. $–$$

WHERE TO EAT

PORT REPUBLIC

Old Field Inn In this converted wood-frame home from the late 1800s, three dining rooms are filled with historic family portraits and linen-covered candlelit tables. Oriental carpets enhance the hardwood floors in two of the rooms. Veal Wellington is a chef's specialty. Another is filet mignon stuffed with herbed cream cheese and a merlot sauce. The seafood sampler—an appetizer for two—includes clams casino, shrimp, and escargot. > 485 Main St., Prince Frederick, tel. 410/535–1054, www.oldfieldinn.com. AE, D, MC, V. No lunch. $$–$$$

Stoney's Seafood House Popular with sailors, this restaurant overlooks Island Creek, which flows into the Patuxent River. There's ample seating—and a tiki bar—outside. Stoney's is worth a visit for its hefty crab cakes alone, made with plenty of back fin meat and little filler. Oyster sandwiches and Stoney's Steamer—handpicked selections of fresh seafood—make other good seafood choices. Homemade desserts such as the strawberry shortcake and the Snickers pie are not for the faint of heart. > Oyster House Rd., tel. 410/586–1888. AE, D, MC, V. Closed Nov.–early Mar. $–$$

SOLOMONS

CD Cafe Fresh flowers on every table make this coffeehouse inviting. The menu is limited but inventive: try the pan-seared chicken breast with pecans, apples, and onions. Vegetarian, pasta, and seafood dishes are also fine, and the desserts, made in-house, are delectable. The restaurant overlooks the main road into Solomons and, beyond that, the Patuxent River. > 14350 Solomons Island Rd., tel. 410/326–3877. MC, V. $–$$

DiGiovanni's Dock of the Bay It's the rare place in which you can enjoy elegant waterside dining and professional service at prices that won't break the bank. The Venetian chef here creates succulent Italian dishes using fresh herbs and spices. The *cacciucco* (seafood soup) alone is worth a special trip, as is the linguine Neri with scallops. A folk singer performs on Wednesday and Friday evenings. > 14556 Solomons Island Rd., tel. 410/394–6400. AE, MC, V. Closed 1st 2 wks Jan. No lunch weekdays. $$–$$$

Dry Dock On the second floor of a bathhouse overlooking Solomons Harbor, this restaurant combines great food with great views. Flags hang from the ceiling, pictures of waterfowl adorn the walls, and the mood is intimate and informal. The menu varies but always includes seafood and meat dishes prepared with flair. Try the grilled rockfish, blackened tenderloin, or crab cakes. > C St. and Back Creek, tel. 410/326–4817. AE, MC, V. No lunch Mon.–Sat. $$$–$$$$

Lighthouse Inn In the bar, a reproduction of an oyster boat, fishing nets, and pictures of old Solomons set the mood. Gas lanterns shine on the polished wood tables and the exposed ceiling beams. Diners on the first floor have a view of Solomons Harbor on Back Creek; on the second floor, you can look onto the creek toward the Patuxent River. The catch of the day is frequently sautéed, and the chef's crab cakes recipe is closely guarded. On weekends in the warmer months you can order lighter fare on the partially covered "quarterdeck." > 14636 Solomons Island Rd., tel. 410/326–2444, www.lighthouse-inn.com. AE, D, DC, MC, V. No lunch. $$–$$$$

WALDORF
Athenian Cafe An unexpected find in an unassuming strip mall just off Route 301, the Athenian Cafe carries an outstanding Greek seafood sampler in addition to spanakopita (a spinach and feta-cheese pie), *kapama* (lamb stew), and calamari. Don't miss the fish of the day, stuffed with the region's specialty—crab. > 10553 Theodore Green Blvd. (Rte. 301), tel. 301/932–1618. AE, D, MC, V. $$–$$$

ESSENTIALS

Getting Here

A car is a must in Southern Maryland; public transportation in the region is very limited.

BY CAR

Washington, D.C., to Southern Maryland can be treacherous if you travel during rush hour: weekdays 6–9 and 3–7. To get here, follow Route 2 South from Annapolis, and Route 5, which continues through Calvert County.

On main roads, expect traffic to be a constant companion. Route 301 through Waldorf and La Plata, Indianhead Highway through Indianhead, and Route 5 across Charles County are major thoroughfares. Allow extra time when traveling on these roads.

Visitor Information

CONTACTS **Calvert County Dept. of Economic Development & Tourism** > County Courthouse, Prince Frederick 20678, tel. 410/535–4583 or 800/331–9771. **Charles County Office of Tourism** > 8190 Port Tobacco Rd., Port Tobacco 20677, tel. 800/766–3386. **Crain Memorial Welcome Center** > U.S. Rte. 301, 12480 Crain Hwy., near Newburg, 1 mi north of Governor Nice bridge over the Potomac River, tel. 301/259–2500. **St. Mary's County Tourism** > 23115 Leonard Hall Dr., Leonardtown 20650, tel. 301/475–4411. **Southern Maryland Heritage Association** > www.southernmdisfun.com.

Maryland's Eastern Shore

Easton is 71 mi southeast of Washington, D.C.

21

Updated by Kristi Delovitch

IT'S ONE OF THE CLOSEST SPOTS TO VISIT for Washingtonians, but the Eastern Shore feels worlds away from the bustle of D.C. life. Shortly after crossing the 4½-mi William Preston Lane Jr. Bridge, also known as the Bay Bridge, the scenery begins to transform. Watermen's towns replace suburbs, romantic inns outnumber big hotels, and the nighttime scenes of city skylines are replaced by the sun setting into the bay. Route 50 itself gives way to one winding road after another, stringing together the area's small towns.

To understand the Eastern Shore, look to the Chesapeake Bay. The Chesapeake, Algonquian for "great shellfish bay," is the nation's largest estuary (a semi-enclosed body of water with free connection to the open sea). An estimated 100,000 rivers and smaller tributaries flow into the bay, ensuring the agricultural wealth of the peninsula as well as the bounty of this 195-mi-long body of water.

The towns dotting the shoreline rely on the bay for their existence, be it for food, trade, or tourism. Water activities include interactive cruises on historic skipjacks or chartered fishing boats. The maze of Chesapeake tributaries and rivers are also great for fishing, kayaking, and canoeing. And because the Eastern Shore is flat, it's a great place for cycling. A well-rounded visit to the shore might consist of exploring the hospitable communities and historic sites, strolling through wildlife parks and refuges, browsing a few shops, dining at third-generation-owned waterfront restaurants, and overnighting at inns and bed-and-breakfasts.

The area cuisine, which relies on seafood caught, prepared, and served on the bay, is often reason enough for a quick visit. Popular variations of crab soup, steamed clams, and Old Bay–seasoned blue crabs steamed in beer are simple pleasures unique to the Eastern Shore. Many who live here take boats across the bay to reach their favorite restaurants.

Your journey begins the moment you cross the Bay Bridge and reach Kent Island, founded in 1631 and Maryland's first permanent English settlement. Many current residents' families have lived in this area for generations.

In order to bypass Route 50's congestion and fast-food restaurants, take a 10-minute detour off the highway to explore Easton. The town now has its own style of urban panache, with fancy inns, a handful of memorable restaurants, and a vaudeville theater that draws popular acts. Well-preserved buildings dating from colonial through Victorian times grace the affluent and genteel downtown. Fine art galleries, antiques shops, and gift shops line North Harrison Street; more stores are clustered in Talbottown, the small midtown mall.

St. Michaels, once a shipbuilding center, is one of the region's major destinations; in warmer months, tourists and boaters crowd its narrow streets and snug harbor. A number of shops, cafés, waterfront restaurants, and inns have begun here in response to its growing popularity.

Unlike its gentrified neighbors, Tilghman Island retains the gritty, relaxed quality of those who still make their living from the bay's bounty—the watermen. A visit to Tilghman Island is a good way to gain insight into the Eastern Shore's remarkable character. Leave your car and explore by bike or kayak. A few working fishing boats use the island's Dogwood Harbor as their home port. This small fleet includes several of the regiona remaining skipjacks, single-masted boats that dredge for oysters.

Tracing its roots to 1683, Oxford remains secluded and unspoiled. Only about 800 live here in this seven-block peninsula between the Tred Avon River and Town Creek. A notable early resident was Robert Morris Jr., a signer of the Declaration of Independence. Morris helped finance the Revolution, but ended up in debtor's prison after land speculation deals soured. When you visit, try to set aside some time to walk the streets and admire the town's five marinas as well as its tiny Victorian and colonial houses.

Cambridge, the Dorchester County seat, was first settled in the 1660s along a Choptank Native American Indian trail. Graceful Georgian, Queen Anne, and colonial-revival churches, schools, businesses, and residences abound in this town, which contains 75 buildings of historic significance; in this living museum of architecture, every exhibit still stands in its original location. According to legend, Annie Oakley aimed at waterfowl from the porch of her waterfront Cambridge home.

The life of the waterman—a term unique to the Chesapeake, defining those who make a living from the bay's bounty—still dominates Tilghman Island as well as nearby Crisfield and Smith Island. Although the shore has a rich history, it has also been changing with the times. Large resort hotels are popping up in and outside small towns, and country inns are expanding. Upscale restaurants with their own nontraditional take on dishes like crab imperial now rub elbows with homey crab shacks.

WHAT TO SEE & DO

CAMBRIDGE

Blackwater National Wildlife Refuge Eight miles south of Cambridge is the nesting spot for the largest bald eagle population north of Florida. The birds often perch on the lifeless tree trunks that poke from the wetlands, which are part of nearly 27,000 acres of woods, open water, marsh, and farmland. In fall and spring, some 35,000 Canada and snow geese pass through in their familiar "V" formations to and from their winter home, joining more than 15,000 ducks. The rest of the year, residents include endangered species such as peregrine falcons and silver-haired Delmarva fox squirrels. Great blue heron stand like sentinels while ospreys dive for meals, birds sing, and tundra swans preen endlessly. By car or bike, you can follow a 5-mi road through several habitats or follow a network of trails on foot. Exhibits and films in the visitor center provide background and insight. > Rte. 335 at Key Wallace Dr., tel. 410/228–2677, blackwater.fws.gov. $3 car, $1 pedestrian or cyclist. Wildlife drive daily dawn–dusk, visitor center weekdays 8–4, weekends 9–5.

James B. Richardson Maritime Museum Celebrating and chronicling Chesapeake boatbuilding, this museum collects impressive, scaled-down versions of boats peculiar to the Chesapeake Bay, including bugeyes, pungies, skipjacks, and log canoes, and the tools used to build them. Photos, a film, and a model boatbuilding workroom complement the models. Besides the arsenal of models, the museum also showcases vintage workboats: a drake tail, a sailing skiff, and a crab boat. > 401 High St., tel. 410/221–1871, www.richardsonmuseum.org. Free. Wed. and weekends 1–4 and by appointment.

EASTON

Academy Art Museum In a former schoolhouse from the 1820s, the museum houses a permanent collection of fine art that includes works by American artists such as Grant Wood, Lichtenstein, and Rauschenberg, as well as Chagall and Dürer. Special exhibitions often cover Eastern Shore artists, and the juried art show the museum holds in early October is one of the finest in the region. > 106 South St., tel. 410/822–2787, www.art-academy.org. $2. Mon., Tues., and Thurs.–Sat. 10–4, Wed. 10–9.

Historic Avalon Theatre This 400-seat theater in downtown Easton, restored in 1989, draws national bluegrass, jazz, and other kinds of musical acts. The former vaudeville house, built in 1921, also hosts the Talbot Chamber Orchestra and the Eastern Shore Chamber Music Festival, as well as films and other performances. > 40 E. Dover St., tel. 410/822–0345, www.avalontheatre.com.

Talbot County Courthouse Rebellious citizens gathered at the Courthouse to protest the 1765 Stamp Act and to adopt the Talbot Resolves, a forerunner of the Declaration of Independence. Today, the courthouse, built in 1712 and expanded in 1794, along with two wings added in the late 1950s, is still in use. The two-tier cupola is topped by a weather vane. > 11 N. Washington St., tel. 410/770–8001. Weekdays 8–5.

Tidedancers Inside the four little buildings that make up the complex is a bit of everything: antiques and imports, decorative accessories, regional foods, and cookbooks and kitchen equipment. Most of what's in this travel emporium–museum–shop is the result of skillful seeking over the whole globe by one of the owners. Don't miss the clearance items. > 28272 St. Michaels Rd. (Rte. 33), tel. 410/763–8630 or 800/329–9139, www.tidedancers.com.

ST. MICHAELS

Chesapeake Bay Maritime Museum One of the region's finest museums covers the bay's history of boatbuilding, commercial fishing, navigating, and hunting in compelling detail. Exhibits, divided among nine buildings on the 18-acre waterfront site, include two of the bay's unique skipjacks as well as more than 80 other historic regional boats. There's also a restored 1879 Hooper Strait lighthouse, a working boatyard, and a "waterman's wharf" with shanties and tools for oystering and crabbing. In the Bay Building, you can see a crabbing skiff and a dugout canoe hewn by Native Americans. The Waterfowl Building contains carved decoys and stuffed birds, including wood ducks, mallards, and swans. > Mill St. at Navy Point, tel. 410/745–2916, www.cbmm.org. $7.50. June–Sept., daily 9–6; Oct., Nov., and Mar.–May, daily 9–5; Dec.–Feb., daily 9–4.

Oxford Museum In what was once the town's soda fountain shop, this museum pays homage to Oxford's maritime past with many pictures and models of sailboats. Some of the boats were built in Oxford, site of one of the first Chesapeake regattas (1860). Check out the full-scale racing boat by the door. Other artifacts include the lamp from a lighthouse on nearby Benoni Point, a sail-maker's bench, and an oyster-shucking stall. Docents elaborate on the exhibits, which set the context for a walking tour of nearby blocks. Oxford is 7 mi southeast of St. Michaels. > Morris and Market Sts., Oxford, tel. 410/226–0191, www.oxfordmuseum.org. Free. Apr.–Sept., Mon., Wed., Fri., and Sat., 10–4, Sun, 11–4; Oct.–mid-Nov., Fri. and Sat., 10–4, Sun. 11–4.

Talbot Street St. Michaels' bustling main street is lined with restaurants, galleries, and all manner of shops, including a hardware store that doubles as a retro gift shop.

The Perfect Stop

KENT ISLAND, *the first part of the shore you reach after crossing the Bay Bridge, makes a good place to rest before continuing into the area's heart. Dining at one of the many waterfront restaurants on Kent Narrows, exploring historic towns like Stevensville, or crossing the scenic Cross Island Trail by foot or cycle—these are all excellent ways to enjoy some of the many pleasures unique to the bay.*

Kent Narrows, the channel that separates Kent Island from the Eastern Shore's mainland, is a popular route for boats traveling between the Chester River and the eastern part of the bay. At the foot of the Kent Narrows Bridge is "the slip," a small area that constantly bustles with activity. Shallow draft workboats, used by generations of watermen, continue to deliver fresh seafood to one of two remaining processing houses. Other boats are used to pull up to waterfront restaurants, whose outdoor decks are packed in the summer.

Just a few miles from the congestion of Route 50, Stevensville is a glimpse into the shore's past. The first English settlement on Maryland soil, from 1631, is commemorated with a stone marker along Route 8. Stevensville, whose heyday was in the early 1900s, thrived as the center of steamboat trade on the East Coast. Its train depot, bank building, and post office all roughly date from this period. Another

significant building is the beautiful Christ Church, a Gothic structure with a steep slate roof that was built with wooden pegs instead of nails.

The Cross Island Trail Park bicycle trail spans Kent Island from west to east, from Terrapin Nature Park on the way to Kent Narrows. The flat, 6-mi trail comes with access to public parks as well as incredible views of the water and the canopied forest. Though there is one bike rental shop in town most bikers bring their own equipment. There are a number of free parking lots off the trail that are open every day from sunrise to sunset: the most convenient are at Terrapin Nature Park, Kent Narrows Boat Launching Ramp, and Chesapeake Exploration Center.

Stroll between Mill Street, the lane to the Chesapeake Bay Maritime Museum, and Willow Street, or head just beyond to Canton Alley. > Talbot St.

Tours

Chesapeake Lights A former U.S. Navy special operations vessel, the merchant vessel *Sharps Island* takes up to 30 passengers on one of three tours of Eastern Shore lighthouses. The eight-hour tour covers 10 lighthouses ($120). A more leisurely half-day tour covers 5 lighthouses ($60), and there's also a two-hour sunset cruise ($35). All trips depart from Knapp's Narrows Marina in front of the Bay Hundred Restaurant. > Knapp's Narrows Marina, Tilghman Island Rd., Tilghman Island, tel. 410/886–2215 or 800/690–5080, www.chesapeakelights.com.
Dockside Express Tours and Shuttles Aboard the *Express Royale*, a 50-foot 49-passenger tour boat, you can also take a 90-minute bird-watching tour with an Audubon specialist ($20). A sunset champagne tour is $25 a person. On land, historic walking

tours include a stop at a waterman's house built in 1860 and a ghost tour, led by a guide in Victorian costume. Tours are held mid-March to mid-November. > 205 Carpenter St., St. Michaels, tel. 410/886–2643, www.cruisinthebay.com.

Lady Patty Sailing aboard this 45-foot bay ketch, built in 1935 and perfectly restored, is a scenic way to experience the Chesapeake Bay and the Choptank River. The sailing schedule includes daily champagne sunset sails ($40) and two-hour, and half- and full-day excursions. > Knapp's Narrows Marina, Tilghman Island Rd., Tilghman Island, tel. 410/886–2215 or 800/690–5080, www.sailladypatty.com.

Nathan of Dorchester Skipjacks were once abundant in the bay but there are now only a few in commercial use. The recently built *Nathan* cruises the Choptank River from Long Wharf at the foot of High Street in Cambridge. In summer the 28-passenger *Nathan* sets sail on most Saturday evenings and Sunday afternoons, April through October. > Long Wharf, 526 Poplar St., Cambridge, tel. 410/228–7141.

The Patriot This large, 65-foot steel-hull yacht departs four times daily, from April through October, for one-hour cruises on the Miles River. The tour covers the ecology and history of the area as it passes along the tranquil riverfront landscape. > Docked near Crab Claw Restaurant and Chesapeake Bay Maritime Museum, St. Michaels, tel. 410/745–3100, www.patriotcruises.com.

Rebecca T. Ruark An interactive tour on this skipjack is essential for a complete visit to Maryland's Eastern Shore. The proud owner of this historic vessel is a sixth-generation dredger and inhabitant of Tilghman Island. The sinking of the *Rebecca* in 1999 and her subsequent rebirth made the front page of the *Washington Post*. For a little hands-on experience you can hoist a dredge into the water or manually lift a sail. The ship can hold 49 passengers. > Dogwood Harbor, Tilghman Island, tel. 410/886–2176 or 410/829–3976, www.skipjack.org.

Sports

BOATING

Fishing Bay Wildlife Management Area In and around these 13,000 acres bordering Blackwater National Wildlife Refuge, you can take a pair of "water trails" through some scenic rivers and streams that are reminiscent of Florida's Everglades. A short canoeing or kayaking trek here, recommended only for paddlers with some experience, is an exceptional way to experience a salt marsh and the wildlife that lives in one. Contact the Dorchester County Department of Tourism for more information, including a waterproof map. > Main entrance: Bestpitch Ferry Rd., Cambridge, tel. 410/376–3236, www.dnr.state.md.us/baylinks/25.html.

Harrisons This down-home restaurant just across the Knapp's Narrows Bridge is also home port for the largest commercial sportfishing fleet on the Eastern Shore. The restaurant's boating packages, which use its fleet of 14 charter boats, are available from April to November. Narrated cruises and hunting packages can also be arranged. > 21551 Chesapeake House Dr., Tilghman Island, tel. 410/886–2121, www.chesapeakehouse.com.

KAYAKING

Robert Morris Inn rents kayaks on a seasonal basis. Harris Creek Kayak, between Tilghman Island and St. Michaels, rents touring kayaks and also organizes ecotours specializing in bird-watching and nature photography.
EQUIPMENT **Harris Creek Kayak** > 7857 Tilghman Island Rd., Sherwood, tel. 410/886–2083, www.harriscreekkayak.com. **Robert Morris Inn** > 314 N. Morris St., Oxford, tel. 410/226–5111, www.robertmorrisinn.com.

Save the Date

APRIL

Oxford Day Increasing the normal town population from 800 to close to 5,000, this annual festival is activity-filled. The day begins with a pancake breakfast, a 10K race, and a street parade with antique cars, the Baltimore Ravens band, and a fife-and-drum corps. Live music bellows from Oxford Tred Avon Park as costumed actors dressed as the patriot Robert Morris roam the streets. You can also expect favorite shore competitions that include boat and crab races. > Oxford, tel. 410/226–5730, www.portofoxford.com/oxday.htm.

JULY

Crabfest In order to honor the Maryland blue crab, this late-July festival includes crab-catching contests and demonstrations of how to cook crabs, live music, and skipjack rides. You can buy steamed crabs, crab cakes, and every variation of crab soup. Children learn to bait crab pots and can watch crabs molt. Admission to the museum serves as a pass to the festivities. > Mill St., St. Michaels, tel. 410/745–2916, www.cbmm.org.

OCTOBER

Tilghman Island Day Crowds fill the tiny streets of Tilghman Island in search of fresh seafood, live music, and boat races. The festivities include sails on historic skipjacks and crab-picking and oyster-shucking contests. Shuttles are available from St. Michaels and Easton. > Tilghman Island, tel. 410/886–2121, www.tilghmanmd.com.

NOVEMBER

Waterfowl Festival For over 30 years this festival has celebrated waterfowl art—and it's timed to coincide with the fall goose migration. The town's school buses shuttle you to venues displaying carvings, decoys, prints, and paintings; prices start at $10 on up to thousands of dollars. You can also participate in decoy-carving classes or the annual duck-calling contest. As many as 20,000 people attend the festival, so make hotel reservations months in advance. > 40 S. Harrison St., Easton, tel. 410/822–4567, www.waterfowlfestival.org.

WHERE TO STAY

CAMBRIDGE

Cambridge House Along a tree-lined row of stately sea captains' homes in the old part of town, this Queen Anne has an interior that's pure Victorian, with a stunning guest parlor with crimson walls, fringed lamps and curtains, and cherubs on the ceiling. A back deck leads to gravel paths and ponds. The spacious rooms have hardwood floors and 10-foot ceilings; most have fireplaces. > 112 High St., 21613, tel. 410/221–7700, fax 410/221–7736, www.cambridgehousebandb.com. 6 rooms. In-room data ports, cable TV, in-room VCRs, pond; no kids under 8, no smoking. AE, MC, V. BP. $

Glasgow Inn A long driveway crossing a broad landscaped lawn leads to this stately white plantation house that evokes its genteel 18th-century beginnings. All rooms are filled with period prints and furniture, including four-poster beds. Front rooms look out over the lawn to the Choptank River. > 1500 Hambrooks Blvd., 21613, tel. 410/228–0575, fax 410/221–0297, www.glasgowinncambridge.com. 10 rooms, 5 with bath. Dining room, croquet, meeting rooms; no room phones, no TV in some rooms, no smoking. No credit cards. BP. $

Hyatt Regency Chesapeake Bay Golf Resort, Spa and Marina Next to the Choptank River to the east of downtown Cambridge, this complex is the Eastern Shore's first full-service, year-round resort. Built on nearly 350 acres, the resort includes an 18-acre nature preserve, a bird sanctuary, an 18,000-square-foot spa, and a golf course designed by Keith Foster. The six-story resort makes optimal use of natural light and has spectacular views of the water. All rooms and suites have a private balcony; those on the upper level have raised ceilings. The resort's restaurants include the self-service Bay Country Market and the Blue Point Provision Company for seafood. Two sandstone fireplaces and a 30-foot-high wall of windows welcome you to the lobby's lounge. > 100 Heron Blvd., 21613, tel. 410/901–1234, fax 410/901–6301, chesapeakebay.hyatt.com. 384 rooms, 16 suites. 4 restaurants, snack bar, room service, in-room data ports, in-room safes, refrigerators, cable TV, 18-hole golf course, 4 tennis courts, indoor-outdoor pool, health club, hot tub, spa, 2 beaches, marina, bar, lounge, shops, Internet, concierge, business services, convention center, meeting rooms. AE, D, DC, MC, V. **$$$$**

EASTON

Bishop's House Built for a former state governor around 1880 and later owned by the Episcopal diocese, this red-trim Victorian house has a wraparound porch, huge bay windows, and fireplaces with tiled mantels. Second-floor guest rooms have 12-foot ceilings and 19th-century oak, walnut, and mahogany furnishings. Three guest rooms have working fireplaces, and two have hot tubs. The third-floor sitting room has a VCR and some kitchen appliances. > 214 Goldsborough St., Box 2217, 21601, tel. 410/820–7290 or 800/223–7290, fax 410/820–7290, www.bishopshouse.com. 5 rooms. In-room data ports, cable TV, bicycles, meeting rooms; no room phones, no kids under 12, no smoking. No credit cards. BP. **$**

Chaffinch House In the heart of the historical district this two-story Queen Anne from 1893 has cozy rooms decorated with wicker and antique period pieces. There's also a massive wraparound porch that comes with the requisite rocking chairs. Four poster or canopy beds complement each room. > 132 S. Harrison St., 21601, tel. 410/822–5074 or 800/861–5074, fax 410/822–5074, www.chaffinchhouse.com. 5 rooms, 1 suite. Internet; no kids under 12, no smoking. AE, D, MC, V. BP. **$**

Inn at Easton Every room in this inn is a marriage of old and new. With a colorful interior that's full of antiques and gracious touches, this circa-1790 federal mansion is a bit like a boutique hotel. Original paintings by the Russian impressionist Nikolai Timkov are hung in the common areas. Upstairs, the seven rooms and suites skillfully combine old-time charm with modern amenities. > 25 S. Harrison St., 21601, tel. 410/822–4910 or 888/800–8091, fax 410/820–6961, www.theinneaston.com. 3 rooms, 4 suites. Restaurant; no room TVs, no kids under 9, no smoking. AE, D, MC, V. BP. **$$–$$$**

OXFORD

Combsberry This 1730 brick home, together with a carriage house, cottage, and formal garden, is set amid magnolias and willows on the banks of Island Creek. Inside are five arched fireplaces, floral chintz fabrics, and polished wood floors. All the rooms and suites of this luxurious B&B have water views and are furnished with English manor–style antiques, including four-poster and canopy beds. Some also have hot tubs and working fireplaces; the two-bedroom carriage house has a kitchen. > 4837 Evergreen Rd., 21654, tel. 410/226–5353, www.combsberry.net. 2 rooms,

2 suites, 1-bedroom cottage, 2-bedroom carriage house. Dining room, library, some pets allowed; no room phones, no room TVs, no kids under 12. AE, MC, V. BP. $$$$

Robert Morris Inn In the early 1700s, this building on the banks of the Tred Avon River was crafted by ships' carpenters, who used ship nails, hand-hewn beams, and pegged paneling. In 1738, it was bought by an English trading company as a house for its Oxford representative, Robert Morris. Four guest rooms have handmade wall paneling and fireplaces built of English bricks (these were used as boat ballast in the trip over). Other buildings in the complex include a newer manor house on a private beach. > 314 N. Morris St., 21654, tel. 410/226–5111, fax 410/226–5744, www.robertmorrisinn.com. 35 rooms. Restaurant, taproom, Internet, meeting rooms; no room phones, no TV in some rooms, no smoking. AE, MC, V. $–$$$$

ST. MICHAELS

Best Western St. Michaels Motor Inn Just on the outskirts of historic St. Michaels, this hotel provides basic accommodations, a convenient location, and competitive rates. Though not as charming as inns in the nearby towns, it's convenient and well run, and the prices remain low even in high season. > 1228 S. Talbot St., 21663, tel. 410/745–3333, fax 410/745–2906. 93 rooms. Restaurant, 2 pools, lounge. AE, D, DC, MC, V. CP. ¢–$

Five Gables Inn & Spa What was once three circa-1860 homes is now a comfortable inn and spa. Some rooms have a private porch or balcony; all are elegantly decorated with working gas fireplaces, antique furnishings, fine linens and towels, and down comforters. Refreshments are served daily at 3. Spa treatments include herbal bath treatments, facials, and even a 15-minute foot massage. > 209 N. Talbot St., 21663, tel. 410/745–0100 or 877/466–0100, fax 410/745–2903, www.fivegables.com. 11 rooms, 3 suites. Dining room, cable TV, some in-room VCRs, pool, sauna, spa, steam room, bicycles, shops, some pets allowed (fee); no phones in some rooms, no smoking. AE, MC, V. CB. $–$$$$

Inn at Perry Cabin Set on 25 acres beside the Miles River, this luxury inn employs a nautical theme throughout. Each guest room has luxurious appointments; standard amenities include heated towel racks, fresh flowers in all rooms, and afternoon tea. Above all, staying here means impeccable service. > 308 Watkins La., 21663, tel. 410/745–2200 or 800/722–2949, fax 410/745–3348, www.perrycabin.com. 54 rooms, 27 suites. Restaurant, in-room data ports, pool, pond, exercise equipment, massage, sauna, steam room, dock, bar, library, concierge, meeting rooms, helipad; no smoking. AE, DC, MC, V. $$$$

The Oaks Antebellum grace defines this 1748 mansion on 17 acres along the banks of Oak Creek, 3 mi from St. Michaels. The antiques-filled inn has a stunning black-and-white tile foyer; its best rooms have fireplaces, private porches, and hot tubs. The day starts with a full country breakfast served in the yellow-and-red dining room. After that, you might want to go fishing off the pier, or head no farther than one of the rockers on the screened porch overlooking the water. > Rte. 329 at Acorn La., Royal Oak 21662, tel. 410/745–5053, www.the-oaks.com. 14 rooms, 1 cottage. Dining room, cable TV, putting green, pool, dock, boating, fishing, bicycles, shuffleboard, volleyball, meeting rooms; no kids (Memorial–Labor Day), no smoking. MC, V. BP. $–$$$$

Wades Point Inn on the Bay Five miles northwest of St. Michaels, three brick colonial and wood-frame Victorian buildings form an exceptional retreat. The stately main house was built in 1819. In 1890, facilities were added for summertime guests, and Wades Point Farm emerged as a bona fide inn. Combining the serenity of the country and the splendor of the Chesapeake Bay, this uncommon complex is at the heart of

120 acres of fields and woodland. Two sun-bright corner rooms in one wing are closest to the water, but each carefully decorated period room has a private porch or balcony. Cows and goats grazing along a 1-mi trail through the property welcome hikers, joggers, and bird-watchers. > Wades Point Rd. (Rte. 33, Box 7), 21663, tel. 410/745–2500, fax 410/745–3443, www.wadespoint.com. 23 rooms. Some kitchenettes, pond, dock, hiking, meeting rooms; no a/c in some rooms, no room phones, no room TVs, no kids under 1, no smoking. MC, V. CP. **$$–$$$$**

Watermark Bed & Breakfast On 7 acres of secluded land between St. Michaels and Tilghman Island, this contemporary log cabin can provide a quiet getaway. Only one room, Turtle Cove, has an exposed log wall, but all three rooms are massive, with a view of the pool's waterfall and the bay. If you take even a short walk around the property, you might see eagles, ospreys, blue heron, swan, deer, and fox. > 8956 Tilghman Island Rd., Whitman 21676, tel. 410/745–2892 or 800/314–7734. 3 rooms. Pool, hot tub, some pets allowed. MC, V. CP. **$$**

TILGHMAN ISLAND

Inn at Knapp's Narrows Marina Light-filled rooms and water views are standard at this budget hotel on the edge of the Knapp's Narrows Marina. A short walk from restaurants, bars, and many water tours, the hotel has an unbeatable location for boaters and families. > 6176 Tilghman Island Rd., 21671, tel. 410/886–2720 or 800/322–5181, www.knappsnarrowsmarina.com. 20 rooms. Pool. D, MC, V. **$**

Lazyjack Inn on Dogwood Harbor One of the island's original 1855 homes has been transformed into this charming B&B, which is beside Dogwood Harbor. Tastefully decorated rooms are equipped with down comforters and candles in the windows; there are also a welcoming vase of fresh flowers and some sherry on the bureau. Both suites include a fireplace and an oversize hot tub. You can reserve a sail on the innkeepers' restored 1935 45-foot boat, the *Lady Patty.* > 5907 Tilghman Island Rd., 21671, tel. 410/886–2215 or 800/690–5080, www.lazyjackinn.com. 2 rooms, 2 suites. Boating; no room phones, no room TVs, no kids under 12, no smoking. AE, MC, V. BP. **$–$$**

Sinclair House Built in the 1920s as a fishermen's inn, Sinclair House became Tilghman's first B&B in 1989. Today, the innkeepers' former lives in international relations (he was a diplomat, and she worked for UNICEF) are tastefully reflected here. Each guest room is decorated with crafts and artwork from a different culture: baskets and tapestries from southern Africa; rattan furniture and puppets from Indonesia; hand-painted headboards and antique mirrors from Morocco; textiles and *retablos* (small devotional paintings) from Peru. American, European, or Latin specialties are served at breakfast. The common room has satellite TV, along with a VCR and tapes of classic films. > 5718 Black Walnut Point Rd., 21671, tel. 410/886–2147, www.sinclairhouse.biz. 4 rooms. Library. AE, D, MC, V. **$**

Tilghman Island Inn Warm, welcoming, and elegant, this compact, modern resort overlooks the Chesapeake Bay (there are also views of a neighboring waterfowl marsh). Five deluxe waterside rooms have hot tubs, fireplaces, fine linens, spacious decks, and fun, urban finishes. The 5-acre complex includes a 20-slip transient marina and a small fleet of tandem and single kayaks available for rent. Themed wine weekends begin with a wine tasting Saturday afternoon, progress to a leisurely six-course dinner, and end with a champagne brunch Sunday morning. > Coopertown Rd., Box B, 21671, tel. 410/886–2141 or 800/866–2141, www.tilghmanislandinn.com. 15 rooms, 5 suites. Restaurant, in-room data ports, cable TV, tennis court, pool, dock, marina, croquet, 2 bars, meeting rooms, some pets allowed; no smoking. AE, D, DC, MC, V. CP. **$$$–$$$$**

WHERE TO EAT

CAMBRIDGE

Snappers Waterfront Cafe The extensive menu at this casual waterside restaurant and bar on the edge of town does have crab cakes but also has a Southwestern flavor. Entrées include steak, which comes in large portions, baked stuffed shrimp, quesadillas, burritos, and a jerk-chicken salad. > 112 Commerce St., tel. 410/228–0112. AE, D, MC, V. $–$$$

EASTON

Alice's Cafe Black-and-white tile floors and bright-color walls set an upbeat tone at this airy sandwich shop just outside the commercial center of Easton. > 22 N. Harrison St., tel. 410/819–8590. No credit cards. No dinner. ¢

Inn at Easton This B&B operates one of the finest restaurants in the country. The chef's studies in Australia shine through in most dishes: you can definitely taste the Pacific Rim influence. Delightfully imaginative creations include green Thai bouillabaisse and char-grilled "Moreton bay bugs" (small lobsters) with a green papaya salad, but the signature dish is roasted lamb sirloin with a Dijon herb crust. > 25 S. Harrison St., tel. 410/822–4910. Reservations essential. AE, D, MC, V. Closed Sun.–Tues. $$$–$$$$

Mason's A family-run landmark since 1966, Mason's uses fresh ingredients from its own garden. Pink snapper, ahi tuna, and Pacific striped marlin from Hawaii are appreciated by seafood lovers, and the restaurant's tenderloin is a very good rendition. Next door is a coffee bar and a food store that sells hard-to-find cheeses and meats, wonderful handcrafted chocolates, and all manner of esoteric foods. > 42 E. Dover St., tel. 410/822–3204. AE, D, MC, V. Closed Sun. $$$–$$$$

Out of the Fire A spare, modern interior sets this neighborhood bistro apart from its colonial neighbors. Of note is the owner's insistence that all equipment and furnishings—including a trompe l'oeil mural, faux-finish walls, and pottery—be obtained locally. One of the more interesting entrées is Caribbean spiced pork with ginger-mango chutney. Breads are baked in a stone-hearth oven; desserts are produced on site. Enjoy one of more than 100 labels at the wine bar or in the lounge area off to one side of the open kitchen. > 22 Goldsborough St., tel. 410/770–4777. AE, D, MC, V. Closed Sun. $$–$$$

OXFORD

Latitude 38 The whimsical red-white-and-green color scheme; painted vines climbing the walls; the polished wood floors—they all set this bistro apart. Weather permitting, you can eat outdoors at wrought-iron tables in a brick courtyard. The creative and diverse menu changes twice a month and includes such dishes as veal scallopini topped with crab and hollandaise sauce, and crab ravioli in an herbed cream sauce. > 26342 Oxford Rd., tel. 410/226–5303. AE, D, MC, V. $$$–$$$$

Robert Morris Inn Chesapeake author James Michener claimed that the best crab cake on the Eastern Shore was served here. The menu, which hasn't changed in over three decades, is famed for its meticulous preparation of Chesapeake Bay's bounty. Popular dishes include seafood au gratin cakes and Black Angus beef. Circa-18th-century murals of river scenes adorn the walls of the main dining room, but you may also eat in the more casual tavern or tap room. > 314 N. Morris St., tel. 410/226–5111. Reservations essential. AE, MD, V. $$$–$$$$

Schooner's Landing An unpretentious waterfront bar and restaurant, Schooner's is a destination for boaters as well as those who just want to relax and watch the boats sail by. The menu is made up mostly sandwiches and standard shore favorites like crab cakes. > 14 Tilghman St., tel. 410/226–0160. AE, D, DC, MC, V. $–$$$

ST. MICHAELS

Bistro St. Michaels A quiet spot on the town's main street, this bistro has dishes that alternate between classic Maryland favorites and French-American comfort food. The house specialty is mussels steamed in a spicy wine and garlic broth. Entrées change daily, but if it's available try the grilled veal loin chop with crispy buttermilk onion rings. > 403 S. Talbot St., tel. 410/745–9111, www.bistrostmichaels.com. Reservations essential. AE, D, DC, MC, V. Closed Tues. and Wed. No lunch. $$$–$$$$

Crab Claw Restaurant Owned and operated by the same family since 1965, this St. Michaels landmark started as a clam- and oyster-shucking house for watermen long before that. Diners at both indoor and outdoor tables have panoramic views over the harbor to the river beyond, but eat dockside if you can. As the name suggests, this is *the* down-home place for fresh steamed and seasoned blue crabs. However, the extensive menu also includes sandwiches and other light fare as well as other seafood and meat dishes. Children's platters are available, too. > End of Mill St., at the Harbor, tel. 410/745–2900 or 410/745–9366. Reservations essential. No credit cards. Closed late Dec.–early Mar. $–$$$

Inn at Perry Cabin Dining at the inn's restaurant with its flawless cuisine and stellar wine selection is an event. Chef Mark Salter uses primarily locally grown and organic ingredients serving classic regional fare along with variations of bay dishes. The signature crab spring roll with pink grapefruit, avocado, and toasted almonds, and the lamb shank glazed with honey and tarragon are both exquisite. The Chesapeake seafood bouillabaisse with Old Bay rouille is a wonderful sampling of many bay treasures. > 308 Watkins La., tel. 410/745–2200 or 800/722–2949. Reservations essential. AE, DC, MC, V.

Tilghman Island Dining alfresco on the sunset deck overlooking the marshes or in the bay-watch room, with Chesapeake views and a strumming classical guitar, you may forget you're only a few hours from home. The alternate dining room, a larger, more spacious area, showcases the work of local artists like the large quilts of a nearby quilter. Built around fresh local ingredients, the menu changes weekly; a springtime dish may be soup primavera, a flavorful dish made with olives and locally grown fiddleheads. Creative main include rabbit braised in sweet-and-sour sauce and the steak Napoléon with stuffed Gorgonzola and Tuscan ham. The wine list has some thoughtful and reasonable wines by the glass. A six-course fixed-price dinner is offered nightly for $50. > Coopertown Rd., tel. 410/886–2141 or 800/866–2141. Reservations essential. AE, D, DC, MC, V. $$$–$$$$

208 Talbot The several intimate dining rooms here have exposed brick walls and brick floors. Seafood specialties include such starters as baked oysters with prosciutto, pistachio nuts, and champagne, and baked salmon in a tomato, mushroom, and tarragon sauce. Entrées, all served with tossed salad, include roasted halibut with lobster and mashed potatoes. On Saturday, there's a prix-fixe menu ($50). > 208 N. Talbot St., St. Michaels, tel. 410/745–3838. D, MC, V. Closed Mon. and Tues. $$$$

ESSENTIALS

Getting Here

The fastest and easiest way to travel to and around the Eastern Shore is by car. Most shore destinations are less than a two-hour drive from Washington, D.C. Try to leave very early in the morning or late in the evening during busy summer months to avoid backups at the Bay Bridge.

BY BUS

Each day Greyhound runs four buses to Cambridge and one to Easton. *DEPOTS* **Fast Stop Convenience Center** > 9543 Ocean Gateway Dr., Rte. 50, Easton 21601, tel. 410/822–3333. **Sunburst Mobile** > 2903 Ocean Gateway Dr., Rte. 50, Cambridge 21613, tel. 410/228–5825. *LINE* **Greyhound** > Tel. 800/229–9424, www.greyhound.com.

BY CAR

To reach the Eastern Shore from Washington, D.C., take the Capital Beltway and travel east on U.S. 50 (U.S. 301) and cross the Chesapeake Bay bridge. The toll of $2.50 is collected heading eastbound only. The drive takes about 1½ hours.

BY FERRY

The Oxford–Bellevue Ferry, begun in 1683, may be the oldest privately owned ferry in continuous operation in the United States. It crosses the Tred Avon River between Bellevue, 7 mi south of St. Michaels via Routes 33 and 329, and Oxford. The 10-minute crossing, besides offering a great view of the town, is a shortcut between St. Michaels and Oxford. *LINE* **Oxford-Bellevue Ferry** > N. Morris St. at the Strand, Oxford, tel. 410/745–9023, www.oxfordmd.com/obf. $5 car and driver 1-way, $1 pedestrian, $2 bicycle, $3 motorcycle. Mar.–Memorial Day and Labor Day–Nov., weekdays 7 AM–sunset, weekends 9 AM–sunset; Memorial Day–Labor Day, weekdays 7 AM–9 PM, weekends 9–9.

Visitor Information

A large sail marks the visitor center at Sailwinds Park, just off Route 50 on the Choptank River and at the entrance of Cambridge. Information is available here on eight Eastern Shore counties. There's also a small beach, a boardwalk, and a playground. *CONTACTS* **Chesapeake Exploration Center** > 2 Rose Hill Pl., Cambridge, tel. 800/522–8687, www.tourdorchester.org. **Sailwinds Park** > 2 Rose Hill Pl., Cambridge, tel. 800/522–8687. **Talbot County Office of Tourism** > 11 N. Washington St., Easton 21601, tel. 410/770–8000, www.tourtalbot.org.

The Lower Eastern Shore

Salisbury is 117 mi southeast of Washington, D.C.

22

Revised by Pete Nelson

THE SMALL TOWNS OF THE LOWER EASTERN SHORE sometimes seem a century away from the oceanfront's summertime bustle. Main Street shops, early-America inns, and nontrendy restaurants are a far cry from the boutiques and galleries, the high-rise hotels and condos, and the eateries that crown the narrow, sandy strip of nearby Ocean City.

The speed limits are pretty much the same here as elsewhere, but with the lightly traveled roads and the beautiful scenery, it's a lot easier to obey them. Even U.S. Route 13, the only north–south highway to run from Salisbury to the tip of Virginia's 70-mi-long Eastern Shore peninsula, is pleasantly low-key, reminiscent of the days before interstates. Part of the fun of this area is exploring the secondary roads that often end in small towns that cling to the shore.

Barges still ply the slow-moving Wicomico River between the Bay and Salisbury, the Eastern Shore's second-largest port after Baltimore, and a town that hundreds of thousands of regional residents pass on their way to Ocean City and Delaware's shore. Antiques shops and galleries, along with some exemplary Victorian architecture, fill the six blocks that make up Salisbury's historic area.

Although Berlin is just 7 mi west of Ocean City, its temperament is much less strident and loud. Magnolias, sycamores, and ginkgo trees line streets filled with predominantly federal- and Victorian-style buildings. Nearby Snow Hill, on the Pocomoke River, is also lined with huge sycamores and stately homes—holdovers from its days as a shipping center in the 18th and 19th centuries.

In his classic study of the Chesapeake Bay, *Beautiful Swimmers*, William W. Warner describes Crisfield as a "town built upon oyster shells, millions of tons of it. A town created by and for the blue crab, cradle of the Chesapeake seafood industries." The number of processing plants here has dwindled to just 3 from a high of 150, but the workers at those that remain still pick crabs and shuck oysters by hand, as they have for more than a century.

During a short visit or overnight stay on Smith Island, reached by ferry from Crisfield, your neighbors include more egrets, heron, osprey, and pelicans than people. For more than three centuries, the fiercely independent but hospitable people who do inhabit the island have made their living by fishing in the Bay. When you're in the tiny island's villages, comprised of simple homes, churches, and a few stores, listen for the residents' distinct accents echoing those of their 17th-century English ancestors. A midday visit by passenger ferry allows ample time for a stroll around the island and a leisurely meal. You might want to stop by Ruke's, a venerable general store that serves excellent fresh seafood.

Virginia's Eastern Shore is a 70-mi-long peninsula between the southernmost reaches of the Chesapeake Bay to the west and the isle-strewn coastline of the

Atlantic Ocean to the east. At its northern edge is its only island resort town, Chincoteague Island. Despite the renown it gained since the publication of the 1947 children's book *Misty of Chincoteague,* the island still gives off an aura of seclusion. Chincoteague's inns, restaurants, and shops are readily reachable by walking, and relatively uncrowded beaches stretch out nearby.

Four miles from Chesapeake Bay, at the mouth of Onancock Creek, the town of Onancock was once the home of a handful of Algonquin families. It was established as a port in 1690 and later emerged as an important ferry link with the burgeoning waterside cities of Maryland and Virginia. Today, this quiet community of 1,600, the second-largest town on Virginia's Eastern Shore, is worth a short visit for a taste of its past as a transfer point between water and land.

Tangier Island, which can be reached from Onancock by ferry, is defined by crab traps stacked 10 feet high, as well as the watermen's shanties on the water. Although you can't take your own car onto Tangier, you can join a guided tour near the boat dock, rent a golf cart to roam the few narrow roads, or simply explore on foot or on bike.

Near the southern tip of Virginia's Eastern Shore, Cape Charles, established in the early 1880s as a railroad-ferry junction, has quieted down considerably after its heyday. However, its very isolation, as well as one of the largest concentrations of late-Victorian and turn-of-the-20th-century buildings in the region, has begun to attract people from farther and farther away. At the peninsula's tip itself, the extraordinary Chesapeake Bay Bridge—Tunnel sweeps 17½ miles across the water to connect with the Virginia Tidewater towns of Hampton Roads, Norfolk, and Virginia Beach.

WHAT TO SEE & DO

ASSATEAGUE ISLAND

Assateague Island National Seashore and Assateague State Park The National Seashore occupies the northern two-thirds of this 37-mi-long barrier island; a small portion of the National Seashore is operated as Assateague State Park. Part of the southern third of the island is taken up by the Chincoteague National Wildlife Refuge, in Virginia. The Seashore is most famous for the small, shaggy, sturdy wild horses, adamantly called "ponies" by the public, that roam freely along the beaches and roads. Behind the dunes, the island's forests and bay-side marshes invite exploration. Swimming, biking, hiking, surf fishing, picnicking, and camping can all be done on the island. The visitor center at the entrance to the park has aquariums and hands-on exhibits about the Seashore's birds and ocean creatures as well as the famous ponies. > 7206 National Seashore La. (Rte. 611), tel. 410/641–1441, www.assateagueisland.com and www.dnr.state.md.us/publiclands. 7-day pass $5 per vehicle, $2 per person for bicycles and pedestrians. Visitor center daily 9–5, park daily 24 hrs.

CAPE CHARLES

Eastern Shore of Virginia and Fisherman Island National Wildlife Refuges The maritime forest, myrtle and bayberry thickets, grasslands and croplands, and ponds in these two refuges are used by such species as bald eagles and peregrine falcons. Each fall, between late August and early November, migrating birds "stage," or gather in large groups, on Refuge lands until favorable winds and weather conditions allow them to easily cross Chesapeake Bay. > Southern extremity of Rte. 13, tel. 757/331–2760, easternshore.fws.gov. Free.

Chesapeake Skipjacks

SETTLEMENT ALONG THE FERTILE shores of the Chesapeake Bay was an obvious choice for 17th-century English immigrants, who soon farmed the cash crop of tobacco and plucked plentiful blue crabs and plump oysters from its bottom. Among the reminders of the Bay's fishing culture, which endures, are its dwindling fleet of native skipjacks: broad, flat-bottom wooden sailing vessels for dredging oysters. Economical to build, skipjacks had the shallowest draft—the distance from the waterline to the lowest point of the keel—of any boat in the Chesapeake Bay. This made them essential for cruising above the grassy shoals favored by oysters.

At first, oyster harvesters would stand in small boats and use simple, long-handle tongs, like a pair of scissored rakes, to grasp clumps of oysters from the bottom and bring them aboard. It was tiresome, difficult work. But in the early 1800s, sturdy Yankee schooners, having left the depleted waters of New England, entered the Chesapeake Bay with dredges, ungainly iron contraptions that dragged up oysters. With their first large harvest, Chesapeake's fishing industry changed forever.

Dredging was banned initially as exploitative and intrusive, first by Virginia and later by Maryland, but after the Civil War drained the region's economy, Maryland changed its mind and legalized the practice, allowing it under certain conditions for boats powered only by sails. By 1875, more than 690 dredging licenses were issued to owners of pungeys, schooners, and sloops. Soon, more sophisticated dredgers emerged, such as "bugeyes" and "brogans." All were loosely called bateaux, French for "boats."

The oyster bounty was not to last. After peaking in 1884 with 15 million bushels, less than a third of that amount was caught in 1891. Despite the growing use of steam and gasoline power on land and water, "only under sail" laws prevailed in the Bay. As the 19th century drew to a close, boatbuilders were forced to experiment with boat designs that were cheap to build and yet had sails that would provide enough power for dredging and transporting the harvests. In 1901, one of these new bateaux appeared in Baltimore's harbor. She caught the eye of a Baltimore Sun newspaper reporter, who wrote that their "quickness to go about may have earned for them the name of skipjack . . . applied by fishermen on the New England coast to the bonita, a flying member of the fish family." The name stuck.

Oysters—and the Chesapeake's renowned blue crab—are still harvested by a dwindling number of watermen, their fleets concentrated in locales such as Crisfield, Kent Narrows, and Smith Island.

Only a dozen sail-powered skipjacks are still working. Taking a ride on one of them (generally from early April through October, when they're not dredging) is an exhilarating way to fully experience the culture and history of the Chesapeake. The region's second-largest working skipjack, the Nellie L. Byrde, is docked in front of Explorer Hall beside Kent Narrows. The Nathan of Dorchester is berthed in Cambridge. The Herman M. Krentz, built in 1955, and the 80-foot Rebecca T. Ruark, originally built in 1886, both sail from Tilghman Island or nearby St. Michaels.

CHINCOTEAGUE ISLAND

Chincoteague National Wildlife Refuge Most of this refuge is made up of the southern third of Assateague Island, directly off of Chincoteague Island. (The northern two-thirds, part of Maryland, is the Assateague Island National Seashore.) Created in 1943 as a resting and breeding area for the imperiled greater snow goose as well as other birds, this refuge's location makes it a prime "flyover" habitat. It also protects native and migratory nonavian wildlife, including the small sika deer that inhabit its interior pine forests. A 3.2-mi self-guided wildlife loop is a great introduction to the refuge. Bike or walk it; it is open to vehicles only between 3 PM and dusk. The Chincoteague ponies occupy a section of the refuge isolated from the public, but they may still be viewed readily from a number of spots. The Herbert H. Bateman Education and Administrative Center, opened in late 2003, includes exhibits on falcon tracking program and the nesting habits of the refuge's burgeoning eagle population.
> Maddox Blvd. at Beach Rd., tel. 757/336–6122, www.assateagueisland.com. $5 per car (valid for 7 days). May–Sept., daily 5 AM–10 PM; Oct. and Apr., daily 6 AM–8 PM; Nov.–Mar., daily 6–6.

Oyster and Maritime Museum This museum chronicles the local oyster trade through displays of mostly homemade tools; elaborate, hand-carved decoys; marine specimens; a diorama; and audio recordings based on museum records. > 7125 Maddox Blvd., tel. 757/336–6117. $3. June–Sept., daily 10–5; Mar.–May, Sat. 10–5, Sun. noon–4.

Wallops Island NASA's Wallops Flight Facility visitor center fires the imagination with full-scale rockets, films on space and aeronautics, and displays on NASA projects. Although this was the site of early rocket launchings and NASA occasionally sends up satellites here, the facility now focuses primarily on atmospheric research. > Rte. 175, 20 mi southwest of Chincoteague, tel. 757/824–2298 or 757/824–1344, www.wff.nasa.gov. Free. July and Aug., daily 10–4; Sept.–June, Thurs.–Mon. 10–4.

CRISFIELD

Ice Cream Gallery The nicely shaded waterside deck of this ice cream parlor can be reached by sail as well as on foot. Ice cream in all its forms is what's here; there's also an arts-and-crafts boutique nearby. > Goodsell Alley between City and County Docks, tel. 410/968–0809.

J. Millard Tawes Historical Museum One of the best small museums on the Eastern Shore, the museum traces the history of the Lower Shore through exhibits on the beginnings of the Chesapeake Bay, the influence of the Native Americans on the early colonists, seafood harvesting and processing, the history of the city of Crisfield, and the evolution of decoy carving and painting. Also be sure to check out the display on Charlie Adams, a local citizen who still sells the *Crisfield Times* from his longtime spot on the corner of 9th and Main streets. > Somers Cove Marina, tel. 410/968–2501. $2.50. May–Oct., daily 9–4:30; Nov.–Apr., weekdays 9–4:30.

Janes Island State Park Nearly surrounded by the waters of the Chesapeake Bay and its inlets, Janes Island has two distinct areas: a developed mainland section with cabins and camping areas (April through October), and a portion accessible only by boat. Miles of isolated shorelines and marsh areas beckon those who enjoy the peacefulness of nature. The original island inhabitants were Native Americans of the Annemessex Nation. > 26280 Alfred Lawson Dr., Crisfield, tel. 410/968–1565 or 410/968–0651, www.dnr.state.md.us.

SALISBURY

Ward Museum of Wildfowl Art Operated in partnership with Salisbury University, this uncommon museum presents realistic marshland and wildfowl displays. Two brothers from Crisfield, Lem and Steve Ward, helped transform decoy making from just a utilitarian pursuit to an art form; their re-created studio is a must-see exhibit. Besides the premier collection of wildfowl art, the 30,000-square-foot museum has some 2,000 other artifacts as well as a gift shop and library. > 3416 Schumaker Pond at Beaglin Park Dr., Salisbury, tel. 410/742–4988, www.wardmuseum.org. $7. Mon.–Sat. 10–5, Sun. noon–5.

SNOW HILL

Furnace Town In the 1800s an industrial village grew up alongside Snow Hill's huge outdoor Nassawango Iron Furnace. This re-creation has a blacksmith shop, a shed used for broom making, a smokehouse, a print shop, a church, and a company store. You can also get a close-up look at nature via the boardwalk and trails that pass through a cypress swamp. Bring insect repellent in summer. > Old Furnace Rd., Rte. 12, tel. 410/632–2032. $3. Apr.–Oct., daily 11–5.

Pocomoke River State Forest and Park With almost 15,000 wooded acres along the banks of the Pocomoke River, this state forest is famous for its stand of loblolly pine and for its Pocomoke Cypress Swamp. White dogwood and pink laurel, river otters and bald eagles, and over 50 species of fish all live in this park's habitats of swamp and upland. The parks includes bike trail, campsites, a swimming pool, and the opportunities for fishing, hiking, and canoeing.

The park is divided into two sections. The Shad Landing area, open year-round, is 3½ mi south of Snow Hill, near Route 113. The Milburn Landing area, closed mid–December through March, is 7 mi northeast of Pocomoke City and can be reached via Route 364 or 12. > Tel. 410/632–2566, www.dnr.state.md.us/publiclands/eastern/pocomokeriver.

Tours

Crisfield Trolley This bus, cleverly painted to look like a trolley, goes on three loops daily around the Crisfield area—it also goes on daily guided tours. The bus departs from the J. Millard Tawes Historical Museum. > 3 9th St., Crisfield, tel. 410/968–2501. Transport 50¢, tour $2.50.

Smith Island Cruises Boats leave Crisfield's Somers Cove Marina for the 60-minute trip to Smith Island at 12:30 PM daily from Memorial Day to mid-October. > Somers Cove Marina, Crisfield, tel. 410/425–2771, www.smithislandcruises.com. $20.

Tangier Island Cruises From May 15 through October, these tours leave Crisfield's City Dock for Tangier Island at 12:30 PM daily. On Tuesday and Saturday during the same period, there's also a two-day cruise from Crisfield to Portsmouth, Virginia. > City Dock, Crisfield, tel. 410/968–2338, www.tangiercruises.com. $22.

Tangier–Onancock Cruises Narrated trips from Onancock to Tangier Island leave at 10 AM daily from Memorial Day to October 15. The return time, 2 PM, leaves ample time to explore. > Onancock, tel. 757/891–2240. $22.

Sports

Places to rent canoes, kayaks, and bikes are common in towns and state and local parks throughout the Lower Eastern Shore, but many of them close in early fall and don't reopen until spring.

BIKING

For a statewide map of prime cycling routes, contact Maryland's Department of Transportation (tel. 800/252–8776).

Viewtrail 100 Flat and friendly, the Eastern Shore is a great biking region. This well-marked 100-mi biking route follows lightly trafficked secondary roads between Berlin and Pocomoke City. For more information, contact the Worcester County Tourism Office.

BIRD-WATCHING

In addition to its many indigenous species, the Lower Eastern Shore is also popular with the many migrating birds and waterfowl that make up the vast Atlantic Flyway. Staffs at local and state parks and preserves have been trained well and can be very helpful in directing birders to the best viewing points. The Maryland Ornithological Society (www.mdbirds.org) and the Maryland section of the Web site Birding.com (www.birding.com/wheretobird/maryland.asp) are both useful sources for more information.

BOATING

Small powerboats may be available for rent in some waterside towns, but take extra care to make sure of their seaworthiness. Storms along the Atlantic coastline can be very violent, and Chesapeake Bay squalls can rise up very suddenly: pay close attention to local weather forecasts. Also be sure to verify that any fishing boat captain you employ is carrying a valid license.

CANOEING

Inn-to-Inn Tours The Bald Cypress tidal river winds gently through miles of pristine woodland. You can paddle a canoe through this environment on a tour arranged by the River House B&B. After a full breakfast at a participating inn, you spend the day drifting past waterside homes, hidden landings, and abundant wildlife. Enjoy a picnic lunch on a quiet bank or in a riverside park. Dinner awaits at your next overnight inn; then continue on for a second day (luggage transfers are included). A standard two-day, two-night, all-inclusive self-paddling trip is $600 for two, and is one of several tours available in spring, summer, and fall. Shorter itineraries are available, and trips can be customized. > River House B&B, tel. 410/632–2722, www.inntours.com.
Pocomoke River Canoe Company This firm rents canoes, gives lessons, and leads tours along the Pocomoke River, a habitat for bald eagles, blue herons, and egrets. > 312 N. Washington St., Snow Hill, tel. 410/632–3971, fax 410/632–2866, www.inntours.com.

FISHING

Island Cruises Departing from the town dock, just south of the Route 175 causeway on Chincoteague Island, these fishing cruises can take you on 1½-hour trips through the waterways of Chincoteague and Assateague. > Town dock south of the Rte. 175 causeway, tel. 757/336–5511.
RENTALS **Barnacle Bill's** > 3691 Main St., tel. 757/336–5188. **Captain Bob's** > 2477 S. Main St., tel. 757/336–6654. **R&R Boats** > 4183 Main St., tel. 757/336–5465.

Save the Date

APRIL

Delmarva Birding Weekend The guided and self-guided tours that take place over two days in late April are in celebration of the spring migration of shorebirds and waterfowl. > 104 W. Market St., Snow Hill, tel. 410/632–3110 or 800/852–0335, skipjack.net/le_shore/birdingweekend.

Fish Hawk Bicycle Festival On this late-April weekend, you can take a bike trip along carefully marked 25-, 50- and 62-mi byways. It's a great chance to see many of the Lower Shore's winged residents. > University of Maryland Eastern Shore Campus, Princess Anne, tel. 410/651–2968 or 800/521–9189, www.skipjack.net/le_shore/fishhawk.

JULY

J. Millard Tawes Crab and Clam Bake This all-you-can-eat feast of crabs, clams, and fish is enhanced by local entertainment. It adds up to one of the most renowned summertime events in the region. > Somers Cove Marina, Crisfield, tel. 410/968–2500 or 800/782–3913, www.crisfield.org.

Pony Swim and Auction What's sometimes called the "Pony Penning" is when Assateague Island's wild horses are rounded up. The foals are auctioned off to support the local volunteer fire department. > Chincoteague Island, tel. 757/336–6161, www.chincoteaguechamber.com.

Smith Island Day Arranged by the Crisfield and Smith Island Cultural Alliance, this afternoon event includes skiff races and a island-wide barbecue. > Ewell, tel. 410/425–3351.

AUGUST

Hard Crab Derby and Fair A quintessential local fair and carnival, this is the place for crab-cooking contests, boat races, and great seafood as well as arts and crafts, fireworks, and a parade. > Somers Cove Marina, Crisfield, tel. 410/968–2500 or 800/782–3913, www.visitsomerset.com/events.html.

SEPTEMBER

Berlin Fiddler Convention Acoustic musicians from all over the country compete in fiddle, banjo, mandolin, guitar, and bluegrass band categories. > Main St., Berlin, tel. 410/641–2998, www.visitworcester.org/events.html.

OCTOBER

Annual Native American Indian Heritage Festival and Pow Wow Native American cultural events like these are becoming more and more rare. In addition to seeing demonstrations of traditional rituals and trades, you can also buy crafts and food made by the local Accohannock tribe. > Bending Water Park, Rte. 413, Marion, tel. 410/623–2660, skipjack.net/le_shore/accohannock.

Chesapeake Celtic Festival The pageantry and heritage of the highlands of Scotland and Wales come to the lowlands of Maryland at this modern gathering of the clans. Music, dance, shepherding demonstrations, a medieval encampment, and a Celtic marketplace are all part of the festival. > Furnace Town Historic Site, Snow Hill, tel. 410/632–2032, www.furnacetown.com/calendar.

Chincoteague Oyster Festival You can savor one of the shore's specialties at this renowned event. Plan ahead: tickets can sell out months in advance. > 6733 Maddox Blvd., Chincoteague Island, tel. 757/787–2460, www.chincoteaguechamber.com.

Terrapin Sands Fish Fry Join the watermen and townsfolk for some grassroots entertainment and fish and chicken. > Side Street Seafood Market, Crisfield, tel. 410/968–2500 or 800/782–3913, www.crisfield.org.

WHERE TO STAY

CAPE CHARLES

Pickett's Harbor Clinging to the southernmost tip of the peninsula, this was part of a 17th-century grant to the owner's family. The current clapboard B&B was built in 1976 according to a colonial-era design, with floors, doors, and cupboards from several old James River farms reinstalled here. All guest rooms overlook small sand dunes and the Chesapeake; the backyard is 27 acres of private beach. The area's long country lanes and untrafficked paved roads are good for running and biking. > Rte. 600, Box 96, Cape Charles 23443, tel. 757/331–2212, www.pickettsharbor.com. 6 rooms, 4 with bath. Beach, bicycles, some pets allowed; no room phones, no room TVs, no smoking. No credit cards. BP. $

Wilson-Lee House A taste of Cape Charles's gilded age lives on in this turn-of-the-20th-century home, built for a businessman. The six rooms are whimsically decorated with a mélange of periods and styles, with a claw-foot tub in one bathroom, a hot tub in another. In good weather the elaborate breakfasts are served on the screened wraparound porch. You may play tennis at a nearby court at no charge; golfing packages for play at the Bay Creek Golf Club are also available. > 403 Tazewell Ave., 23310, tel. 757/331–1954, www.wilsonleehouse.com. 6 rooms. Golf privileges, boating, fishing, bicycles; no room phones, no room TVs, no kids under 12, no smoking. MC, V. $–$$

CHINCOTEAGUE ISLAND

Cedar Gables Seaside Inn In the northeast of town, this stunning, modern waterfront B&B is a refreshing alternative to those that are more traditional. The professionally designed rooms each have their own unique character. The Captain's Quarters, with a brass king-size bed, occupies the third floor by itself. > 6095 Hopkins La., 23336, tel. 757/336–1096 or 888/491–2944, www.cedargable.com. 3 rooms, 1 suite. Fans, in-room data ports, refrigerators, cable TV, in-room VCRs, pool, outdoor hot tub; no kids under 14, no smoking. D, MC. V. $$

Channel Bass Inn This three-story, beige clapboard house just off Chincoteague Bay was built in the 1870s, then expanded and converted to an inn 50 years later. Its luxurious rooms all have comfortable sitting areas. In addition to its full breakfast, the inn serves afternoon tea daily in the public tearoom. Delicacies such as *apfel kuchen* (German apple cake), firm scones, and an extraordinary multilayer trifle, all homemade, are served on Wedgwood china. > 6228 Church St., 23336, tel. 757/336–6148 or 800/249–0818, www.channelbass-inn.com. 8 rooms, 1 suite. Shop, some pets allowed; no room phones, no room TVs, no kids under 6, no smoking. AE, D, MC, V. BP. $–$$

Inn at Poplar Corner and the Watson House Both of these stately structures, across the street from each other, look Victorian. But although the Watson House is from the 1890s, the Inn at Poplar Corner was built a century later. Both contain impressive Victorian furniture. All four of the Poplar Corner rooms have hot tubs and private showers. Rates include breakfast, served at the Poplar Corner's antique dining table or on the inviting side porch. For visits to the National Wildlife Refuge, you can borrow beach chairs and binoculars. > 4240 Main St. (Box 905), 23336, tel. 757/336–1564 or 800/336–6787, fax 757/336–5776, www.watsonhouse.com. 10 rooms. Bicycles; no room phones, no room TVs, no kids under 10, no smoking. MC, V. Closed Dec.–Mar. BP. $–$$

Island Manor House Along with period mirrors and oil paintings, this three-story white frame federal-style house from 1848 contains several stunning items, including a sea chest from 1736 and a Scottish tall clock dated 1790. About half of its rooms have views of the Intercoastal Waterway (the best are in the Mark Twain and the Joseph Kenny rooms). The breakfast here stands out from others on the island. > 4160 Main St., 23336, tel. 757/336–5436 or 800/852–1505, fax 757/336–1338, www.islandmanor.com. 8 rooms, 6 with bath. No room phones, no room TVs, no kids under 6, no smoking. AE, MC, V. Closed Jan. BP. ¢–$

Miss Molly's Operated by the same innkeepers as the Channel Bass Inn, this unassuming 1886 Victorian inn claims fame as the temporary home of author Marguerite Henry, who wrote *Misty of Chincoteague*. Here, in 1946, she spent two of her six weeks in Chincoteague preparing the background for her children's novel. Miss Molly, the daughter of the home's builder, spent most of her life here. High tea is served every afternoon at the Channel Bass. > 4141 Main St., 23336, tel. 757/336–6686 or 800/221–5620, fax 757/336–0600, www.missmollys-inn.com. 7 rooms. No room phones, no room TVs, no kids under 6, no smoking. AE, D, MC, V. Closed Jan. and Feb. BP. $–$$

CRISFIELD

Bea's B&B Sunshine streaming through the stained-glass windows in this 1909 home is as cheerful as Bea's hospitality. The wallpapered rooms are all done in a Victorian style. A wide, screened porch is a welcoming retreat in summertime, and fireplaces crackle inside when it's cold. A steam room adds a touch of modernity. > 10 S. Somerset Ave., 21817, tel. 410/968–0423, www.beasbandb.com. 3 rooms. Cable TV; no room phones, no kids under 10, no smoking. No credit cards. BP. ¢

ONANCOCK

76 Market Street Near the ferry to Tangier Island, this circa-1840s Victorian house is pleasant and simple. The three warmly welcoming rooms—Blue, Rose, and Yellow—all have queen-size beds. There's cable TV with a VCR in the common room. Those who stay here often praise the breakfasts. > 76 Market St., 23417, tel. 757/787–7600 or 888/751–7600, fax 757/787–2744, www.76marketst.com. 3 rooms. Croquet, volleyball; no room phones, no TV, no kids under 6, no smoking. MC, V. BP. $

PRINCESS ANNE

Alexander House Booklovers B&B Each of the rooms in this historic district B&B is done in an interpretation of what a famous author's own room may have appeared in his or her time. You can immerse yourself in the jazzy Harlem Renaissance of the Langston Hughes Room, the high-seas adventure of Robert Louis Stevenson, or the Regency England romance of Jane Austen. The Mark Twain Reading Parlor has an extensive library. Breakfast as well as afternoon tea and dinner are served in Colette's Cafe. > 30535 Linden Ave., 21853, tel. 410/651–5195, www.bookloversbnb.com. 3 rooms. Café, library; no kids, no smoking. AE, D, MC, V. Closed Mon.–Wed. BP. ¢–$

Hayman House This elegant three-story 1898 house with a widow's walk retains the touches of the lumber baron who built it: high ceilings, gleaming oak trim, and double-mantel fireplaces. Floor-to-ceiling oak bookshelves line red walls in the library, just across the foyer from a parlor with a velvet sofa. The wonderful wraparound porch is filled with green wicker furniture. The single suite has a fireplace and cable TV, and a parlor on each floor contains a data port. > 30491 Prince William St., 21853, tel. 410/651–1107, www.haymanhouse.com. 5 rooms, 1 suite. Dining room, library; no room phones, no room TVs, no kids under 14, no smoking. MC, V. BP. ¢–$

Waterloo Country Inn Built in 1750, this rural Georgian brick mansion with gardens and a pool once served as the county almshouse. Restored throughout, it has served as an inn since 1996, its rooms carefully furnished with a mixture of Victorian antiques, reproductions, and modern amenities that include a microwave in one room.

Most rooms have fireplaces, and its suites have VCRs, refrigerators, coffeemakers, and hot tubs. Canoes are available free of charge. > 28822 Mt. Vernon Rd., 21853, tel. 410/651–0883, fax 410/651–5592, www.waterloocountryinn.com. 4 rooms, 2 suites. In-room data ports, cable TV, pool, pond, bicycles, some pets allowed; no smoking. AE, D, MC, V. BP. **$–$$$$**

SMITH ISLAND

Ewell Tide B&B On the northern tip of Smith Island, down-home hospitality is heartily extended by a licensed ferry- and charter-boat captain and his wife. Dinner is available, but you must order it in advance. The inn welcomes children, as well as pets, on weekdays. Complimentary snacks and beverages, including beer and wine, are available in the kitchen. > Ewell 21824, tel. 410/425–2141 or 888/699–2141, www.smithisland.net. 4 rooms, 2 with bath. Dining room, in-room data ports, cable TV, dock, bicycles, pub, meeting rooms, some pets allowed; no room phones, no smoking. AE, MC, V. CP. **¢–$**

Inn of Silent Music In a town that's separated by water from the other two villages on Smith Island, this remote English cottage–style inn takes its soothing name from a phrase in a poem by St. John of the Cross, a Carmelite monk. Tylerton has no restaurants, but the innkeepers will cook a fresh seafood dinner for those staying here for an extra $15. The rooms here are all sunny and furnished with a mix of antiques and flea market items. > Tylerton 21866, tel. 410/425–3541, www.innofsilentmusic.com. 3 rooms. Dining room, dock, bicycles; no room phones, no room TVs, no kids under 6, no smoking. No credit cards. Closed mid-Nov.–early Mar. BP. **$**

SNOW HILL

Chanceford Hall This mansion's Georgian front section was begun in 1759. Chimneys seem to soar from every corner. Ten working fireplaces and the contrast of cool colonial-era greens and blues welcome you throughout the guest rooms and public areas. A huge fireplace mantel moved from the ballroom overlooks a 12-place dining table and a breakfront bookcase crafted of yew wood. > 209 W. Federal St., 21863, tel. 410/632–2900, www.chancefordhall.com. 4 rooms. Pool, bicycles, croquet, volleyball, meeting rooms; no room phones, no room TVs, no smoking. MC, V. BP. **$–$$**

River House The welcoming icon for this National Register Victorian home on the Pocomoke River is the prancing carousel horse on the front porch. All rooms, suites, and cottages have working fireplaces, and the cottage rooms come with a hot tub. The rooms are spread out among a former barn and three other buildings. > 201 E. Market St., 21863, tel. 410/632–2722, www.riverhouseinn.com. 2 room, 2 suites, 2 cottage rooms. Microwaves, refrigerators, cable TV with VCR, meeting rooms, some pets allowed (fee); no room phones, no smoking. AE, D, MC, V. BP. **$$–$$$**

TANGIER ISLAND

Shirley's Bay View Inn You may stay in one of two guest rooms in one of the oldest houses on the island and have breakfast on 100-year-old china, hosted by members of the home's original family, or you may stay in one of the adjacent cottages. Either way, an overnight on Tangier Island is an uncommon experience. A visit to Shirley's should include a visit to her ice cream parlor, where music from the 1950s plays. > 16408 W. Ridge Rd., 23440, tel. 757/891–2396, www.tangierisland.net. 2 rooms, 7 cottages. Refrigerators, cable TV, beach; no room phones, no smoking. No credit cards. **¢**

WHERE TO EAT

CHINCOTEAGUE ISLAND
Etta's Channel Side Restaurant On the eastern side of the island, along the Assateague Channel, this well-maintained family-friendly restaurant has a vista as soothing as its food. Its dishes include pastas and popular meat dishes as well as typical fish and shellfish creations. Its signature dish is flounder stuffed with crab imperial. > 7452 East Side Dr., tel. 757/336–5644. D, MC, V. Closed Jan. and Feb. No lunch Mon.–Thurs. $–$$

Shucking House Cafe This is just the place to unwind after a day on the water. With oyster, crab, and fish sandwiches along with fish-and-chips, the Shucking House is a pleasant change from fancy restaurants or fast-food franchises. Be sure to try the rich New England or Manhattan clam chowder, both prepared with local mollusks. > Landmark Pl., tel. 757/336–5145. AE, D, MC, V. $–$$

CRISFIELD
Cove Restaurant Overlooking Somers Cove Marina and within easy walking distance of Main Street, this popular place serves such favorites as grilled porterhouse steaks as well as the freshest Bay seafood. > 718 Broadway, tel. 410/968–9532. AE, D, MC, V. No lunch. $–$$$

Watermen's Inn Since 1988, the Johnson & Wales–trained chef here has prided himself on using fresh, seasonal, local and regional seafood and organically grown fruits and vegetables. His weekend specials include entrées enhanced by unique combinations of herbs and sauces. But whenever you might visit, check out the desserts before you commit to your main meal. > 901 W. Main St., tel. 410/968–2119. Reservations not accepted. AE, D, MC, V. Closed Mon. and Tues. $$–$$$

TANGIER ISLAND
Islander Seafood Restaurant The soft-shell crabs here are excellent, no matter which of the many ways you choose to have them prepared. > 4414 Chamber La., tel. 757/891–2249. No credit cards. Closed Nov.–Apr. No dinner. ¢–$

Waterfront Sandwich Shop Sometimes a great sandwich is the perfect meal; the specialty is a crab-cake sandwich here, but a seafood platter is also available. > 6125 Main St., tel. 757/891–2248. No credit cards. Closed Nov.–mid–May. No dinner. ¢–$

ESSENTIALS

Getting Here

You can get to Salisbury by bus. To the south, however, public transportation is nonexistent; a vehicle—or at least a bike—is essential. The flat landscape and light traffic make for unhurried exploring whichever method you choose.

Smith and Tangier islands can be reached by ferry, but private vehicles are not permitted onto either island. Bikes, however, are welcome on both islands. Virtually all Chesapeake Bay– and Atlantic Ocean–side communities have public marinas and can be visited by private boat.

BY BUS

Carolina Trailways makes several round-trip runs daily between Washington and Salisbury. There is no regularly scheduled bus service between Salisbury and points south.

DEPOT **Salisbury** > 350 Cypress St., tel. 410/749–4121.

LINE **Carolina Trailways** > Tel. 800/231–2222.

BY CAR

A car is indispensable for touring the region. To reach the Eastern Shore from Washington, D.C., travel east on U.S. 50 (U.S. 301) and cross the 4½-mi Chesapeake Bay bridge (toll collected eastbound only, $2.50) northeast of Annapolis. Note that on the first Sunday in May, one span of the bridge is closed virtually all day for the Annual Bay Bridge Walk. Unless you want to participate, avoid the bridge that day.

TRAFFIC In summer, Friday-afternoon eastbound (beach-bound) traffic can be very heavy; conversely, Sunday- and sometimes Saturday-afternoon westbound traffic (from the beaches toward Baltimore and Washington, D.C.) can be equally congested.

BY FERRY

Ferries run between the mainland and both Smith and Tangier islands. Neither island permits private cars to land, but both are so small that vehicles are unnecessary. Service is regular and reliable, but infrequent; call ahead for departure and return times.

The *Captain Jason* freight boats as well as the *Island Belle,* a mail boat, can take you to Smith Island for $20 round-trip. All three boats depart daily at 12:30 PM and return to Crisfield at 5:15 PM, year-round, weather permitting. If you prefer, you can travel to Smith Island on one of the *Captain Jason* boats later in the evening, stay overnight, and return the next morning; both captains live on the island.

CONTACTS **Captain Jason I** and **Captain Jason II.** > Tel. 410/425–4471. *Island Belle* > Tel. 410/968–1118.

Visitor Information

Because virtually all of the towns on the Lower Eastern Shore are eminently walkable, most have prepared walking tour maps that allow you to explore at your own pace. These are available through tourism offices and visitor centers.

CONTACTS **Chincoteague Chamber of Commerce** > 6733 Maddox Blvd., Chincoteague, VA 23336, tel. 757/336–6161, fax 757/336–1242, www.chincoteaguechamber.com. **Eastern Shore of Virginia Chamber of Commerce & Tourism** > 19056 Industrial Pkwy. (off Rte. 13), Melfa, VA 23410, tel. 757/787–2460, fax 757/787–8687, www.esvachamber.org. **Salisbury Chamber of Commerce** > 300 E. Main St., Salisbury, MD, tel. 410/749–0144. **Somerset County Tourism Office and Visitors Center** > 11440 Ocean Hwy., Princess Anne, MD 21853, tel. 410/651–2968 or 800/521–9189, fax 410/651–3917, www.visitsomerset.com. **U.S. 13 Welcome Center** > 144 Ocean Hwy. (U.S. 13; 15 mi south of Snow Hill), Pocomoke City, MD, tel. 410/957–2484. **Wicomico County Convention & Visitors Bureau and Visitors Center** > 8480 Ocean Hwy., Delmar, MD 21875, tel. 410/548–4914 or 800/332–8687, fax 410/341–4996, www.wicomicotourism.org. **Worcester County Tourism Office** > 105 Pearl St., Snow Hill, MD 21863, tel. 410/632–3617 or 800/852–0335, fax 410/632–3158, www.visitworcester.org.

Ocean City

150 mi east of Washington, D.C.

23

Updated by Kristi Delovitch

AN ISLAND RESORT TOWN, Ocean City is known for its wide, well-kept beaches, rowdy, honky-tonk Boardwalk, and, in recent years, soaring real-estate prices. Along with the increase in the housing have come many new and attractive restaurants and hotels. This combination of new and old charms makes for a weekend destination that rivals the towns along the Eastern Shore and the Delaware Shore.

Ocean City stretches 10 mi along a narrow barrier island just off Maryland's Atlantic coast, drawing millions of people each year to its broad beaches and quiet bay side. Whether you come to relax or to get some stimulation, Ocean City offers plenty of options.

A timeless attraction, the 3-mi Boardwalk was built in 1910 on the older, southern end of the island. In the off-season and early morning it's a great place for a relaxing oceanside stroll or easy bike ride. Those up for more action prefer the sensory overload of summer days and evenings on the Boardwalk, where an abundance of stomach-churning rides can be found in two amusement parks. Need a break from the crowds? People-watch from a sideline bench, take a ride on a restored 19th-century carousel, fish from the pier, or try your hand at Skee-Ball, the Boardwalk sport of choice.

Coastal Highway (Route 1) bisects the town, with the Atlantic Ocean to the east and the Assawoman Bay to the west. Catching a glimpse of the ocean or bay can be difficult through the conglomerations of hotels, condos, restaurants, amusement parks, and trinket stores selling everything from tacky T-shirts to hermit crabs. As a rule, vehicle and pedestrian traffic thickens near the Boardwalk.

Kayaking can be done easily in Ocean City, and an abundance of marinas and public boat ramps makes most other water sports handy. Area charter boats offer bay tours and ocean-fishing and crabbing excursions. Sun-loving beachgoers will find Ocean City's usually mild waves perfect for swimming or bodysurfing. Biking and golfing are both popular sports. Many of the 12 or so courses have spectacular greens right on the bay. If you prefer a more lighthearted game, head for one of the many miniature-golf courses that line the highway.

Make reservations for summertime lodging well in advance: places fill up quickly. Options include modern high-rise hotels, sleepy motels, two small bed-and-breakfasts, a few chic inns, and several landmark hotels whose oceanfront porches are lined with rocking chairs. Beyond the northern end of the Boardwalk at 27th Street, high-rise condos and less-congested beaches prevail. Camping, although possible in Ocean City, is much more popular on nearby Assateague Island.

For many Marylanders, Ocean City's cuisine is emblematic of that of the whole state. Local favorites include fried chicken, piles of steamed blue crabs (generally accompanied with a side of cold beer), and Maryland crab soup. Despite somewhat depleted levels of blue crabs, they're still easy to find: just be prepared to pay a premium. The Boardwalk itself contains many treats for children of all ages, from Thrasher's french fries and Dayton's fried chicken to Dolle's saltwater taffy and Dumser's soft-serve ice cream. Don't be fooled—great meals are sometimes served in humble surroundings. A market shack might sell incredible house-smoked fish and have a waiting list a month long, a kitschy hotel restaurant might have an impressive wine list or serve urbane meals on the floor above its rowdy bar.

Head to West Ocean City for spectacular views and a glimpse of the waterman's town that preceded the resort. Fishermen still dock in the marina each evening with their live catch, but only one fish market remains, surrounded by bar and restaurant hangouts and million-dollar bay-front properties.

Despite Ocean City's recent growth, a down-home quality remains in the casual style of the local festivals. Springfest, over Memorial Day weekend, kicks off the season with arts, crafts, and festivities; September's Sunfest marks the season's end. In summer there are Fourth of July festivities with bay-side and ocean-side fireworks, boat shows, and classic car shows. Weekly bonfires, events at Northside Park, and free concerts on the beach are also popular.

A year-round destination, Ocean City is particularly appealing in fall and early winter, then again in late winter and early spring, when the weather is relatively mild and other tourists scarce. In the high-season months of summer, Ocean City has about 10,000 hotel rooms available. Most hotels and better restaurants remain open year-round, although the latter may operate on abbreviated schedules in the off-season.

A narrow island means that nowhere is very far from either the ocean or the bay. Rates vary dramatically through the year, with the lowest typically between mid-November and mid-March, and the highest in July and August. A room with an ocean view will almost always come with a premium rate.

WHAT TO SEE & DO

Boardwalk The original Boardwalk, constructed from 1900 to 1915, was once taken up board by board for winter storage. Today's permanent walkway is an institution, lined with shops, pubs, restaurants, hotels, a fishing pier, and two amusement parks; it's the hub of all tourist activities in town. The 3-mi Boardwalk stretches from the inlet in South Ocean City to 27th Street and can be seen by tram as well as walked. > Inlet to 27th St., tel. 410/250–0125, www.ococean.com. Free. Daily.

Jolly Roger Amusement Park This massive complex houses two miniature-golf courses, Splash Mountain Water Park, a roller coaster, kids' rides, petting zoo, and miniature racing cars. The "rain forest" comes fully outfitted with an arsenal of water guns and slides. Of the two golf courses, Treasure Golf is more challenging and larger, spanning the width of the park. Jungle Golf is more manageable with small children. > Coastal Hwy. at 30th St., tel. 410/289–4902. Rides and golf priced individually. Easter–Apr., weekends noon–midnight; May–Sept., daily 11 AM–1 AM.

Kite Loft This store is hard to miss: every summer it advertises its presence by flying kites in the shape of animals and other designs on the beach in front of the store. Inside, in addition to the many kites, are banners, flags, wind socks, hammocks and SKY chairs, whirligigs, and wind chimes. The Kite Loft has another branch at 45th Street Village. > 5th St. at the Boardwalk, tel. 410/289–7855, www.kiteloft.com. Feb.–Nov.

Ocean City Beach The 10 mi of beach that stretch along this coastal town are the major attraction for millions of annual visitors. Lifeguards patrol the beach from 10 to

Boardwalk Snacks

OCEAN CITY WOULDN'T BE THE same without its famous junk food. Luckily, most of the classics can be tasted in the few short blocks of the Boardwalk that are closest to the southern inlet. Many of the businesses are original, still making the timeless beach foods that they always have. Start at the inlet, walk north, and make a stop every few blocks for another classic treat.

At Thrashers French Fries (801 Boardwalk, 410/289–4150), patrons wait patiently for the steaming-hot fries to be finished. The Idaho potatoes are deep fried in peanut oil and then dashed with salt. Not only do you not need ketchup, you can't even get it. The fixin's are limited to salt and vinegar.

Dumser's original Boardwalk location (Atlantic St. and Boardwalk, 410/289–0934) has been serving ice cream since 1939. It's hard to choose between the hand-dipped and the soft serve, and the thick milk shake is another timeless favorite, especially the chocolate.

If you want a creamy treat, try the Kohr Brothers' (401 S. Atlantic Ave., 410/289–1178) famous frozen custard. The kosher recipe hasn't changed since 1919. A classic flavor is orange and vanilla twist, and new favorites include the peanut butter and chocolate twirl.

Dolle's Candyland (Boardwalk and Wicomico St., 410/289–6000) has been serving saltwater taffy and caramel corn on this same corner since 1910. Everything's made right here. To make the caramel corn, brown sugar, syrup, butter, and salt are cooked to 280° and poured over freshly popped, large-kernel popcorn. When you order a tub, it's brought over to the window, poured into a bin, and then tossed in the air to cool. Over 1,500 pounds of taffy are sold every summer day.

The bright pink-and-white Candy Kitchens (Somerset and Boardwalk, 410/289–9003) dot the shore. The many fudge flavors include the King Tut, made with caramel and nuts and then sandwiched between thick layers of milk chocolate and heavenly hash, with massive chunks of marshmallow. Licorice, colorful foot-long lollipops, saltwater taffy, and gummies galore all pack each store.

5:30 daily, in season. Surfing is permitted on two beaches, which is announced daily on local radio stations. Body-boarding is abundant throughout the entire beach. Neither sports nor animals are permitted on the beach in season. > www.ococean.com. Free. Daily.

Ocean City Life-Saving Station Museum On the southernmost tip of the island, the museum traces the resort's roots back to its days as a tiny fishing village in the late 1800s. Housed in an 1891 building that once held the U.S. Lifesaving Service and the Coast Guard, the museum's exhibits include models of the grand old hotels, artifacts from shipwrecks, boat models, and even itchy wool swimsuits and an old Boardwalk automaton, Laughing Sal. Press the button, and have a laugh with her. > Boardwalk at the inlet, tel. 410/289–4991, www.ocmuseum.org. $2. June–Sept., daily 11–10; May and Oct., daily 10–4; Nov.–Apr., weekends 10–4.

Old Pro Golf Miniature golf is a staple in Ocean City, and Old Pro is the largest chain in town. Most of the company's seven courses line Route 1; Old Pro owns Undersea Adventure, the city's only year-round indoor course, which is at 68th Street. If you're planning to have a golfing marathon, opt for the unlimited-play day pass ($12). The 27-hole course Medieval Castle, on 28th Street, was made by combining two courses. > Undersea Adventure and Dinosaurs, 68th St., tel. 410/524–2645, www.oldprogolf.com. $6.50. Daily 9 AM–1 AM.

Seacrets Bar and Grill Everything about this sprawling bay-side bar is over the top. Tiki bars, grill-style restaurants, and spots with live music are all part of this block-long venue. The waitresses even wade into the bay to deliver tropical drinks to patrons floating in yellow inner tubes. Thousands pack into Seacrets in a single summer day—be prepared to wait in long lines on weekend nights. > 49th St. at the bay, tel. 410/524–4900, www.seacrets.com. Cover charge $5–$20. Daily 11 AM–2 AM.

Shantytown Village This faux village holds some 20 shops selling holiday gifts and souvenirs, candy, collectibles, flowers, and wine. > Rte. 50 at Shantytown Rd., West Ocean City, www.shantytownvillage.com.

Sportland Arcade Although many of the arcades and amusement parks on the Boardwalk house older games and Skee-Ball, Sportland contains modern games. Adults and kids alike wait in lines to try out the latest in virtual-reality gaming. > Worcester St. and the Boardwalk.

Trimper's Amusement Park At the south end of the Boardwalk, this small park has more than 100 rides, games, and amusements. Highlights include an antique carousel from 1902, a double-loop roller coaster, an arcade, and miniature golf. The view of the inlet and the Boardwalk from the top of the carousel is one of the best in town. Most of the rides are outdoors, but an indoor section has rides for little kids. The park has been owned by the Trimper family since it opened in 1890. > Boardwalk at S. 1st St., tel. 410/289–8617, www.beach-net.com/trimpers. Rides priced individually. Memorial Day–Labor Day, daily 1–midnight; Labor Day–May, indoor park weekends noon–4.

Wheels of Yesterday This museum of antique and otherwise collectible cars has famed comedian Jack Benny's Overland and other cars and trucks, including an 1830 postal wagon and a 1930 race car. All but a handful of the vehicles make up a private collection—and all are roadworthy. > 12708 Ocean Gateway (Rte. 50), tel. 410/213–7329, www.wheelsofyesterday.com. $4. Oct.–May, daily 9–5; June–Sept., daily 9–9.

Tours

Discovery Educational ecotours give you hands-on experience of the waters between Ocean City and Assateague Island. You get to hoist a net or drop a crab pot into the water—an onboard expert identifies the day's catch. From the boat you can observe fauna native to Assateague Island, such as pelicans and ospreys, as well as the famous ponies. Cruises last 1½ hours. In summer tours leave at 8:30 AM, 10 AM, noon, 2 PM, and 4 PM. > 1st St. on the bay, next to BJ's Bayfront Bar and Restaurant, tel. 410/289–2700, www.ocean-city.com/ocsbest/discovery.

Sports

BIKING

A portion of the Coastal Highway has been designated for bus and bicycle traffic. Bicycle riding is allowed on the Ocean City Boardwalk from 2 AM to 10 AM in summer and 5 AM to 4 PM the rest of the year. The bike route from Ocean City to Assateague Island (U.S. 50 to Rte. 611) is a 9-mi trek, and Assateague itself is crisscrossed by a number of clearly marked, paved trails.

Bike rentals are available throughout Ocean City, "every three blocks" according to some. Rates start at $5 for the first hour and $3 for every hour thereafter for regular adult bikes and go up to $20 an hour for a "surrey" that will hold six passengers and two toddlers. One of the most venerable places for bike rental, sales, and service enterprises is Mike's Bikes. In addition to normal rental, the firm also rents "fun cycles": low-riding, bright-yellow, three-wheeled bikes that cost $7 for the first hour. *EQUIPMENT* **Mike's Bikes** > N. 1st St. at the Boardwalk, tel. 410/289–4637, www.mikesbikesoc.com; N. Division St. and Baltimore Ave., tel. 410/289–5404.

FISHING

Founded as a fishing village in 1875, Ocean City continues to lure anglers to its waters. A violent storm that hit the town in 1933 created the inlet that connects the ocean and the bay.

No fishing licenses are required in Ocean City. If you're hoping to catch some marlin, bluefish, tuna, or wahoo, take one of the many boats that head out to sea daily. Smaller vessels stay in the bay and fish for flounder, sea bass, and trout. If you prefer to keep your feet firmly on the ground, cast a line from one of the several fishing piers or surf-fish (fish from the beach). You can get bait and rent a rod from most of the marinas or smaller tackle shops. Amateur fishing contests award weekly prizes to anglers with the largest flounder, trout, bluefish, sea bass, and rockfish.

Bahia Marina With a fleet of over a dozen vessels, this bay-side company can organize sportfishing trips that include chumming for shark and trolling for bottom fish. Bahia also arranges deep-sea charters to fish for marlin, shark, and tuna. Box lunches are available from the tackle shop. > 21st St. at the bay, tel. 410/289–7438, www.bahiamarina.com.

Ocean City Fishing Center Ocean City's largest deep-sea charter boat marina has some 30 vessels and professional captains licensed by the Coast Guard. In addition to assisting preformed groups, the Fishing Center will also form fishing groups of individuals who are on their own. > U.S. 50 and Shantytown Rd., West Ocean City, tel. 410/213–1121, www.ocfishing.com.

Public Piers Public fishing piers on the Assawoman Bay and Isle of Wight Bay are at 3rd, 9th, 40th, and 125th streets and at the inlet in Ocean City. Other fishing and crabbing areas include the U.S. 50 bridge, Oceanic Pier, Ocean City Pier at Wicomico Street and the Boardwalk, and Shantytown Village. > Tel. 410/213–0463 Dept. of Natural Resources.

GOLF

Now rivaling premier golfing destinations around the United States, Ocean City is within easy driving distance of no fewer than 17 golf courses.

Eagle's Landing Golf Course This par-72 course (7,003/4,896; 73.6/67.9), the first Audubon-sanctioned golf course in the state of Maryland, remains an inexpensive alternative to some of the pricier new courses in and around Ocean City. The maximum in-season rate is $69 with a cart and $49 without. Six of the 18 holes on this par-72 coastal course run throughout the marshland of the Sinepuxent Bay. The 17th hole has great views of Assateague Island. > 12367 Eagle's Nest Rd., Berlin, tel. 410/213–7277 or 800/283–3846.

Links at Lighthouse Sound This par-72 links-style course (7,031/4,553; 73.3/67.1) overlooks the Assawoman Bay and has spectacular views of the Ocean City Skyline. The course winds through marsh, river, and the bay. A 1,500-foot cart bridge is built over the marsh to take you from one side of the course to the other. The beautiful clubhouse, which has a full-service restaurant, sits on a small peninsula that juts into the bay. The weekend green fee ranges from $75 to $165. > 12723 St. Martin's Neck Rd., Bishopville, tel. 410/352–5767 or 888/554–4557, www.lighthousesound.com.

TENNIS

There are public tennis courts scattered throughout Ocean City. The courts on 41st and 61st streets require reservations. Courts on 14th, 94th, and 136th streets are first-come, first-served.

Ocean City Tennis Center This outdoor tennis center, open from early May to September, is available for hourly court rental, tennis lessons, and children camps. Three clay courts and six Omni courts, with artificial turf, are available daily from 7 AM to 8 PM for $8–$14, depending on surface and time of day. Two tennis pros offer private lessons at $45 an hour, and in every season there are four four-day sessions of an ace tennis camp for children ages 6 to 15. An unlimited-use weekly pass is $40. > 61 St. and the bay, tel. 410/524–8337, www.ococean.com.

WATER SPORTS

Sailing Etc. Outfitters & Mellow Beach Watersports Center rents sailboats, wind boards, single and double kayaks, and paddleboats. Individual and group sailing and windsurfing lessons are available; there's also a 27-foot stiletto catamaran that comes with a captain. The sail is $150 for the first 1½ hours and $100 for each additional hour. The sails are for eight to 10 adults.
EQUIPMENT **Sailing Etc. Outfitters & Mellow Beach Watersports Center** > 46th St. on the bay, tel. 410/723–1144.

Save the Date

MAY

Springfest The unofficial start to summer, Springfest brings classic shore food, regional arts and crafts, and live music. Huge tents span the south tip of Ocean City between the water, Trimper's Amusement Park, and the Boardwalk. National acts such as the Village People and Diamond Rio perform during the four-day festival. > Inlet parking lot, tel. 410/250–0125 or 800/626–2326, www.ococean.com.

JULY

Fourth of July Celebration Two fireworks displays, on the bay and ocean side, light up the skies on the Fourth. Bay-side festivities begin at 1 PM, with Northside Park's Jamboree. Highlights of this daylong, family-oriented celebration are pie-eating contests and games. The ocean-side celebration starts with live music on the beach at 8 PM with a performance of the United States Army Band and Chorus. Bay-side and ocean-side fireworks explode over the Assawoman Bay and the ocean at 9:30 PM, in simultaneous displays. > Caroline St. and the beach, and Northside Park at 127th, tel. 410/250–0125 or 800/626–2326, www.ococean.com.

JULY–AUGUST

Sundaes in the Park Northside Park Recreation Center, a popular park on the edge of Assawoman Bay, is the place for free outdoor concerts at 6 PM on Sunday. You can also buy the fixings for a make-your-own sundae. > 125th St. at the bay, tel. 410/250–0125 or 800/626–2326, www.ococean.com. Free.

AUGUST

White Marlin Open Ocean City is the "White Marlin Capital of the World," and it's also host to one of the world's largest billfish tournaments. Thousands of spectators come to watch 350 boats and anglers compete for over $2 million in cash awards. The largest prize is reserved for the contestant catching the largest white marlin, but prizes are also awarded for blue marlin, wahoo, mahimahi, shark, and tuna. > Harbor Island Marina, 14th St. and the bay, tel. 410/289–9229, www.whitemarlinopen.com.

SEPTEMBER

Sunfest Marking the end of the summer season, Sunfest brings with it live music, regional arts and crafts, and classic Ocean City cuisine. More quirky activities include scarecrow making, a pie-eating contest, and a beach treasure hunt. > Inlet lot, tel. 410/250–0125 or 800/626–2326, www.ococean.com.

NOVEMBER–DECEMBER

Winterfest of Lights Nearly 300,000 people come to see the thousands of lights twinkling on stationary and animated displays throughout the seaside resort. > Tel. 410/250–0125 or 800/626–2326.

WHERE TO STAY

Atlantic Hotel You can trace the history of this resort town by looking at the pictures from the 1920s and 1930s that hang in the lobby of this hotel, the oldest in town. Family-owned and -operated, the three-story, H-shape frame hotel is a replacement of the original Victorian hotel that burned in 1922. Rooms are as plainly furnished and decorated as they were originally, but now with modern comforts that include air-conditioning. This is ocean-side vacationing as it was in a calmer era. The annual Fourth of July fireworks are ignited from the beach just steps from the hotel, making their block-long sundeck a popular spot. > Boardwalk and Wicomico St., 21843, tel. 410/289–9111 or 800/328–5268, fax 410/289–2221, www.atlantichotelocmd.com. 80 rooms. Cable TV, beach. AE, D, MC, V. Closed Oct.–Apr. **$**

Clarion Resort This high-rise hotel is on the "Golden Mile," Ocean City's strip of high-rise hotels and condominiums. The rooms are done in floral patterns, and some have ocean views. Live entertainment performs nightly in-season in the on-site nightclub and at the two oceanfront restaurants, which have a massive wine list. Outside there are a beach bar and grill and a huge deck bar with live entertainment. > 10100 Coastal Hwy., 21842, tel. 410/524–3535 or 800/638–2100, fax 410/524–3834, www.clarionoc.com. 250 rooms, 69 apartments. 3 restaurants, in-room data ports, some kitchenettes, microwaves, refrigerators, cable TV, indoor pool, gym, hot tub, beach, bar, nightclub, business services, airport shuttle, some pets allowed (fee). AE, D, DC, MC, V. **$$$$**

Commander Hotel Built where the original 1930 Ocean City mainstay once stood, the current Commander opened in 1998. Family-owned and -operated since its inception, the hotel is owned by the fourth generation of the Lynch family. All suites and efficiencies have private balconies with ocean views. Rooms have carpeting and tile and are decorated in a blue-and-white motif that employs photos of the original hotel. > 14th St. at the Boardwalk, 21842, tel. 410/289–6166 or 888/289–6166, www.commanderhotel.com. 109 suites. Restaurant, microwaves, refrigerators, cable TV in some rooms, pool, indoor pool, lounge, free parking; no TV in some rooms. MC, V. Closed Dec.–Feb., and weekdays Mar. and Nov. **$$–$$$$**

Dunes Manor Hotel The Victorian-style lobby, with immense crystal chandeliers and a carved ceiling, sets the tone for the rest of the hotel: it was built in 1987 to replicate a 19th-century seashore resort. You can step beyond the lobby and settle into a green rocking chair on the porch, which overlooks the ocean. All rooms face the ocean and have two double beds, pickled-pine furniture, and private balconies; suites include a full kitchen. Tea and homemade cookies are served each afternoon. The hotel is a block beyond the north end of the Boardwalk. > 28th St. at the Boardwalk, 21842, tel.

410/289–1100 or 800/523–2888, fax 410/289–4905, www.dunesmanor.com. 160 rooms, 10 suites. Restaurant, microwaves, refrigerators, cable TV, gym, hot tub, bar, free parking, no-smoking rooms. D, MC, V. $$$–$$$$

The Edge This boutique hotel, opened in 2002, has accommodations that exude quality and style. Each of the rooms is uniquely furnished to evoke such locales as Bali or the Caribbean, the French Riviera or southern Italy, a safari and even the *Orient Express*. The Island Monkey Room is filled with simian statuettes and pictures. Amenities here include special windows that take up the entire west-facing room walls. > 56th St. at the bay, 21842, tel. 410/524–5400 or 888/371–5400, fax 410/524–3928, www.fagers.com. 12 suites. In-room hot tubs, minibars, refrigerators, cable TV, conceirge; no smoking. AE, D, DC, MC, V. CP. $$$$

Holiday Inn Hotel & Suites This luxurious all-suites hotel is packed with amenities. The spacious rooms have a Jacuzzi, a double-sink vanity, and a full kitchen stocked with cookware, dishes, and utensils. The rooms are furnished in a tasteful fusion of French country and island motifs. Each room has an oversize balcony, and most have ocean views. There's also a gorgeous outdoor deck overlooking the ocean and the Boardwalk that has both an adult and a children's pool (with fountains and water slides). > 1701 Atlantic Ave. (17th St. and the Boardwalk), 21842, tel. 410/289–7263 or 866/627–8483, fax 410/289–3381, www.ocsuites.com. 210 suites. Restaurant, café, in-room data ports, kitchens, cable TV3 pools (1 indoor), hot tub, outdoor hot tub, bar, laundry facilities. AE, D, DC, MC, V. CP. $$$–$$$$

Hotel Monte Carlo This small hotel is in the pulsing heart of southern Ocean City. One highlight: the spectacular ocean and bay views from the pool or from the roof deck's hot tub. The compact rooms, which all have balconies, are basic, with simple furnishings. The hotel is very family-friendly, with a small shaded indoor pool and cribs available at no extra charge. A two-minute walk will get you to the beach or the Boardwalk. > 216 N. Baltimore Ave., 21842, tel. 410/289–7101 or 877/375–6537, fax 410/289–4464, www.montecarlo-2000.com. 70 rooms. Restaurant, in-room data ports, some in-room hot tubs, microwaves, refrigerators, cable TV, 2 pools (1 indoor), hot tub, free parking. AE, D, MC, V. $$–$$$

Inn on the Ocean Small, elegant, and romantic, Maryland's only beachfront B&B has a fireplace in the living room to warm you up and a wraparound veranda to cool you off. Wood and wicker furnishings give the 1938 Victorian cottage a relaxed charm. Afternoon refreshments, which often include freshly baked chocolate-chip cookies or miniature cheesecakes, are available. In good weather the full breakfast is served on the veranda. Interesting dishes, such as French toast made with Grand Marnier and then topped with orange slices and strawberries, are often served. > 1001 Atlantic Ave., 21842, tel. 410/289–8894 or 888/226–6223, fax 410/289–8215, www.innontheocean.com. 6 rooms. Dining room, cable TV, hot tub, beach, bicycles, free parking; no kids, no smoking. AE, D, MC, V. BP. $$$–$$$$

Lighthouse Club Hotel Built to resemble a Chesapeake Bay "screwpile" lighthouse, this elegant hotel is just blocks from the busy Coastal Highway. Its airy, contemporary suites have high ceilings and views of sand dunes that slope to the Assawoman Bay. Rooms are furnished with white-cushioned rattan furniture and have marble bathrooms with two-person hot tubs. Sliding glass doors lead to private decks with steamer chairs. It all makes for a luxurious and uncommonly quiet hotel. > 56th St. at the bay, 21842, tel. 410/524–5400 or 888/371–5400, fax 410/524–3928, www.fagers.com. 23 suites. In-room hot tubs, minibars, refrigerators, cable TV; no kids. AE, D, DC, MC, V. CP. $$$–$$$$

Phillips Beach Plaza This oceanfront hotel is near everything you're likely to seek in Ocean City—restaurants, shops, the beach, and the Boardwalk. Victorian-style furnishings add to its retro charm; it's one of the older hotels on the strip. The rooms with queen beds have classic four-poster beds. Some rooms have spectacular ocean views, and you can also watch the Boardwalk crowds from your window. It's a great location if you want to be in the middle of the action. > 13th St. at the Boardwalk, 21842, tel. 410/289–9121 or 800/492–5834, fax 410/289–3041, www.phillipsbeachplaza.com. 96 units. Restaurant, bar, some kitchenettes, cable TV, beach, business services. AE, D, DC, MC, V. Closed Jan. and Feb., and weekdays in Mar. $–$$

Princess Royale This ocean-side, 10-story hotel has five levels of condos, an ocean deck, a private boardwalk, and an Olympic-size heated pool in a four-story atrium. Warm colors and beach paintings make the suites a relaxing place to kick off your sandals after a long day at the beach. Some have heart-shape hot tubs, and all are equipped with a living room and private balcony. > 91st St. at the ocean, 21842, tel. 410/524–7777 or 800/476–9253, fax 410/524–7787, www.princessroyale.com. 310 units. Restaurant, in-room data ports, some in-room hot tubs, kitchenettes, microwaves, cable TV, tennis court, indoor pool, exercise equipment, hair salon, hot tub, beach, video game room, bar, laundry facilities, business services. AE, D, DC, MC, V. $$–$$$$

CAMPING

Ocean City Campground A block from the beach, the only campground in Ocean City is convenient to the ocean, many amusements, and the municipal bus service. A boat ramp and slips are on the property; pets on a leash are allowed. > 105 70th St., 21842, tel. 410/524–7601, fax 410/524–4329, www.occamping.com. 56 tent or RV sites with hookups, 14 tent sites. Flush toilets, full hookups, drinking water, laundry facilities, showers, electricity, general store, play area, swimming (ocean). AE, MC, V. Closed Oct.–Jan. ¢

WHERE TO EAT

Bagels N' Buns In season, this popular bagel shop is open until 4 AM on weekdays and all night on weekends. The fresh bagels baked throughout the day are served with numerous spreads that include pineapple and mandarin orange. The typical deli fare includes corned beef, pastrami, and Reuben sandwiches. Omelets, burgers, and gyros are served all day, and kosher meats are available. > 7111 Coastal Hwy., tel. 410/723–2253. No credit cards. ¢

Bull on the Beach This laid-back restaurant and bar has true Maryland flair. It serves beef sandwiches and ice-cold draft beer as well as many raw-bar offerings. It's a comfortable respite from the bustle of a resort town. You can play a game or two of air hockey as you wait to be served. Additional branches are at U.S. 50 and Keyser Point Road and at 211 Boardwalk. > 94th St. and Coastal Hwy., tel. 410/524–2455. AE, MC, V. ¢–$$$

Captain's Galley The claim to fame of this harborside restaurant is its crab cakes, the best in town. Locals pack the many dining rooms, but the open-air deck is the most popular place in summer. On the menu are favorites such as the crab imperial sandwiches and a plethora of dock-fresh fish. > West Ocean City Harbor, 12817 S. Harbor Rd., West Ocean City, tel. 410/213–2525. AE, D, DC, MC, V. $$–$$$$

Crab Alley Sitting at the edge of the harbor in West Ocean City, where commercial fisherman dock nightly, Crab Alley is a local favorite for fresh seafood, especially steamed blue crabs. Clams, served steamed on the half shell, or casino style with cheese, bread crumbs, and bacon, are also favorites, and so is the in-house smoked fish. The typically Maryland soups available here include clam chowder and Maryland crab. The seafood market, open May through September, serves fresh seafood carry-out and prepared favorites such as the cream of crab soup. > 9703 Golf Course Rd., West Ocean City, tel. 410/213–7800. D, MC, V. Closed mid-Nov.–Dec. $$–$$$

Dumser's Drive-In Making ice cream since 1939, Dumser's whips up such flavors as strawberry, peanut butter fudge, and butter pecan daily. Don't leave without trying an ice cream soda or a thick milk shake made with hand-dipped ice cream. If you want something a bit more substantial at this '50s-style diner, go for the subs, burgers, and fries. There's another branch at 123rd Street and Coastal Highway. > 49th St. and Coastal Hwy., tel. 410/524–1588. MC, V. ¢–$

Fager's Island This swanky bay-side restaurant gives you white-linen treatment along with large windows perfect for viewing sunsets and the wetlands. White stucco walls and white columns contrast with red tile floors and brass chandeliers. Entrées include lobster, prime rib, crab cakes, and salmon. There's an outside deck for more informal dining and a raw bar with lighter fare. In summer, Tchaikovsky's 1812 Overture is played every evening, with the tumultuous finale whimsically timed to coincide with the setting of the sun. > 60th St. at the bay, tel. 410/524–5500. AE, D, DC, MC, V. $$–$$$

Fractured Prune Freshly baked doughnuts are the signature offering at this tiny bakery. Every morning patrons wait in line for hand-dipped, piping-hot doughnuts in their choice of glazes (like banana and honey) and toppings (crushed Oreo and sprinkles, for instance). > North Bay Shopping Center, 127th St. and Coastal Hwy., tel. 410/250–4400. No credit cards. Closed Dec.–Feb. ¢

Galaxy Bar & Grille The canary-yellow-and-cobalt-blue exterior of this modern, urban-style restaurant sets the stage for what's inside: towering ceilings, eclectic furnishings, and a hip clientele that dines on modern versions of filet mignon and lobster tail, among other dishes. The menu changes frequently and emphasizes local ingredients. > 6601 Coastal Hwy., tel. 410/723–6762. Reservations essential. AE, D, DC, MC, V. $$$–$$$$

Grove Market Smokehouse Eatery What might be Ocean City's best-kept secret is inside a tiny fish shack on an old country road. A reservation is hard to come by; potential patrons call months ahead to claim one of the handful of tables. Small charms abound here. The staff greets you by reciting what's available that day: there are no printed menus. True to its smokehouse roots, the restaurant has house-smoked fish available nightly; another option might be filet mignon stuffed with massive oysters. The wine list is well chosen and fairly priced. > 12402 St. Martin's Neck Rd., Bishopville, tel. 410/352–5055. Reservations essential. No credit cards. $$–$$$

Harrison's Harbor Watch Restaurant and Raw Bar Overlooking the island's southernmost tip, this sprawling, two-story seafood restaurant includes only freshly prepared sauces, soups, breads, and dressings on its menu, with fish and meat cut and prepared daily. A raw bar is also available. Comfortable booths have tile tabletops and clear ocean views, and the dining room has seashell-pattern carpeting, ocean scenes on the walls, and huge fish-market signs and lobster artwork hanging from a sloped wood-beam ceiling. > Boardwalk at the inlet, tel. 410/289–5121. AE, D, MC, V. Closed Jan. and Feb. $$–$$$$

The Hobbit Dedicated to Bilbo Baggins and the other literary creations of J. R. R. Tolkien, this bay-side dining room has scenes from the book painted on the wall and wood table lamps carved in the shape of hobbits. The deck is popular in summer. One favorite entrée is veal and pistachios sautéed in a sauce of Madeira, veal stock, prosciutto, mushrooms, shallots, and cream. The fish of the day ("Hobbit Catch") is typically salmon, swordfish, or tuna. Light fare is served in the adjoining bar as well as in the café. There's a gift shop full of hobbit-related T-shirts and gifts. > 101 81st St., at the bay, tel. 410/524–8100. AE, D, MC, V. **$$$–$$$$**

Ocean Club You can see the ocean through the oval windows in this ample dining room, which is decorated with wooden pillars and wicker furnishings. Look for a diverse menu of seafood, chicken, beef, and veal dishes. A palm-shaded beach provides a restful spot for outdoor dining. The popular Crow's Nest rooftop bar has entertainment nightly. > 49th St. at the ocean, tel. 410/524–7500. AE, D, DC, MC, V. Closed Tues. Nov.–Mar. No lunch weekdays Sept.–May. **$$$**

Reflections When you enter this dimly lit restaurant, it seems a bit as if you've entered a maze; mirrors cover every surface. Standout dishes include steak Diane, with shallots and Dijon mustard in a cream sauce, and the Seafood Symphonia, a melting pot of lobster, scallops, and shrimp prepared table-side. Other offerings are predominately surf-and-turf local favorites such as rainbow trout and veal marsala. > Holiday Inn, 67th St. and Coastal Hwy., tel. 410/524–5252. AE, D, DC, MC, V. **$$$–$$$$**

Rio Grande Cafe and Tiki Bar This seasonal restaurant with indoor and outdoor seating is known for its overstuffed sandwiches, salads, and grilled tuna. Other popular selections include the boneless pork chops with cranberry and the chicken Rio Grande, topped with bacon, provolone, and barbecue sauce. Breakfast at this sunny little restaurant is sometimes so popular that lines circle the deck. > 145th St. at Coastal Hwy., tel. 410/250–0409. AE, D, MC, V. Closed weekdays Sept.–May. No dinner Sept.–May. **$–$$**

Windows on the Bay As the name implies, the picture windows here allow expansive views of Assawoman Bay to the west. The restaurant has tables adorned with white linen and flowers within a mauve-and-green dining room. The dishes served, a cut above those at similar restaurants, include the much-sought-after crab imperial, a mixture of crab meat, spices, and mayonnaise. > 61st St. at the bay, tel. 410/723–3463. AE, MC, V. **$–$$$**

ESSENTIALS

Getting Here

BY BUS

Greyhound's daily bus trips from Washington to Ocean City take 4½ to 5 hours. Once in Ocean City, the local transportation provides easy, efficient, and inexpensive ways to get around.

Municipal buses travel in the far right-hand lane on Coastal Highway. An unlimited ride day-pass is $2. From Memorial Day to Labor Day, buses run roughly every 10 minutes and stop every other block along Coastal Highway, Philadelphia Avenue, and Baltimore Avenue from the inlet to the Delaware state line. Services run 24 hours daily. After Labor Day until Memorial Day, buses run every 30 minutes.

If you want to avoid driving in town altogether, consider heading to the West Ocean City Park and Ride on U.S. 50 and shuttle into town for $1. The shuttle drops passengers off at the South Division Street Transit Center. For an additional $1, passengers can purchase an unlimited use day-pass for travel within Ocean City. Shuttle service is available April to October.

A tram runs along 2½ mi of Boardwalk, from the inlet to 27th Street. From Memorial Day to Labor Day the tram operates daily from 10 AM to midnight; you can get on or off it at any point along its route.

DEPOT **Bus Terminal** > 2nd St. and Philadelphia Ave., 21842, tel. 410/289–9307. *LINES* **Boardwalk Tram** > Tel. 410/723–1606. **Greyhound** > Tel. 800/229–9424, www.greyhound.com.

BY CAR

A car is indispensable for touring the region. To reach the Eastern Shore from Washington, D.C., travel east on U.S. 50 (U.S. 301) and cross the 4½-mi Chesapeake Bay bridge ($2.50 toll, eastbound only) northeast of Annapolis. The drive from Washington takes approximately three hours, but if you're heading there for a weekend, plan to leave the city late Friday evening or before sunrise Saturday morning to avoid massive backups at the Bay Bridge and beyond.

When driving in town, keep out of the right lane on the Coastal Highway, which is for buses only. Parking, available in private lots, city lots, and at signed areas on public streets, can be tough to find in season. City lots are metered 24 hours a day.

The Hugh Cropper Inlet Lot is at the southernmost point in the city. Close to the Boardwalk, the pier, the beach, and other amusements, this parking lot is almost always full. The first hour is $1 and 25¢ for every 15 minutes thereafter.

Visitor Information

CONTACT **Ocean City Dept. of Tourism and Visitor Information Center** > 4001 Coastal Hwy., at 41st St., 21842, tel. 410/289–8181 or 800/626–2326, www.ococean.com.

Delaware's Atlantic Coast

Rehoboth Beach is 120 mi east of Washington, D.C.

24

Revised by Kristi Delovitch

BEGINNING WITH CAPE HENELOPEN and extending 23 mi south to Fenwick Island, Delaware's shore along the Atlantic is known for its beachfront resort towns. Rehoboth Beach is the largest and the most expensive. New restaurants and bars open here each season, going after the discerning and well-heeled—the area is especially popular with the gay community. Rehoboth is also known for its old-fashioned boardwalk, made for strolling, and its nightlife (it's the only Shore town with an appreciable amount), as well as for its excellent boutique and outlet shopping. Nearby Lewes, a 1631 Dutch settlement at the mouth of Delaware Bay, is a step into the past. From its plentiful antique stores to its many inns, this village has a sense of history not typically found in the newer, more developed beach towns.

Bethany Beach and Fenwick Island are known as the "quiet resorts." Sleepy Bethany has a family focus, with great beaches and a main street that leads right into the sand. It's not for everyone: with the exception of a few restaurants, everything here closes very early, and lodging options are limited to two family-owned beach-front motels, a B&B, and the massive Sea Colony complex, which leases condos. Most eateries serve old-fashioned beach favorites like pizza, fried chicken, and saltwater taffy.

The raucous nightlife of Dewey Beach, which has open-air bars where popular bands perform, makes it a sort of Georgetown of the Shore, with crowds of singles in their twenties and early thirties. Lodging and dining options are limited to no-frills oceanfront motels and good, basic bar food. One of the prettiest stretches of shoreline is south of Dewey Beach: the sand dunes and wide, white-sand beaches seem to be just an arm's reach away from Route 1, the Coastal Highway.

Founded as a church camp, Fenwick Island stretches south along Route 1, to Ocean City, then splits to the west along the bay. Its commercial district is in a small pocket near the Maryland border, and unspoiled national parkland, gorgeous white dunes, and expansive summer homes take up the rest of the island.

Although there is ample public access to the miles of Atlantic surf and sand, crowds do pour in from D.C. and points nearby on holidays and on summer weekends. Broadkill River, Rehoboth Bay, Indian River Bay, and Little Assawoman Bay all have sheltered coves for boating, water sports, and fishing.

Just west of the beaches are some of the state's historic villages and scenic bayside parks. At the head of the Broadkill River is Milton, which was a major shipbuilding center. Its entire downtown is now a historic district of 18th- and 19th-century buildings, including old cypress-shingle houses.Although it's a short drive to the Atlantic Shore from Washington, traffic can be horrendous during the summer season. If you plan to visit then, try to leave the city late Friday evening or before sunrise on Saturday to avoid massive backups at the Bay Bridge and beyond. The quickest way to get to the Atlantic Shore is Route 1, but if you have the time, take Route 9. As it meanders down from New Castle to Dover, it passes farm fields, 10-foot-high grasses, and roadside produce stands.

WHAT TO SEE & DO

DEWEY BEACH

Bottle and Cork Famous for live music, this grungy, partially open-air maze of stages and bars is one reason for Dewey Beach's popularity among young, single Washingtonians. The heart of Dewey's nightlife, the bar draws national and regional acts and thousands of customers on some summer weekends. > 1807 Hwy. 1, Dewey Beach, tel. 302/227–7272, www.deweybeachlife.com. Closed Oct.–Apr.

Ruddertown A massive entertainment complex, Ruddertown is in the heart of Dewey Beach, just off Highway 1 on the bay. The complex houses a bookstore, a pub, a game room, a few restaurants, and the only water-sports rental store in town. > Dickinson St. on the bay, Dewey Beach, tel. 302/227–3888, www.deweybeachlife.com.

Rusty Rudder Barnlike and with a nautical theme, the Rusty Rudder has the same owner as the Bottle and Cork. It's a restaurant, but it's best known for its rowdy after-dinner crowd. Late-night live music's the specialty here: it has the best light-and-sound system at the beach and often draws big national acts. > 113 Dickinson St., Dewey Beach, tel. 302/227–3888, www.deweybeachlife.com.

Starboard Restaurant The line begins to form around the building at breakfast time. Most of those in the crowd are heading for the Bloody Mary bar, loaded with hot sauce, horseradish, vegetables, and hundreds of other ingredients. On weekend nights in summer, live bands play on the front porch. > 2009 Hwy. 1, Dewey Beach, tel. 302/227–4600, www.thestarboard.com.

FENWICK ISLAND

Discover-Sea Museum Sometimes small treasures hide in unlikely places—such as the top floor of the Sea Shell City tourist shop. Jewelry and porcelain dishes from the *Titanic* as well as objects from ships wrecked off the coast of Assateague are on display here. The interactive exhibits map shipwrecks and their eventual recovery. > 706 Ocean Hwy., Fenwick Island, tel. 888/743–5524, www.discoversea.com. Donations accepted. June–Aug., daily 10–9; Sept.–May weekends 11–4.

Fenwick Island Lighthouse Built in 1859, this restored lighthouse marks two boundaries. It distinguishes Fenwick Island from Ocean City, and a 1751 marker of the Mason-Dixon line lies just a few feet from the lighthouse. A descendant of the original keepers lives in the quarters. The lighthouse is not open for tours. > 146th St., west of Rte. 1, Fenwick Island.

Fenwick Island State Park The smallest of the state parks in southern Delaware, this is a 3-mi stretch of barrier island between Bethany Beach and Fenwick Island. There are a beach with lifeguards on duty, an area set aside for surfing, a bathhouse, and boats available for rental. A large brown sign in the middle of Highway 1 marks the entrance to the bathhouse. > Coastal Hwy. 1, Fenwick Island, tel. 302/539–1055, www.destateparks.com. $5 ($2.50 for Delaware residents). Memorial Day–Labor Day; lifeguarded beach daily 9–5.

REHOBOTH

Art League Inside Rehoboth's wealthiest neighborhood, this small gallery complex exhibits paintings, pottery, and sculpture from local and regional artists. The Homestead, built 1743, serves as one of the galleries. Summer seminars and workshops are available but fill up quickly, so make reservations ahead of time. > 12 Dodds La., Rehoboth, tel. 302/227–8408, www.rehobothartleague.org. Free. Mon.–Sat. 10–4, Sun. noon–4.

Bandstand Live bands perform with an ocean backdrop at this tiny pavilion in the center of town. Free weekend concerts begin at 8 PM. The performers, announced in the special-events section of local papers, are often jazz and string quartets. > Rehoboth Ave. and the boardwalk, tel. 302/227–6181, www.cityofrehoboth.com. Free.

Cape Henelopen State Park One of the first public lands in the nation, this 5,193-acre park encompass many bay and ocean beaches. The two swimming beaches have lifeguards on patrol from Memorial Day through Labor Day; the more northern one also has a food stand, a bathhouse, showers, and a changing room. Famous for birdwatching, the park provides a habitat for rare protected fowl that include the piping plover. Because of its strategic location at the mouth of the Delaware Bay, the Department of Defense built bunkers and towers here during World War II. One vestige, a 132-step concrete observation tower, provides a 360-degree view from the top. > 42 Cape Henelopen Dr., Lewes, tel. 302/645–8983, www.destateparks.com. $5 ($2.50 for Delaware residents). Beaches Memorial Day–Labor Day.

Delaware Seashore State Park You're always surrounded by water here. Most people come to swim at one of the two guarded beaches or to fish for flounder, rockfish (striped bass), and bluefish in the Indian River Inlet. The full-service Indian River Marina is in the heart of the park. Surf-fishing permits, which allow you to take your vehicle on the beach, are $100 ($50 for vehicles registered in Delaware). Bathhouses have showers, and you can rent umbrellas, chairs, and rafts on the beach. > Inlet 850, Rehoboth, tel. 302/227–2800, www.destateparks.com. $5 ($2.50 for Delaware residents). Memorial Day–Labor Day; lifeguarded beaches daily 9–5.

Jungle Jim's Adventure World Whether you want miniature golf, go-carts, or a "Lazy River" to lounge in, this complex combines them all. Besides conventional beach favorites there's also a rock climbing wall and the largest local selection of rides outside of Ocean City. > Rte. 1 and Country Club Rd., Rehoboth, tel. 302/227–8444. $26 water park, $6 go-carts, $7 miniature golf, $5 bumper boats, $5 for 3 climbs on rock-climbing wall. Memorial Day–Labor Day, daily 10–7:30.

Rehoboth Boardwalk The largest and liveliest boardwalk on the Delaware shore, this oceanfront stretch is packed with restaurants, game rooms, and the smells of saltwater and french fries. If you find yourself wistful for the familiar beeping of electronic games harmonized with the thunderous rolling of a Skee-Ball, head to **Funland** (tel. 302/227–2785), a small collection of inexpensive beach games and rides. > Boardwalk, Rehoboth, tel. 302/227–6181, www.cityofrehoboth.com.

Tours

Coastal Kayak This organizer of ecotours of the waterways and coastal waters of Fenwick Island State Park also rents kayaks and sailboats. > Fenwick Island State Park on the bay, Fenwick Island, tel. 302/539–7999 or 877/445–2925, www.c-kayak.com.

Jolly Rover This topsail schooner leaves Lewes for three-hour sunset cruises and two-hour sailing trips daily from May through September. > Front St. by the drawbridge, Lewes, tel. 302/644–1501.

Sports

BOATING

From mid-April through October, Vines Creek Marina rents pontoons for use in the bay and the Indian River Inlet. Rates range from $45 for an hour to $225 for a full day. Gas, not included in the rental, can be purchased at the marina.

Rehoboth Bay Marina rents pontoons, skiffs, and other equipment for fishing, crabbing, and clamming. The boats range in cost from $125 to $300 for a full day. *RENTALS* **Rehoboth Bay Marina** > 1115 Rte. 1, Dewey Beach, tel. 302/226–2012. **Vines Creek Marina** > Pepper Creek Rd. off Falling Point Rd., Dagsboro, tel. 302/732–6043.

FISHING

Delaware Division of Fish and Wildlife In addition to providing information on boating and fishing, this agency also sells special surf-fishing licenses for Delaware Seashore State Park. > Tel. 302/739–5296, www.dnrec.state.de.us.
Fisherman's Wharf Charter boats for either deep-sea or bay fishing can be booked for full-day ($45) or half-day ($25) trips, which include necessary gear and bait. Regular trips are scheduled from Memorial Day to Labor Day, but some limited trips are organized in the off-season. > Anglers and Savannah Rds., Lewes, tel. 302/645–8862.

WATER SPORTS

Baseboards rents large water trampolines for the young and the active. With one of them, you can jump to your heart's content in the middle of the bay.
EQUIPMENT **Baseboards** > Ruddertown, Dickinson St. on the bay, Dewey Beach, tel. 302/227–3888, www.deweybeachlife.com. **Coastal Kayak** > Fenwick Island State Park on the bay, Fenwick Island, tel. 302/539–7999 or 877/445–2925, www.c-kayak.com. **Rehoboth Bay Sailing Association** > Rte. 1, Indian Beach, tel. 302/227–9008, www.rbsa.org.

Shopping

Elegant Slumming Home French countryside meets Park Avenue in this stylish boutique tucked in a small alley in downtown Rehoboth. Though the inventory changes regularly, typical offerings include stylish leather chairs, Andy Warhol prints, and throw pillows covered in exotic fabric. On the way to the little cove is the sister store **Elegant Slumming Jewels and Gifts** (tel. 302/227–5551). Stop in; there's a good selection of jewelry. The owner also does interesting custom work. > 33 Baltimore Ave., Rehoboth Beach, tel. 302/227–3097.
Rehoboth Outlets One of the main draws of this massive outlet complex on Coastal Highway is Delaware's sales-tax–free shopping. A total of 140 stores sprawl along both sides of Highway 1 in three separate areas. In the first, the bayside outlets include Coach, Nine West, and Disney. Travel a little farther north to reach a newer section selling popular clothing by Banana Republic, Brooks Brothers, and Polo. Farther north, on the southbound side of the highway, is a 35-unit outlet mall anchored by an L. L. Bean factory store. > Rte. 1, Rehoboth Beach, tel. 302/226–9223, www.shoprehoboth.com.
Second Street A small strip of antiques stores and boutiques makes up Lewes's main street. **Lewes Mercantile Antique Gallery** (tel. 302/645–7900), one of the many antiques shops in town, has a large selection of vintage posters, newspapers, and jewelry. > 2nd St., Lewes.

Save the Date

MAY

Hoopla Antiques and classic cars fill the parking lot of Ruddertown during this weekend festival. The juried car competitions are supplemented with many activities for kids. > Ruddertown, Coastal Hwy. 1, Dewey Beach, tel. 302/227–2233 Ext. 12, www.beach-fun.com.

Mid-Atlantic Regional Surfing Championships Spectators line up along Dewey Beach to watch over 350 surfing and body-boarding competitors take part in a weekend's worth of competitions, which start at 5 AM and end at dusk. Held on the same weekend as Hoopla, the festival also includes nightly beach bonfires. > Dewey Beach, tel. 302/227–4011, www.beach-fun.com.

JULY

Rehoboth Beach Downtown Fireworks On the Sunday of the Fourth of July weekend, thousands of spectators gather on the beach for a spectacular fireworks display ignited from a huge barge. Rather than trying to park in town, take one of the shuttles that run regularly from the outlets on Route 1. > Rehoboth Ave. and the boardwalk, Rehoboth, tel. 302/227–2772, www.beach-fun.com.

OCTOBER

Rehoboth Beach Autumn Jazz Festival A showcase of traditional and contemporary jazz, this annual festival has included shows by living legends like Patti Austin and Shaka Khan. Performances are held at Rehoboth and Dewey Beach. > Tel. 800/296–8742, www.rehobothjazz.com.

Seawitch **Halloween Fiddler's Festival** Two thousand costumed participants march down the center of Rehoboth in search of the *Seawitch,* a legendary local ship that is said to have been the fastest one in 1846—it traveled to China in record time. Other events at this weekend festival include dueling fiddlers and a best-dressed pet contest (one year the contestants included a goat). > Rehoboth Ave., Rehoboth, tel. 302/227–2233, www.beach-fun.com.

NOVEMBER

Punkin Chunkin' The first week in November, thousands gather in a huge field to see which competitors will be able to hoist pumpkins the fastest, farthest, and highest. > Millsboro, tel. 302/934–6777, www.punkinchunkin.com.

Rehoboth Independent Film Festival With over 200 screenings of independent films from 20 countries, this is the largest movie festival on the shore. The shorts, documentaries, and features are all shown in a single complex, Movies at Midway, with simultaneous screenings in eight different theaters. An opening-night gala kicks off the four-day festival. Individual tickets cost $7.50 (multiview packages are available). Free screenings of prospective movies are shown in summer, and it's those viewers' ratings that determine festival finalists. > Midway Shopping Center, Rte. 1, Rehoboth, tel. 302/645–9095, www.rehobothfilm.com.

WHERE TO STAY

BETHANY BEACH

Addy Sea Bed & Breakfast A front-row view of the ocean and personalized service are the perks of this oceanfront inn, the only B&B in town. Built in 1901, the three-story Victorian has a wraparound veranda with rocking chairs. Two corner rooms on the second floor have great views of the ocean. Most restaurants and shops are just a quick walk away. > 99 Ocean View Pkwy., at Atlantic Ave., Bethany Beach 19930, tel. 302/539–3707 or 800/418–6764, fax 302/539–7263, www.addysea.com. 13 rooms. Free parking; no smoking, no kids under 12. AE, D, MC, V. BP. **$$$$**

Best Western Gold Leaf The rooms are standard and traditionally styled at this Best Western. But the location, a half block from the beach and a short walk from the bay or the Rusty Rudder directly across the street, is unbeatable. A few rooms have water views. Be aware that from June until late August Dewey's rowdy nightlife scene can mean noise into the night. > 1400 Rte. 1, Dewey Beach 19971, tel. 302/226–1100 or 800/422–8566, fax 302/226–9785, www.bestwesterngoldleaf.com. 76 rooms. Microwaves, refrigerators, pool. AE, D, DC, MC, V. CP. **$$–$$$**

Blue Surf Motel At this family-owned, no-frills motel, you have a first-class view of the ocean. You can step out of the motel and right onto the beach or the quiet boardwalk. The location is convenient to the main drag, with its shopping and restaurants. Rooms on the second floor have unobstructed views of the ocean. > Box 999, Bethany Beach 19930, tel. 302/539–7531, fax 302/539–7605, www.bethanycam.com. 36 rooms. Some kitchens, microwaves, refrigerators, no smoking rooms. AE, MC, V. Closed Oct.–Apr. **$–$$**

LEWES

Blue Water House Playfully furnished in bright, tropical hues, this Caribbean-style B&B sits high on stilts, with views of the bay from its fourth-floor observation deck. Every room manages to be cheerful yet tasteful. The inn provides beach essentials from bicycles to beach chairs, and there's even an outdoor shower for when you return. There are individual porches with hammocks off most rooms and a communal wraparound porch. You can eat breakfast in the living room, overlooking the marsh; in your room; or in the garden outside. The inn encourages families and shows child friendly movies each evening. > 407 E. Market St., Lewes 19958, tel. 302/645–7832 or 800/493–2080, fax 302/645–2173, www.lewes-beach.com. 6 rooms, 2 suites. Bicycles, bar, recreation room. AE, MC, V. BP. **$$**

Inn at Canal Square Prized for its waterfront location, this large inn has many rooms with balconies overlooking the Lewes harbor. The rooms are homey and comfortable, and the spacious suites have a full kitchen, fireplace, and Jacuzzi. Harbor views are best from the fourth floor, but there is at least a partial view from nearly every room. The inn is a short walk from shops and restaurants. > 122 Market St., Lewes 19958, tel. 302/644–3377 or 888/644–1911, fax 302/645–7083. 19 rooms. AE, MC, V. CP. **$$$–$$$$**

Inns on the Mispillion The Marshall House, a restored Victorian bank building, and the Towers, on the National Register of Historic Places, make up this hotel. Charming details include the carved sycamore ceiling and a circa-1899 grand piano in the music room, a common room on the first floor of the Towers. The guest rooms, each with a fireplace, are decorated in French Victorian style. > 112 N.W. Front St., Milford 19963, tel. 800/366–3814, fax 302/422–4703, www.mispillion.com. 9 rooms. Restaurant. DC, MC, V. BP. **$**

Zwaanendael Inn At the end of 2nd Street, the main commercial street of Lewes, is this inn, built in 1926 and on the National Register of Historic Places. In keeping with the Dutch name, which refers to the ill-fated first settlement of 1631, the interiors are spartan and manage to evoke an earlier era. (On the other hand, rooms now do have two phone lines and data ports, and there is a health club and restaurant on the premises.) The lobby and parlor hold many fine early-American pieces. > 142 2nd St., Lewes 19958, tel. 302/645–6466 or 800/824–8754, fax 302/645–7196, www.zwaanendaelinn.com. 23 rooms. Restaurant, in-room data ports, health club. AE, D, MC, V. CP. $

REHOBOTH

Atlantic Sands Hotel and Conference Center The first thing that catches your eye about this ocean-side hotel is its corner rooms: their floor-to-ceiling pyramid-like windows make the rooms resemble giant fishbowls. All rooms are clean and modern, but the hotel's best feature remains its location. You can step out of the pool onto the beach or take a short walk to restaurants and shops. > 101 N. Boardwalk, Rehoboth 19971, tel. 302/227–2511 or 800/422–0600, fax 302/227–9476, www.atlanticsandshotel.com. 181 rooms, 78 suites. Restaurant, pool, health club, bar, free parking. AE, D, DC, MC, V. CP. $$–$$$$

Avenue Inn and Spa From the lobby onward this inn puts a lot of effort into making you feel at home. There's wine in the afternoon, and even cookies at bedtime. Each room is simply and tastefully decorated with light-color walls and floral linens. The Jacuzzi suites come with poster beds, a fireplace, and a Jacuzzi, and a bottle of champagne. Check out the heated indoor pool, which has a striking stainless-steel bottom. > 33 Wilmington Ave., Rehoboth 19971, tel. 302/226–2900 or 800/433–5870, fax 302/226–7549, www.avenueinn.com. 60 rooms, 14 suites. Indoor pool, health club, hair salon, hot tub, sauna, steam room. AE, D, MC, V. CP. $$–$$$

The Bellmoor It seems as if no detail was left to chance at this luxurious hotel, from the hunt-country–style library, done in soft leather, to the shady garden, the perfect spot for some afternoon tea. Near the garden is a pool that's only for those 25 and older. Each room has a classic, homelike feel, decorated in a soft, Southern manner—the bed linens and wallpaper are made of fine fabrics in an interesting mix of color and texture. In the suites many of the couches have been covered in white fabric interwoven with bright red hunt-country scenes. All the suites have fireplaces, and most rooms have marble baths. Although it may feel removed, the Bellmoor is just blocks from restaurants, shops, and the ocean. > 6 Christian St., Rehoboth 19971, tel. 302/227–5800 or 800/425–2355, fax 302/227–0323, www.thebellmoor.com. 53 rooms, 22 suites. Pool, health club, hot tub, spa, library, Internet, free parking; no smoking. AE, D, MC, V. BP. $$–$$$$

Chesapeake Landing Bed & Breakfast Inside a residential neighborhood in Rehoboth, this inn sits beside a lake and near a bird sanctuary. It's a good place for those who want a break at the end of the day from the pulsing activity of this resort town. The tasteful furnishings include unusual outdoor sculptures and a large collection of American pottery. The eclectic rooms are furnished with whimsical bright-color oil paintings, comfortably worn furniture, and unique pottery pieces. You can take the inn's dinghy or paddleboat out on the lake, and the ocean is just a short walk away. > 101 Chesapeake St., Rehoboth Beach 19971, tel. 302/227–2973, fax 302/227–0301, www.chesapeakelanding.com. 4 rooms. Pool. MC, V. Closed Jan.–Mar. BP. $$–$$$$

Oceanus Motel Although this small hotel shares owners with the luxurious Bellmoor across the street, the two are quite different. The rooms, which form a sort of L around the outdoor pool, were remodeled in 2003 and are extremely clean and family friendly. All rooms also come with refrigerator and a microwave, which can go a long way toward reducing dining expenses. The beach is just two blocks away. > 6 2nd St., Rehoboth 19971, tel. 302/227–8200 or 800/852–5011, www.oceanusmotel.com. 38 rooms. Microwaves, refrigerators, pool. D, MC, V. Closed Dec.–Feb. ¢–$$

CAMPING

Cape Henelopen State Park The sites here, part of the Coastal Defense System during World War II, are near pine-covered dunes. A nature center and fishing pier are on-site, and you're less than half a mile from the ocean. A swimming beach with lifeguards is about a mile away (campers do not have to pay the entrance fee to the beach). While at the park explore the famous dune, which you can walk and play on. Make sure to bring bug spray with DEET—mosquitoes, biting flies, and deer ticks are all common to the area. > 42 Cape Henelopen Dr., Lewes 19958, tel. 302/645–8983 information, 877/987–2757 reservations, fax 302/645–0588, www.destateparks.com. 17 tent sites without hookups, 139 tent or RV sites with water hookups. Flush toilets, dump station, drinking water, laundry facilities, showers, public telephone. Reservations essential. D, MC, V. Closed Dec.–Feb. ¢

Delaware Seashore State Park Directly on the Indian River Inlet, this campground is filled with fishing fans casting from rocks just yards from their tent or RV. The inlet, where the bay water meets the ocean, is known for its abundant flounder, rockfish (striped bass), and bluefish. The park has 6 mi of beaches and two beaches with lifeguards, one within walking distance of the campground. The full service Indian River Marina is in the park. Be sure to bring bug spray. No campfires are permitted in the park. > 850 Inlet Dr., Rehoboth 19971, tel. Reservations: 302/227–2800 or 877/987–2757, fax 302/227–3930, www.destateparks.com. 133 sites without hookups, 145 sites with full hookups, 156 overflow sites without bathhouses. Flush toilets, dump station, drinking water, laundry facilities, showers, public telephone, swimming (ocean). Reservations essential. MC, V. Closed Dec.–Feb. ¢

WHERE TO EAT

BETHANY BEACH

DiFibo's Restaurant & Deli The smell of basil and garlic and the sound of children fill this casual family-owned trattoria at night. Dishes such as veal Parmesan scallopini and fresh ravioli topped with a walnut-currant cream sauce are common offerings. The expansive wine list has offerings from $20 on up. Carryout is also available. > 789 Garfield Pkwy., Bethany Beach, tel. 302/539–4550. MC, V. $–$$$$

Redfin Sitting on the bay side of Route 1, the red-shingle roof of this seafood grill and fish market stands out. Inside, the bright, stylish interior has large windows that give broad bay views. The menu here is one of the most extensive and interesting on the shore, often including dishes made from wolffish (a bottom dweller that eats lobster and other sea creatures in the wild) and other unusual seafood. More straightforward fare includes pan-seared grouper, blackened swordfish, and tuna grilled with a balsamic and rosemary glaze. To the right of the entrance is a carryout fish market. > Coastal Hwy. 1, N. Bethany Beach, tel. 302/537–0100. Reservations not accepted. AE, MC, V. Closed Mon. and Tues. No lunch Oct.–Apr. $$–$$$$

Sedona What was once a Southwestern restaurant now serves New American food. The only thing that menu items like Yaquina Bay oysters, fresh skate, and foie gras have in common is that they are all supreme ingredients brought together from all over the globe. Creative takes on dishes like shepherd's pie (theirs is made with merguez sausage, potatoes whipped with bacalao and Vermont shepherd's cheese) are the order of day here. It's expensive, but Sedona is the only place in Bethany serving food of such quality, and that's kept loyal followers filling it up year-round. In summer call well in advance to make reservations. > 26 Pennsylvania Ave., Bethany Beach, tel. 302/539–1200. Reservations essential. AE, DC, MC, V. Closed Nov.–Jan. $$$–$$$$

FENWICK ISLAND

Harpoon Hannah's What originally earned this restaurant renown are the sunsets seen from its tiki bar. Almost as appealing are its breads and coconut muffins, which draw people inside to dine. The menu, dominated by seafood and steak, has other traditional ocean-side favorites such as ribs and a raw bar. > 142nd St. on the bay, Fenwick Island, tel. 302/539–3095 or 800/227–0525. Reservations not accepted. AE, D, MC, V. $–$$$$

Nantucket's New England–style Continental cuisine is what's on this local favorite's menu. Specialties include spicy corn chowder, bouillabaisse, and filet mignon encrusted with blue cheese and herbs and spices. Because Nantucket's is a bit expensive, you might wish to consider eating in the bar during happy hour, when all food is 20% off. The staff is exceedingly helpful and friendly. > Rte. 1 and Atlantic Ave., Fenwick Island, tel. 302/539–2607 or 800/362–3463. D, DC, MC, V. Closed Dec. $$$$

LEWES

Buttery Restaurant Inside a large Victorian on the edge of the historic district, Buttery serves basic versions of everything from seafood to steaks to sandwiches. Its old-fashioned Sunday brunch includes a basket of fresh bread, a huge plate of fresh fruit, and one of 12 entrées. > 2nd and Savannah Sts., Lewes, tel. 302/645–7755. Reservations essential. D, MC, V. $$$–$$$$

Striper Bites In a town where everything seems historical, this small seafood bistro with a bright interior, young owner, and energetic waitstaff is a breath of fresh air. The menu is as fun as the interior, where the polished pine makes it seem as if you're dining on the deck of a fine yacht. One thing you can always expect, hinted at in the name, is lots of striped bass, also known as rockfish. Blackened rockfish on sourdough, smoked rockfish, and even rockfish braised with fresh dill and fennel are all here. The rest of the menu also emphasizes seafood, with additions such as New York strip and gumbo here and there. Opt for the fries seasoned with Old Bay: they're a sure thing. > 107 Savannah Rd., Lewes, tel. 302/645–4657. Reservations not accepted. D, MC, V. Closed Wed. Labor Day–mid-June. $$–$$$

REHOBOTH BEACH

Chez La Mare Since 1980, Chez La Mare has been serving fine French cooking that makes good use of the local seafood. Specialties include veal marsala and a country-style pâté. You can dine in the French country dining room, the enclosed sunporch, or atop the roof deck of this remodeled beach house. > 2nd St. at Wilmington Ave., Rehoboth, tel. 302/227–6494. Reservations essential. AE, D, DC, MC, V. Closed Mon.–Wed. Nov.–Mar. $$$–$$$$

Dogfish Head Brewing and Eats Delaware's first brewpub, Dogfish Head keeps everyone happy with a changing menu of in-house brews, pizzas, and musical performers on Friday and Saturday nights. Dogfish is also a "micro-distillery," producing Blue Hen vodka, a gin, and two kinds of rum. Private tours of the brewing and distillery process are available by appointment. > 320 Rehoboth Ave., Rehoboth, tel. 302/226–2739, www.dogfish.com. AE, MC, V. Closed Tues. and Wed. Sept.–May. $–$$$$

Espuma In a town where some people seem to change their favorite restaurant as often as they change their sunscreen, Espuma has remained in good standing. The signature dish, paella, is an extensive medley of seafood, rice, saffron, and two kinds of chorizo. Starter options include the expected pan-seared jumbo lump crab cake and a more adventurous escargot potpie. As for main courses, you may find the menu listing lobster, shrimp, and scallop marsala next to veal ossa bucco. > 28 Wilmington Ave., at 1st St., Rehoboth Beach, tel. 302/227–4199. Reservations essential. AE, DC, V. Closed Tues. and Wed. $$$–$$$$

Fusion Festively decorated with hanging illuminated stars, this lively restaurant in the heart of downtown has an equally playful attitude toward the food it serves. The relatively small menu of three starters and six entrées still works in many extremely creative twists on modern American cuisine. An Angus fillet might be served with a potato pancake, the lobster and shrimp prepared in a potent Thai curry, and a traditional jumbo lump crab cake might be accompanied with a wasabi reduction. Watch for happy-hour offers that reduce prices on the night's menu. > 50 Wilmington Ave., Rehoboth, tel. 302/226–1940. AE, D, DC, MC, V. Closed Jan.–mid-Feb. $$$$

Louie's Pizza The crossroads of Rehoboth Avenue and the boardwalk is where you can find some of the most famous food on the shore. Louie's, open since 1974, is to grinders (hot sub sandwiches) what Thrasher's, next door, is to french fries. Choose one of 17 varieties: they're made to order and served piping hot. Sit down at a booth for table-side service or order at the counter for carryout. As the name partially implies, Louie's also serves pizzas, fries, and other casual fare. > 11 Rehoboth Ave., Rehoboth, tel. 302/227–6002. No credit cards. Closed Thanksgiving–early Mar. ¢

Planet X This unique conglomeration of zebra-striped fabric, mismatched furniture, sheer curtains, and candlelight keeps you wondering, What's next? The menu is equally daring, building poultry, meat, and seafood dishes around spices like tarragon, cumin, thyme, and jasmine. Vegetarian cuisine is a specialty, with dishes such as red Thai curry with organic tofu. From the bar, you can get drinks like mango Bellinis and smoothies made of strawberry, yogurt, and honey. The à la carte Sunday brunch includes lobster rolls, homemade granola, and hummus made with organic ingredients. > 35 Wilmington Ave., Rehoboth, tel. 302/226–1928. Reservations not accepted. MC, V. Closed Jan–mid-Feb. $$$–$$$$

Sydney's Blues and Jazz The New Orleans–influenced American cooking coming from this kitchen includes such specialties as oysters Rockefeller and authentic gumbo and jambalaya. Wine-flight tastings—samples of three wines served in small portions—are also available. The innovative "grazing" menu is great for light eaters; the bar menu includes po'boys. There are live blues and jazz music on Wednesday, Friday, and Saturday. > 25 Christian St., Rehoboth, tel. 302/227–1339 or 800/808–1924. AE, D, DC, MC, V. Closed Mon. and Tues. Memorial Day–Labor Day. $$$–$$$$

ESSENTIALS

Getting Here

BY BUS

A trip on Greyhound to the Shorestop Express depot in Rehoboth Beach takes about four hours.

DART First State operates a bus service from Memorial Day to Labor Day that stops at routes along Route 1 between Lewes, Rehoboth, Dewey, and Fenwick Island. The bus also travels to the outlet stores, the Rehoboth Boardwalk, and into historic Lewes, and then makes its final stop in Ocean City. The service, available from 6 AM to 2:30 AM the next morning, costs $2.10 and includes parking at the Park & Ride off Route 1.

Jolly Trolley of Rehoboth runs from the Rehoboth Boardwalk to Dewey Beach, with stops throughout the area, from Memorial Day to Labor Day, 8 AM–2 AM. A pass is $1.50 per ride and free for under. Rides after midnight are $3. *DEPOT* **Shorestop Express** > 801 Rehoboth Ave., Rehoboth, tel. 302/227–1080. *LINES* **DART First State** > Tel. 800/553–3278, www.beachbus.com. **Greyhound** > Tel. 800/224–9424. **Jolly Trolley of Rehoboth** > Tel. 302/227–1197, www.jollytrolley.com.

BY CAR

To get to the area from D.C., take Capital Beltway to U.S. 50 East to the Bay Bridge, which has a $2.50 toll. Continue on U.S. 50 East when it splits off from Route 301. Take a left on the MD 404 East (Queen Anne Highway). Continue 45 mi.

Exit onto U.S. 9 East at the circle in Georgetown. Travel approximately 13 mi to Route 1 South to Rehoboth Beach, and follow Route 1A into Rehoboth. Follow Route 1A, Rehoboth Avenue, to the beach. To reach Dewey Beach, Bethany Beach, and Fenwick Island, continue along Route 1 South toward Ocean City, Maryland. To reach Lewes, take Route 1 North from Rehoboth Beach.

Visitor Information

The Lewes Chamber of Commerce publishes a brochure mapping a self-guided walking tour of almost 50 historical buildings in town.
CONTACTS **Bethany Beach-Fenwick Island Chamber of Commerce** > Rte. 1 N, Fenwick Island 19930, tel. 302/539–2100 or 800/962–7873, www.bethany-fenwick.org. **Lewes Chamber of Commerce** > Savannah Rd. and Kings Hwy., Box 1, Lewes 19958, tel. 302/645–8073, www.leweschamber.com. **Milton Chamber of Commerce** > 104 Federal St., Milton 19968, tel. 302/684–1101, www.historicmilton.com. **Rehoboth Beach–Dewey Beach Chamber of Commerce** > 501 Rehoboth Ave., Box 216, Rehoboth Beach 19971, tel. 302/227–2233 or 800/441–1329, www.beach-fun.com.

Index

Notes